20TH–CENTURY POETRY & POETICS

EDITED BY GARY GEDDES

THIRD EDITION

Toronto
Oxford University Press
1985

CANADIAN CATALOGUING IN PUBLICATION DATA
Main entry under title:
20th-century poetry & poetics
Includes bibliographies and index.
ISBN 0-19-540488-2
1. English poetry — 20th century.   2. American Poetry — 20th century.
3. Canadian poetry (English) — 20th century.*   4. Poetics.
I. Geddes, Gary, 1940-
PN6101.T93 1985   821'.9108   C85-098998-1

© Oxford University Press Canada 1985
OXFORD is a trademark of Oxford University Press
1 2 3 4 — 8 7 6 5
Printed in Canada by
John Deyell Company

CONTENTS

PREFACE TO THE THIRD EDITION

My decision to edit this anthology in the late 1960s was a response to two impulses: the desire for a new anthology that contained the best in British, American, and Canadian poetry from the beginnings of the twentieth century to the present; and a determination to provide enough first-rate commentary by the poets on their art to excite and direct readers towards a deeper understanding of the nature and importance of the poetic act—what Dylan Thomas called his 'craft or sullen art'. I believed, with Auden, that

> In our age, the mere making of a work of art is itself a political act. So long as artists exist, making what they please and think they ought to make, even if it is not terribly good, even if it appeals only to a handful of people, they remind the Management of something managers need to be reminded of, namely, that the managed are a people with faces, not anonymous members, that *Homo Laborens* is also *Homo Ludens*.

I still hold that conviction; in fact the necessity of poetry seems to me now greater than ever.

My initial editorial decisions have, to some extent, been confirmed by the long success of the anthology at various levels, from advanced high-school classes to Honours seminars. Everywhere I go teachers and students tell me how useful and important the selection has been to them; and the occasional stranger has been moved to forgive my foibles on the strength of my association with this book. Association is the right word, since I know how much my judgement is a product of the combined wisdom of all those who taught me, in books and in classrooms. I know, too, how excellent poets have trained my ear to find the best in what Ted Hughes describes as 'ragged dirty undated letters from remote battles and weddings'.

When the time came for another revision it seemed appropriate to consult those who use the anthology. Questionnaires were sent out and many discussions were conducted with teachers and writers. The prevailing wisdom of the responses was not to change the book significantly. I have accepted this suggestion, out of respect for the original integrity of the anthology and in consideration of its audience. Still, in the intervening years between the first and third editions my own tastes in poetry have altered somewhat; so, too, has my sense of what a textbook ought to accomplish. I have lost some of the innocence and catholicity that once made me smile favourably on poetic fashions that I now regard as interesting but of limited significance. Imagists, Beats, Black Mountain poets, and Concrete poets have all had their say, reminding us with their various gestures that poetry touches on many subjects and modes and should never forget its power to image in words, to conjure with its music, and to perform the dance of feelings and intellect in its structures. Each has made its claim for the importance of ear, eye, mind, breathing, and the body politic. However, the poetic groups and movements of this century now seem less important than the brilliance and performance of their best practitioners. The token section on Concrete poetry has been dropped—as well as a number of poems by individual authors that now seem to me to be weak or redundant—in order to make room for good recent work and for new poets or poets overlooked the first time around. However, neither learning nor guilt has permitted me to make all the changes I would like to make in the anthology. Though I now feel, for example, that Denise Levertov is the most interesting of the poets to emerge from the Black Mountain milieu, I respect the best work of Creeley and Olson and know that they are both favourites among many readers of the anthology. Also, despite the admirable social and political gestures inherent in the work of Allen Ginsberg and Lawrence Ferlinghetti, I find that their poems do not age well. The new additions will surprise few informed readers. Elizabeth Bishop, Seamus Heaney, Adrienne Rich, Phyllis Webb, Michael Ondaatje, and P. K. Page have achieved considerable stature since 1969 (Bishop posthumously); or, to put the matter more honestly, I have finally become attuned to the wonderful sounds several of them were making even then. A much longer book might have included Robert Bly, W. S. Merwin, Galway Kinnell, and Robert Kroetsch.

It is satisfying to see that poetry continues to be widely enjoyed and studied and that this anthology has been instrumental in deepening both the enjoyment of, and exposure to, a broad range of twentieth-century poetry. The third edition should not go out into the world, however, without the warning I made in 1969; *caveat emptor*. Buyer beware. Anthologies by their very nature are selective, subjective, and can therefore be misleading. A major limitation of this anthology is the absence of a good cross-section of long poems. Some of the best writing today is to be found in narratives, meditations, and poem-sequences that can seldom be included in such confined quarters. I recommend supplementing your reading here and there with the complete works of poets, and with other anthologies devoted to longer works.

Karl Shapiro once described poetry as a way of seeing things. His intention was to suggest that the poetic impulse underlies all the arts and, perhaps, all our lives: the urge to sing and the urge to order being evident in places where words have never travelled. Shelley believed poets to be the 'unacknowledged legislators of the world', who might be counted on to give us moral and spiritual direction; and Albert Camus went one step further when he wrote in 1937: 'Politics, and the fate of mankind, are shaped by men without ideals and without greatness. Men who have greatness don't go in for politics. The same is true for everything. But our task is to create a new man within ourselves. We must make our men of action into men of ideals, our poets into captains of industry. We must learn to live out our dreams and transform them into action.' I'm not convinced

that poets in public offices would act other than as politicians;
the shambles of their domestic and financial lives suggests that
they would not. However, we can trust the best of them with
our language, which seems a sufficiently enchanting and exacting mistress to keep them in line. Denise Levertov has put the
matter beautifully:

'. . . it is the poet who has language in his care; the poet
who more than others recognizes language also as a form of
life and a common resource to be cherished and served as we
should serve and cherish earth and its waters, animal and
vegetable life, and each other. The would-be poet who looks on
language merely as something to be used, as the bad farmer or
the rapacious industrialist looks on the soil or on rivers merely
as things to be used, will not discover a deep poetry; he will
only, according to the degree of his skill, construct a counter-
feit more or less acceptable—a sub-poetry, at best, efficiently
representative of his thought or feeling—a reference, not an
incarnation. And he will be contributing even if not in any immediately apparent way, to the erosion of language, just as
the irresponsible, irreverent farmer and industrialist erode the
land and pollute the rivers.'

I am more grateful than ever to those who have pushed,
nudged, and guided me towards work I might not have noticed,
poems that were too subtle or complex or honest for the mood
of an editorial moment: Phyllis Bruce, Susan Crowdy, Bill
Keith, Bob Rogers, Don Priestman, William Toye, and the many
friends, teachers and students who have taken the time to share
with me their impressions of, and pleasures in, the text.

March 1985   GARY GEDDES

ACKNOWLEDGEMENTS

MARGARET ATWOOD Reprinted by permission of Oxford University Press Canada: 'Backdrop Addresses Cowboy', 'Progressive Insanities of a Pioneer', 'It Is Dangerous to Read Newspapers' from *The Animals in That Country*; 'Death of a Young Son by Drowning' from *The Journals of Susanna Moodie*; 'Notes Towards a Poem That Can Never Be Written', 'Variations on the Word Sleep' from *True Stories*; and 'Marrying the Hangman' from *Two-Headed Poems*. 'You Take my Hand' from *Power Politics* by Margaret Atwood reprinted by permission of The House of Anansi Press Ltd. W.H. AUDEN 'The Unknown Citizen', 'In Memory of W.B. Yeats', 'Musée des Beaux Arts', 'Lullaby', 'As I Walked Out One Evening' reprinted by permission of Faber and Faber Ltd. from *Collected Poems* by W.H. Auden. 'The Shield of Achilles', 'In Praise of Limestone' copyright 1951, 1952 by W.H. Auden. Reprinted from W.H. Auden *Collected Poems* edited by Edward Mendelson, by permission of Random House, Inc. 'From The Poet and the City', 'From The Virgin and the Dynamo' copyright 1950, © 1962 by W.H. Auden. Reprinted from *The Dyer's Hand and Other Essays*, by W.H. Auden, by permission of Random House, Inc. MARGARET AVISON 'The World Still Needs', 'To Professor X, Year Y', 'The Swimmer's Moment', 'Voluptuaries and Others', 'Pace', 'Black-White Under Green: May 18, 1965', 'July Man', 'The Absorbed', 'In a Season of Unemployment', 'A Nameless One' from *Winter Sun/The Dumbfounding* by Margaret Avison. Used by permission of The Canadian Publishers, McClelland and Stewart Limited, Toronto. JOHN BERRYMAN Reprinted by permission of Farrar, Straus and Giroux, Inc.: 'Dream Songs #1, 8, 14, 26, 29, 40, 49, 50, 52' from *The Dream Songs* by John Berryman, copyright © 1959, 1962, 1963, 1964 by John Berryman; excerpts from *Homage to Mistress Bradstreet* by John Berryman, copyright © 1956 by John Berryman; 'A Professor's Song', 'The Dispossessed' from *Short Poems* by John Berrryman, copyright © 1948, 1958 by John Berryman. EARLE BIRNEY 'Vancouver Lights', 'Anglosaxon Street', 'From the Hazel Bough', 'Bushed', 'A Walk in Kyoto', 'The Bear on the Delhi Road', 'Twenty-Third Flight', 'Haiku for a Young Waitress', 'Cartagena de Indias' from *Collected Poems* © 1975 by Earle Birney. Used by permission of The Canadian Publishers, McClelland and Stewart Limited, Toronto. ELIZABETH BISHOP Reprinted by permission of Farrar, Straus and Giroux, Inc.: 'Santarém', '12 O'Clock News', 'Squatter's Children', 'Questions of Travel', 'Arrival at Santos', 'Cape Breton', 'At the Fishhouses', 'The Imaginary Iceberg', 'The Map' from *Elizabeth Bishop: The Complete Poems 1927-1979*, copyright © 1983 by Alice Helen Methfessel, copyright © 1947, 1949, 1952, 1956, 1957, 1973, 1976, 1978 by Elizabeth Bishop, copyright renewed © 1974 by Elizabeth Bishop, copyright renewed © 1980 by Alice Methfessel. LEONARD COHEN 'Elegy', 'Story', 'You have the lovers', 'As the mist leaves no scar', 'Now of Sleeping', 'The Genius', 'Style', 'The Bus', 'The Music Crept by Us', 'Disguises' from *Selected Poems, 1956-1968* by Leonard Cohen. Used by permission of The Canadian Publishers, McClelland and

Stewart Limited, Toronto. ROBERT CREELEY 'The Immoral Proposition', 'The Way', 'The Awakening', The Rain', 'For Love' from *For Love: Poems 1950-1960*. Copyright © 1962 Robert Creeley. Reprinted with the permission of Charles Scribner's Sons. 'A Place', 'I keep to myself such measures', 'The Rhythm' from *Words*. 'To Define' from *A Quick Graph*. Reprinted with permission. E.E. CUMMINGS Introduction to *Complete Poems 1913-1962* by E.E. Cummings, renewed 1966 by Marion Morehouse Cummings; and 'i thank You God for most this amazing', 'dying is fine)but Death', 'true lovers in each happening of their hearts', ' love is more thicker than forget', 'my father moved through dooms of love', 'anyone lived in a pretty how town' copyright 1939, 1940, 1944, 1947, 1948 by E.E. Cummings, renewed 1967, 1968 by Marion Morehouse Cummings, 1972, 1975 by Nancy T. Andrews, reprinted from *Complete Poems 1913-1962* by E.E. Cummings by permission of Harcourt Brace Jovanovich, Inc. Reprinted by permission of Liveright Publishing Corporation: 'May i feel said he' from *No Thanks* by E.E. Cummings, copyright © 1968 by Marion Morehouse Cummings, copyright © 1973, 1978 by the Trustees for the E.E. Cummings Trust, copyright © 1973, 1978 by George James Firmage; 'somewhere i have never travelled, gladly beyond', 'i sing of Olaf' from *ViVa* by E.E. Cummings, copyright 1931, © 1959 by E.E. Cummings, copyright © 1979, 1973 by the Trustees for the E.E. Cummings Trust, copyright © 1979, 1973 by George James Firmage; 'my sweet old etcetera', 'Forward from Is 5' from *Is 5* by E.E. Cummings, copyright © 1985 by E.E. Cummings Trust, copyright 1926 by Horace Liveright, copyright © 1964 by E.E. Cummings, copyright © 1985 by George James Firmage; 'Chanson Innocentes' (I 'in Just-', II 'hist whist', V 'Tumbling-hair') from *Tulips and Chimneys* by E.E. Cummings, copyright 1923, 1925 and renewed 1951, 1953 by E.E. Cummings, copyright © 1973, 1976 by the Trustees for the E.E. Cummings Trust, copyright © 1973, 1976 by George James Firmage; 'A Poet's Advice to Students' appeared originally in the Ottawa Hills *Spectator*, reprinted from *e.e. cummings: A Miscellany Revised* edited by George J. Firmage, copyright 1955 by E.E. Cummings, copyright © 1965 by Marion Morehouse Cummings, copyright © 1958, 1965 by George J. Firmage. T.S. ELIOT Reprinted by permission of Faber and Faber Ltd.: 'The Love Song of J. Alfred Prufrock', 'Preludes', 'The Hollow Men', 'Journey of the Magi', 'Burnt Norton' from *Collected Poems 1909-1962* by T.S. Eliot; 'Tradition and the Individual Talent', 'From Hamlet and his Problems' from *Selected Essays* by T.S. Eliot; and 'From The Music of Poetry' from *On Poetry and Poets* by T.S. Eliot. LAWRENCE FERLINGHETTI 'In Goya's greatest scenes we seem to see', 'Don't let that horse eat that violin', 'Constantly risking absurdity and death', 'The pennycandystore beyond the El', 'Dog', 'Junkman's Obbligato' from Lawrence Ferlinghetti, *A Coney Island of the Mind*. Copyright © 1958 by Lawrence Ferlinghetti. Reprinted by permission of New Directions Publishing Corporation, New York. ROBERT FROST All poems from *The Poetry of Robert Frost* edited by Edward Connery Lathem. Copyright 1916, 1923, 1928, 1930, 1939, 1947, © 1969 by Holt, Rinehart and Winston. Copyright 1936, 1944, 1951, © 1956, 1958 by Robert Frost. Copyright © 1964, 1967, 1975 by Lesley Frost Ballantine. Reprinted by permission of Holt, Rinehart and Winston, Publishers. 'The Figure a Poem Makes' from *Selected Prose of Robert Frost* edited by Hyde Cox and Edward Connery Lathem. Copyright 1939, © 1967 by Holt, Rinehart and Winston. Reprinted by permission of Holt, Rinehart and Winston, Publishers. ALLEN GINSBERG Reprinted by permission of Harper & Row, Publishers, Inc., from *Collected Poems 1947-1980* by Allen Ginsberg: 'Sunflower Sutra', 'A Supermarket in California', 'Howl' copyright © 1955 by Allen Ginsberg; 'America' copyright © 1956, 1959 by Allen Ginsberg. ROBERT GRAVES Used by permission of Robert Graves and AP Watt Ltd.: 'Rocky Acres', 'The Pier-Glass', 'Warning to Children', 'The Cool Web', 'Pure Death', 'In Broken Images', 'Down, Wanton, Down!', 'With Her Lips Only', 'The Terraced Valley', and 'To Juan at the Winter Solstice' from *Collected Poems*; 'From The Poet and his Public' from *The Crowning Privilege*; and 'From Poetic Craft and Principle' from *Poetic Craft and Principle*. THOM GUNN Reprinted by permission of Faber and Faber Ltd.: 'The Wound', 'The Beach Head' from *Fighting Terms* by Thom Gunn; 'On the Move', 'Lines for a Book', 'Thoughts on Unpacking' from *The Sense of Movement* by Thom Gunn; 'In Santa Maria Del Popolo', 'Innocence' from *My Sad Captain* by Thom Gunn; and 'In the Tank' from *Touch* by Thom Gunn. SEAMUS HEANEY Reprinted by permission of Faber and Faber Ltd.: 'Digging', 'Death of a Naturalist', 'Mid-Term Break', 'Personal Helicon' from *Death of a Naturalist* by Seamus Heaney; 'Requiem for the Croppies', 'Bogland' from *Door Into The Dark* by Seamus Heaney; 'The Tollund Man', 'Summer Home' from *Wintering Out* by Seamus Heaney; and 'Bog Queen', 'Act of Union' from *North* by Seamus Heaney. TED HUGHES Reprinted by permission of Harper & Row, Publishers, Inc.: 'Macaw and Little Miss' 'Invitation to the Dance' from *The Hawk in the Rain* by Ted Hughes, copyright © 1957 by Ted Hughes; 'The Thought-Fox' copyright © 1957 by Ted Hughes (originally appeared in *The New Yorker*), and 'Six Young Men' copyright © 1957 by Ted Hughes from *New Selected Poems* by Ted Hughes. Reprinted by permission of Faber & Faber Ltd.: 'A Childish Prank', 'Crow's First Lesson', 'A Disaster' from *Crow* by Ted Hughes; 'Pike', 'Hawk Roosting' from *Lupercal* by Ted Hughes; and 'Dehorning' from *Moortown* by Ted Hughes. 'On Poetry' from *Ted Hughes: The Unaccommodated Universe*, used by permission of Black Sparrow Press. A.M. KLEIN 'Heirloom', '*In re* Solomon Warshawer', 'Political Meeting', 'Lone Bather', 'Portrait of the Poet as Landscape' 'Autobiographical' from *The Collected Poems of A.M. Klein*. Reprinted by permission of McGraw-Hill Ryerson Limited. PHILIP LARKIN 'Lines on a Young Lady's Photograph Album', 'Wants', 'Church Going', 'Toads', 'Poetry of Departures', 'If, My Darling' are reprinted from *The Less Deceived* by permission of The Marvell Press, England. 'Faith Healing', 'An Arundel Tomb' are reprinted by permission of Faber and Faber Ltd., from *The Whitsun Weddings* by Philip Larkin. IRVING LAYTON All poems are reprinted from *Collected Poems* by Irving Layton. Used by permission of The Canadian Publishers, McClelland & Stewart Limited, Toronto. ROBERT LOWELL 'The Holy Innocents', 'Christmas in Black Rock, 'After the Surprising Conversations', 'New Year's Day', 'The Quaker Graveyard in November', 'Mr Edwards and the Spider' from *Lord Weary's Castle*, copyright 1946, 1974 by Robert Lowell. Reprinted by permission of Harcourt Brace Jovanovich, Inc. Reprinted by permission of Farrar, Straus and Giroux, Inc.: 'For the Union Dead' from *For The Union Dead* by Robert Lowell, copyright © 1960, 1964 by Robert Lowell; and 'Skunk Hour', 'Memories of West Street and Lepke' from *Life Studies* by Robert Lowell, copyright © 1956, 1959 by Robert Lowell. 'From An Interview' from *Writers at Work: The Paris Review*

Interviews, 2nd Series. Edited by George Plimpton. Copyright © 1963 by
The Paris Review, Inc. Reprinted by permission of Viking Penguin Inc.
CHARLES OLSON 'The Kingfishers', 'As the Dead Prey Upon Us', 'Variations
Done for Gerald Van de Wiele', 'Projective Verse', 'Letter to Elaine Fein-
stein' from *Selected Writings* by Charles Olson, copyright 1950 by Poetry
New York, copyright © 1959, 1960 by Charles Olson. Reprinted by per-
mission of New Directions Publishing Corporation, New York. 'Maximus,
to Himself' from *The Maximus Poems*, Charles Butterick, ed. (1983). Re-
printed by permission of The University of California Press. MICHAEL
ONDAATJE Reprinted by permission of Michael Ondaatje: 'The Yellow
Room', 'To a Sad Daughter', 'The Cinnamon Peeler' from *Secular Love*
(Coach House Press, 1984); *'From* Billy the Kid' from *Billy the Kid;*
'Light', 'Bearhug', 'White Dwarfs', 'Letters & Other Worlds', 'Peter',
'Elizabeth', 'Signature' from *There's A Trick with a Knife I'm Learning
to Do*. WILFRED OWEN 'Strange Meeting', 'Greater Love', 'Arms and the
Boy', 'Anthem for Doomed Youth', 'Dulce Et Decorum Est', 'Futility' from
The Collected Poems of Wilfred Owen edited by C.D. Lewis. Used by
permission of Chatto & Windus. P.K. PAGE All poems reprinted by per-
mission of the author. SYLVIA PLATH Reprinted by permission of Olwyn
Hughes: 'Two Views of a Cadaver Room', 'The Colossus', 'Black Rook in
Rainy Weather', 'Blue Moles', 'The Disquieting Muses' from *The Colossus*
by Sylvia Plath, published by Faber and Faber, copyright Ted Hughes
1967; 'Lady Lazarus', 'Tulips', 'Ariel', 'Getting There', 'Daddy' from *Ariel*,
published by Faber and Faber, copyright Ted Hughes 1965; and 'Two
Campers in Cloud Country' from *Crossing the Water* by Sylvia Plath,
published by Faber and Faber, copyright Ted Hughes 1971. 'An Interview'
from *The Poet Speaks* edited by Peter Orr. Used by permission of the
publisher Routledge & Kegan Paul PLC. EZRA POUND Reprinted by permission of New Directions Publishing Corporation, New York: 'Canto I',
'Canto XIII', 'Canto XLV' from *The Cantos* by Ezra Pound, copyright
1934, 1937 by Ezra Pound; 'Portrait d'une Femme', 'The Garden', 'Com-
mission', 'Dance Figure', 'In a Station of the Metro', 'Alba', 'L'Art, 1910',
'The Tea Shop', 'The River-Merchant's Wife: A Letter', 'Exile's Letter',
'From *Hugh Selwyn Mauberley*: E.P. Ode pour l'élection de son sépulchre',
'Mr Nixon' from *Personae* by Ezra Pound, copyright 1926 by Ezra Pound;
and 'A Retrospect' from *The Literary Essays* by Ezra Pound, copyright
1918 by Ezra Pound. ALFRED PURDY 'Eskimo Graveyard' used by permis-
sion of the author. All other poems from *Selected Poems* by Al Purdy.
Used by permission of The Canadian Publishers, McClelland and Stewart
Limited, Toronto. ADRIENNE RICH 'At a Bach Concert', 'Snapshots of a
Daughter-in-Law', 'Necessities of Life', 'The Burning of Paper Instead of
Children', 'A Valediction Forbidding Mourning', 'Diving into the Wreck',
'The Phenomenology of Anger', 'Integrity', 'Frame' reprinted from *The
Face of a Doorframe, Poems Selected and New, 1950-1984*, by Adrienne
Rich, by permission of W.W. Norton & Company, Inc. Copyright © 1984
by Adrienne Rich. Copyright © 1975, 1978 by W.W. Norton & Company,
Inc. Copyright © 1981 by Adrienne Rich. THEODORE ROETHKE Reprinted
by permission of Doubleday & Company, Inc., from *The Collected Poems
of Theodore Roethke* by Theodore Roethke: 'In a Dark Time', copyright
© 1960 by Beatrice Roethke, as Administratrix of the Estate of Theodore

Roethke; 'The Far Field', copyright © 1964 by Beatrice Roethke, as Administratrix of the Estate of Theodore Roethke; 'Prayer', 'The Waking', 'Praise to the End', 'Old Lady's Winter Words', 'I Knew a Woman', copyright 1935, 1948, 1950, 1952, 1953, 1954 by Theodore Roethke; 'Dolor' copyright 1943 by Modern Poetry Association, Inc.; and 'Big Wind' copyright 1947 by The United Chapter of Phi Beta Kappa. 'From Some Remarks on Rhythm', 'From Open Letter' from *On the Poet and His Craft*, used by permission of University of Washington Press. GARY SNYDER Reprinted by permission of Gary Snyder: 'Anasazi' from *Manzanita*; 'Journeys (Section Six)' from *Six Sections from Mountain and Rivers Without End*; 'Riprap', 'Piute Creek' from *Riprap and Cold Mountain: Poems*; and 'Some Yips & Barks in the Dark' from *Naked Poetry*. Reprinted by permission of New Directions Publishing Corporation, New York: 'Song of the Taste' (first published in *Poetry*) and 'Kai, Today' from *Regarding Wave* by Gary Snyder, copyright © 1968 by Gary Snyder; 'Poetry of the Primitive' from *Earth House Hold* by Gary Snyder, copyright © 1967 by Gary Snyder. WALLACE STEVENS Reprinted by permission of Alfred A. Knopf, Inc.: from *The Collected Poems of Wallace Stevens* 'The Emperor of Ice-Cream', 'Sunday Morning' copyright 1923 and renewed 1951 by Wallace Stevens, 'The Idea of Order at Key West' copyright 1936 by Wallace Stevens and renewed 1964 by Holly Stevens, 'The Man on the Dump' copyright 1942 by Wallace Stevens and renewed 1970 by Holly Stevens, 'The Motive for Metaphor', 'Credences of Summer' copyright 1947 by Wallace Stevens, and 'The Poem that Took the Place of a Mountain' copyright 1952 by Wallace Stevens; from *Opus Posthumous*, by Wallace Stevens, edited by Samuel French Morse, copyright © 1957 by Elsie Stevens and Holly Stevens 'Selections from Adagia'. DYLAN THOMAS All poems from *Collected Poems, 1934-1952*, (J.M. Dent & Sons Ltd.), and 'Notes on the Art of Poetry' from *Texas Quarterly* (winter 1961) reprinted by permission of David Higham Associates Ltd., London. PHYLLIS WEBB All poems and poetics reprinted by permission of the author. RICHARD WILBUR Reprinted by permission of Harcourt Brace Jovanovich, Inc.: 'In the Smoking-Car' copyright 1960 by Richard Wilbur (first published in *The New Yorker*) and 'She' copyright 1958 by Richard Wilbur from his volume *Advice to a Prophet and Other Poems*; 'Love Calls Us to the Things of This World', 'Beasts' copyright © 1956 by Richard Wilbur, and 'Exeunt' copyright 1952, 1980 by Richard Wilbur from his volume *The Things of This World*; 'A Glance from the Bridge', 'Giacometti' from *Ceremony and Other Poems*, copyright 1950, 1978 by Richard Wilbur; and 'Place Pigalle' from *The Beautiful Changes*, copyright 1947, 1975 by Richard Wilbur. WILLIAM CARLOS WILLIAMS Reprinted by permission of New Directions Publishing Corporation, New York: 'Aux Imagistes' from *The Lost Poems of William Carlos Williams*, copyright © 1957 by Florence H. Williams; 'Danse Russe', 'This is Just to Say', 'To Waken an Old Lady', 'Tract', 'Spring and All', 'The Red Wheelbarrow', 'Nantucket', 'The Yachts' from *Collected Earlier Poems*, copyright 1938 by New Directions Publishing Corporation; 'The Dance', 'The Rewaking', 'To a Dog Injured in the Street', 'The Host' from *Pictures from Breughel and Other Poems*, copyright 1954, 1955, 1962 by William Carlos Williams; and

'On Measure—Statement for Sid Corman' from *Selected Essays*, copyright 1954 by William Carlos Williams. WILLIAM BUTLER YEATS Used by permission of Michael Yeats, Macmillan London Ltd., and A.P. Watt Ltd.: 'When You Are Old', 'Who Goes with Fergus?', 'The Folly of Being Comforted', 'The Wild Swans at Coole', 'The Fisherman', 'Easter 1916', 'The Second Coming', 'A Prayer for my Daughter', 'Sailing to Byzantium', 'Leda and the Swan', 'Among School Children', 'For Anne Gregory', 'Crazy Jane Talks with the Bishop', 'News for the Delphic Oracle', 'Long-Legged Fly', 'The Circus Animals' Desertion', 'Politics' from *Collected Poems* by W.B. Yeats; 'From Magic' from *Ideas of Good and Evil* by W.B. Yeats; 'From The Symbolism of Poetry' from *The Symbolism of Poetry* by W.B. Yeats; and 'From A General Introduction to my Work' from *Essays and Introductions* by W.B. Yeats.

There are a few poems whose copyright owners have not been located after diligent inquiry. The publishers would be grateful for information enabling them to make suitable acknowledgements in future printings.

William Butler Yeats

When You Are Old

When you are old and grey and full of sleep,
And nodding by the fire, take down this book,
And slowly read, and dream of the soft look
Your eyes had once, and of their shadows deep;

How many loved your moments of glad grace,
And loved your beauty with love false or true,
But one man loved the pilgrim soul in you,
And loved the sorrows of your changing face;

And bending down beside the glowing bars,
Murmur, a little sadly, how Love fled
And paced upon the mountains overhead
And hid his face amid a crowd of stars.

Who Goes with Fergus?

Who will go drive with Fergus now,
And pierce the deep wood's woven shade,
And dance upon the level shore?
Young man, lift up your russet brow,
And lift your tender eyelids, maid,
And brood on hopes and fear no more.

And no more turn aside and brood
Upon love's bitter mystery;
For Fergus rules the brazen cars,
And rules the shadows of the wood,
And the white breast of the dim sea
And all dishevelled wandering stars.

The Folly of Being Comforted

One that is ever kind said yesterday:
'Your well-belovèd's hair has threads of grey,
And little shadows come about her eyes;
Time can but make it easier to be wise
Though now it seems impossible, and so
All that you need is patience.'
                       Heart cries, 'No,
I have not a crumb of comfort, not a grain.
Time can but make her beauty over again:
Because of that great nobleness of hers
The fire that stirs about her, when she stirs,
Burns but more clearly. O she had not these ways
When all the wild summer was in her gaze.'

O heart! O heart! if she'd but turn her head,
You'd know the folly of being comforted.

The Wild Swans at Coole

The trees are in their autumn beauty,
The woodland paths are dry,
Under the October twilight the water
Mirrors a still sky;
Upon the brimming water among the stones
Are nine-and-fifty swans.

The nineteenth autumn has come upon me
Since I first made my count;
I saw, before I had well finished,
All suddenly mount
And scatter wheeling in great broken rings
Upon their clamorous wings.

I have looked upon those brilliant creatures,
And now my heart is sore.
All's changed since I, hearing at twilight,
The first time on this shore,
The bell-beat of their wings above my head,
Trod with a lighter tread.

Unwearied still, lover by lover,
They paddle in the cold
Companionable streams or climb the air;
Their hearts have not grown old;
Passion or conquest, wander where they will,
Attend upon them still.

But now they drift on the still water,
Mysterious, beautiful;
Among what rushes will they build,
By what lake's edge or pool
Delight men's eyes when I awake some day
To find they have flown away?

The Fisherman

Although I can see him still,
The freckled man who goes
To a grey place on a hill
In grey Connemara clothes
At dawn to cast his flies,
It's long since I began
To call up to the eyes
This wise and simple man.
All day I'd looked in the face
What I had hoped 'twould be
To write for my own race
And the reality;

The living men that I hate,
The dead man that I loved,
The craven man in his seat,
The insolent unreproved,
And no knave brought to book
Who has won a drunken cheer,
The witty man and his joke
Aimed at the commonest ear,
The clever man who cries
The catch-cries of the clown,
The beating down of the wise
And great Art beaten down.

Maybe a twelvemonth since
Suddenly I began,
In scorn of this audience,
Imagining a man,
And his sun-freckled face,
And grey Connemara cloth,
Climbing up to a place
Where stone is dark under froth,
And the down-turn of his wrist
When the flies drop in the stream;
A man who does not exist,
A man who is but a dream;
And cried, 'Before I am old
I shall have written him one
Poem maybe as cold
And passionate as the dawn.'

Easter 1916

I have met them at close of day
Coming with vivid faces
From counter or desk among grey
Eighteenth-century houses.

I have passed with a nod of the head
Or polite meaningless words,
Or have lingered awhile and said
Polite meaningless words,
And thought before I had done
Of a mocking tale or a gibe
To please a companion
Around the fire at the club,
Being certain that they and I
But lived where motley is worn:
All changed, changed utterly:
A terrible beauty is born.

That woman's days were spent
In ignorant good-will,
Her nights in argument
Until her voice grew shrill.
What voice more sweet than hers
When, young and beautiful,
She rode to harriers?
This man had kept a school
And rode our wingèd horse;
This other his helper and friend
Was coming into his force;
He might have won fame in the end,
So sensitive his nature seemed,
So daring and sweet his thought.
This other man I had dreamed
A drunken, vainglorious lout.
He had done most bitter wrong
To some who are near my heart,
Yet I number him in the song;
He, too, has resigned his part
In the casual comedy;
He, too, has been changed in his turn,
Transformed utterly:
A terrible beauty is born.

Hearts with one purpose alone
Through summer and winter seem
Enchanted to a stone
To trouble the living stream.
The horse that comes from the road,
The rider, the birds that range
From cloud to tumbling cloud,
Minute by minute they change;
A shadow of cloud on the stream
Changes minute by minute;
A horse-hoof slides on the brim,
And a horse plashes within it;
The long-legged moor-hens dive,
And hens to moor-cocks call;
Minute by minute they live:
The stone's in the midst of all.

Too long a sacrifice
Can make a stone of the heart.
O when may it suffice?
That is Heaven's part, our part
To murmur name upon name,
As a mother names her child
When sleep at last has come
On limbs that had run wild.
What is it but nightfall?
No, no, not night but death;
Was it needless death after all?
For England may keep faith
For all that is done and said.
We know their dream; enough
To know they dreamed and are dead;
And what if excess of love
Bewildered them till they died?
I write it out in a verse—
MacDonagh and MacBride
And Connolly and Pearse
Now and in time to be,

Wherever green is worn,
Are changed, changed utterly:
A terrible beauty is born.

The Second Coming

Turning and turning in the widening gyre
The falcon cannot hear the falconer;
Things fall apart; the centre cannot hold;
Mere anarchy is loosed upon the world,
The blood-dimmed tide is loosed, and everywhere
The ceremony of innocence is drowned;
The best lack all conviction, while the worst
Are full of passionate intensity.

Surely some revelation is at hand;
Surely the Second Coming is at hand.
The Second Coming! Hardly are those words out
When a vast image out of *Spiritus Mundi*
Troubles my sight: somewhere in sands of the desert
A shape with lion body and the head of a man,
A gaze blank and pitiless as the sun,
Is moving its slow thighs, while all about it
Reel shadows of the indignant desert birds.
The darkness drops again; but now I know
That twenty centuries of stony sleep
Were vexed to nightmare by a rocking cradle,
And what rough beast, its hour come round at last,
Slouches towards Bethlehem to be born?

A Prayer for my Daughter

Once more the storm is howling, and half hid
Under this cradle-hood and coverlid
My child sleeps on. There is no obstacle

But Gregory's wood and one bare hill
Whereby the haystack- and roof-levelling wind,
Bred on the Atlantic, can be stayed;
And for an hour I have walked and prayed
Because of the great gloom that is in my mind.

I have walked and prayed for this young child an hour
And heard the sea-wind scream upon the tower,
And under the arches of the bridge, and scream
In the elms above the flooded stream;
Imagining in excited reverie
That the future years had come,
Dancing to a frenzied drum,
Out of the murderous innocence of the sea.

May she be granted beauty and yet not
Beauty to make a stranger's eye distraught,
Or hers before a looking-glass, for such,
Being made beautiful overmuch,
Consider beauty a sufficient end,
Lose natural kindness and maybe
The heart-revealing intimacy
That chooses right, and never find a friend.

Helen being chosen found life flat and dull
And later had much trouble from a fool,
While that great Queen, that rose out of the spray,
Being fatherless could have her way
Yet chose a bandy-leggèd smith for man.
It's certain that fine women eat
A crazy salad with their meat
Whereby the Horn of Plenty is undone.

In courtesy I'd have her chiefly learned;
Hearts are not had as a gift but hearts are earned
By those that are not entirely beautiful;
Yet many, that have played the fool
For beauty's very self, has charm made wise,

And many a poor man that has roved,
Loved and thought himself beloved,
From a glad kindness cannot take his eyes.

May she become a flourishing hidden tree
That all her thoughts may like the linnet be,
And have no business but dispensing round
Their magnanimities of sound,
Nor but in merriment begin a chase,
Nor but in merriment a quarrel.
O may she live like some green laurel
Rooted in one dear perpetual place.

My mind, because the minds that I have loved,
The sort of beauty that I have approved,
Prosper but little, has dried up of late,
Yet knows that to be choked with hate
May well be of all evil chances chief.
If there's no hatred in a mind
Assault and battery of the wind
Can never tear the linnet from the leaf.

An intellectual hatred is the worst,
So let her think opinions are accursed.
Have I not seen the loveliest woman born
Out of the mouth of Plenty's horn,
Because of her opinionated mind
Barter that horn and every good
By quiet natures understood
For an old bellows full of angry wind?

Considering that, all hatred driven hence,
The soul recovers radical innocence
And learns at last that it is self-delighting,
Self-appeasing, self-affrighting,
And that its own sweet will is Heaven's will;
She can, though every face should scowl
And every windy quarter howl
Or every bellows burst, be happy still.

And may her bridegroom bring her to a house
Where all's accustomed, ceremonious;
For arrogance and hatred are the wares
Peddled in the thoroughfares.
How but in custom and in ceremony
Are innocence and beauty born?
Ceremony's a name for the rich horn,
And custom for the spreading laurel tree.

Sailing to Byzantium

I

That is no country for old men. The young
In one another's arms, birds in the trees
—Those dying generations—at their song,
The salmon-falls, the mackerel-crowded seas,
Fish, flesh, or fowl, commend all summer long
Whatever is begotten, born, and dies.
Caught in that sensual music all neglect
Monuments of unageing intellect.

II

An aged man is but a paltry thing,
A tattered coat upon a stick, unless
Soul clap its hands and sing, and louder sing
For every tatter in its mortal dress,
Nor is there singing school but studying
Monuments of its own magnificence;
And therefore I have sailed the seas and come
To the holy city of Byzantium.

III

O sages standing in God's holy fire
As in the gold mosaic of a wall,
Come from the holy fire, perne in a gyre,

And be the singing-masters of my soul.
Consume my heart away; sick with desire
And fastened to a dying animal
It knows not what it is; and gather me
Into the artifice of eternity.

IV

Once out of nature I shall never take
My bodily form from any natural thing,
But such a form as Grecian goldsmiths make
Of hammered gold and gold enamelling
To keep a drowsy Emperor awake;
Or set upon a golden bough to sing
To lords and ladies of Byzantium
Of what is past, or passing, or to come.

Leda and the Swan

A sudden blow: the great wings beating still
Above the staggering girl, her thighs caressed
By the dark webs, her nape caught in his bill,
He holds her helpless breast upon his breast.

How can those terrified vague fingers push
The feathered glory from her loosening thighs?
And how can body, laid in that white rush,
But feel the strange heart beating where it lies?

A shudder in the loins engenders there
The broken wall, the burning roof and tower
And Agamemnon dead.
                          Being so caught up,
So mastered by the brute blood of the air,
Did she put on his knowledge with his power
Before the indifferent beak could let her drop?

Among School Children

I

I walk through the long schoolroom questioning;
A kind old nun in a white hood replies;
The children learn to cipher and to sing,
To study reading-books and histories,
To cut and sew, be neat in everything
In the best modern way—the children's eyes
In momentary wonder stare upon
A sixty-year-old smiling public man.

II

I dream of a Ledaean body, bent
Above a sinking fire, a tale that she
Told of a harsh reproof, or trivial event
That changed some childish day to tragedy—
Told, and it seemed that our two natures blent
Into a sphere from youthful sympathy,
Or else, to alter Plato's parable,
Into the yolk and white of the one shell.

III

And thinking of that fit of grief or rage
I look upon one child or t'other there
And wonder if she stood so at that age—
For even daughters of the swan can share
Something of every paddler's heritage—
And had that colour upon cheek or hair,
And thereupon my heart is driven wild:
She stands before me as a living child.

IV

Her present image floats into the mind—
Did Quattrocento finger fashion it
Hollow of cheek as though it drank the wind
And took a mess of shadows for its meat?
And I though never of Ledaean kind

Had pretty plumage once—enough of that,
Better to smile on all that smile, and show
There is a comfortable kind of old scarecrow.

V

What youthful mother, a shape upon her lap
Honey of generation had betrayed,
And that must sleep, shriek, struggle to escape
As recollection or the drug decide,
Would think her son, did she but see that shape
With sixty or more winters on its head,
A compensation for the pang of his birth,
Or the uncertainty of his setting forth?

VI

Plato thought nature but a spume that plays
Upon a ghostly paradigm of things;
Solider Aristotle played the taws
Upon the bottom of a king of kings;
World-famous golden-thighed Pythagoras
Fingered upon a fiddle-stick or strings
What a star sang and careless Muses heard:
Old clothes upon old sticks to scare a bird.

VII

Both nuns and mothers worship images,
But those the candles light are not as those
That animate a mother's reveries,
But keep a marble or a bronze repose.
And yet they too break hearts—O Presences
That passion, piety or affection knows,
And that all heavenly glory symbolise—
O self-born mockers of man's enterprise;

VIII

Labour is blossoming or dancing where
The body is not bruised to pleasure soul,
Nor beauty born out of its own despair,

Nor blear-eyed wisdom out of midnight oil.
O chestnut-tree, great-rooted blossomer,
Are you the leaf, the blossom or the bole?
O body swayed to music, O brightening glance,
How can we know the dancer from the dance?

For Anne Gregory

'Never shall a young man,
Thrown into despair
By those great honey-coloured
Ramparts at your ear,
Love you for yourself alone
And not your yellow hair.'

'But I can get a hair-dye
And set such colour there,
Brown, or black, or carrot,
That young men in despair
May love me for myself alone
And not my yellow hair.'

'I heard an old religious man
But yesternight declare
That he had found a text to prove
That only God, my dear,
Could love you for yourself alone
And not your yellow hair.'

Crazy Jane Talks with the Bishop

I met the Bishop on the road
And much said he and I.
'Those breasts are flat and fallen now,

Those veins must soon be dry;
Live in a heavenly mansion,
Not in some foul sty.'

'Fair and foul are near of kin,
And fair needs foul,' I cried.
'My friends are gone, but that's a truth
Nor grave nor bed denied,
Learned in bodily lowliness
And in the heart's pride.

'A woman can be proud and stiff
When on love intent;
But love has pitched his mansion in
The place of excrement;
For nothing can be sole or whole
That has not been rent.'

News for the Delphic Oracle

I

There all the golden codgers lay,
There the silver dew,
And the great water sighed for love,
And the wind sighed too.
Man-picker Niamh leant and sighed
By Oisin on the grass;
There sighed amid his choir of love
Tall Pythagoras.
Plotinus came and looked about,
The salt-flakes on his breast,
And having stretched and yawned awhile
Lay sighing like the rest.

II

Straddling each a dolphin's back
And steadied by a fin,

Those Innocents re-live their death,
Their wounds open again.
The ecstatic waters laugh because
Their cries are sweet and strange,
Through their ancestral patterns dance,
And the brute dolphins plunge
Until, in some cliff-sheltered bay
Where wades the choir of love
Proffering its sacred laurel crowns,
They pitch their burdens off.

III

Slim adolescence that a nymph has stripped,
Peleus on Thetis stares.
Her limbs are delicate as an eyelid,
Love has blinded him with tears;
But Thetis' belly listens.
Down the mountain walls
From where Pan's cavern is
Intolerable music falls.
Foul goat-head, brutal arm appear,
Belly, shoulder, bum,
Flash fishlike; nymphs and satyrs
Copulate in the foam.

Long-Legged Fly

That civilisation may not sink,
Its great battle lost,
Quiet the dog, tether the pony
To a distant post;
Our master Caesar is in the tent
Where the maps are spread,
His eyes fixed upon nothing,
A hand under his head.
Like a long-legged fly upon the stream
His mind moves upon silence.

That the topless towers be burnt
And men recall that face,
Move most gently if move you must
In this lonely place.
She thinks, part woman, three parts a child,
That nobody looks; her feet
Practise a tinker shuffle
Picked up on a street.
Like a long-legged fly upon the stream
Her mind moves upon silence.

That girls at puberty may find
The first Adam in their thought,
Shut the door of the Pope's chapel
Keep those children out.
There on that scaffolding reclines
Michael Angelo.
With no more sound than the mice make
His hand moves to and fro.
Like a long-legged fly upon the stream
His mind moves upon silence.

The Circus Animals' Desertion

I

I sought a theme and sought for it in vain,
I sought it daily for six weeks or so.
Maybe at last, being but a broken man,
I must be satisfied with my heart, although
Winter and summer till old age began
My circus animals were all on show,
Those stilted boys, that burnished chariot,
Lion and woman and the Lord knows what.

II

What can I but enumerate old themes?
First that sea-rider Oisin led by the nose
Through three enchanted islands, allegorical dreams,
Vain gaiety, vain battle, vain repose,
Themes of the embittered heart, or so it seems,
That might adore old songs or courtly shows;
But what cared I that set him on to ride,
I, starved for the bosom of his faery bride?

And then a counter-truth filled out its play,
The Countess Cathleen was the name I gave it;
She, pity-crazed, had given her soul away,
But masterful Heaven had intervened to save it.
I thought my dear must her own soul destroy,
So did fanaticism and hate enslave it,
And this brought forth a dream and soon enough
This dream itself had all my thought and love.

And when the Fool and Blind Man stole the bread
Cuchulain fought the ungovernable sea;
Heart-mysteries there, and yet when all is said
It was the dream itself enchanted me:
Character isolated by a deed
To engross the present and dominate memory.
Players and painted stage took all my love,
And not those things that they were emblems of.

III

Those masterful images because complete
Grew in pure mind, but out of what began?
A mound of refuse or the sweepings of a street,
Old kettles, old bottles, and a broken can,
Old iron, old bones, old rags, that raving slut
Who keeps the till. Now that my ladder's gone,
I must lie down where all the ladders start,
In the foul rag-and-bone shop of the heart.

Politics

'In our time the destiny of man presents its meaning in political terms.'—
THOMAS MANN

How can I, that girl standing there,
My attention fix
On Roman or on Russian
Or on Spanish politics?
Yet here's a travelled man that knows
What he talks about,
And there's a politician
That has read and thought,
And maybe what they say is true
Of war and war's alarms,
But O that I were young again
And held her in my arms!

Ezra Pound

Portrait d'une Femme

Your mind and you are our Sargasso Sea,
London has swept about you this score years
And bright ships left you this or that in fee:
Ideas, old gossip, oddments of all things,
Strange spars of knowledge and dimmed wares of price.
Great minds have sought you—lacking someone else.
You have been second always. Tragical?
No. You preferred it to the usual thing:
One dull man, dulling and uxorious,
One average mind—with one thought less, each year.
Oh, you are patient, I have seen you sit
Hours, where something might have floated up.
And now you pay one. Yes, you richly pay.
You are a person of some interest, one comes to you
And takes strange gain away:
Trophies fished up; some curious suggestion;
Fact that leads nowhere; and a tale or two,
Pregnant with mandrakes, or with something else
That might prove useful and yet never proves,
That never fits a corner or shows use,
Or finds its hour upon the loom of days:
The tarnished, gaudy, wonderful old work;
Idols and ambergris and rare inlays,
These are your riches, your great store; and yet
For all this sea-hoard of deciduous things,
Strange woods half-sodden, and new brighter stuff:
In the slow float of differing light and deep,
No! there is nothing! In the whole and all,
Nothing that's quite your own.
                              Yet this is you.

The Garden

'En robe de parade.'—SAMAIN

Like a skein of loose silk blown against a wall
She walks by the railing of a path
          in Kensington Gardens,
And she is dying piece-meal
          of a sort of emotional anæmia.

And round about there is a rabble
Of the filthy, sturdy, unkillable infants of the very poor.
They shall inherit the earth.

In her is the end of breeding.
Her boredom is exquisite and excessive.
She would like some one to speak to her,
And is almost afraid that I
          will commit that indiscretion.

Commission

Go, my songs, to the lonely and the unsatisfied,
Go also to the nerve-racked, go to the enslaved-by-convention,
Bear to them my contempt for their oppressors.
Go as a great wave of cool water,
Bear my contempt of oppressors.

Speak against unconscious oppression,
Speak against the tyranny of the unimaginative,
Speak against bonds.
Go to the bourgeoise who is dying of her ennuis,
Go to the women in suburbs.
Go to the hideously wedded,
Go to them whose failure is concealed,
Go to the unluckily mated,

Go to the bought wife,
Go to the woman entailed.

Go to those who have delicate lust,
Go to those whose delicate desires are thwarted,
Go like a blight upon the dullness of the world;
Go with your edge against this,
Strengthen the subtle cords,
Bring confidence upon the algæ and the tentacles of the soul.

Go in a friendly manner,
Go with an open speech.
Be eager to find new evils and new good,
Be against all forms of oppression.
Go to those who are thickened with middle age,
To those who have lost their interest.

Go to the adolescent who are smothered in family—
Oh how hideous it is
To see three generations of one house gathered together!
It is like an old tree with shoots,
And with some branches rotted and falling.

Go out and defy opinion,
Go against this vegetable bondage of the blood.
Be against all sorts of mortmain.

Dance Figure

For the Marriage in Cana of Galilee

Dark eyed,
O woman of my dreams,
Ivory sandalled,
There is none like thee among the dancers,
None with swift feet.
I have not found thee in the tents,

In the broken darkness.
I have not found thee at the well-head
Among the women with pitchers.

Thine arms are as a young sapling under the bark;
Thy face as a river with lights.

White as an almond are thy shoulders;
As new almonds stripped from the husk.
They guard thee not with eunuchs;
Not with bars of copper.

Gilt turquoise and silver are in the place of thy rest.
A brown robe, with threads of gold woven in
        patterns, hast thou gathered about thee,
O Nathat-Ikanaie, 'Tree-at-the-river'.

As a rillet among the sedge are thy hands upon me;
Thy fingers a frosted stream.

Thy maidens are white like pebbles;
Their music about thee!

There is none like thee among the dancers;
None with swift feet.

In a Station of the Metro

The apparition of these faces in the crowd;
Petals on a wet, black bough.

Alba

As cool as the pale wet leaves
                    of lily-of-the-valley
She lay beside me in the dawn.

L'Art, 1910

Green arsenic smeared on an egg-white cloth,
Crushed strawberries! Come, let us feast our eyes.

The Tea Shop

The girl in the tea shop
                          Is not so beautiful as she was,
The August has worn against her.
She does not get up the stairs so eagerly;
Yes, she also will turn middle-aged,
And the glow of youth that she spread about us
                          As she brought us our muffins
Will be spread about us no longer.
                          She also will turn middle-aged.

The River-Merchant's Wife: A Letter

While my hair was still cut straight across my forehead
I played about the front gate, pulling flowers.
You came by on bamboo stilts, playing horse,
You walked about my seat, playing with blue plums.
And we went on living in the village of Chokan:
Two small people, without dislike or suspicion.

At fourteen I married My Lord you.
I never laughed, being bashful.
Lowering my head, I looked at the wall.
Called to, a thousand times, I never looked back.

At fifteen I stopped scowling,
I desired my dust to be mingled with yours

For ever and for ever and for ever.
Why should I climb the look out?

At sixteen you departed,
You went into far Ku-to-yen, by the river of swirling eddies,
And you have been gone five months.
The monkeys make sorrowful noise overhead.

You dragged your feet when you went out.
By the gate now, the moss is grown, the different mosses,
Too deep to clear them away!
The leaves fall early this autumn, in wind.
The paired butterflies are already yellow with August
Over the grass in the West garden;
They hurt me. I grow older.
If you are coming down through the narrows of the river Kiang,
Please let me know beforehand,
And I will come out to meet you
          As far as Cho-fu-Sa.

By Rihaku
A.D. 800

Exile's Letter

To So-Kin of Rakuyo, ancient friend, Chancellor of Gen.
Now I remember that you built me a special tavern
By the south side of the bridge at Ten-Shin.
With yellow gold and white jewels, we paid for songs and
     laughter
And we were drunk for month on month, forgetting the kings
     and princes.
Intelligent men came drifting in from the sea and from the west
     border,
And with them, and with you especially
There was nothing at cross purpose,
And they made nothing of sea-crossing or of mountain-crossing,

If only they could be of that fellowship,
And we all spoke out our hearts and minds, without regret.
And then I was sent off to South Wei,
        smothered in laurel groves,
And you to the north of Raku-hoku
Till we had nothing but thoughts and memories in common.
And then, when separation had come to its worst,
We met, and travelled into Sen-Go,
Through all the thirty-six folds of the turning and twisting
    waters.
Into a valley of the thousand bright flowers,
That was the first valley;
And into ten thousand valleys full of voices and pine-winds.
And with silver harness and reins of gold,
Out came the East of Kan foreman and his company
And there came also the 'True man' of Shi-yo to meet me,
Playing on a jewelled mouth-organ.
In the storied houses of San-Ko they gave us more Sennin music,
Many instruments, like the sound of young phoenix broods.
The foreman of Kan Chu, drunk, danced
        because his long sleeves wouldn't keep still
With that music playing,
And I, wrapped in brocade, went to sleep with my head on his
    lap,
And my spirit so high it was all over the heavens,
And before the end of the day we were scattered like stars, or
    rain.
I had to be off to So, far away over the waters,
You back to your river-bridge.

And your father, who was as brave as a leopard,
Was governor in Hei Shu, and put down the barbarian rabble.
And one May he had you send for me,
        despite the long distance.
And what with broken wheels and so on, I won't say it wasn't
    hard going,
Over roads twisted like sheep's guts.
And I was still going, late in the year,
        in the cutting wind from the North,

And thinking how little you cared for the cost,
        and you caring enough to pay it.
And what a reception:
Red jade cups, food well set on a blue jewelled table,
And I was drunk, and had no thought of returning.
And you would walk out with me to the western corner of the
    castle,
To the dynastic temple, with water about it clear as blue jade,
With boats floating, and the sound of mouth-organs and drums,
With ripples like dragon-scales, going grass-green on the water,
Pleasure lasting, with courtesans, going and coming without
    hindrance,
With the willow flakes falling like snow,
And the vermilioned girls getting drunk about sunset,
And the water, a hundred feet deep, reflecting green eyebrows
—Eyebrows painted green are a fine sight in young moonlight,
Gracefully painted—
And the girls singing back at each other,
Dancing in transparent brocade,
And the wind lifting the song, and interrupting it,
Tossing it up under the clouds.
            And all this comes to an end.
            And is not again to be met with.
I went up to the court for examination,
Tried Layu's luck, offered the Choyo song,
And got no promotion,
            and went back to the East Mountains
            White-headed.
And once again, later, we met at the South bridge-head.
And then the crowd broke up, you went north to San palace,
And if you ask how I regret that parting:
It is like the flowers falling at Spring's end
            Confused, whirled in a tangle.
What is the use of talking, and there is no end of talking,
There is no end of things in the heart.
I call in the boy,
Have him sit on his knees here
            To seal this,
And send it a thousand miles, thinking.

By Rihaku

From *Hugh Selwyn Mauberley*

I

For three years, out of key with his time,
He strove to resuscitate the dead art
Of poetry; to maintain 'the sublime'
In the old sense. Wrong from the start—

No, hardly, but seeing he had been born
In a half-savage country, out of date;
Bent resolutely on wringing lilies from the acorn;
Capaneus; trout for factitious bait;

'Ιδμεν γάρ τοι πάνθ', ὅσ' ἐνὶ Τροίη
Caught in the unstopped ear;
Giving the rocks small lee-way
The chopped seas held him, therefore, that year.

His true Penelope was Flaubert,
He fished by obstinate isles;
Observed the elegance of Circe's hair
Rather than the mottoes on sundials.

Unaffected by 'the march of events',
He passed from men's memory in *l'an trentiesm*
De son eage; the case presents
No adjunct to the Muses' diadem.

II

The age demanded an image
Of its accelerated grimace,
Something for the modern stage,
Not, at any rate, an Attic grace;

Not, not certainly, the obscure reveries

Of the inward gaze;
Better mendacities
Than the classics in paraphrase!

The 'age demanded' chiefly a mould in plaster,
Made with no loss of time,
A prose kinema, not, not assuredly, alabaster
Or the 'sculpture' of rhyme.

III

The tea-rose tea-gown, etc.
Supplants the mousseline of Cos,
The pianola 'replaces'
Sappho's barbitos.

Christ follows Dionysus,
Phallic and ambrosial
Made way for macerations;
Caliban casts out Ariel.

All things are a flowing,
Sage Heracleitus says;
But a tawdry cheapness
Shall outlast our days.

Even the Christian beauty
Defects—after Samothrace;
We see τὸ καλὸν
Decreed in the market-place.

Faun's flesh is not to us,
Nor the saint's vision.
We have the Press for wafer;
Franchise for circumcision.

All men, in law, are equals.
Free of Pisistratus,
We choose a knave or an eunuch
To rule over us.

O bright Apollo,
τίν' ἀνδρα, τίν' ἦρωα. τίνα θεὸν,
What god, man, or hero
Shall I place a tin wreath upon!

MR NIXON

In the cream gilded cabin of his steam yacht
Mr Nixon advised me kindly, to advance with fewer
Dangers of delay. 'Consider
        Carefully the reviewer.

'I was as poor as you are;
When I began I got, of course,
Advance on royalties, fifty at first,' said Mr Nixon,
'Follow me, and take a column,
Even if you have to work free.

'Butter reviewers. From fifty to three hundred
I rose in eighteen months;
The hardest nut I had to crack
Was Dr Dundas.

'I never mentioned a man but with the view
Of selling my own works.
The tip's a good one, as for literature
It gives no man a sinecure.

'And no one knows, at sight, a masterpiece.
And give up verse, my boy,
There's nothing in it.'

   .   .   .

Likewise a friend of Blougram's once advised me:
Don't kick against the pricks,
Accept opinion. The 'Nineties' tried your game
And died, there's nothing in it.

Canto I

And then went down to the ship,
Set keel to breakers, forth on the godly sea, and
We set up mast and sail on that swart ship,
Bore sheep aboard her, and our bodies also
Heavy with weeping, so winds from sternward
Bore us out onward with bellying canvas,
Circe's this craft, the trim-coifed goddess.
Then sat we amidships, wind jamming the tiller,
Thus with stretched sail, we went over sea till day's end.
Sun to his slumber, shadows o'er all the ocean,
Came we then to the bounds of deepest water,
To the Kimmerian lands, and peopled cities
Covered with close-webbed mist, unpiercèd ever
With glitter of sun-rays
Nor with stars stretched, nor looking back from heaven
Swartest night stretched over wretched men there.
The ocean flowing backward, came we then to the place
Aforesaid by Circe.
Here did they rites, Perimedes and Eurylochus,
And drawing sword from my hip
I dug the ell-square pitkin;
Poured we libations unto each the dead,
First mead and then sweet wine, water mixed with white flour.
Then prayed I many a prayer to the sickly death's-heads;
As set in Ithaca, sterile bulls of the best
For sacrifice, heaping the pyre with goods,
A sheep to Tiresias only, black and a bell-sheep.
Dark blood flowed in the fosse,
Souls out of Erebus, cadaverous dead, of brides,
Of youths and of the old who had borne much;
Souls stained with recent tears, girls tender,
Men many, mauled with bronze lance heads,
Battle spoil, bearing yet dreory arms,
These many crowded about me; with shouting,
Pallor upon me, cried to my men for more beasts;
Slaughtered the herds, sheep slain of bronze;

Poured ointment, cried to the gods,
To Pluto the strong, and praised Proserpine;
Unsheathed the narrow sword,
I sat to keep off the impetuous impotent dead,
Till I should hear Tiresias.
But first Elpenor came, our friend Elpenor,
Unburied, cast on the wide earth,
Limbs that we left in the house of Circe,
Unwept, unwrapped in sepulchre, since toils urged other.
Pitiful spirit. And I cried in hurried speech:
'Elpenor, how art thou come to this dark coast?
Cam'st thou afoot, outstripping seamen?'
                And he in heavy speech:
'Ill fate and abundant wine. I slept in Circe's ingle.
Going down the long ladder unguarded,
I fell against the buttress,
Shattered the nape-nerve, the soul sought Avernus.
But thou, O King, I bid remember me, unwept, unburied,
Heap up mine arms, be tomb by sea-board, and inscribed:
A man of no fortune and with a name to come."
And set my oar up, that I swung mid fellows.'

And Anticlea came, whom I beat off, and then Tiresias Theban,
Holding his golden wand, knew me, and spoke first:
'A second time? why? man of ill star,
Facing the sunless dead and this joyless region?
Stand from the fosse, leave me my bloody bever
For soothsay.'
                And I stepped back,
And he strong with the blood, said then: 'Odysseus
Shalt return through spiteful Neptune, over dark seas,
Lose all companions.' And then Anticlea came.
Lie quiet Divus. I mean that is Andreas Divus,
In officina Wecheli, 1538, out of Homer.
And he sailed, by Sirens and thence outward and away
And unto Circe.
                Venerandam,
In the Cretan's phrase, with the golden crown, Aphrodite,

Cypri munimenta sortita est, mirthful, oricalchi, with golden
Girdles and breast bands, thou with dark eyelids
Bearing the golden bough of Argicida.

Canto XIII

Kung walked
            by the dynastic temple
and into the cedar grove,
            and then out by the lower river,
And with him Khieu Tchi
            and Tian the low speaking
And 'we are unknown,' said Kung,
You will take up charioteering?
            'Then you will become known,
Or perhaps I should take up charioteering, or archery?
Or the practice of public speaking?'
And Tseu-lou said, 'I would put the defences in order,'
And Khieu said, 'If I were lord of a province
I would put it in better order than this is.'
And Tchi said, 'I should prefer a small mountain temple,
With order in the observances,
            with a suitable performance of the ritual,'
And Tian said, with his hand on the strings of his lute
The low sounds continuing
            after his hand left the strings,
And the sound went up like smoke, under the leaves,
And he looked after the sound:
            'The old swimming hole,
And the boys flopping off the planks,
Or sitting in the underbrush playing mandolins.'
            And Kung smiled upon all of them equally.
And Thseng-sie desired to know:
            'Which had answered correctly?'

And Kung said, 'They have all answered correctly,
That is to say, each in his nature.'
And Kung raised his cane against Yuan Jang,
        Yuan Jang being his elder,
For Yuan Jang sat by the roadside pretending to
        be receiving wisdom.
And Kung said
        'You old fool, come out of it,
Get up and do something useful.'
        And Kung said
'Respect a child's faculties
From the moment it inhales the clear air,
But a man of fifty who knows nothing
        Is worthy of no respect.'
And 'When the prince has gathered about him
All the savants and artists, his riches will be fully employed.'
And Kung said, and wrote on the bo leaves:
        'If a man have not order within him
He cannot spread order about him;
And if a man have not order within him
His family will not act with due order;
        And if the prince have not order within him
He cannot put order in his dominions.'
And Kung gave the words 'order'
and 'brotherly deference'
And said nothing of the 'life after death'.
And he said
        'Anyone can run to excesses,
It is easy to shoot past the mark,
It is hard to stand firm in the middle.'

And they said: 'If a man commit murder
        Should his father protect him, and hide him?'
And Kung said:
        'He should hide him.'

And Kung gave his daughter to Kong-Tchang
        Although Kong-Tchang was in prison.

And he gave his niece to Nan-Young
        although Nan-Young was out of office.
And Kung said 'Wang ruled with moderation,
        In his day the State was well kept,
And even I can remember
A day when the historians left blanks in their writings,
I mean for things they didn't know,
But that time seems to be passing.'
And Kung said, 'Without character you will
        be unable to play on that instrument
Or to execute the music fit for the Odes.
The blossoms of the apricot
        blow from the east to the west,
And I have tried to keep them from falling.'

Canto XLV

WITH USURA

With usura hath no man a house of good stone
each block cut smooth and well fitting
that design might cover their face,
with usura
hath no man a painted paradise on his church wall
harpes et luthes
or where virgin receiveth message
and halo projects from incision,
with usura
seeth no man Gonzaga his heirs and his concubines
no picture is made to endure nor to live with
but it is made to sell and sell quickly
with usura, sin against nature,
is thy bread ever more of stale rags
is thy bread dry as paper,
with no mountain wheat, no strong flour
with usura the line grows thick
with usura is no clear demarcation

and no man can find site for his dwelling.
Stone cutter is kept from his stone
weaver is kept from his loom
WITH USURA
wool comes not to market
sheep bringeth no gain with usura
Usura is a murrain, usura
blunteth the needle in the maid's hand
and stoppeth the spinner's cunning. Pietro Lombardo
came not by usura
Duccio came not by usura
nor Pier della Francesca; Zuan Bellin' not by usura
nor was 'La Calunnia' painted.
Came not by usura Angelico; came not Ambrogio Praedis,
Came no church of cut stone signed: *Adamo me fecit.*
Not by usura St Trophime
Not by usura Saint Hilaire,
Usura rusteth the chisel
It rusteth the craft and the craftsman
It gnaweth the thread in the loom
None learneth to weave gold in her pattern;
Azure hath a canker by usura; cramoisi is unbroidered
Emerald findeth no Memling
Usura slayeth the child in the womb
It stayeth the young man's courting
It hath brought palsey to bed, lyeth
between the young bride and her bridegroom
                              CONTRA NATURAM
They have brought whores for Eleusis
Corpses are set to banquet
at behest of usura.

William Carlos Williams

Aux Imagistes

I think I have never been so exalted
As I am now by you,
O frost bitten blossoms,
That are unfolding your wings
From out the envious black branches.

Bloom quickly and make much of the sunshine
The twigs conspire against you!
Hear them!
They hold you from behind!

You shall not take wing
Except wing by wing, brokenly,
And yet—
Even they
Shall not endure for ever.

Danse Russe

If I when my wife is sleeping
and the baby and Kathleen
are sleeping
and the sun is a flame-white disc
in silken mists
above shining trees,—
if I in my north room
dance naked, grotesquely
before my mirror
waving my shirt round my head
and singing softly to myself:

'I am lonely, lonely.
I was born to be lonely,
I am best so!'
If I admire my arms, my face
my shoulders, flanks, buttocks
against the yellow drawn shades,—

Who shall say I am not
the happy genius of my household?

This is Just to Say

I have eaten
the plums
that were in
the icebox

and which
you were probably
saving
for breakfast

Forgive me
they were delicious
so sweet
and so cold

To Waken an Old Lady

Old age is
a flight of small
cheeping birds
skimming
bare trees
above a snow glaze.
Gaining and failing
they are buffetted
by a dark wind—

But what?
On harsh weedstalks
the flock has rested,
the snow
is covered with broken
seedhusks
and the wind tempered
by a shrill
piping of plenty.

Tract

I will teach you my townspeople
how to perform a funeral—
for you have it over a troop
of artists—
unless one should scour the world—
you have the ground sense necessary.

See! the hearse leads.
I begin with a design for a hearse.
For Christ's sake not black—
nor white either—and not polished!
Let it be weathered—like a farm wagon—
with gilt wheels (this could be
applied fresh at small expense)
or no wheels at all:
a rough dray to drag over the ground.

Knock the glass out!
My God—glass, my townspeople!
For what purpose? Is it for the dead
to look out or for us to see
how well he is housed or to see
the flowers or the lack of them—
or what?
To keep the rain and snow from him?

He will have a heavier rain soon:
pebbles and dirt and what not.
Let there be no glass—
and no upholstery! phew!
and no little brass rollers
and small easy wheels on the bottom—
my townspeople what are you thinking of!
A rough plain hearse then
with gilt wheels and no top at all.
On this the coffin lies
by its own weight.

                No wreaths please—
especially no hot-house flowers.
Some common memento is better,
something he prized and is known by:
his old clothes—a few books perhaps—
God knows what! You realize
how we are about these things,
my townspeople—
something will be found—anything—
even flowers if he had come to that.
So much for the hearse.

For heaven's sake though see to the driver!
Take off the silk hat! In fact
that's no place at all for him
up there unceremoniously
dragging our friend out to his own dignity!
Bring him down—bring him down!
Low and inconspicuous! I'd not have him ride
on the wagon at all—damn him—
the undertaker's understrapper!
Let him hold the reins
and walk at the side
and inconspicuously too!

Then briefly as to yourselves:
Walk behind—as they do in France,

seventh class, or if you ride
Hell take curtains! Go with some show
of inconvenience; sit openly—
to the weather as to grief.
Or do you think you can shut grief in?
What—from us? We who have perhaps
nothing to lose? Share with us
share with us—it will be money
in your pockets.
                    Go now
I think you are ready.

By the road to the contagious hospital

By the road to the contagious hospital
under the surge of the blue
mottled clouds driven from the
northeast—a cold wind. Beyond, the
waste of broad, muddy fields
brown with dried weeds, standing and fallen

patches of standing water
the scattering of tall trees

All along the road the reddish
purplish, forked, upstanding, twiggy
stuff of bushes and small trees
with dead, brown leaves under them
leafless vines—

Lifeless in appearance, sluggish
dazed spring approaches—

They enter the new world naked,
cold, uncertain of all
save that they enter. All about them
the cold, familiar wind—

Now the grass, tomorrow
the stiff curl of wildcarrot leaf
One by one objects are defined—
It quickens: clarity, outline of leaf

But now the stark dignity of
entrance—Still, the profound change
has come upon them: rooted, they
grip down and begin to awaken

The Red Wheelbarrow

so much depends
upon

a red wheel
barrow

glazed with rain
water

beside the white
chickens.

Nantucket

Flowers through the window
lavender and yellow

changed by white curtains—
Smell of cleanliness—

Sunshine of late afternoon—
On the glass tray

a glass pitcher, the tumbler
turned down, by which

a key is lying—And the
immaculate white bed

The Yachts

contend in a sea which the land partly encloses
shielding them from the too heavy blows
of an ungoverned ocean which when it chooses

tortures the biggest hulls, the best man knows
to pit against its beatings, and sinks them pitilessly.
Mothlike in mists, scintillant in the minute

brilliance of cloudless days, with broad bellying sails
they glide to the wind tossing green water
from their sharp prows while over them the crew crawls

ant like, solicitously grooming them, releasing,
making fast as they turn, lean far over and having
caught the wind again, side by side, head for the mark.

In a well guarded arena of open water surrounded by
lesser and greater craft which, sycophant, lumbering
and flittering follow them, they appear youthful, rare

as the light of a happy eye, live with the grace
of all that in the mind is fleckless, free and
naturally to be desired. Now the sea which holds them

is moody, lapping their glossy sides, as if feeling
for some slightest flaw but fails completely.
Today no race. Then the wind comes again. The yachts

move, jockeying for a start, the signal is set and they

are off. Now the waves strike at them but they are too
well made, they slip through, though they take in canvas.

Arms with hands grasping seek to clutch at the prows.
Bodies thrown recklessly in the way are cut aside.
It is a sea of faces about them in agony, in despair

until the horror of the race dawns staggering the mind,
the whole sea become an entanglement of watery bodies
lost to the world bearing what they cannot hold. Broken,

beaten, desolate, reaching from the dead to be taken up
they cry out, failing, failing! their cries rising
in waves still as the skillful yachts pass over.

The Dance

When the snow falls the flakes
spin upon the long axis
that concerns them most intimately
two and two to make a dance

the mind dances with itself,
taking you by the hand,
your lover follows
there are always two,

yourself and the other,
the point of your shoe setting the pace,
if you break away and run
the dance is over

Breathlessly you will take
another partner
better or worse who will keep
at your side, at your stops

whirls and glides until he too
leaves off
on his way down as if
there were another direction

gayer, more carefree
spinning face to face but always down
with each other secure
only in each other's arms

But only the dance is sure!
make it your own.
Who can tell
what is to come of it?

in the woods of your
own nature whatever
twig interposes, and bare twigs
have an actuality of their own

this flurry of the storm
that holds us,
plays with us and discards us
dancing, dancing as may be credible.

The Rewaking

Sooner or later
we must come to the end
of striving

to re-establish
the image the image of
the rose

but not yet
you say extending the
time indefinitely

by
your love until a whole
spring

rekindle
the violet to the very
lady's-slipper

and so by
your love the very sun
itself is revived

To a Dog Injured in the Street

It is myself,
            not the poor beast lying there
                        yelping with pain
that brings me to myself with a start—
            as at the explosion
                        of a bomb, a bomb that has laid
all the world waste.
            I can do nothing
                        but sing about it
and so I am assuaged
            from my pain.

A drowsy numbness drowns my sense
            as if of hemlock
                        I had drunk. I think
of the poetry
            of René Char
                        and all he must have seen

and suffered
        that has brought him
             to speak only of
sedgy rivers,
        of daffodils and tulips
             whose roots they water,
even to the free-flowing river
        that laves the rootlets
             of those sweet-scented flowers
that people the
        milky

            way

I remember Norma
        our English setter of my childhood
             her silky ears
and expressive eyes.
        She had a litter
             of pups one night
in our pantry and I kicked
        one of them
             thinking, in my alarm,
that they
        were biting her breasts
             to destroy her.

I remember also
        a dead rabbit
             lying harmlessly
on the outspread palm
        of a hunter's hand.
             As I stood by
watching
        he took a hunting knife
             and with a laugh
thrust it
        up into the animal's private parts.
             I almost fainted.

Why should I think of that now?
          The cries of a dying dog
                    are to be blotted out
as best I can.
          René Char
                    you are a poet who believes
in the power of beauty
          to right all wrongs.
                    I believe it also.
With invention and courage
          we shall surpass
                    the pitiful dumb beasts,
let all men believe it,
          as you have taught me also
                    to believe it.

The Host

According to their need,
          this tall Negro evangelist
                    (at a table separate from the
                    rest of his party);
these two young Irish nuns
          (to be described subsequently);
                    and this white-haired Anglican
have come witlessly
          to partake of the host
                    laid for them (and for me)
  by the tired waitresses.

It is all
          (since eat we must)
                    made sacred by our common need.
  The evangelist's assistants
          are most open in their praise
                    though covert

as would be seemly
            in such a public
                        place. The nuns
are all black, a side view.
            The cleric,
                        his head bowed to reveal
his unruly poll
            dines alone.

My eyes are restless.
            The evangelists eat well,
                        fried oysters and what not
at this railway restaurant. The Sisters
            are soon satisfied. One
                        on leaving,
looking straight before her under steadfast brows,
            reveals
                        blue eyes. I myself
have brown eyes
            and a milder mouth.

There is nothing to eat,
            seek it where you will,
                        but of the body of the Lord.
The blessed plants
            and the sea, yield it
                        to the imagination
intact. And by that force
            it becomes real,
                        bitterly
to the poor animals
            who suffer and die
                        that we may live.

The well-fed evangels,
            the narrow-lipped and bright-eyed nuns,
                        the tall,
white-haired Anglican,
            proclaim it by their appetites

as do I also,
chomping with my worn-out teeth:
the Lord is my shepherd
I shall not want.

No matter how well they are fed,
how daintily
they put the food to their lips,
it is all
according to the imagination!
Only the imagination
is real! They have imagined it,
therefore it is so:
of the evangels,
with the long legs characteristic of the race—
only the docile women
of the party smiled at me
when, with my eyes
I accosted them.
The nuns—but after all
I saw only a face, a young face
cut off at the brows.
It was a simple story.
The cleric, plainly
from a good school,
interested me more,
a man with whom I might
carry on a conversation.

No one was there
save only for
the food. Which I alone,
being a poet,
could have given them.
But I
had only my eyes
with which to speak.

Robert Frost

Mending Wall

Something there is that doesn't love a wall,
That sends the frozen-ground-swell under it,
And spills the upper boulders in the sun;
And makes gaps even two can pass abreast.
The work of hunters is another thing:
I have come after them and made repair
Where they have left not one stone on a stone,
But they would have the rabbit out of hiding,
To please the yelping dogs. The gaps I mean,
No one has seen them made or heard them made,
But at spring mending-time we find them there.
I let my neighbor know beyond the hill;
And on a day we meet to walk the line
And set the wall between us once again.
We keep the wall between us as we go.
To each the boulders that have fallen to each.
And some are loaves and some so nearly balls
We have to use a spell to make them balance:
'Stay where you are until our backs are turned!'
We wear our fingers rough with handling them.
Oh, just another kind of outdoor game,
One on a side. It comes to little more:
There where it is we do not need the wall:
He is all pine and I am apple orchard.
My apple trees will never get across
And eat the cones under his pines, I tell him
He only says, 'Good fences make good neighbors.'
Spring is the mischief in me, and I wonder
If I could put a notion in his head:
'*Why* do they make good neighbors? Isn't it

Where there are cows? But here there are no cows.
Before I built a wall I'd ask to know
What I was walling in or walling out,
And to whom I was like to give offense.
Something there is that doesn't love a wall,
That wants it down.' I could say 'Elves' to him,
But it's not elves exactly, and I'd rather
He said it for himself. I see him there
Bringing a stone grasped firmly by the top
In each hand, like an old-stone savage armed.
He moves in darkness as it seems to me,
Not of woods only and the shade of trees.
He will not go behind his father's saying,
And he likes having thought of it so well
He says again, 'Good fences make good neighbors.'

After Apple-Picking

My long two-pointed ladder's sticking through a tree
Toward heaven still,
And there's a barrel that I didn't fill
Beside it, and there may be two or three
Apples I didn't pick upon some bough.
But I am done with apple-picking now.
Essence of winter sleep is on the night,
The scent of apples: I am drowsing off.
I cannot rub the strangeness from my sight
I got from looking through a pane of glass
I skimmed this morning from the drinking trough
And held against the world of hoary grass.
It melted, and I let it fall and break.
But I was well
Upon my way to sleep before it fell,
And I could tell
What form my dreaming was about to take.
Magnified apples appear and disappear,
Stem end and blossom end,

And every fleck of russet showing clear.
My instep arch not only keeps the ache,
It keeps the pressure of a ladder-round.
I feel the ladder sway as the boughs bend.
And I keep hearing from the cellar bin
The rumbling sound
Of load on load of apples coming in.
For I have had too much
Of apple-picking: I am overtired
Of the great harvest I myself desired.
There were ten thousand thousand fruit to touch,
Cherish in hand, lift down, and not let fall.
For all
That struck the earth,
No matter if not bruised or spiked with stubble,
Went surely to the cider-apple heap
As of no worth.
One can see what will trouble
This sleep of mine, whatever sleep it is.
Were he not gone,
The woodchuck could say whether it's like his
Long sleep, as I describe its coming on,
Or just some human sleep.

Birches

When I see birches bend to left and right
Across the lines of straighter darker trees,
I like to think some boy's been swinging them.
But swinging doesn't bend them down to stay
As ice-storms do. Often you must have seen them
Loaded with ice a sunny winter morning
After a rain. They click upon themselves
As the breeze rises, and turn many-colored
As the stir cracks and crazes their enamel.
Soon the sun's warmth makes them shed crystal shells
Shattering and avalanching on the snow-crust—

Such heaps of broken glass to sweep away
You'd think the inner dome of heaven had fallen.
They are dragged to the withered bracken by the load,
And they seem not to break; though once they are bowed
So low for long, they never right themselves:
You may see their trunks arching in the woods
Years afterwards, trailing their leaves on the ground
Like girls on hands and knees that throw their hair
Before them over their heads to dry in the sun.
But I was going to say when Truth broke in
With all her matter-of-fact about the ice-storm
I should prefer to have some boy bend them
As he went out and in to fetch the cows—
Some boy too far from town to learn baseball,
Whose only play was what he found himself,
Summer or winter, and could play alone.
One by one he subdued his father's trees
By riding them down over and over again
Until he took the stiffness out of them,
And not one but hung limp, not one was left
For him to conquer. He learned all there was
To learn about not launching out too soon
And so not carrying the tree away
Clear to the ground. He always kept his poise
To the top branches, climbing carefully
With the same pains you use to fill a cup
Up to the brim, and even above the brim.
Then he flung outward, feet first, with a swish,
Kicking his way down through the air to the ground.
So was I once myself a swinger of birches.
And so I dream of going back to be.
It's when I'm weary of considerations,
And life is too much like a pathless wood
When your face burns and tickles with the cobwebs
Broken across it, and one eye is weeping
From a twig's having lashed across it open.
I'd like to get away from earth awhile
And then come back to it and begin over.

May no fate willfully misunderstand me
And half grant what I wish and snatch me away
Not to return. Earth's the right place for love:
I don't know where it's likely to go better.
I'd like to go by climbing a birch tree,
And climb black branches up a snow-white trunk
Toward heaven, till the tree could bear no more,
But dipped its top and set me down again.
That would be good both going and coming back.
One could do worse than be a swinger of birches.

The Witch of Coös

I stayed the night for shelter at a farm
Behind the mountain, with a mother and son,
Two old-believers. They did all the talking.

MOTHER. Folks think a witch who has familiar spirits
She could call up to pass a winter evening,
But won't, should be burned at the stake or something.
Summoning spirits isn't 'Button, button,
Who's got the button,' I would have them know.

SON. Mother can make a common table rear
And kick with two legs like an army mule.

MOTHER. And when I've done it, what good have I done?
Rather than tip a table for you, let me
Tell you what Ralle the Sioux Control once told me.
He said the dead had souls, but when I asked him
How could that be—I thought the dead were souls,
He broke my trance. Don't that make you suspicious
That there's something the dead are keeping back?
Yes, there's something the dead are keeping back.

SON. You wouldn't want to tell him what we have
Up attic, mother?

MOTHER. Bones—a skeleton.

SON. But the headboard of mother's bed is pushed
Against the attic door: the door is nailed.
It's harmless. Mother hears it in the night
Halting perplexed behind the barrier
Of door and headboard. Where it wants to get
Is back into the cellar where it came from.

MOTHER. We'll never let them, will we, son! We'll never!

SON. It left the cellar forty years ago
And carried itself like a pile of dishes
Up one flight from the cellar to the kitchen,
Another from the kitchen to the bedroom,
Another from the bedroom to the attic,
Right past both father and mother, and neither stopped it.
Father had gone upstairs; mother was downstairs.
I was a baby: I don't know where I was.

MOTHER. The only fault my husband found with me—
I went to sleep before I went to bed,
Especially in winter when the bed
Might just as well be ice and the clothes snow.
The night the bones came up the cellar-stairs
Toffile had gone to bed alone and left me,
But left an open door to cool the room off
So as to sort of turn me out of it.
I was just coming to myself enough
To wonder where the cold was coming from,
When I heard Toffile upstairs in the bedroom
And thought I heard him downstairs in the cellar.
The board we had laid down to walk dry-shod on
When there was water in the cellar in spring
Struck the hard cellar bottom. And then someone

Began the stairs, two footsteps for each step,
The way a man with one leg and a crutch,
Or a little child, comes up. It wasn't Toffile:
It wasn't anyone who could be there.
The bulkhead double-doors were double-locked
And swollen tight and buried under snow.
The cellar windows were banked up with sawdust
And swollen tight and buried under snow.
It was the bones. I knew them—and good reason.
My first impulse was to get to the knob
And hold the door. But the bones didn't try
The door; they halted helpless on the landing,
Waiting for things to happen in their favor.
The faintest restless rustling ran all through them.
I never could have done the thing I did
If the wish hadn't been too strong in me
To see how they were mounted for this walk.
I had a vision of them put together
Not like a man, but like a chandelier.
So suddenly I flung the door wide on him.
A moment he stood balancing with emotion,
And all but lost himself. (A tongue of fire
Flashed out and licked along his upper teeth.
Smoke rolled inside the sockets of his eyes.)
Then he came at me with one hand outstretched,
The way he did in life once; but this time
I struck the hand off brittle on the floor,
And fell back from him on the floor myself.
The finger-pieces slid in all directions.
(Where did I see one of those pieces lately?
Hand me my button-box—it must be there.)
I sat on the floor and shouted, 'Toffile,
It's coming up to you.' It had its choice
Of the door to the cellar or the hall.
It took the hall door for the novelty,
And set off briskly for so slow a thing,
Still going every which way in the joints, though,
So that it looked like lightning or a scribble,

From the slap I had just now given its hand.
I listened till it almost climbed the stairs
From hall to the only finished bedroom,
Before I got up to do anything;
Then ran and shouted, 'Shut the bedroom door,
Toffile, for my sake!' 'Company?' he said,
'Don't make me get up; I'm too warm in bed.'
So lying forward weakly on the handrail
I pushed myself upstairs, and in the light
(The kitchen had been dark) I had to own
I could see nothing. 'Toffile, I don't see it.
It's with us in the room though. It's the bones.'
'What bones?' 'The cellar bones—out of the grave.'
That made him throw his bare legs out of bed
And sit up by me and take hold of me.
I wanted to put out the light and see
If I could see it, or else mow the room,
With our arms at the level of our knees,
And bring the chalk-pile down. 'I'll tell you what—
It's looking for another door to try.
The uncommonly deep snow has made him think
Of his old song, *The Wild Colonial Boy*,
He always used to sing along the tote road.
He's after an open door to get outdoors.
Let's trap him with an open door up attic.'
Toffile agreed to that, and sure enough,
Almost the moment he was given an opening,
The steps began to climb the attic stairs.
I heard them. Toffile didn't seem to hear them.
'Quick!' I slammed to the door and held the knob.
'Toffile, get nails.' I made him nail the door shut
And push the headboard of the bed against it.
Then we asked was there anything
Up attic that we'd ever want again.
The attic was less to us than the cellar.
If the bones liked the attic, let them have it.
Let them stay in the attic. When they sometimes
Come down the stairs at night and stand perplexed

Behind the door and headboard of the bed,
Brushing their chalky skull with chalky fingers,
With sounds like the dry rattling of a shutter,
That's what I sit up in the dark to say—
To no one any more since Toffile died.
Let them stay in the attic since they went there.
I promised Toffile to be cruel to them
For helping them be cruel once to him.

SON. We think they had a grave down in the cellar.

MOTHER. We know they had a grave down in the cellar.

SON. We never could find out whose bones they were.

MOTHER. Yes, we could too, son. Tell the truth for once.
They were a man's his father killed for me.
I mean a man he killed instead of me.
The least I could do was to help dig their grave.
We were about it one night in the cellar.
Son knows the story: but 'twas not for him
To tell the truth, suppose the time had come.
Son looks surprised to see me end a lie
We'd kept all these years between ourselves
So as to have it ready for outsiders.
But tonight I don't care enough to lie—
I don't remember why I ever cared.
Toffile, if he were here, I don't believe
Could tell you why he ever cared himself. . . .

She hadn't found the finger-bone she wanted
Among the buttons poured out in her lap.
I verified the name next morning: Toffile.
The rural letter box said Toffile Lajway.

Fire and Ice

Some say the world will end in fire,
Some say in ice.
From what I've tasted of desire
I hold with those who favor fire.
But if it had to perish twice,
I think I know enough of hate
To say that for destruction ice
Is also great
And would suffice.

Stopping by Woods on a
Snowy Evening

Whose woods these are I think I know.
His house is in the village though;
He will not see me stopping here
To watch his woods fill up with snow.

My little horse must think it queer
To stop without a farmhouse near
Between the woods and frozen lake
The darkest evening of the year.

He gives his harness bells a shake
To ask if there is some mistake.
The only other sound's the sweep
Of easy wind and downy flake.

The woods are lovely, dark and deep,
But I have promises to keep,
And miles to go before I sleep,
And miles to go before I sleep.

Acquainted with the Night

I have been one acquainted with the night.
I have walked out in rain—and back in rain.
I have outwalked the furthest city light.

I have looked down the saddest city lane.
I have passed by the watchman on his beat
And dropped my eyes, unwilling to explain.

I have stood still and stopped the sound of feet
When far away an interrupted cry
Came over houses from another street,

But not to call me back or say good-bye;
And further still at an unearthly height,
One luminary clock against the sky

Proclaimed the time was neither wrong nor right.
I have been one acquainted with the night.

Departmental

An ant on the tablecloth
Ran into a dormant moth
Of many times his size.
He showed not the least surprise.
His business wasn't with such.
He gave it scarcely a touch,
And was off on his duty run.
Yet if he encountered one
Of the hive's enquiry squad
Whose work is to find out God
And the nature of time and space,
He would put him onto the case.
Ants are a curious race;

One crossing with hurried tread
The body of one of their dead
Isn't given a moment's arrest—
Seems not even impressed.
But he no doubt reports to any
With whom he crosses antennae,
And they no doubt report
To the higher up at court.
Then word goes forth in Formic:
'Death's come to Jerry McCormic,
Our selfless forager Jerry.
Will the special Janizary
Whose office it is to bury
The dead of the commissary
Go bring him home to his people.
Lay him in state on a sepal.
Wrap him for shroud in a petal.
Embalm him with ichor of nettle.
This is the word of your Queen.'
And presently on the scene
Appears a solemn mortician;
And taking formal position
With feelers calmly atwiddle,
Seizes the dead by the middle,
And heaving him high in air,
Carries him out of there.
No one stands round to stare.
It is nobody else's affair.

It couldn't be called ungentle.
But how thoroughly departmental.

Desert Places

Snow falling and night falling fast, oh, fast
In a field I looked into going past,

And the ground almost covered smooth in snow,
But a few weeds and stubble showing last.

The woods around it have it—it is theirs.
All animals are smothered in their lairs.
I am too absent-sprited to count;
The loneliness includes me unawares.

And lonely as it is that loneliness
Will be more lonely ere it will be less—
A blanker whiteness of benighted snow
With no expression, nothing to express.

They cannot scare me with their empty spaces
Between stars—on stars where no human race is.
I have it in me so much nearer home
To scare myself with my own desert places.

Neither Out Far Nor In Deep

The people along the sand
All turn and look one way.
They turn their back on the land.
They look at the sea all day.

As long as it takes to pass
A ship keeps raising its hull;
The wetter ground like glass
Reflects a standing gull.

The land may vary more;
But wherever the truth may be—
The water comes ashore,
And the people look at the sea.

They cannot look out far.
They cannot look in deep.
But when was that ever a bar
To any watch they keep?

Design

I found a dimpled spider, fat and white,
On a white heal-all, holding up a moth
Like a white piece of rigid satin cloth—
Assorted characters of death and blight
Mixed ready to begin the morning right,
Like the ingredients of a witches' broth—
A snow-drop spider, a flower like a froth,
And dead wings carried like a paper kite.

What had that flower to do with being white,
The wayside blue and innocent heal-all?
What brought the kindred spider to that height,
Then steered the white moth thither in the night?
What but design of darkness to appall?—
If design govern in a thing so small.

Provide, Provide

The witch that came (the withered hag)
To wash the steps with pail and rag,
Was once the beauty Abishag,

The picture pride of Hollywood.
Too many fall from great and good
For you to doubt the likelihood.

Die early and avoid the fate.
Or if predestined to die late,
Make up your mind to die in state.

Make the whole stock exchange your own!
If need be occupy a throne,
Where nobody can call *you* crone.

Some have relied on what they knew;
Others on being simply true.
What worked for them might work for you.

No memory of having starred
Atones for later disregard,
Or keeps the end from being hard.

Better to go down dignified
With boughten friendship at your side
Than none at all. Provide, provide!

One Step Backward Taken

Not only sands and gravels
Were once more on their travels,
But gulping muddy gallons
Great boulders off their balance
Bumped heads together dully
And started down the gully.
Whole capes caked off in slices.
I felt my standpoint shaken
In the universal crisis.
But with one step backward taken
I saved myself from going.
A world torn loose went by me.
Then the rain stopped and the blowing
And the sun came out to dry me.

Directive

Back out of all this now too much for us,
Back in a time made simple by the loss
Of detail, burned, dissolved, and broken off
Like graveyard marble sculpture in the weather,
There is a house that is no more a house
Upon a farm that is no more a farm
And in a town that is no more a town.
The road there, if you'll let a guide direct you
Who only has at heart your getting lost,
May seem as if it should have been a quarry—
Great monolithic knees the former town
Long since gave up pretense of keeping covered.
And there's a story in a book about it:
Besides the wear of iron wagon wheels
The ledges show lines ruled southeast northwest,
The chisel work of an enormous Glacier
That braced his feet against the Arctic Pole.
You must not mind a certain coolness from him
Still said to haunt this side of Panther Mountain
Nor need you mind the serial ordeal
Of being watched from forty cellar holes
As if by eye pairs out of forty firkins.
As for the woods' excitement over you
That sends light rustle rushes to their leaves,
Charge that to upstart inexperience.
Where were they all not twenty years ago?
They think too much of having shaded out
A few old pecker-fretted apple trees.
Make yourself up a cheering song of how
Someone's road home from work this once was,
Who may be just ahead of you on foot
Or creaking with a buggy load of grain.
The height of the adventure is the height
Of country where two village cultures faded
Into each other. Both of them are lost.
And if you're lost enough to find yourself

By now, pull in your ladder road behind you
And put a sign up CLOSED to all but me.
Then make yourself at home. The only field
Now left's no bigger than a harness gall.
First there's the children's house of make believe,
Some shattered dishes underneath a pine,
The playthings in the playhouse of the children.
Weep for what little things could make them glad.
Then for the house that is no more a house,
But only a belilaced cellar hole,
Now slowly closing like a dent in dough.
This was no playhouse but a house in earnest.
Your destination and your destiny's
A brook that was the water of the house,
Cold as a spring as yet so near its source,
Too lofty and original to rage.
(We know the valley streams that when aroused
Will leave their tatters hung on barb and thorn.)
I have kept hidden in the instep arch
Of an old cedar at the waterside
A broken drinking goblet like the Grail
Under a spell so the wrong ones can't find it,
So can't get saved, as Saint Mark says they mustn't.
(I stole the goblet from the children's playhouse.)
Here are your waters and your watering place.
Drink and be whole again beyond confusion.

Robert Graves

Rocky Acres

This is a wild land, country of my choice,
With harsh craggy mountain, moor ample and bare.
Seldom in these acres is heard any voice
But voice of cold water that runs here and there
Through rocks and lank heather growing without care.
No mice in the heath run, no song-birds fly
For fear of the buzzard that floats in the sky.

He soars and he hovers, rocking on his wings,
He scans his wide parish with a sharp eye,
He catches the trembling of small hidden things,
He tears them in pieces, dropping them from the sky;
Tenderness and pity the heart will deny,
Where life is but nourished by water and rock—
A hardy adventure, full of fear and shock.

Time has never journeyed to this lost land,
Crakeberry and heather bloom out of date,
The rocks jut, the streams flow singing on either hand,
Careless if the season be early or late,
The skies wander overhead, now blue, now slate;
Winter would be known by his cutting snow
If June did not borrow his armour also.

Yet this is my country, beloved by me best,
The first land that rose from Chaos and the Flood,
Nursing no valleys for comfort or rest,
Trampled by no shod hooves, bought with no blood.
Sempiternal country whose barrows have stood
Stronghold for demigods when on earth they go,
Terror for fat burghers on far plains below.

The Pier-Glass

Lost manor where I walk continually
A ghost, though yet in woman's flesh and blood.
Up your broad stairs mounting with outspread fingers
And gliding steadfast down your corridors
I come by nightly custom to this room,
And even on sultry afternoons I come
Drawn by a thread of time-sunk memory.

Empty, unless for a huge bed of state
Shrouded with rusty curtains drooped awry
(A puppet theatre where malignant fancy
Peoples the wings with fear). At my right hand
A ravelled bell-pull hangs in readiness
To summon me from attic glooms above
Service of elder ghosts; here, at my left,
A sullen pier-glass, cracked from side to side,
Scorns to present the face (as do new mirrors)
With a lying flush, but shows it melancholy
And pale, as faces grow that look in mirrors.

Is there no life, nothing but the thin shadow
And blank foreboding, never a wainscot rat
Rasping a crust? Or at the window-pane
No fly, no bluebottle, no starveling spider?
The windows frame a prospect of cold skies
Half-merged with sea, as at the first creation—
Abstract, confusing welter. Face about,
Peer rather in the glass once more, take note
Of self, the grey lips and long hair dishevelled,
Sleep-staring eyes. Ah, mirror, for Christ's love
Give me one token that there still abides
Remote—beyond this island mystery,
So be it only this side Hope, somewhere,
In streams, on sun-warm mountain pasturage—
True life, natural breath; not this phantasma.

Warning to Children

Children, if you dare to think
Of the greatness, rareness, muchness,
Fewness of this precious only
Endless world in which you say
You live, you think of things like this:
Blocks of slate enclosing dappled
Red and green, enclosing tawny
Yellow nets, enclosing white
And black acres of dominoes,
Where a neat brown paper parcel
Tempts you to untie the string.
In the parcel a small island,
On the island a large tree,
On the tree a husky fruit.
Strip the husk and pare the rind off:
In the kernel you will see
Blocks of slate enclosed by dappled
Red and green, enclosed by tawny
Yellow nets, enclosed by white
And black acres of dominoes,
Where the same brown paper parcel—
Children, leave the string alone!
For who dares undo the parcel
Finds himself at once inside it,
On the island, in the fruit,
Blocks of slate about his head,
Finds himself enclosed by dappled
Green and red, enclosed by yellow
Tawny nets, enclosed by black
And white acres of dominoes,
With the same brown paper parcel
Still untied upon his knee.
And, if he then should dare to think
Of the fewness, muchness, rareness,
Greatness of this endless only
Precious world in which he says
He lives—he then unties the string.

The Cool Web

Children are dumb to say how hot the day is,
How hot the scent is of the summer rose,
How dreadful the black wastes of evening sky,
How dreadful the tall soldiers drumming by.

But we have speech, to chill the angry day,
And speech, to dull the rose's cruel scent.
We spell away the overhanging night,
We spell away the soldiers and the fright.

There's a cool web of language winds us in,
Retreat from too much joy or too much fear:
We grow sea-green at last and coldly die
In brininess and volubility.

But if we let our tongues lose self-possession,
Throwing off language and its watery clasp
Before our death, instead of when death comes,
Facing the wide glare of the children's day,
Facing the rose, the dark sky, and the drums
We shall go mad no doubt and die that way.

Pure Death

We looked, we loved, and therewith instantly
Death became terrible to you and me.
By love we disenthralled our natural terror
From every comfortable philosopher
Or tall, grey doctor of divinity:
Death stood at last in his true rank and order.

It happened soon, so wild of heart were we,
Exchange of gifts grew to a malady:

Their worth rose always higher on each side
Till there seemed nothing but ungivable pride
That yet remained ungiven, and this degree
Called a conclusion not to be denied.

Then we at last bethought ourselves, made shift
And simultaneously this final gift
Gave: each with shaking hands unlocks
The sinister, long, brass-bound coffin-box,
Unwraps pure death, with such bewilderment
As greeted our love's first acknowledgement.

In Broken Images

He is quick, thinking in clear images;
I am slow, thinking in broken images.

He becomes dull, trusting to his clear images;
I become sharp, mistrusting my broken images.

Trusting his images, he assumes their relevance;
Mistrusting my images, I question their relevance.

Assuming their relevance, he assumes the fact;
Questioning their relevance, I question the fact.

When the fact fails him, he questions his senses;
When the fact fails me, I approve my senses.

He continues quick and dull in his clear images;
I continue slow and sharp in my broken images.

He in a new confusion of his understanding;
I in a new understanding of my confusion.

Down, Wanton, Down!

Down, wanton, down! Have you no shame
That at the whisper of Love's name,
Or Beauty's, presto! up you raise
Your angry head and stand at gaze?

Poor bombard-captain, sworn to reach
The ravelin and effect a breach—
Indifferent what you storm or why,
So be that in the breach you die!

Love may be blind, but Love at least
Knows what is man and what mere beast;
Or Beauty wayward, but requires
More delicacy from her squires.

Tell me, my witless, whose one boast
Could be your staunchness at the post,
When were you made a man of parts
To think fine and profess the arts?

Will many-gifted Beauty come
Bowing to your bald rule of thumb,
Or Love swear loyalty to your crown?
Be gone, have done! Down, wanton, down!

With Her Lips Only

This honest wife, challenged at dusk
At the garden gate, under a moon perhaps,
In scent of honeysuckle, dared to deny
Love to an urgent lover: with her lips only,
Not with her heart. It was no assignation;
Taken aback, what could she say else?

For the children's sake, the lie was venial;
'For the children's sake', she argued with her conscience.

Yet a mortal lie must follow before dawn:
Challenged as usual in her own bed,
She protests love to an urgent husband,
Not with her heart but with her lips only;
'For the children's sake', she argues with her conscience,
'For the children'—turning suddenly cold towards them.

The Terraced Valley

In a deep thought of you and concentration
I came by hazard to a new region:
The unnecessary sun was not there,
The necessary earth lay without care—
For more than sunshine warmed the skin
Of the round world that was turned outside-in.

Calm sea beyond the terraced valley
Without horizon easily was spread,
As it were overhead,
Washing the mountain-spurs behind me:
The unnecessary sky was not there,
Therefore no heights, no deeps, no birds of the air.

Neat outside-inside, neat below-above,
Hermaphrodizing love.
Neat this-way-that-way and without mistake:
On the right hand could slide the left glove.
Neat over-under: the young snake
Through an unyielding shell his path could break.
Singing of kettles, like a singing brook,
Made out-of-doors a fireside nook.

But you, my love, where had you then your station?
Seeing that on this counter-earth together
We go not distant from each other;
I knew you near me in that strange region,
So searched for you, in hope to see you stand
On some near olive-terrace, in the heat,
The left-hand glove drawn on your right hand,
The empty snake's egg perfect at your feet—

But found you nowhere in the wide land,
And cried disconsolately, until you spoke
Immediate at my elbow, and your voice broke
This trick of time, changing the world about
To once more inside-in and outside-out.

To Juan at the Winter Solstice

There is one story and one story only
That will prove worth your telling,
Whether as learned bard or gifted child;
To it all lines or lesser gauds belong
That startle with their shining
Such common stories as they stray into.

Is it of trees you tell, their months and virtues,
Or strange beasts that beset you,
Of birds that croak at you the Triple will?
Or of the Zodiac and how slow it turns
Below the Boreal Crown,
Prison of all true kings that ever reigned?

Water to water, ark again to ark,
From woman back to woman:
So each new victim treads unfalteringly
The never altered circuit of his fate,
Bringing twelve peers as witness
Both to his starry rise and starry fall.

Or is it of the Virgin's silver beauty,
All fish below the thighs?
She in her left hand bears a leafy quince;
When with her right she crooks a finger, smiling,
How may the King hold back?
Royally then he barters life for love.

Or of the undying snake from chaos hatched,
Whose coils contain the ocean,
Into whose chops with naked sword he springs,
Then in black water, tangled by the reeds,
Battles three days and nights,
To be spewed up beside her scalloped shore?

Much snow is falling, winds roar hollowly,
The owl hoots from the elder,
Fear in your heart cries to the loving-cup:
Sorrow to sorrow as the sparks fly upward.
The log groans and confesses:
There is one story and one story only.

Dwell on her graciousness, dwell on her smiling,
Do not forget what flowers
The great boar trampled down in ivy time.
Her brow was creamy as the crested wave,
Her sea-blue eyes were wild
But nothing promised that is not performed.

T. S. Eliot

The Love Song of J. Alfred Prufrock

S'io credesse che mia risposta fosse
A persona che mai tornasse al mondo,
Questa fiamma staria senza più scosse.
Ma perciocche giammai di questo fondo
Non tornò vivo alcun, s'i'odo il vero,
Senza tema d'infamia ti rispondo.

Let us go then, you and I,
When the evening is spread out against the sky
Like a patient etherised upon a table;
Let us go, through certain half-deserted streets,
The muttering retreats
Of restless nights in one-night cheap hotels
And sawdust restaurants with oyster-shells:
Streets that follow like a tedious argument
Of insidious intent
To lead you to an overwhelming question . . .
Oh, do not ask, 'What is it?'
Let us go and make our visit.

In the room the women come and go
Talking of Michelangelo.

The yellow fog that rubs its back upon the window-panes,
The yellow smoke that rubs its muzzle on the window-panes
Licked its tongue into the corners of the evening,
Lingered upon the pools that stand in drains,
Let fall upon its back the soot that falls from chimneys,
Slipped by the terrace, made a sudden leap,
And seeing that it was a soft October night,
Curled once about the house, and fell asleep.

And indeed there will be time
For the yellow smoke that slides along the street
Rubbing its back upon the window-panes;
There will be time, there will be time
To prepare a face to meet the faces that you meet;
There will be time to murder and create,
And time for all the works and days of hands
That lift and drop a question on your plate;
Time for you and time for me,
And time yet for a hundred indecisions,
And for a hundred visions and revisions,
Before the taking of a toast and tea.

In the room the women come and go
Talking of Michelangelo.

And indeed there will be time
To wonder, 'Do I dare?' and, 'Do I dare?'
Time to turn back and descend the stair,
With a bald spot in the middle of my hair—
[They will say: 'How his hair is growing thin!']
My morning coat, my collar mounting firmly to the chin,
My necktie rich and modest, but asserted by a simple pin—
[They will say: 'But how his arms and legs are thin!']
Do I dare
Disturb the universe?
In a minute there is time
For decisions and revisions which a minute will reverse.

For I have known them all already, known them all—
Have known the evenings, mornings, afternoons,
I have measured out my life with coffee spoons;
I know the voices dying with a dying fall
Beneath the music from a farther room.
    So how should I presume?

And I have known the eyes already, known them all—
The eyes that fix you in a formulated phrase,

And when I am formulated, sprawling on a pin,
When I am pinned and wriggling on the wall,
Then how should I begin
To spit out all the butt-ends of my days and ways?
   And how should I presume?

And I have known the arms already, known them all—
Arms that are braceleted and white and bare
[But in the lamplight, downed with light brown hair!]
Is it perfume from a dress
That makes me so digress?
Arms that lie along a table, or wrap about a shawl.
   And should I then presume?
   And how should I begin?
    .   .   .

Shall I say, I have gone at dusk through narrow streets
And watched the smoke that rises from the pipes
Of lonely men in shirt-sleeves, leaning out of windows? . . .

I should have been a pair of ragged claws
Scuttling across the floors of silent seas.
    .   .   .

And the afternoon, the evening, sleeps so peacefully!
Smoothed by long fingers,
Asleep . . . tired . . . or it malingers,
Stretched on the floor, here beside you and me.
Should I, after tea and cakes and ices,
Have the strength to force the moment to its crisis?
But though I have wept and fasted, wept and prayed,
Though I have seen my head [grown slightly bald]
   brought in upon a platter,
I am no prophet—and here's no great matter;
I have seen the moment of my greatness flicker,
And I have seen the eternal Footman hold my coat, and snicker,
And in short, I was afraid.

And would it have been worth it, after all,
After the cups, the marmalade, the tea,

Among the porcelain, among some talk of you and me,
Would it have been worth while,
To have bitten off the matter with a smile,
To have squeezed the universe into a ball
To roll it toward some overwhelming question,
To say: 'I am Lazarus, come from the dead,
Come back to tell you all, I shall tell you all'—
If one, settling a pillow by her head,
    Should say: 'That is not what I meant at all.
    That is not it, at all.'

And would it have been worth it, after all,
Would it have been worth while,
After the sunsets and the dooryards and the sprinkled streets,
After the novels, after the teacups, after the skirts that
    trail along the floor—
And this, and so much more?—
It is impossible to say just what I mean!
But as if a magic lantern threw the nerves in patterns on a screen:
Would it have been worth while
If one, settling a pillow or throwing off a shawl,
And turning toward the window, should say:
    'That is not it at all,
    That is not what I meant, at all.'

              .   .   .

No! I am not Prince Hamlet, nor was meant to be;
Am an attendant lord, one that will do
To swell a progress, start a scene or two,
Advise the prince; no doubt, an easy tool,
Deferential, glad to be of use,
Politic, cautious, and meticulous;
Full of high sentence, but a bit obtuse;
At times, indeed, almost ridiculous—
Almost, at times, the Fool.

I grow old . . . I grow old . . .
I shall wear the bottoms of my trousers rolled.

Shall I part my hair behind? Do I dare to eat a peach?
I shall wear white flannel trousers, and walk upon the beach.
I have heard the mermaids singing, each to each.

I do not think that they will sing to me.

I have seen them riding seaward on the waves
Combing the white hair of the waves blown back
When the wind blows the water white and black.

We have lingered in the chambers of the sea
By sea-girls wreathed with seaweed red and brown
Till human voices wake us, and we drown.

Preludes

I

The winter evening settles down
With smell of steaks in passageways.
Six o'clock.
The burnt-out ends of smoky days.
And now a gusty shower wraps
The grimy scraps
Of withered leaves about your feet
And newspapers from vacant lots;
The showers beat
On broken blinds and chimney-pots,
And at the corner of the street
A lonely cab-horse steams and stamps.
And then the lighting of the lamps.

II

The morning comes to consciousness
Of faint stale smells of beer
From the sawdust-trampled street

With all its muddy feet that press
To early coffee-stands.
With the other masquerades
That time resumes,
One thinks of all the hands
That are raising dingy shades
In a thousand furnished rooms.

III

You tossed a blanket from the bed,
You lay upon your back, and waited;
You dozed, and watched the night revealing
The thousand sordid images
Of which your soul was constituted;
They flickered against the ceiling.
And when all the world came back
And the light crept up between the shutters
And you heard the sparrows in the gutters,
You had such a vision of the street
As the street hardly understands;
Sitting along the bed's edge, where
You curled the papers from your hair,
Or clasped the yellow soles of feet
In the palms of both soiled hands.

IV

His soul stretched tight across the skies
That fade behind a city block,
Or trampled by insistent feet
At four and five and six o'clock;
And short square fingers stuffing pipes,
And evening newspapers, and eyes
Assured of certain certainties,
The conscience of a blackened street
Impatient to assume the world.

I am moved by fancies that are curled
Around these images, and cling:
The notion of some infinitely gentle
Infinitely suffering thing.

Wipe your hand across your mouth, and laugh;
The worlds revolve like ancient women
Gathering fuel in vacant lots.

The Hollow Men

Mistah Kurtz—he dead.

A penny for the Old Guy

I

We are the hollow men
We are the stuffed men
Leaning together
Headpiece filled with straw. Alas!
Our dried voices, when
We whisper together
Are quiet and meaningless
As wind in dry grass
Or rats' feet over broken glass
In our dry cellar

Shape without form, shade without colour,
Paralysed force, gesture without motion;

Those who have crossed
With direct eyes, to death's other Kingdom
Remember us—if at all—not as lost
Violent souls, but only
As the hollow men
The stuffed men.

II

Eyes I dare not meet in dreams
In death's dream kingdom
These do not appear:
There, the eyes are
Sunlight on a broken column
There, is a tree swinging
And voices are
In the wind's singing
More distant and more solemn
Than a fading star.

Let me be no nearer
In death's dream kingdom
Let me also wear
Such deliberate disguises
Rat's coat, crowskin, crossed staves
In a field
Behaving as the wind behaves
No nearer—

Not that final meeting
In the twilight kingdom

III

This is the dead land
This is the cactus land
Here the stone images
Are raised, here they receive
The supplication of a dead man's hand
Under the twinkle of a fading star.

Is it like this
In death's other kingdom
Waking alone
At the hour when we are
Trembling with tenderness

Lips that would kiss
Form prayers to broken stone.

IV

The eyes are not here
There are no eyes here
In this valley of dying stars
In this hollow valley
This broken jaw of our lost kingdoms

In this last of meeting places
We grope together
And avoid speech
Gathered on this beach of the tumid river

Sightless, unless
The eyes reappear
As the perpetual star
Multifoliate rose
Of death's twilight kingdom
The hope only
Of empty men.

V

Here we go round the prickly pear
Prickly pear prickly pear
Here we go round the prickly pear
At five o'clock in the morning.

Between the idea
And the reality
Between the motion
And the act
Falls the Shadow
                    For Thine is the Kingdom

Between the conception
And the creation
Between the emotion
And the response
Falls the Shadow

Life is very long

Between the desire
And the spasm
Between the potency
And the existence
Between the essence
And the descent
Falls the Shadow

For Thine is the Kingdom

For Thine is
Life is
For Thine is the

This is the way the world ends
This is the way the world ends
This is the way the world ends
Not with a bang but a whimper.

Journey of the Magi

'A cold coming we had of it,
Just the worst time of the year
For a journey, and such a long journey:
The ways deep and the weather sharp,
The very dead of winter.'
And the camels galled, sore-footed, refractory,
Lying down in the melting snow.
There were times we regretted
The summer palaces on slopes, the terraces,

And the silken girls bringing sherbet.
Then the camel men cursing and grumbling
And running away, and wanting their liquor and women,
And the night-fires going out, and the lack of shelters,
And the cities hostile and the towns unfriendly
And the villages dirty and charging high prices:
A hard time we had of it.
At the end we preferred to travel all night,
Sleeping in snatches,
With the voices singing in our ears, saying
That this was all folly.

Then at dawn we came down to a temperate valley,
Wet, below the snow line, smelling of vegetation;
With a running stream and a water-mill beating the darkness,
And three trees on the low sky,
And an old white horse galloped away in the meadow.
Then we came to a tavern with vine-leaves over the lintel,
Six hands at an open door dicing for pieces of silver,
And feet kicking the empty wine-skins.
But there was no information, and so we continued
And arrived at evening, not a moment too soon
Finding the place; it was (you may say) satisfactory.

All this was a long time ago, I remember,
And I would do it again, but set down
This set down
This: were we led all that way for
Birth or Death? There was a Birth, certainly,
We had evidence and no doubt. I had seen birth and death,
But had thought they were different; this Birth was
Hard and bitter agony for us, like Death, our death.
We returned to our places, these Kingdoms,
But no longer at ease here, in the old dispensation,
With an alien people clutching their gods.
I should be glad of another death.

Burnt Norton

τοῦ λόγου δ'ἐόντος ξυνοῦ ζώουσιν
οἱ πολλοὶ ὡς ἰδίαν ἔχοντες φρό-
νησιν.

I. p. 77. Fragment 2.

ὁδὸς ἄνω κάτω μία καὶ ὠυτή

I. p. 89. Fragment 60.

—Diels: *Die Fragmente der Vorsokratiker*

(Herakleitos).

I

Time present and time past
Are both perhaps present in time future,
And time future contained in time past.
If all time is eternally present
All time is unredeemable.
What might have been is an abstraction
Remaining a perpetual possibility
Only in a world of speculation.
What might have been and what has been
Point to one end, which is always present.
Footfalls echo in the memory
Down the passage which we did not take
Towards the door we never opened
Into the rose-garden. My words echo
Thus, in your mind.
                          But to what purpose
Disturbing the dust on a bowl of rose-leaves
I do not know.
                          Other echoes
Inhabit the garden. Shall we follow?
Quick, said the bird, find them, find them,
Round the corner. Through the first gate,
Into our first world, shall we follow
The deception of the thrush? Into our first world.

There they were, dignified, invisible,
Moving without pressure, over the dead leaves,
In the autumn heat, through the vibrant air,
And the bird called, in response to
The unheard music hidden in the shrubbery,
And the unseen eyebeam crossed, for the roses
Had the look of flowers that are looked at.
There they were as our guests, accepted and accepting.
So we moved, and they, in a formal pattern,
Along the empty alley, into the box circle,
To look down into the drained pool.
Dry the pool, dry concrete, brown edged,
And the pool was filled with water out of sunlight,
And the lotos rose, quietly, quietly,
The surface glittered out of heart of light,
And they were behind us, reflected in the pool.
Then a cloud passed, and the pool was empty.
Go, said the bird, for the leaves were full of children,
Hidden excitedly, containing laughter.
Go, go, go, said the bird: human kind
Cannot bear very much reality.
Time past and time future
What might have been and what has been
Point to one end, which is always present.

II

Garlic and sapphires in the mud
Clot the bedded axle-tree.
The trilling wire in the blood
Sings below inveterate scars
Appeasing long forgotten wars.
The dance along the artery
The circulation of the lymph
Are figured in the drift of stars
Ascend to summer in the tree
We move above the moving tree
In light upon the figured leaf
And hear upon the sodden floor

Below, the boarhound and the boar
Pursue their pattern as before
But reconciled among the stars.

At the still point of the turning world. Neither flesh nor
     fleshless;
Neither from nor towards; at the still point, there the dance is,
But neither arrest nor movement. And do not call it fixity,
Where past and future are gathered. Neither movement
     from nor towards,
Neither ascent nor decline. Except for the point, the still point,
There would be no dance, and there is only the dance.
I can only say, *there* we have been: but I cannot say where.
And I cannot say, how long, for that is to place it in time.
The inner freedom from the practical desire,
The release from action and suffering, release from the inner
And the outer compulsion, yet surrounded
By a grace of sense, a white light still and moving,
Erhebung without motion, concentration
Without elimination, both a new world
And the old made explicit, understood
In the completion of its partial ecstasy,
The resolution of its partial horror.
Yet the enchainment of past and future
Woven in the weakness of the changing body,
Protects mankind from heaven and damnation
Which flesh cannot endure.
                                        Time past and time future
Allow but a little consciousness.
To be conscious is not to be in time
But only in time can the moment in the rose-garden,
The moment in the arbour where the rain beat,
The moment in the draughty church at smokefall
Be remembered; involved with past and future.
Only through time time is conquered.

III

Here is a place of disaffection
Time before and time after
In a dim light: neither daylight
Investing form with lucid stillness
Turning shadow into transient beauty
With slow rotation suggesting permanence
Nor darkness to purify the soul
Emptying the sensual with deprivation
Cleansing affection from the temporal.
Neither plenitude nor vacancy. Only a flicker
Over the strained time-ridden faces
Distracted from distraction by distraction
Filled with fancies and empty of meaning
Tumid apathy with no concentration
Men and bits of paper, whirled by the cold wind
That blows before and after time,
Wind in and out of unwholesome lungs
Time before and time after.
Eructation of unhealthy souls
Into the faded air, the torpid
Driven on the wind that sweeps the gloomy hills of London,
Hampstead and Clerkenwell, Campden and Putney,
Highgate, Primrose and Ludgate. Not here
Not here the darkness, in this twittering world.

Descend lower, descend only
Into the world of perpetual solitude,
World not world, but that which is not world,
Internal darkness, deprivation
And destitution of all property,
Desiccation of the world of sense,
Evacuation of the world of fancy,
Inoperancy of the world of spirit;
This is the one way, and the other
Is the same, not in movement
But abstention from movement; while the world moves
In appetency, on its metalled ways
Of time past and time future.

IV

Time and the bell have buried the day,
The black cloud carries the sun away.
Will the sunflower turn to us, will the clematis
Stray down, bend to us; tendril and spray
Clutch and cling?
Chill
Fingers of yew be curled
Down on us? After the kingfisher's wing
Has answered light to light, and is silent, the light is still
At the still point of the turning world.

V

Words move, music moves
Only in time; but that which is only living
Can only die. Words, after speech, reach
Into the silence. Only by the form, the pattern,
Can words or music reach
The stillness, as a Chinese jar still
Moves perpetually in its stillness.
Not the stillness of the violin, while the note lasts,
Not that only, but the co-existence,
Or say that the end precedes the beginning,
And the end and the beginning were always there
Before the beginning and after the end.
And all is always now. Words strain,
Crack and sometimes break, under the burden,
Under the tension, slip, slide, perish,
Decay with imprecision, will not stay in place,
Will not stay still. Shrieking voices
Scolding, mocking, or merely chattering,
Always assail them. The Word in the desert
Is most attacked by voices of temptation,
The crying shadow in the funeral dance,
The loud lament of the disconsolate chimera.

The detail of the pattern is movement,
As in the figure of the ten stairs.
    Desire itself is movement
    Not in itself desirable;
    Love is itself unmoving,
    Only the cause and end of movement,
    Timeless, and undesiring
    Except in the aspect of time
    Caught in the form of limitation
    Between un-being and being.
    Sudden in a shaft of sunlight
    Even while the dust moves
    There rises the hidden laughter
    Of children in the foliage
    Quick now, here, now, always—
    Ridiculous the waste sad time
    Stretching before and after.

Wilfred Owen

Strange Meeting

It seemed that out of battle I escaped
Down some profound dull tunnel, long since scooped
Through granites which titanic wars had groined.
Yet also there encumbered sleepers groaned,
Too fast in thought or death to be bestirred.
Then, as I probed them, one sprang up, and stared
With piteous recognition in fixed eyes,
Lifting distressful hands as if to bless.
And by his smile, I knew that sullen hall,
By his dead smile I knew we stood in Hell.
With a thousand pains that vision's face was grained;
Yet no blood reached there from the upper ground,
And no guns thumped, or down the flues made moan.
'Strange friend,' I said, 'here is no cause to mourn.'
'None,' said the other, 'save the undone years,
The hopelessness. Whatever hope is yours,
Was my life also; I went hunting wild
After the wildest beauty in the world,
Which lies not calm in eyes, or braided hair,
But mocks the steady running of the hour,
And if it grieves, grieves richlier than here.
For of my glee might many men have laughed,
And of my weeping something had been left,
Which must die now. I mean the truth untold,
The pity of war, the pity war distilled.
Now men will go content with what we spoiled,
Or, discontent, boil bloody, and be spilled.
They will be swift with swiftness of the tigress.
None will break ranks, though nations trek from progress.

Courage was mine, and I had mystery,
Wisdom was mine, and I had mastery:
To miss the march of this retreating world
Into vain citadels that are not walled.
Then, when much blood had clogged their chariot-wheels,
I would go up and wash them from sweet wells,
Even with truths that lie too deep for taint.
I would have poured my spirit without stint
But not through wounds; not on the cess of war.
Foreheads of men have bled where no wounds were.
I am the enemy you killed, my friend.
I knew you in this dark: for so you frowned
Yesterday through me as you jabbed and killed.
I parried; but my hands were loath and cold.
Let us sleep now. . . .

Greater Love

Red lips are not so red
   As the stained stones kissed by the English dead.
Kindness of wooed and wooer
Seems shame to their love pure.
O Love, your eyes lose lure
   When I behold eyes blinded in my stead!

Your slender attitude
   Trembles not exquisite like limbs knife-skewed,
Rolling and rolling there
Where God seems not to care;
Till the fierce love they bear
   Cramps them in death's extreme decrepitude.

Your voice sings not so soft,—
   Though even as wind murmuring through raftered loft,—
Your dear voice is not dear,
Gentle, and evening clear,

As theirs whom none now hear,
    Now earth has stopped their piteous mouths that coughed.

Heart, you were never hot
    Nor large, nor full like hearts made great with shot;
And though your hand be pale,
Paler are all which trail
Your cross through flame and hail:
    Weep, you may weep, for you may touch them not.

Arms and the Boy

Let the boy try along this bayonet-blade
How cold steel is, and keen with hunger of blood;
Blue with all malice, like a madman's flash;
And thinly drawn with famishing for flesh.

Lend him to stroke these blind, blunt bullet-heads
Which long to nuzzle in the hearts of lads,
Or give him cartridges of fine zinc teeth,
Sharp with the sharpness of grief and death.

For his teeth seem for laughing round an apple.
There lurk no claws behind his fingers supple;
And God will grow no talons at his heels,
Nor antlers through the thickness of his curls.

Anthem for Doomed Youth

What passing-bells for these who die as cattle?
    Only the monstrous anger of the guns.
    Only the stuttering rifles' rapid rattle
Can patter out their hasty orisons.
No mockeries now for them; no prayers nor bells,
    Nor any voice of mourning save the choirs,—

The shrill, demented choirs of wailing shells;
   And bugles calling for them from sad shires.

What candles may be held to speed them all?
   Not in the hands of boys, but in their eyes
Shall shine the holy glimmers of good-byes.
   The pallor of girls' brows shall be their pall;
Their flowers the tenderness of patient minds,
And each slow dusk a drawing-down of blinds.

Dulce Et Decorum Est

Bent double, like old beggars under sacks,
Knock-kneed, coughing like hags, we cursed through sludge,
Till on the haunting flares we turned our backs
And towards our distant rest began to trudge.
Men marched asleep. Many had lost their boots
But limped on, blood-shod. All went lame; all blind;
Drunk with fatigue; deaf even to the hoots
Of tired, outstripped Five-Nines that dropped behind.

Gas! Gas! Quick, boys!—An ecstasy of fumbling,
Fitting the clumsy helmets just in time;
But someone still was yelling out and stumbling
And flound'ring like a man in fire or lime . . .
Dim, through the misty panes and thick green light,
As under a green sea, I saw him drowning.

In all my dreams, before my helpless sight,
He plunges at me, guttering, choking, drowning.

If in some smothering dreams you too could pace
Behind the wagon that we flung him in,
And watch the white eyes writhing in his face,
His hanging face, like a devil's sick of sin;
If you could hear, at every jolt, the blood

Come gargling from the froth-corrupted lungs,
Obscene as cancer, bitter as the cud
Of vile, incurable sores on innocent tongues,—
My friend, you would not tell with such high zest
To children ardent for some desperate glory,
The old Lie: Dulce et decorum est
Pro patria mori.

Futility

Move him into the sun—
Gently its touch awoke him once,
At home, whispering of fields unsown.
Always it woke him, even in France,
Until this morning and this snow.
If anything might rouse him now
The kind old sun will know.

Think how it wakes the seeds,—
Woke, once, the clays of a cold star.
Are limbs, so dear-achieved, are sides,
Full-nerved—still warm—too hard to stir?
Was it for this the clay grew tall?
—O what made fatuous sunbeams toil
To break earth's sleep at all?

Mental Cases

Who are these? Why sit they here in twilight?
Wherefore rock they, purgatorial shadows,
Drooping tongues from jaws that slob their relish,
Baring teeth that leer like skulls' teeth wicked?
Stroke on stroke of pain,—but what slow panic,
Gouged these chasms round their fretted sockets?
Ever from their hair and through their hands' palms

Misery swelters. Surely we have perished
Sleeping, and walk hell; but who these hellish?

—These are men whose minds the Dead have ravished.
Memory fingers in their hair of murders,
Multitudinous murders they once witnessed.
Wading sloughs of flesh these helpless wander,
Treading blood from lungs that had loved laughter.
Always they must see these things and hear them,
Batter of guns and shatter of flying muscles,
Carnage incomparable, and human squander
Rucked too thick for these men's extrication.

Therefore still their eyeballs shrink tormented
Back into their brains, because on their sense
Sunlight seems a blood-smear; night comes blood-black;
Dawn breaks open like a wound that bleeds afresh.
—Thus their heads wear this hilarious, hideous,
Awful falseness of set-smiling corpses.
—Thus their hands are plucking at each other;
Picking at the rope-knouts of their scourging;
Snatching after us who smote them, brother,
Pawing us who dealt them war and madness.

e. e. cummings

Chansons Innocentes

I

in Just-
spring   when the world is mud-
luscious the little
lame balloonman

whistles   far   and wee

and eddieandbill come
running from marbles and
piracies and it's
spring

when the world is puddle-wonderful

the queer
old balloonman whistles
far   and   wee
and bettyandisbel come dancing

from hop-scotch and jump-rope and
it's
spring
and
    the
        goat-footed

balloonMan   whistles
far
and
wee

II

hist   whist
little ghostthings
tip-toe
twinkle-toe

little twitchy
witches and tingling
goblins
hob-a-nob   hob-a-nob

little hoppy happy
toad in tweeds
tweeds
little itchy mousies

with scuttling
eyes   rustle and run   and
hidehidehide
whisk

whisk   look·out for the old woman
with the wart on her nose
what she'll do to yer
nobody knows

for she knows the devil   ooch
the devil   ouch
the devil
ach   the great
green
dancing
devil
devil

devil
devil
          wheeEEE

III

Tumbling-hair
                  picker of buttercups
                                    violets
dandelions
And the big bullying daisies
                        through the field wonderful
with eyes a little sorry
Another comes
                  also picking flowers

my sweet old etcetera

my sweet old etcetera
aunt lucy during the recent

war could and what
is more did tell you just
what everybody was fighting

for,
my sister
isabel created hundreds
(and
hundreds) of socks not to
mention shirts fleaproof earwarmers

etcetera wristers etcetera, my
mother hoped that

i would die etcetera
bravely of course my father used
to become hoarse talking about how it was
a privilege and if only he
could meanwhile my

self etcetera lay quietly
in the deep mud et

cetera
(dreaming,
et
    cetera, of
Your smile
eyes knees and of your Etcetera)

i sing of Olaf

i sing of Olaf glad and big
whose warmest heart recoiled at war:
a conscientious object-or

his wellbelovéd colonel (trig
westpointer most succinctly bred)
took erring Olaf soon in hand;
but—though an host of overjoyed
noncoms (first knocking on the head
him) do through icy waters roll
that helplessness which others stroke
with brushes recently employed
anent this muddy toiletbowl,
while kindred intellects evoke
allegiance per blunt instruments—
Olaf (being to all intents
a corpse and wanting any rag
upon what God unto him gave)
responds, without getting annoyed
'I will not kiss your f.ing flag'

straightway the silver bird looked grave
(departing hurriedly to shave)

but—though all kinds of officers
(a yearning nation's blueeyed pride)
their passive prey did kick and curse
until for wear their clarion
voices and boots were much the worse,
and egged the firstclassprivates on
his rectum wickedly to tease
by means of skilfully applied
bayonets roasted hot with heat—
Olaf (upon what were once knees)
does almost ceaselessly repeat
'there is some s. I will not eat'

our president,being of which
assertions duly notified
threw the yellowsonofabitch
into a dungeon,where he died

Christ(of His mercy infinite)
i pray to see;and Olaf,too

preponderatingly because
unless statistics lie he was
more brave than me:more blond than you.

somewhere i have never travelled,gladly beyond

somewhere i have never travelled,gladly beyond
any experience,your eyes have their silence:
in your most frail gesture are things which enclose me,
or which i cannot touch because they are too near

your slightest look easily will unclose me
though i have closed myself as fingers,
you open always petal by petal myself as Spring opens
(touching skilfully, mysteriously)her first rose

or if your wish be to close me,i and
my life will shut very beautifully,suddenly,
as when the heart of this flower imagines
the snow carefully everywhere descending;

nothing which we are to perceive in this world equals
the power of your intense fragility:whose texture
compels me with the colour of its countries,
rendering death and forever with each breathing

(i do not know what it is about you that closes
and opens;only something in me understands
the voice of your eyes is deeper than all roses)
nobody,not even the rain,has such small hands

may i feel said he

may i feel said he
(i'll squeal said she
just once said he)
it's fun said she

(may i touch said he
how much said she
a lot said he)
why not said she

(let's go said he
not too far said she
what's too far said he
where you are said she)

may i stay said he
(which way said she
like this said he
if you kiss said she

may i move said he
is it love said she)
if you're willing said he
(but you're killing said she

but it's life said he
but your wife said she
now said he)
ow said she

(tiptop said he
don't stop said she
oh no said he)
go slow said she

(cccome?said he
ummm said she)
you're divine!said he
(you are Mine said she)

anyone lived in a pretty how town

anyone lived in a pretty how town
(with up so floating many bells down)
spring summer autumn winter
he sang his didn't he danced his did.

Women and men(both little and small)
cared for anyone not at all
they sowed their isn't they reaped their same
sun moon stars rain

children guessed(but only a few
and down they forgot as up they grew
autumn winter spring summer)
that noone loved him more by more

when by now and tree by leaf
she laughed his joy she cried his grief
bird by snow and stir by still
anyone's any was all to her

someones married their everyones
laughed their cryings and did their dance
(sleep wake hope and then)they
said their nevers they slept their dream

stars rain sun moon
(and only the snow can begin to explain
how children are apt to forget to remember
with up so floating many bells down)

one day anyone died i guess
(and noone stooped to kiss his face)
busy folk buried them side by side
little by little and was by was

all by all and deep by deep
and more by more they dream their sleep
noone and anyone earth by april
wish by spirit and if by yes.

Women and men(both dong and ding)
summer autumn winter spring
reaped their sowing and went their came
sun moon stars rain

my father moved through dooms of love

my father moved through dooms of love
through sames of am through haves of give,
singing each morning out of each night
my father moved through depths of height

this motionless forgetful where
turned at his glance to shining here;
that if(so timid air is firm)
under his eyes would stir and squirm

newly as from unburied which
floats the first who,his april touch
drove sleeping selves to swarm their fates
woke dreamers to their ghostly roots

and should some why completely weep
my father's fingers brought her sleep:
vainly no smallest voice might cry
for he could feel the mountains grow.

Lifting the valleys of the sea
my father moved through griefs of joy;
praising a forehead called the moon
singing desire into begin

joy was his song and joy so pure
a heart of star by him could steer
and pure so now and now so yes
the wrists of twilight would rejoice

keen as midsummer's keen beyond
conceiving mind of sun will stand,
so strictly(over utmost him
so hugely)stood my father's dream

his flesh was flesh his blood was blood:
no hungry man but wished him food;
no cripple wouldn't creep one mile
uphill to only see him smile.

Scorning the pomp of must and shall
my father moved through dooms of feel;
his anger was as right as rain
his pity was as green as grain

septembering arms of year extend
less humbly wealth to foe and friend
than he to foolish and to wise
offered immeasurable is

proudly and(by octobering flame
beckoned)as earth will downward climb,
so naked for immortal work
his shoulders marched against the dark

his sorrow was as true as bread:
no liar looked him in the head;
if every friend became his foe
he'd laugh and build a world with snow.

My father moved through theys of we,
singing each new leaf out of each tree
(and every child was sure that spring
danced when she heard my father sing)

then let men kill which cannot share,
let blood and flesh be mud and mire,
scheming imagine,passion willed,
freedom a drug that's bought and sold

giving to steal and cruel kind,
a heart to fear,to doubt a mind,
to differ a disease of same,
conform the pinnacle of am

though dull were all we taste as bright,
bitter all utterly things sweet,
maggoty minus and dumb death
all we inherit,all bequeath

and nothing quite so least as truth
—i say though hate were why men breathe—
because my father lived his soul
love is the whole and more than all

love is more thicker than forget

love is more thicker than forget
more thinner than recall
more seldom than a wave is wet
more frequent than to fail

it is most mad and moonly
and less it shall unbe
than all the sea which only
is deeper than the sea

love is less always than to win
less never than alive
less bigger than the least begin
less littler than forgive

it is most sane and sunly
and more it cannot die
than all the sky which only
is higher than the sky

true lovers in each happening of their hearts

true lovers in each happening of their hearts
live longer than all which and every who;
despite what fear denies,what hope asserts,
what falsest both disprove by proving true

(all doubts,all certainties,as villains strive
and heroes through the mere mind's poor pretend
—grim comics of duration:only love
immortally occurs beyond the mind)

such a forever is love's any now
and her each here is such an everywhere,

even more true would truest lovers grow
if out of midnight dropped more suns than are

(yes;and if time should ask into his was
all shall,their eyes would never miss a yes)

dying is fine) but Death

dying is fine)but Death

?o
baby
i

wouldn't like

Death if Death
were
good:for

when(instead of stopping to think)you

begin to feel of it,dying
's miraculous
why?be

cause dying is

perfectly natural;perfectly
putting
it mildly lively(but

Death

is strictly
scientific
& artificial &

evil & legal)

we thank thee
god
almighty for dying

(forgive us,o life!the sin of Death

i thank You God for most this amazing

i thank You God for most this amazing
day:for the leaping greenly spirits of trees
and a blue true dream of sky;and for everything
which is natural which is infinite which is yes

(i who have died am alive again today,
and this is the sun's birthday;this is the birth
day of life and of love and wings:and of the gay
great happening illimitably earth)

how should tasting touching hearing seeing
breathing any—lifted from the no
of all nothing—human merely being
doubt unimaginable You?

(now the ears of my ears awake and
now the eyes of my eyes are opened)

Wallace Stevens

The Emperor of Ice-Cream

Call the roller of big cigars,
The muscular one, and bid him whip
In kitchen cups concupiscent curds.
Let the wenches dawdle in such dress
As they are used to wear, and let the boys
Bring flowers in last month's newspapers.
Let be be finale of seem.
The only emperor is the emperor of ice-cream.

Take from the dresser of deal,
Lacking the three glass knobs, that sheet
On which she embroidered fantails once
And spread it so as to cover her face.
If her horny feet protrude, they come
To show how cold she is, and dumb.
Let the lamp affix its beam.
The only emperor is the emperor of ice-cream.

Sunday Morning

I

Complacencies of the peignoir, and late
Coffee and oranges in a sunny chair,
And the green freedom of a cockatoo
Upon a rug mingle to dissipate
The holy hush of ancient sacrifice.
She dreams a little, and she feels the dark
Encroachment of that old catastrophe,

As a calm darkens among water-lights.
The pungent oranges and bright, green wings
Seem things in some procession of the dead,
Winding across wide water, without sound.
The day is like wide water, without sound,
Stilled for the passing of her dreaming feet
Over the seas, to silent Palestine,
Dominion of the blood and sepulchre.

II

Why should she give her bounty to the dead?
What is divinity if it can come
Only in silent shadows and in dreams?
Shall she not find in comforts of the sun,
In pungent fruit and bright, green wings, or else
In any balm or beauty of the earth,
Things to be cherished like the thought of heaven?
Divinity must live within herself:
Passions of rain, or moods in falling snow;
Grievings in loneliness, or unsubdued
Elations when the forest blooms; gusty
Emotions on wet roads on autumn nights;
All pleasures and all pains, remembering
The bough of summer and the winter branch.
These are the measures destined for her soul.

III

Jove in the clouds had his inhuman birth.
No mother suckled him, no sweet land gave
Large-mannered motions to his mythy mind
He moved among us, as a muttering king,
Magnificent, would move among his hinds,
Until our blood, commingling, virginal,
With heaven, brought such requital to desire
The very hinds discerned it, in a star.
Shall our blood fail? Or shall it come to be
The blood of paradise? And shall the earth
Seem all of paradise that we shall know?

The sky will be much friendlier then than now,
A part of labor and a part of pain,
And next in glory to enduring love,
Not this dividing and indifferent blue.

IV

She says, 'I am content when wakened birds,
Before they fly, test the reality
Of misty fields, by their sweet questionings;
But when the birds are gone, and their warm fields
Return no more, where, then, is paradise?'
There is not any haunt of prophecy,
Nor any old chimera of the grave,
Neither the golden underground, nor isle
Melodious, where spirits gat them home,
Nor visionary south, nor cloudy palm
Remote on heaven's hill, that has endured
As April's green endures; or will endure
Like her remembrance of awakened birds,
Or her desire for June and evening, tipped
By the consummation of the swallow's wings.

V

She says, 'But in contentment I still feel
The need of some imperishable bliss.'
Death is the mother of beauty; hence from her,
Alone, shall come fulfilment to our dreams
And our desires. Although she strews the leaves
Of sure obliteration on our paths,
The path sick sorrow took, the many paths
Where triumph rang its brassy phrase, or love
Whispered a little out of tenderness,
She makes the willow shiver in the sun
For maidens who were wont to sit and gaze
Upon the grass, relinquished to their feet.
She causes boys to pile new plums and pears
On disregarded plate. The maidens taste
And stray impassioned in the littering leaves.

VI

Is there no change of death in paradise?
Does ripe fruit never fall? Or do the boughs
Hang always heavy in that perfect sky,
Unchanging, yet so like our perishing earth,
With rivers like our own that seek for seas
They never find, the same receding shores
That never touch with inarticulate pang?
Why set the pear upon those river-banks
Or spice the shores with odors of the plum?
Alas, that they should wear our colors there,
The silken weavings of our afternoons,
And pick the strings of our insipid lutes!
Death is the mother of beauty, mystical,
Within whose burning bosom we devise
Our earthly mothers waiting, sleeplessly.

VII

Supple and turbulent, a ring of men
Shall chant in orgy on a summer morn
Their boisterous devotion to the sun,
Not as a god, but as a god might be,
Naked among them, like a savage source.
Their chant shall be a chant of paradise,
Out of their blood, returning to the sky;
And in their chant shall enter, voice by voice,
The windy lake wherein their lord delights,
The trees, like serafin, and echoing hills,
That choir among themselves long afterward.
They shall know well the heavenly fellowship
Of men that perish and of summer morn.
And whence they came and whither they shall go
The dew upon their feet shall manifest.

VIII

She hears, upon that water without sound,
A voice that cries, 'The tomb in Palestine
Is not the porch of spirits lingering.

It is the grave of Jesus, where he lay.'
We live in an old chaos of the sun,
Or old dependency of day and night,
Or island solitude, unsponsored, free,
Of that wide water, inescapable.
Deer walk upon our mountains, and the quail
Whistle about us their spontaneous cries;
Sweet berries ripen in the wilderness;
And, in the isolation of the sky,
At evening, casual flocks of pigeons make
Ambiguous undulations as they sink,
Downward to darkness, on extended wings.

The Idea of Order at Key West

She sang beyond the genius of the sea.
The water never formed to mind or voice,
Like a body wholly body, fluttering
Its empty sleeves; and yet its mimic motion
Made constant cry, caused constantly a cry,
That was not ours although we understood,
Inhuman, of the veritable ocean.

The sea was not a mask. No more was she.
The song and water were not medleyed sound
Even if what she sang was what she heard,
Since what she sang was uttered word by word.
It may be that in all her phrases stirred
The grinding water and the gasping wind;
But it was she and not the sea we heard.

For she was the maker of the song she sang.
The ever-hooded, tragic-gestured sea
Was merely a place by which she walked to sing.
Whose spirit is this? we said, because we knew
It was the spirit that we sought and knew
That we should ask this often as she sang.

If it was only the dark voice of the sea
That rose, or even colored by many waves;
If it was only the outer voice of sky
And cloud, of the sunken coral water-walled,
However clear, it would have been deep air,
The heaving speech of air, a summer sound
Repeated in a summer without end
And sound alone. But it was more than that,
More even than her voice, and ours, among
The meaningless plungings of water and the wind,
Theatrical distances, bronze shadows heaped
On high horizons, mountainous atmospheres
Of sky and sea.
                        It was her voice that made
The sky acutest at its vanishing.
She measured to the hour its solitude.
She was the single artificer of the world
In which she sang. And when she sang, the sea,
Whatever self it had, became the self
That was her song, for she was the maker. Then we,
As we beheld her striding there alone,
Knew that there never was a world for her
Except the one she sang and, singing, made.

Ramon Fernandez, tell me, if you know,
Why, when the singing ended and we turned
Toward the town, tell why the glassy lights,
The lights in the fishing boats at anchor there,
As the night descended, tilting in the air,
Mastered the night and portioned out the sea,
Fixing emblazoned zones and fiery poles,
Arranging, deepening, enchanting night.

Oh! Blessed rage for order, pale Ramon,
The maker's rage to order words of the sea,
Words of the fragrant portals, dimly-starred,
And of ourselves and of our origins,
In ghostlier demarcations, keener sounds.

The Man on the Dump

Day creeps down. The moon is creeping up.
The sun is a corbeil of flowers the moon Blanche
Places there, a bouquet. Ho-ho . . . The dump is full
Of images. Days pass like papers from a press.
The bouquets come here in the papers. So the sun,
And so the moon, both come, and the janitor's poems
Of every day, the wrapper on the can of pears,
The cat in the paper-bag, the corset, the box
From Esthonia: the tiger chest, for tea.

The freshness of night has been fresh a long time.
The freshness of morning, the blowing of day, one says
That it puffs as Cornelius Nepos reads, it puffs
More than, less than or it puffs like this or that.
The green smacks in the eye, the dew in the green
Smacks like fresh water in a can, like the sea
On a cocoanut—how many men have copied dew
For buttons, how many women have covered themselves
With dew, dew dresses, stones and chains of dew, heads
Of the floweriest flowers dewed with the dewiest dew.
One grows to hate these things except on the dump.

Now, in the time of spring (azaleas, trilliums,
Myrtle, viburnums, daffodils, blue phlox),
Between that disgust and this, between the things
That are on the dump (azaleas and so on)
And those that will be (azaleas and so on),
One feels the purifying change. One rejects
The trash.

            That's the moment when the moon creeps up
To the bubbling of bassoons. That's the time
One looks at the elephant-colorings of tires.
Everything is shed; and the moon comes up as the moon
(All its images are in the dump) and you see
As a man (not like an image of a man),
You see the moon rise in the empty sky.

One sits and beats an old tin can, lard pail.
One beats and beats for that which one believes.
That's what one wants to get near. Could it after all
Be merely oneself, as superior as the ear
To a crow's voice? Did the nightingale torture the ear,
Pack the heart and scratch the mind? And does the ear
Solace itself in peevish birds? Is it peace,
Is it a philosopher's honeymoon, one finds
On the dump? Is it to sit among mattresses of the dead,
Bottles, pots, shoes and grass and murmur *aptest eve:*
Is it to hear the blatter of grackles and say
Invisible priest; is it to eject, to pull
The day to pieces and cry *stanza my stone*?
Where was it one first heard of the truth? The the.

The Motive for Metaphor

You like it under the trees in autumn,
Because everything is half dead.
The wind moves like a cripple among the leaves
And repeats words without meaning.

In the same way, you were happy in spring,
With the half colors of quarter-things,
The slightly brighter sky, the melting clouds,
The single bird, the obscure moon—

The obscure moon lighting an obscure world
Of things that would never be quite expressed,
Where you yourself were never quite yourself
And did not want nor have to be,

Desiring the exhilarations of changes:
The motive for metaphor, shrinking from
The weight of primary noon,
The A B C of being,

The ruddy temper, the hammer
Of red and blue, the hard sound—
Steel against intimation—the sharp flash,
The vital, arrogant, fatal, dominant X.

Credences of Summer

I

Now in midsummer come and all fools slaughtered
And spring's infuriations over and a long way
To the first autumnal inhalations, young broods
Are in the grass, the roses are heavy with a weight
Of fragrance and the mind lays by its trouble.

Now the mind lays by its trouble and considers.
The fidgets of remembrance come to this.
This is the last day of a certain year
Beyond which there is nothing left of time.
It comes to this and the imagination's life.

There is nothing more inscribed nor thought nor felt
And this must comfort the heart's core against
Its false disasters—these fathers standing round,
These mothers touching, speaking, being near,
These lovers waiting in the soft dry grass.

II

Postpone the anatomy of summer, as
The physical pine, the metaphysical pine.
Let's see the very thing and nothing else.
Let's see it with the hottest fire of sight.
Burn everything not part of it to ash.

Trace the gold sun about the whitened sky
Without evasion by a single metaphor.

Look at it in its essential barrenness
And say this, this is the centre that I seek.
Fix it in an eternal foliage

And fill the foliage with arrested peace,
Joy of such permanence, right ignorance
Of change still possible. Exile desire
For what it is not. This is the barrenness
Of the fertile thing that can attain no more.

III

It is the natural tower of all the world,
The point of survey, green's green apogee,
But a tower more precious than the view beyond,
A point of survey squatting like a throne,
Axis of everything, green's apogee

And happiest folk-land, mostly marriage-hymns.
It is the mountain on which the tower stands,
It is the final mountain. Here the sun,
Sleepless, inhales his proper air, and rests.
This is the refuge that the end creates.

It is the old man standing on the tower,
Who reads no book. His ruddy ancientness
Absorbs the ruddy summer and is appeased,
By an understanding that fulfils his age,
By a feeling capable of nothing more.

IV

One of the limits of reality
Presents itself in Oley when the hay,
Baked through long days, is piled in mows. It is
A land too ripe for enigmas, too serene.
There the distant fails the clairvoyant eye

And the secondary senses of the ear
Swarm, not with secondary sounds, but choirs,

Not evocations but last choirs, last sounds
With nothing else compounded, carried full,
Pure rhetoric of a language without words.

Things stop in that direction and since they stop
The direction stops and we accept what is
As good. The utmost must be good and is
And is our fortune and honey hived in the trees
And mingling of colors at a festival.

V

One day enriches a year. One woman makes
The rest look down. One man becomes a race,
Lofty like him, like him perpetual.
Or do the other days enrich the one?
And is the queen humble as she seems to be,

The charitable majesty of her whole kin?
The bristling soldier, weather-foxed, who looms
In the sunshine is a filial form and one
Of the land's children, easily born, its flesh,
Not fustian. The more than casual blue

Contains the year and other years and hymns
And people, without souvenir. The day
Enriches the year, not as embellishment.
Stripped of remembrance, it displays its strength—
The youth, the vital son, the heroic power.

VI

The rock cannot be broken. It is the truth.
It rises from land and sea and covers them.
It is a mountain half way green and then,
The other immeasurable half, such rock
As placid air becomes. But it is not

A hermit's truth nor symbol in hermitage.
It is the visible rock, the audible,

The brilliant mercy of a sure repose,
On this present ground, the vividest repose,
Things certain sustaining us in certainty.

It is the rock of summer, the extreme,
A mountain luminous half way in bloom
And then half way in the extremest light
Of sapphires flashing from the central sky,
As if twelve princes sat before a king.

VII

Far in the woods they sang their unreal songs,
Secure. It was difficult to sing in face
Of the object. The singers had to avert themselves
Or else avert the object. Deep in the woods
They sang of summer in the common fields.

They sang desiring an object that was near,
In face of which desire no longer moved,
Nor made of itself that which it could not find . . .
Three times the concentred self takes hold, three times
The thrice concentred self, having possessed

The object, grips it in savage scrutiny,
Once to make captive, once to subjugate
Or yield to subjugation, once to proclaim
The meaning of the capture, this hard prize,
Fully made, fully apparent, fully found.

VIII

The trumpet of morning blows in the clouds and through
The sky. It is the visible announced,
It is the more than visible, the more
Than sharp, illustrious scene. The trumpet cries
This is the successor of the invisible.

This is its substitute in stratagems
Of the spirit. This, in sight and memory,

Must take its place, as what is possible
Replaces what is not. The resounding cry
Is like ten thousand tumblers tumbling down

To share the day. The trumpet supposes that
A mind exists, aware of division, aware
Of its cry as clarion, its diction's way
As that of a personage in a multitude:
Man's mind grown venerable in the unreal.

IX

Fly low, cock bright, and stop on a bean pole. Let
Your brown breast redden, while you wait for warmth.
With one eye watch the willow, motionless.
The gardener's cat is dead, the gardener gone
And last year's garden grows salacious weeds.

A complex of emotions falls apart,
In an abandoned spot. Soft, civil bird,
The decay that you regard: of the arranged
And of the spirit of the arranged, *douceurs*,
Tristesses, the fund of life and death, suave bush

And polished beast, this complex falls apart.
And on your bean pole, it may be, you detect
Another complex of other emotions, not
So soft, so civil, and you make a sound,
Which is not part of the listener's own sense.

X

The personae of summer play the characters
Of an inhuman author, who meditates
With the gold bugs, in blue meadows, late at night.
He does not hear his characters talk. He sees
Them mottled, in the moodiest costumes,

Of blue and yellow, sky and sun, belted
And knotted, sashed and seamed, half pales of red,

Half pales of green, appropriate habit for
The huge decorum, the manner of the time,
Part of the mottled mood of summer's whole,

In which the characters speak because they want
to speak, the fat, the roseate characters,
Free, for a moment, from malice and sudden cry,
Complete in a completed scene, speaking
Their parts as in a youthful happiness.

The Poem that Took the Place of a Mountain

There it was, word for word,
The poem that took the place of a mountain.

He breathed its oxygen,
Even when the book lay turned in the dust of his table.

It reminded him how he had needed
A place to go to in his own direction,

How he had recomposed the pines,
Shifted the rocks and picked his way among clouds,

For the outlook that would be right,
Where he would be complete in an unexplained completion:

The exact rock where his inexactnesses
Would discover, at last, the view toward which they had edged,

Where he could lie and, gazing down at the sea,
Recognize his unique and solitary home.

W. H. Auden

As I Walked Out One Evening

As I walked out one evening,
   Walking down Bristol Street,
The crowds upon the pavement
   Were fields of harvest wheat.

And down by the brimming river
   I heard a lover sing
Under an arch of the railway:
   'Love has no ending.

'I'll love you, dear, I'll love you
   Till China and Africa meet,
And the river jumps over the mountain
   And the salmon sing in the street,

'I'll love you till the ocean
   Is folded and hung up to dry
And the seven stars go squawking
   Like geese about the sky.

The years shall run like rabbits,
   For in my arms I hold
The Flower of the Ages,
   And the first love of the world.'

But all the clocks in the city
   Began to whirr and chime:
'O let not Time deceive you,
   You cannot conquer Time.

'In the burrows of the Nightmare
   Where Justice naked is,
Time watches from the shadow
   And coughs when you would kiss.

'In headaches and in worry
   Vaguely life leaks away,
And Time will have his fancy
   To-morrow or to-day.

'Into many a green valley
   Drifts the appalling snow;
Time breaks the threaded dances
   And the diver's brilliant bow.

'O plunge your hands in water,
   Plunge them in up to the wrist;
Stare, stare in the basin
   And wonder what you've missed.

'The glacier knocks in the cupboard,
   The desert sighs in the bed,
And the crack in the tea-cup opens
   A lane to the land of the dead.

'Where the beggars raffle the banknotes
   And the Giant is enchanting to Jack,
And the Lily-white Boy is a Roarer,
   And Jill goes down on her back.

'O look, look in the mirror,
   O look in your distress;
Life remains a blessing
   Although you cannot bless.

'O stand, stand at the window
   As the tears scald and start;
You shall love your crooked neighbour
   With your crooked heart.'

It was late, late in the evening,
  The lovers they were gone;
The clocks had ceased their chiming,
  And the deep river ran on.

Lullaby

Lay your sleeping head, my love,
Human on my faithless arm;
Time and fevers burn away
Individual beauty from
Thoughtful children, and the grave
Proves the child ephemeral:
But in my arms till break of day
Let the living creature lie,
Mortal, guilty, but to me
The entirely beautiful.

Soul and body have no bounds:
To lovers as they lie upon
Her tolerant enchanted slope
In their ordinary swoon,
Grave the vision Venus sends
Of supernatural sympathy,
Universal love and hope;
While an abstract insight wakes
Among the glaciers and the rocks
The hermit's carnal ecstasy.

Certainty, fidelity
On the stroke of midnight pass
Like vibrations of a bell
And fashionable madmen raise
Their pedantic boring cry:
Every farthing of the cost,
All the dreaded cards foretell,

Shall be paid, but from this night
Not a whisper, not a thought,
Not a kiss nor look be lost.

Beauty, midnight, vision dies:
Let the winds of dawn that blow
Softly round your dreaming head
Such a day of welcome show
Eye and knocking heart may bless,
Find our mortal world enough;
Noons of dryness find you fed
By the involuntary powers,
Nights of insult let you pass
Watched by every human love.

Musée des Beaux Arts

About suffering they were never wrong,
The Old Masters: how well they understood
Its human position; how it takes place
While someone else is eating or opening a window or just walking
    dully along;
How, when the aged are reverently, passionately waiting
For the miraculous birth, there always must be
Children who did not specially want it to happen, skating
On a pond at the edge of the wood:

They never forgot
That even the dreadful martyrdom must run its course
Anyhow in a corner, some untidy spot
Where the dogs go on with their doggy life and the torturer's
    horse
Scratches its innocent behind on a tree.

In Brueghel's *Icarus*, for instance: how everything turns away
Quite leisurely from the disaster; the ploughman may

Have heard the splash, the forsaken cry,
But for him it was not an important failure; the sun shone
As it had to on the white legs disappearing into the green
Water; and the expensive delicate ship that must have seen
Something amazing, a boy falling out of the sky,
Had somewhere to get to and sailed calmly on.

In Memory of W. B. Yeats

(d. Jan. 1939)

I

He disappeared in the dead of winter:
The brooks were frozen, the airports almost deserted,
And snow disfigured the public statues;
The mercury sank in the mouth of the dying day.
What instruments we have agree
The day of his death was a dark cold day.

Far from his illness
The wolves ran on through the evergreen forests,
The peasant river was untempted by the fashionable quays;
By mourning tongues
The death of the poet was kept from his poems.

But for him it was his last afternoon as himself,
An afternoon of nurses and rumours;
The provinces of his body revolted,
The squares of his mind were empty,
Silence invaded the suburbs,
The current of his feeling failed; he became his admirers.

Now he is scattered among a hundred cities
And wholly given over to unfamiliar affections,
To find his happiness in another kind of wood

And be punished under a foreign code of conscience.
The words of a dead man
Are modified in the guts of the living.

But in the importance and noise of to-morrow
When the brokers are roaring like beasts on the floor of the
    Bourse,
And the poor have the sufferings to which they are fairly
    accustomed,
And each in the cell of himself is almost convinced of his
    freedom,
A few thousand will think of this day
As one thinks of a day when one did something slightly unusual.
What instruments we have agree
The day of his death was a dark cold day.

II

You were silly like us; your gift survived it all:
The parish of rich women, physical decay,
Yourself. Mad Ireland hurt you into poetry.
Now Ireland has her madness and her weather still,
For poetry makes nothing happen: it survives
In the valley of its making where executives
Would never want to tamper, flows on south
From ranches of isolation and the busy griefs,
Raw towns that we believe and die in; it survives,
A way of happening, a mouth.

III

Earth, receive an honoured guest:
William Yeats is laid to rest.
Let the Irish vessel lie
Emptied of its poetry.

In the nightmare of the dark
All the dogs of Europe bark,
And the living nations wait,
Each sequestered in its hate;

Intellectual disgrace
Stares from every human face,
And the seas of pity lie
Locked and frozen in each eye.

Follow, poet, follow right
To the bottom of the night,
With your unconstraining voice
Still persuade us to rejoice;

With the farming of a verse
Make a vineyard of the curse,
Sing of human unsuccess
In a rapture of distress;

In the deserts of the heart
Let the healing fountain start,
In the prison of his days
Teach the free man how to praise.

The Unknown Citizen

(To JS/07/M/378
This Marble Monument
Is Erected by the State

He was found by the Bureau of Statistics to be
One against whom there was no official complaint,
And all the reports on his conduct agree
That, in the modern sense of an old-fashioned word, he was a
    saint,
For in everything he did he served the Greater Community.
Except for the War till the day he retired
He worked in a factory and never got fired,
But satisfied his employers, Fudge Motors Inc.
Yet he wasn't a scab or odd in his views,
For his Union reports that he paid his dues,

(Our report on his Union shows it was sound)
And our Social Psychology workers found
That he was popular with his mates and liked a drink.
The Press are convinced that he bought a paper every day
And that his reactions to advertisements were normal in every
  way.
Policies taken out in his name prove that he was fully insured,
And his Health-card shows he was once in hospital but left it
  cured.
Both Producers Research and High-Grade Living declare
He was fully sensible to the advantages of the Instalment Plan
And had everything necessary to the Modern Man,
A phonograph, a radio, a car, and a frigidaire.
Our researchers into Public Opinion are content
That he held the proper opinions for the time of year;
When there was peace, he was for peace; when there was war,
  he went.
He was married and added five children to the population,
Which our Eugenist says was the right number for a parent of
  his generation,
And our teachers report that he never interfered with their
  education.
Was he free? Was he happy? The question is absurd:
Had anything been wrong, we should certainly have heard.

In Praise of Limestone

If it form the one landscape that we, the inconstant ones,
    Are consistently homesick for, this is chiefly
Because it dissolves in water. Mark these rounded slopes
    With their surface fragrance of thyme and, beneath,
A secret system of caves and conduits; hear the springs
    That spurt out everywhere with a chuckle,
Each filling a private pool for its fish and carving
    Its own little ravine whose cliffs entertain
The butterfly and the lizard; examine this region

Of short distances and definite places:
What could be more like Mother or a fitter background
    For her son, the flirtatious male who lounges
Against a rock in the sunlight, never doubting
    That for all his faults he is loved; whose works are but
Extensions of his power to charm? From weathered outcrop
    To hill-top temple, from appearing waters to
Conspicuous fountains, from a wild to a formal vineyard,
    Are ingenious but short steps that a child's wish
To receive more attention than his brothers, whether
    By pleasing or teasing, can easily take.

Watch, then, the band of rivals as they climb up and down
    Their steep stone gennels in twos and threes, at times
Arm in arm, but never, thank God, in step; or engaged
    On the shady side of a square at midday in
Voluble discourse, knowing each other too well to think
    There are any important secrets, unable
To conceive a god whose temper-tantrums are moral
    And not to be pacified by a clever line
Or a good lay: for, accustomed to a stone that responds,
    They have never had to veil their faces in awe
Of a crater whose blazing fury could not be fixed;
    Adjusted to the local needs of valleys
Where everything can be touched or reached by walking,
    Their eyes have never looked into infinite space
Through the lattice-work of a nomad's comb; born lucky,
    Their legs have never encountered the fungi
And insects of the jungle, the monstrous forms and lives
    With which we have nothing, we like to hope, in common.
So, when one of them goes to the bad, the way his mind works
    Remains comprehensible: to become a pimp
Or deal in fake jewellery or ruin a fine tenor voice
    For effects that bring down the house, could happen to all
But the best and the worst of us . . .
                                        That is why, I suppose,
    The best and worst never stayed here long but sought
Immoderate soils, where the beauty was not so external,

The light less public and the meaning of life
Something more than a mad camp. 'Come!' cried the granite
      wastes,
   'How evasive is your humour, how accidental
Your kindest kiss, how permanent is death.' (Saints-to-be
   Slipped away sighing.) 'Come!' purred the clays and gravels.
'On our plains there is room for armies to drill; rivers
   Wait to be tamed and slaves to construct you a tomb
In the grand manner: soft as the earth is mankind and both
   Need to be altered.' (Intendant Caesars rose and
Left, slamming the door.) But the really reckless were fetched
   By an older colder voice, the oceanic whisper:
'I am the solitude that asks and promises nothing;
   That is how I shall set you free. There is no love;
There are only the various envies, all of them sad.'
   They were right, my dear, all those voices were right
And still are; this land is not the sweet home that it looks,
   Nor its peace the historical calm of a site
Where something was settled once and for all: A backward
   And dilapidated province, connected
To the big busy world by a tunnel, with a certain
   Seedy appeal, is that all it is now? Not quite:
It has a worldly duty which in spite of itself
   It does not neglect, but calls into question
All the Great Powers assume; it disturbs our rights. The poet,
   Admired for his earnest habit of calling
The sun the sun, his mind Puzzle, is made uneasy
   By these marble statues which so obviously doubt
His antimythological myth; and these gamins,
   Pursuing the scientist down the tiled colonnade
With such lively offers, rebuke his concern for Nature's
   Remotest aspects: I, too, am reproached, for what
And how much you know. Not to lose time, not to get caught,
   Not to be left behind, not, please! to resemble
The beasts who repeat themselves, or a thing like water
   Or stone whose conduct can be predicted, these
Are our Common Prayer, whose greatest comfort is music
   Which can be made anywhere, is invisible,

And does not smell. In so far as we have to look forward
    To death as a fact, no doubt we are right: But if
Sins can be forgiven, if bodies rise from the dead,
    These modifications of matter into
Innocent athletes and gesticulating fountains,
    Made solely for pleasure, make a further point:
The blessed will not care what angle they are regarded from,
    Having nothing to hide. Dear, I know nothing of
Either, but when I try to imagine a faultless love
    Or the life to come, what I hear is the murmur
Of underground streams, what I see is a limestone landscape.

The Shield of Achilles

      She looked over his shoulder
        For vines and olive trees,
      Marble well-governed cities
        And ships upon untamed seas,
      But there on the shining metal
        His hands had put instead
      An artificial wilderness
        And a sky like lead.

A plain without a feature, bare and brown,
    No blade of grass, no sign of neighbourhood,
Nothing to eat and nowhere to sit down,
    Yet, congregated on its blankness, stood
    An unintelligible multitude,
A million eyes, a million boots in line,
Without expression, waiting for a sign.

Out of the air a voice without a face
    Proved by statistics that some cause was just
In tones as dry and level as the place:
    No one was cheered and nothing was discussed;
    Column by column in a cloud of dust

They marched away enduring a belief
Whose logic brought them, somewhere else, to grief.

      She looked over his shoulder
        For ritual pieties,
     White flower-garlanded heifers,
        Libation and sacrifice,
     But there on the shining metal
        Where the altar should have been,
     She saw by his flickering forge-light
        Quite another scene.

Barbed wire enclosed an arbitrary spot
   Where bored officials lounged (one cracked a joke)
And sentries sweated for the day was hot:
   A crowd of ordinary decent folk
   Watched from without and neither moved nor spoke
As three pale figures were led forth and bound
To three posts driven upright in the ground.

The mass and majesty of this world, all
   That carries weight and always weighs the same
Lay in the hands of others; they were small
   And could not hope for help and no help came:
   What their foes liked to do was done, their shame
Was all the worst could wish; they lost their pride
And died as men before their bodies died.

      She looked over his shoulder
        For athletes at their games,
     Men and women in a dance
        Moving their sweet limbs
     Quick, quick, to music,
        But there on the shining shield
     His hands had set no dancing-floor
        But a weed-choked field.

A ragged urchin, aimless and alone,
   Loitered about that vacancy, a bird

Flew up to safety from his well-aimed stone:
   That girls are raped, that two boys knife a third,
   Were axioms to him, who'd never heard
Of any world where promises were kept,
Or one could weep because another wept.

      The thin-lipped armourer,
        Hephaestos hobbled away,
      Thetis of the shining breasts
        Cried out in dismay
      At what the god had wrought
        To please her son, the strong
      Iron-hearted man-slaying Achilles
        Who would not live long.

Dylan Thomas

The force that through the green fuse
drives the flower

The force that through the green fuse drives the flower
Drives my green age; that blasts the roots of trees
Is my destroyer.
And I am dumb to tell the crooked rose
My youth is bent by the same wintry fever.

The force that drives the water through the rocks
Drives my red blood; that dries the mouthing streams
Turns mine to wax.
And I am dumb to mouth unto my veins
How at the mountain spring the same mouth sucks.

The hand that whirls the water in the pool
Stirs the quicksand; that ropes the blowing wind
Hauls my shroud sail.
And I am dumb to tell the hanging man
How of my clay is made the hangman's lime.

The lips of time leech to the fountain head;
Love drips and gathers, but the fallen blood
Shall calm her sores.
And I am dumb to tell a weather's wind
How time has ticked a heaven round the stars.

And I am dumb to tell the lover's tomb
How at my sheet goes the same crooked worm.

If I were tickled by the rub of love

If I were tickled by the rub of love,
A rooking girl who stole me for her side,
Broke through her straws, breaking my bandaged string,
If the red tickle as the cattle calve
Still set to scratch a laughter from my lung,
I would not fear the apple nor the flood
Nor the bad blood of spring.

Shall it be male or female? say the cells,
And drop the plum like fire from the flesh.
If I were tickled by the hatching hair,
The winging bone that sprouted in the heels,
The itch of man upon the baby's thigh,
I would not fear the gallows nor the axe
Nor the crossed sticks of war.

Shall it be male or female? say the fingers
That chalk the walls with green girls and their men.
I would not fear the muscling-in of love
If I were tickled by the urchin hungers
Rehearsing heat upon a raw-edged nerve.
I would not fear the devil in the loin
Nor the outspoken grave.

If I were tickled by the lovers' rub
That wipes away not crow's-foot nor the lock
Of sick old manhood on the fallen jaws,
Time and the crabs and the sweethearting crib
Would leave me cold as butter for the flies,
The sea of scums could drown me as it broke
Dead on the sweethearts' toes.

This world is half the devil's and my own,
Daft with the drug that's smoking in a girl
And curling round the bud that forks her eye.
An old man's shank one-marrowed with my bone,

And all the herrings smelling in the sea,
I sit and watch the worm beneath my nail
Wearing the quick away.

And that's the rub, the only rub that tickles.
The knobbly ape that swings along his sex
From damp love-darkness and the nurse's twist
Can never raise the midnight of a chuckle,
Nor when he finds a beauty in the breast
Of lover, mother, lovers, or his six
Feet in the rubbing dust.

And what's the rub? Death's feather on the nerve?
Your mouth, my love, the thistle in the kiss?
My Jack of Christ born thorny on the tree?
The words of death are dryer than his stiff,
My wordy wounds are printed with your hair.
I would be tickled by the rub that is:
Man be my metaphor.

And death shall have no dominion

And death shall have no dominion.
Dead men naked they shall be one
With the man in the wind and the west moon;
When their bones are picked clean and the clean bones gone,
They shall have stars at elbow and foot;
Though they go mad they shall be sane,
Though they sink through the sea they shall rise again;
Though lovers be lost love shall not;
And death shall have no dominion.

And death shall have no dominion.
Under the windings of the sea
They lying long shall not die windily;
Twisting on racks when sinews give way,

Strapped to a wheel, yet they shall not break;
Faith in their hands shall snap in two,
And the unicorn evils run them through;
Split all ends up they shan't crack;
And death shall have no dominion.

And death shall have no dominion.
No more may gulls cry at their ears
Or waves break loud on the seashores;
Where blew a flower may a flower no more
Lift its head to the blows of the rain;
Though they be mad and dead as nails,
Heads of the characters hammer through daisies;
Break in the sun till the sun breaks down,
And death shall have no dominion.

After the Funeral

IN MEMORY OF ANN JONES

After the funeral, mule praises, brays,
Windshake of sailshaped ears, muffle-toed tap
Tap happily of one peg in the thick
Grave's foot, blinds down the lids, the teeth in black,
The spittled eyes, the salt ponds in the sleeves,
Morning smack of the spade that wakes up sleep,
Shakes a desolate boy who slits his throat
In the dark of the coffin and sheds dry leaves,
That breaks one bone to light with a judgment clout,
After the feast of tear-stuffed time and thistles
In a room with a stuffed fox and a stale fern,
I stand, for this memorial's sake, alone
In the snivelling hours with dead, humped Ann
Whose hooded, fountain heart once fell in puddles
Round the parched worlds of Wales and drowned each sun
(Though this for her is a monstrous image blindly

Magnified out of praise; her death was a still drop;
She would not have me sinking in the holy
Flood of her heart's fame; she would lie dumb and deep
And need no druid of her broken body).
But I, Ann's bard on a raised hearth, call all
The seas to service that her wood-tongued virtue
Babble like a bellbuoy over the hymning heads,
Bow down the walls of the ferned and foxy woods
That her love sing and swing through a brown chapel,
Bless her bent spirit with four, crossing birds.
Her flesh was meek as milk, but this skyward statue
With the wild breast and blessed and giant skull
Is carved from her in a room with a wet window
In a fiercely mourning house in a crooked year.
I know her scrubbed and sour humble hands
Lie with religion in their cramp, her threadbare
Whisper in a damp word, her wits drilled hollow,
Her fist of a face died clenched on a round pain;
And sculptured Ann is seventy years of stone.
These cloud-sopped, marble hands, this monumental
Argument of the hewn voice, gesture and psalm,
Storm me forever over her grave until
The stuffed lung of the fox twitch and cry Love
And the strutting fern lay seeds on the black sill.

Twenty-Four Years

Twenty-four years remind the tears of my eyes.
(Bury the dead for fear that they walk to the grave in labour.)
In the groin of the natural doorway I crouched like a tailor
Sewing a shroud for a journey
By the light of the meat-eating sun.
Dressed to die, the sensual strut begun,
With my red veins full of money,
In the final direction of the elementary town
I advance for as long as forever is.

A Refusal to Mourn the Death, by Fire, of a Child in London

Never until the mankind making
Bird beast and flower
Fathering and all humbling darkness
Tells with silence the last light breaking
And the still hour
Is come of the sea tumbling in harness

And I must enter again the round
Zion of the water bead
And the synagogue of the ear of corn
Shall I let pray the shadow of a sound
Or sow my salt seed
In the least valley of sackcloth to mourn

The majesty and burning of the child's death.
I shall not murder
The mankind of her going with a grave truth
Nor blaspheme down the stations of the breath
With any further
Elegy of innocence and youth.

Deep with the first dead lies London's daughter,
Robed in the long friends,
The grains beyond age, the dark veins of her mother,
Secret by the unmourning water
Of the riding Thames.
After the first death, there is no other.

Do not go gentle into that good night

Do not go gentle into that good night,
Old age should burn and rave at close of day;
Rage, rage against the dying of the light.

Though wise men at their end know dark is right,
Because their words had forked no lightning they
Do not go gentle into that good night.

Good men, the last wave by, crying how bright
Their frail deeds might have danced in a green bay,
Rage, rage against the dying of the light.

Wild men who caught and sang the sun in flight,
And learn, too late, they grieved it on its way,
Do not go gentle into that good night.

Grave men, near death, who see with blinding sight
Blind eyes could blaze like meteors and be gay,
Rage, rage against the dying of the light.

And you, my father, there on the sad height,
Curse, bless, me now with your fierce tears, I pray.
Do not go gentle into that good night.
Rage, rage against the dying of the light.

In my craft or sullen art

In my craft or sullen art
Exercised in the still night
When only the moon rages
And the lovers lie abed
With all their griefs in their arms,
I labour by singing light
Not for ambition or bread
Or the strut and trade of charms
On the ivory stages
But for the common wages
Of their most secret heart.

Not for the proud man apart
From the raging moon I write

On these spindrift pages
Nor for the towering dead
With their nightingales and psalms
But for the lovers, their arms
Round the griefs of the ages,
Who pay no praise or wages
Nor heed my craft or art.

Fern Hill

Now as I was young and easy under the apple boughs
About the lilting house and happy as the grass was green,
      The night above the dingle starry,
         Time let me hail and climb
      Golden in the heydays of his eyes,
And honoured among wagons I was prince of the apple towns
And once below a time I lordly had the trees and leaves
         Trail with daisies and barley
      Down the rivers of the windfall light.

And as I was green and carefree, famous among the barns
About the happy yard and singing as the farm was home,
      In the sun that is young once only,
         Time let me play and be
      Golden in the mercy of his means,
And green and golden I was huntsman and herdsman, the calves
Sang to my horn, the foxes on the hills barked clear and cold,
         And the sabbath rang slowly
      In the pebbles of the holy streams.

All the sun long it was running, it was lovely, the hay
Fields high as the house, the tunes from the chimneys, it was air
      And playing, lovely and watery
         And fire green as grass.
      And nightly under the simple stars
As I rode to sleep the owls were bearing the farm away,

All the moon long I heard, blessed among stables, the nightjars
     Flying with the ricks, and the horses
        Flashing into the dark.

And then to awake, and the farm, like a wanderer white
With the dew, come back, the cock on his shoulder: it was all
     Shining, it was Adam and maiden,
        The sky gathered again
     And the sun grew round that very day.
So it must have been after the birth of the simple light
In the first, spinning place, the spellbound horses walking
          warm
     Out of the whinnying green stable
       On to the fields of praise.

And honoured among foxes and pheasants by the gay house
Under the new made clouds and happy as the heart was long,
     In the sun born over and over,
       I ran my heedless ways,
     My wishes raced through the house high hay
And nothing I cared, at my sky blue trades, that time allows
In all his tuneful turning so few and such morning songs
     Before the children green and golden
       Follow him out of grace,

Nothing I cared, in the lamb white days, that time would take me
Up to the swallow thronged loft by the shadow of my hand,
     In the moon that is always rising,
       Nor that riding to sleep
     I should hear him fly with the high fields
And wake to the farm forever fled from the childless land.
Oh as I was young and easy in the mercy of his means,
       Time held me green and dying
     Though I sang in my chains like the sea.

A. M. Klein

Heirloom

My father bequeathed me no wide estates;
No keys and ledgers were my heritage;
Only some holy books with *yahrzeit* dates
Writ mournfully upon a blank front page—

Books of the Baal Shem Tov, and of his wonders;
Pamphlets upon the devil and his crew;
Prayers against road demons, witches, thunders;
And sundry other tomes for a good Jew.

Beautiful: though no pictures on them, save
The Scorpion crawling on a printed track;
The Virgin floating on a scriptural wave,
Square letters twinkling in the Zodiac.

The snuff left on this page, now brown and old,
The tallow stains of midnight liturgy—
These are my coat of arms, and these unfold
My noble lineage, my proud ancestry!

And my tears, too, have stained this heirloomed ground,
When reading in these treatises some weird
Miracle, I turned a leaf and found
A white hair fallen from my father's beard.

Autobiographical

I

Out of the ghetto streets where a Jewboy
Dreamed pavement into pleasant bible-land,
Out of the Yiddish slums where childhood met
The friendly beard, the loutish Sabbath-goy,
Or followed, proud, the Torah-escorting band
Out of the jargoning city I regret
Rise memories, like sparrows rising from
The gutter-scattered oats,
Like sadness sweet of synagogal hum,
Like Hebrew violins
Sobbing delight upon their eastern notes.

II

Again they ring their little bells, those doors
Deemed by the tender-year'd, magnificent:
Old Ashkenazi's cellar, sharp with spice;
The widow's double-parloured candy-stores
And nuggets sweet bought for one sweaty cent;
The warm fresh-smelling bakery, its pies,
Its cakes, its navel'd bellies of black bread;
The lintels candy-poled
Of barber-shop, bright-bottled, green, blue, red;
And fruit-stall piled, exotic,
And the big synagogue door, with letters of gold.

III

Again my kindergarten home is full—
Saturday night—with kin and compatriot:
My brothers playing Russian card-games; my
Mirroring sisters looking beautiful
Humming the evening's imminent fox-trot;
My uncle Mayer, of blessed memory,
Still murmuring Maariv, counting holy words;
And the two strangers, come

Fiery from Volhynia's murderous hordes—
The cards and humming stop.
And I too swear revenge for that pogrom.

IV

Occasions dear: the four-legged aleph named
And angel pennies dropping on my book;
The rabbi patting a coming scholar-head;
My mother, blessing candles, Sabbath-flamed,
Queenly in her Warsovian perruque;
My father pickabacking me to bed
To tell tall tales about the Baal Shem Tov,
Letting me curl his beard.
O memory of unsurpassing love,
Love leading a brave child
Thorough childhood's ogred corridors, unfear'd.

V

The week in the country at my brother's (May
He own fat cattle in the fields of heaven!)
Its picking of strawberries from grassy ditch,
Its odour of dogrose and of yellowing hay,—
Dusty, adventurous, sunny days, all seven!—
Still follow me, still warm me, still are rich
With the cow-tinkling peace of pastureland.
The meadow'd memory
Is sodded with its clover, and is spanned
By that same pillow'd sky
A boy on his back one day watched enviously.

VI

And paved again the street; the shouting boys
Oblivious of mothers on the stoops
Playing the robust robbers and police,
The corn-cob battle,—all high-spirited noise
Competitive among the lot-drawn groups.
Another day, of shaken apple-trees
In the rich suburbs, and a furious dog

And guilty boys in flight;
Hazelnut games, and games in the synagogue.
The burrs, the Haman rattle,
The Torah-dance on Simchas-Torah night.

VII

Immortal days of the picture-calendar
Dear to me always with the virgin joy
Of the first flowing of senses five
Discovering birds, or textures, or a star,
Or tastes sweet, sour, acid, those that cloy,
And perfumes. Never was I more alive.
All days thereafter are a dying-off,
A wandering away
From home and the familiar. The years doff
Their innocence.
No other day is ever like that day.

VIII

I am no old man fatuously intent
On memoirs, but in memory I seek
The strength and vividness of nonage days,
Not tranquil recollection of event.
It is a fabled city that I seek;
It stands in space's vapours and Time's haze;
Thence comes my sadness in remembered joy
Constrictive of the throat;
Thence do I hear, as heard by a Jewboy
The Hebrew violins,
Delighting in the sobbed oriental note.

In re *Solomon Warshawer*

On Wodin's day, sixth of December, thirty-nine,
I, Friedrich Vercingetorix, attached
to the viith Eavesdroppers-behind-the-Line,

did cover my beat, when, suddenly, the crowd I
    watched
surrounded, in a cobbled lane one can't pass
    through,
a bearded man, in rags, disguised, a Jew.

In the said crowd there were a number of Poles.
Mainly, however, there were Germans there:
blood-brothers of our Reich, true Aryan souls,
breathing at last—in Warsaw—Nordic air.

These were the words the Jew was shouting:
I took them down verbatim:

Whom have I hurt? Against whose silk have I
    brushed?
On which of your women looked too long?
I tell you I have done no wrong!
Send home your children, lifting hardened dung,
And let your curs be hushed!
For I am but beard and breathlessness, and chased
    enough.
Leave me in peace, and let me go my way.

At this the good folk laughed. The Jew continued
    to say
he was no thief; he was a man for hire;
worked for his bread, artist or artisan;
a scribe if you wished; a vendor; even buyer;
work of all kinds, and anything at all:
paint a mural, scour a latrine,
indite an ode, repair an old machine,
anything, to repeat,
anything at all,
so that he might eat
and have his pallet in his abandoned stall.

Asked for his papers, he made a great to-do
of going through the holes in his rags, whence he
     withdrew
a Hebrew pamphlet and a signet-ring,
herewith produced, Exhibits 1 and 2.

I said: No documents in a civilized tongue?
He replied:

Produce, O Lord, my wretched fingerprint!
Bring forth, O angel in the heavenly court,
My dossier, full, detailed, both fact and hint,
Felony, misdemeanour, tort!

I refused to be impressed by talk of that sort.

From further cross-examination, it appeared,
immediate history: a beggar in Berlin;
chased, as a vagrant, from the streets of Prague;
kept, as a leper, in forced quarantine;
shunned as the pest, avoided like the plague;
then had escaped, mysteriously come
by devious routes and stolen frontiers to
the *nalewkas* of Warsaw's sheenydom.

Pressed to reveal his true identity,
he lied:
One of the anthropophagi was he,
or, if we wished, a denizen of Mars,
the ghost of *my* father, Conscience—aye,
the anatomy of Reason, naked, and with scars;
even became insulting, said he was
Aesop the slave among the animals . . .
Sir Incognito . . . Rabbi Alias . . .
The eldest elder of Zion . . . said we knew
his numerous varied oriental shapes,
even as we ought to know his present guise—
the man in the jungle, and beset by apes.

It was at this point the s.s. man arrived.
The Jew was interrupted. When he was revived,
he deposed as follows:

At low estate, a beggar, and in flight,
Still do I wear my pride like purple. I
Do fear you, yes, but founder not from fright.
Already I breathe your unfuturity.
For you are not the first whom I have met—
O I have known them all,
The dwarf dictators, the diminutive dukes,
The heads of straw, the hearts of gall,
Th' imperial plumes of eagles covering rooks!

It is not necessary to name names,
But it may serve anon,
Now to evoke from darkness some dark frames,
Evoke
Armada'd Spain, that gilded jettison;
And Russia's last descended Romanov,
Descending a dark staircase
To a dank cellar at Ekaterinoslov;
Evoke
The peacock moulted from the Persian loom . . .
Babylon tumbled from its terraces . . .
Decrescent and debased Mizraim, remembered
    only
By that one star that sentries Pharaoh's tomb . . .
Evoke
O Greece! O broken marble! . . .
And disinterred unresurrected Rome . . .

They would have harried me extinct, these
    thrones!
Set me, archaic, in their heraldries,
Blazon antique! . . . For they were Powers . . .
    Once!
But I, though still exilian, rest extant,

And on my cicatrices tally off
Their undone dynasties!
Shall I dread you—who overlived all these?

Here impudence was duly rebuked, and the Jew
confronted with Exhibit 2.

Yes, but that signet ring! . . . Freiherr, that seal
Once flashed the pleasure majestical!
For I, who in tatters stand investitured,
Who, to these knightly men, am dislodged pawn,
Abdicate and abjured,
I was, I am, the Emperor Solomon!
O, to and fro upon the face of the earth,
I wandered, crying: Ani Shlomo, *but—*
But no one believed my birth.

For he now governs in my place and stead,
He who did fling me from Jerusalem
Four hundred parasangs!
Who stole the crown from off my head!
Who robed him in my robes! Beneath whose hem
The feet of the cock extend, the tail of the demon
*   hangs!*
Asmodeus!

Mistake me not: I am no virtuous saint;
Only a man, and like all men, not god-like . . .
From birth beset by his own heart's constraint,
Its brimstone pride, the cinders of its greed,
(Brazier behind the ribs that will not faint!)
Beset, inflamed, besooted, charred, indeed,—
Only a man, and like all men, not god-like,
Damned by desire—
But I at least fought down that bellows'd greed,
Tried to put out the sulphurs of that fire! . . .
At least craved wisdom, how to snuff the blaze,
Sought knowledge, to unravel good from evil,
Sought guidance from the Author of my Days.

The understanding heart, and its enthymemes,
Being granted me, I learned from beast . . . bird
   . . . man;
Would know; and eavesdropped nest . . . and
  house . . . and lair.
The wild beasts spoke to me, told me their dreams,
Which, always biped, towards the human ran . . .
O, how that flesh did long to doff its fur! . . .
The fluttering birds, the twittering birds of the air:
'Would you cast off from your feet,' they said,
  'earth's mass,
That weighted globe of brass,
And soar into your own?
With azure fill your heart! . . . Be hollow of bone!'
And from my self, and from the breed of Adam,
I fathom'd that heart's depths, how it may sink
Down to the deep and ink of genesis,
And lie there, that once could the heavens explore,
A sponge and pulse of hunger on the
  ocean-floor . . .
Saw also, and praised, for then knew possible,
The heart's saltations! . . .
That always—vanitatum vanitas!—
That always after back to grossness fell.
Thus taught, thus prompted, upward I essay'd,—
Some not mean triumphs scored,
Spread truth, spread song, spread justice, which
  prevailed,
Builded that famous footstool for the Lord,—
Yet human, human among mortals, failed!
Was thwarted the greater yearning, the jubilee
Wherein the race might at the last be hailed
Transcendent of its own humanity!
For I, Ooheleth, King in Jerusalem,
Ecclesiast of the troubled apothegm,
Concluding the matter, must affirm mankind
Still undivined.
However, though worsted, I had wrestled, but
  he—

Our royal Jew, now questioned *in camera*,
was not, this time, molested. It was thought
some enemy intelligence might come through
from his distractions, some inkling of the plot
now being pursued by his ten losing tribes.
Therefore the record, as ordered, here gives the
    whole Jew,—
for which the subscribing officer subscribes
apology.

But he, unspeakable prince of malice!
Usurper of my throne, pretender to the Lord's!
Wicked, demoniac, lycanthropous,
Goad of the succubi, horrific hordes!
Master of the worm, pernicious, that cleaves
    rocks,
The beast that talks,
Asmodeus!—

Who has not felt his statutes? . . . His scientists,
Mastering for him the lethal mysteries;
His surgeons of doctrine, cutting, like vile cysts
From off the heart, all pities and sympathies;
His judges, trembling over their decrees,
Lest insufficient injustice displease;
And his psychiaters, guarding against relapse,
For fear the beast, within the man, collapse.

His statecraft, and its modes and offices?
Here motive is appetite; and oestric hate
The force that freaks and fathers all device.
All love's venereal; or excess; or bait.
Ambush all policy, and artifice;
And all reward conferred, all honour
Hierarchical to the degrees of Hate.

Upon his lych-throne, robed in bloodied purple,
Listening to those harmonies where the sigh

Exhaling greets the groan, the groan is pitched to
    the cry,
Asmodeus sits;
And I—

At this point the s.s. men departed.
The Jew was not revived. He was carried and
    carted,
and to his present gaoler brought;
awaiting higher pleasure.
                            And further deponent saith not.

Political Meeting

FOR CAMILLIEN HOUDE

On the school platform, draping the folding seats,
they wait the chairman's praise and glass of water.
Upon the wall the agonized Y initials their faith.

Here all are laic; the skirted brothers have gone.
Still, their equivocal absence is felt, like a breeze
that gives curtains the sounds of surplices.

The hall is yellow with light, and jocular;
suddenly some one lets loose upon the air
the ritual bird which the crowd in snares of singing

catches and plucks, throat, wings, and little limbs.
Fall the feathers of sound, like *alouette's*.
The chairman, now, is charming, full of asides and wit,

building his orators, and chipping off
the heckling gargoyles popping in the hall.
(Outside, in the dark, the street is body-tall,

flowered with faces intent on the scarecrow thing
that shouts to thousands the echoing
of their own wishes.) The Orator has risen!

Worshipped and loved, their favourite visitor,
a country uncle with sunflower seeds in his pockets,
full of wonderful moods, tricks, imitative talk,

he is their idol: like themselves, not handsome,
not snobbish, not of the *Grande Allée! Un homme!*
Intimate, informal, he makes bear's compliments

to the ladies; is gallant; and grins;
goes for the balloon, his opposition, with pins;
jokes also on himself, speaks of himself

in the third person, slings slang, and winks with folklore;
and knows now that he has them, kith and kin.
Calmly, therefore, he begins to speak of war,

praises the virtue of being *Canadien*,
of being at peace, of faith, of family,
and suddenly his other voice: *Where are your sons?*

He is tearful, choking tears; but not he
would blame the clever English; in their place
he'd do the same; maybe.

Where *are* your sons?
                    The whole street wears one face,
shadowed and grim; and in the darkness rises
the body-odour of race.

Lone Bather

Upon the ecstatic diving board the diver,
poised for parabolas, lets go
lets go his manshape to become a bird.
Is bird, and topsy-turvy
the pool floats overhead, and the white tiles snow

their crazy hexagons. Is dolphin. Then
is plant with lilies bursting from his heels.

Himself, suddenly mysterious and marine,
bobs up a merman leaning on his hills.

Plashes and plays alone the deserted pool;
as those, is free, who think themselves unseen.
He rolls in his heap of fruit,
he slides his belly over
the melonrinds of water, curved and smooth and green.
Feels good: and trains, like little acrobats
his echoes dropping from the galleries;
circles himself over a rung of water;
swims fancy and gay; taking a notion, hides
under the satins of his great big bed,—
and then comes up to float until he thinks
the ceiling at his brow, and nowhere any sides.

His thighs are a shoal of fishes: scattered: he
turns with many gloves of greeting
towards the sunnier water and the tiles.

Upon the tiles he dangles from his toes
lazily the eight reins of his ponies.

An afternoon, far from the world
a street sound throws like a stone, with paper, through the glass.
Up, he is chipped enamel, grained with hair.
The gloss of his footsteps follows him to the showers,
the showers, and the male room, and the towel
which rubs the bird, the plant, the dolphin back again
personable plain.

Portrait of the Poet as Landscape

I

Not an editorial-writer, bereaved with bartlett,
mourns him, the shelved Lycidas.
No actress squeezes a glycerine tear for him.
The radio broadcast lets his passing pass.
And with the police, no record. Nobody, it appears,
either under his real name or his alias,
missed him enough to report.

It is possible that he is dead, and not discovered.
It is possible that he can be found some place
in a narrow closet, like the corpse in a detective story,
standing, his eyes staring, and ready to fall on his face.
It is also possible that he is alive
and amnesiac, or mad, or in retired disgrace,
or beyond recognition lost in love.

We are sure only that from our real society
he has disappeared; he simply does not count,
except in the pullulation of vital statistics—
somebody's vote, perhaps, an anonymous taunt
of the Gallup poll, a dot in a government table—
but not felt, and certainly far from eminent—
in a shouting mob, somebody's sigh.

O, he who unrolled our culture from his scroll—
the prince's quote, the rostrum-rounding roar—
who under one name made articulate
heaven, and under another the seven-circled air,
is, if he is at all, a number, an x,
a Mr Smith in a hotel register,—
incognito, lost, lacunal.

II

The truth is he's not dead, but only ignored—
like the mirroring lenses forgotten on a brow

that shine with the guilt of their unnoticed world.
The truth is he lives among neighbours, who, though they will
    allow
him a passable fellow, think him eccentric, not solid,
a type that one can forgive, and for that matter, forego.

Himself he has his moods, just like a poet.
Sometimes, depressed to nadir, he will think all lost,
will see himself as throwback, relict, freak,
his mother's miscarriage, his great-grandfather's ghost,
and he will curse his quintuplet senses, and their tutors
in whom he put, as he should not have put, his trust.

Then he will remember his travels over that body—
the torso verb, the beautiful face of the noun,
and all those shaped and warm auxiliaries!
A first love it was, the recognition of his own.
Dear limbs adverbial, complexion of adjective,
dimple and dip of conjugation!

And then remember how this made a change in him
affecting for always the glow and growth of his being;
how suddenly was aware of the air, like shaken tinfoil,
of the patents of nature, the shock of belated seeing,
the lonelinesses peering from the eyes of crowds;
the integers of thought; the cube-roots of feeling.

Thus, zoomed to zenith, sometimes he hopes again,
and sees himself as a character, with a rehearsed role:
the Count of Monte Cristo, come for his revenges;
the unsuspected heir, with papers; the risen soul;
or the chloroformed prince awaking from his flowers;
or—deflated again—the convict on parole.

III

He is alone; yet not completely alone.
Pins on a map of a colour similar to his,
each city has one, sometimes more than one;

here, caretakers of art, in colleges;
in offices, there, with arm-bands, and green-shaded;
and there, pounding their catalogued beats in libraries,—

everywhere menial, a shadow's shadow.
And always for their egos—their outmoded art.
Thus, having lost the bevel in the ear,
they know neither up nor down, mistake the part
for the whole, curl themselves in a comma,
talk technics, make a colon their eyes. They distort—

such is the pain of their frustration—truth
to something convolute and cerebral.
How they do fear the slap of the flat of the platitude!
Now Pavlov's victims, their mouths water at bell,
the platter empty.
                    See they set twenty-one jewels
into their watches; the time they do not tell!

Some, patagonian in their own esteem,
and longing for the multiplying word,
join party and wear pins, now have a message,
an ear, and the convention-hall's regard.
Upon the knees of ventriloquists, they own,
of their dandled brightness, only the paint and board.

And some go mystical, and some go mad.
One stares at a mirror all day long, as if
to recognize himself; another courts
angels,—for here he does not fear rebuff;
and a third, alone, and sick with sex, and rapt,
doodles him symbols convex and concave.

O schizoid solitudes! O purities
curdling upon themselves! Who live for themselves,
or for each other, but for nobody else;
desire affection, private and public loves;
are friendly, and then quarrel and surmise
the secret perversions of each other's lives.

IV

He suspects that something has happened, a law
been passed, a nightmare ordered. Set apart,
he finds himself, with special haircut and dress,
as on a reservation. Introvert.
He does not understand this; sad conjecture
muscles and palls thrombotic on his heart.

He thinks an impostor, having studied his personal biography,
his gestures, his moods, now has come forward to pose
in the shivering vacuums his absence leaves.
Wigged with his laurel, that other, and faked with his face,
he pats the heads of his children, pecks his wife,
and is at home, and slippered, in his house.

So he guesses at the impertinent silhouette
that talks to his phone-piece and slits open his mail.
Is it the local tycoon who for a hobby
plays poet, he so epical in steel?
The orator, making a pause? Or is that man
he who blows his flash of brass in the jittering hall?

Or is he cuckolded by the troubadour
rich and successful out of celluloid?
Or by the don who unrhymes atoms? Or
the chemist death built up? Pride, lost impostor'd pride,
it is another, another, whoever he is,
who rides where he should ride.

V

Fame, the adrenalin: to be talked about;
to be a verb; to be introduced as *The:*
to smile with endorsement from slick paper; make
caprices anecdotal; to nod to the world; to see
one's name like a song upon the marquees played;
to be forgotten with embarrassment; to be—
to be.

It has its attractions, but is not the thing;
nor is it the ape mimesis who speaks from the tree
ancestral; nor the merkin joy. . .
Rather it is stark infelicity
which stirs him from his sleep, undressed, asleep
to walk upon roofs and window-sills and defy
the gape of gravity.

VI

Therefore he seeds illusions. Look, he is
the nth Adam taking a green inventory
in world but scarcely uttered, naming, praising,
the flowering fiats in the meadow, the
syllabled fur, stars aspirate, the pollen
whose sweet collision sounds eternally.
For to praise

the world—he, solitary man—is breath
to him. Until it has been praised, that part
has not been. Item by exciting item—
air to his lungs, and pressured blood to his heart,—
they are pulsated, and breathed, until they map,
not the world's, but his own body's chart!

And now in imagination he has climbed
another planet, the better to look
with single camera view upon this earth—
its total scope, and each afflated tick,
its talk, its trick, its tracklessness—and this,
this he would like to write down in a book!

To find a new function for the declassé craft
archaic like the fletcher's; to make a new thing;
to say the word that will become sixth sense;
perhaps by necessity and indirection bring
new forms to life, anonymously, new creeds—
O, somehow pay back the daily larcenies of the lung!

These are not mean ambitions. It is already something
merely to entertain them. Meanwhile, he
makes of his status as zero a rich garland,
a halo of his anonymity,
and lives alone, and in his secret shines
like phosphorus. At the bottom of the sea.

Theodore Roethke

Prayer

If I must of my Senses lose,
I pray Thee, Lord, that I may choose
Which of the Five I shall retain
Before oblivion clouds the brain.
My Tongue is generations dead,
My Nose defiles a comely head;
For hearkening to carnal evils
My Ears have been the very devil's.
And some have held the Eye to be
The instrument of lechery,
More furtive than the Hand in low
And vicious venery—Not so!
Its rape is gentle, never more
Violent than a metaphor.
In truth, the Eye's the abettor of
The holiest platonic love:
Lip, Breast, and Thigh cannot possess
So singular a blessedness.
Therefore, O Lord, let me preserve
The Sense that does so fitly serve,
Take Tongue and Ear—all else I have—
Let Light attend me to the grave!

Big Wind

Where were the greenhouses going,
Lunging into the lashing
Wind driving water
So far down the river

All the faucets stopped?—
So we drained the manure-machine
For the steam plant,
Pumping the stale mixture
Into the rusty boilers,
Watching the pressure gauge
Waver over to red,
As the seams hissed
And the live steam
Drove to the far
End of the rose-house,
Where the worst wind was,
Creaking the cypress window-frames,
Cracking so much thin glass
We stayed all night,
Stuffing the holes with burlap;
But she rode it out,
That old rose-house,
She hove into the teeth of it,
The core and pith of that ugly storm,
Ploughing with her stiff prow,
Bucking into the wind-waves
That broke over the whole of her,
Flailing her sides with spray,
Flinging long strings of wet across the roof-top,
Finally veering, wearing themselves out, merely
Whistling thinly under the wind-vents;
She sailed until the calm morning,
Carrying her full cargo of roses.

Dolor

I have known the inexorable sadness of pencils,
Neat in their boxes, dolor of pad and paper-weight,
All the misery of manilla folders and mucilage,
Desolation in immaculate public places,

Lonely reception room, lavatory, switchboard,
The unalterable pathos of basin and pitcher,
Ritual of multigraph, paper-clip, comma,
Endless duplication of lives and objects.
And I have seen dust from the walls of institutions,
Finer than flour, alive, more dangerous than silica,
Sift, almost invisible, through long afternoons of tedium,
Dropping a fine film on nails and delicate eyebrows,
Glazing the pale hair, the duplicate grey standard faces.

Praise to the End!

I

It's dark in this wood, soft mocker.
For whom have I swelled like a seed?
What a bone-ache I have.
Father of tensions, I'm down to my skin at last.

It's a great day for the mice.
Prickle-me, tickle-me, close stems.
Bumpkin, he can dance alone.
Ooh, ooh, I'm a duke of eels.

> Arch my back, pretty-bones, I'm dead at both ends.
> Softly softly, you'll wake the clams.
> I'll feed the ghost alone.
> Father, forgive my hands.

The rings have gone from the pond.
The river's alone with its water.
All risings
Fall.

II

Where are you now, my bonny beating gristle,
My blue original dandy, numb with sugar?

Once I fished from the banks, leaf-light and happy:
On the rocks south of quiet, in the close regions of kissing,
I romped, lithe as a child, down the summery streets of my veins,
Strict as a seed, nippy and twiggy.
Now the water's low. The weeds exceed me.
It's necessary, among the flies and bananas, to keep a constant
    vigil,
For the attacks of false humility take sudden turns for the worse.
Lacking the candor of dogs, I kiss the departing air;
I'm untrue to my own excesses.

Rock me to sleep, the weather's wrong.
Speak to me, frosty beard.
Sing to me, sweet.

> Mips and ma the mooly moo,
> The likes of him is biting who,
> A cow's a care and who's a coo?—
> What footie does is final.

> My dearest dear my fairest fair,
> Your father tossed a cat in air,
> Though neither you nor I was there,—
> What footie does is final.

> Be large as an owl, be slick as a frog,
> Be good as a goose, be big as a dog,
> Be sleek as a heifer, be long as a hog,—
> What footie will do will be final.

I conclude! I conclude!
My dearest dust, I can't stay here.
I'm undone by the flip-flap of odious pillows.
An exact fall of waters has rendered me impotent.
I've been asleep in a bower of dead skin.
It's a piece of a prince I ate.
This salt can't warm a stone.
These lazy ashes.

III

The stones were sharp,
The wind came at my back;
Walked along the highway,
Mincing like a cat.

The sun came out;
The lake turned green;
Romped upon the goldy grass,
Aged thirteen.

The sky cracked open
The world I knew;
Lay like the cats do
Sniffing the dew.

    I dreamt I was all bones;
    The dead slept in my sleeve;
    Sweet Jesus tossed me back:
    I wore the sun with ease.

    The several sounds were low;
    The river ebbed and flowed:
    Desire was winter-calm,
    A moon away.

Such owly pleasures! Fish come first, sweet bird.
Skin's the least of me. Kiss this.
Is the eternal near, fondling?
I hear the sound of hands.

Can the bones breathe? This grave has an ear.
It's still enough for the knock of a worm.
I feel more than a fish.
Ghost, come closer.

IV

Arch of air, my heart's original knock,
I'm awake all over:
I've crawled from the mire, alert as a saint or a dog;
I know the back-stream's joy, and the stone's eternal pulseless
    longing.
Felicity I cannot hoard.
My friend, the rat in the wall, brings me the clearest messages;
I bask in the bower of change;
The plants wave me in, and the summer apples;
My palm-sweat flashes gold;
Many astounds before, I lost my identity to a pebble;
The minnows love me, and the humped and spitting creatures.

I believe! I believe!—
In the sparrow, happy on gravel;
In the winter-wasp, pulsing its wings in the sunlight;
I have been somewhere else; I remember the sea-faced uncles.
I hear, clearly, the heart of another singing,
Lighter than bells,
Softer than water.

Wherefore, O birds and small fish, surround me.
Lave me, ultimate waters.
The dark showed me a face.
My ghosts are all gay.
The light becomes me.

Old Lady's Winter Words

To seize, to seize,—
I know that dream.
Now my ardors sleep in a sleeve.
My eyes have forgotten.
Like the half-dead, I hug my last secrets.
O for some minstrel of what's to be,

A bird singing into the beyond,
The marrow of God, talking,
Full merry, a gleam
Gracious and bland,
On a bright stone.
Somewhere, among the ferns and birds,
The great swamps flash.
I would hold high converse
Where the winds gather,
And leap over my eye,
An old woman
Jumping in her shoes.
If only I could remember
The white grass bending away,
The doors swinging open,
The smells, the moment of hay,—
When I went to sea in a sigh,
In a boat of beautiful things.
The good day has gone:
The fair house, the high
Elm swinging around
With its deep shade, and birds.
I have listened close
For the thin sound of the windy chimney,
The fall of the last ash
From the dying ember.
I've become a sentry of small seeds,
Poking alone in my garden.
The stone walks, where are they?
Gone to bolster a road.
The shrunken soil
Has scampered away in a dry wind.
Once I was sweet with the light of myself,
A self-delighting creature,
Leaning over a rock,
My hair between me and the sun,
The waves rippling near me.
My feet remembered the earth,

The loam heaved me
That way and this.
My looks had a voice;
I was careless in growing.

If I were a young man,
I could roll in the dust of a fine rage.

The shadows are empty, the sliding externals.
The wind wanders around the house
On its way to the back pasture.
The cindery snow ticks over stubble.
My dust longs for the invisible.
I'm reminded to stay alive
By the dry rasp of the recurring inane,
The fine soot sifting through my south windows.
It is hard to care about corners,
And the sound of paper tearing.
I fall, more and more,
Into my own silences.
In the cold air,
The spirit
Hardens.

The Waking

I wake to sleep, and take my waking slow.
I feel my fate in what I cannot fear.
I learn by going where I have to go.

We think by feeling. What is there to know?
I hear my being dance from ear to ear.
I wake to sleep, and take my waking slow.

Of those so close beside me, which are you?
God bless the Ground! I shall walk softly there,
And learn by going where I have to go.

Light takes the Tree; but who can tell us how?
The lowly worm climbs up a winding stair;
I wake to sleep, and take my waking slow.

Great Nature has another thing to do
To you and me; so take the lively air,
And, lovely, learn by going where to go.

This shaking keeps me steady. I should know.
What falls away is always. And is near.
I wake to sleep, and take my waking slow.
I learn by going where I have to go.

I Knew a Woman

I knew a woman, lovely in her bones,
When small birds sighed, she would sigh back at them;
Ah, when she moved, she moved more ways than one:
The shapes a bright container can contain!
Of her choice virtues only gods should speak,
Or English poets who grew up on Greek
(I'd have them sing in chorus, cheek to cheek).

How well her wishes went! She stroked my chin,
She taught me Turn, and Counter-turn, and Stand;
She taught me Touch, that undulant white skin;
I nibbled meekly from her proffered hand;
She was the sickle; I, poor I, the rake,
Coming behind her for her pretty sake
(But what prodigious mowing we did make).

Love likes a gander, and adores a goose:
Her full lips pursed, the errant note to seize;
She played it quick, she played it light and loose;
My eyes, they dazzled at her flowing knees;

Her several parts could keep a pure repose,
Or one hip quiver with a mobile nose
(She moved in circles, and those circles moved).

Let seed be grass, and grass turn into hay:
I'm martyr to a motion not my own;
What's freedom for? To know eternity.
I swear she cast a shadow white as stone.
But who would count eternity in days?
These old bones live to learn her wanton ways:
(I measure time by how a body sways).

The Far Field

I

I dream of journeys repeatedly:
Of flying like a bat deep into a narrowing tunnel,
Of driving alone, without luggage, out a long peninsula,
The road lined with snow-laden second growth,
A fine dry snow ticking the windshield,
Alternate snow and sleet, no on-coming traffic,
And no lights behind, in the blurred side-mirror,
The road changing from glazed tarface to a rubble of stone,
Ending at last in a hopeless sand-rut,
Where the car stalls,
Churning in a snowdrift
Until the headlights darken.

II

At the field's end, in the corner missed by the mower,
Where the turf drops off into a grass-hidden culvert,
Haunt of the cat-bird, nesting-place of the field-mouse,
Not too far away from the ever-changing flower-dump,
Among the tin cans, tires, rusted pipes, broken machinery,—
One learned of the eternal;
And in the shrunken face of a dead rat, eaten by rain and
    ground-beetles

(I found it lying among the rubble of an old coal bin)
And the tom-cat, caught near the pheasant-run,
Its entrails strewn over the half-grown flowers,
Blasted to death by the night watchman.

I suffered for birds, for young rabbits caught in the mower,
My grief was not excessive.
For to come upon warblers in early May
Was to forget time and death:
How they filled the oriole's elm, a twittering restless cloud, all one
    morning,
And I watched and watched till my eyes blurred from the bird
    shapes,—
Cape May, Blackburnian, Cerulean, —
Moving, elusive as fish, fearless,
Hanging, bunched like young fruit, bending the end branches,
Still for a moment,
Then pitching away in half-flight,
Lighter than finches,
While the wrens bickered and sang in the half-green hedgerows,
And the flicker drummed from his dead tree in the chicken-yard.

—Or to lie naked in sand,
In the silted shallows of a slow river,
Fingering a shell,
Thinking:
Once I was something like this, mindless,
Or perhaps with another mind, less peculiar;
Or to sink down to the hips in a mossy quagmire;
Or, with skinny knees, to sit astride a wet log,
Believing:
I'll return again,
As a snake or a raucous bird,
Or, with luck, as a lion.

I learned not to fear infinity,
The far field, the windy cliffs of forever,
The dying of time in the white light of tomorrow,

The wheel turning away from itself,
The sprawl of the wave,
The on-coming water.

III

The river turns on itself,
The tree retreats into its own shadow.
I feel a weightless change, a moving forward
As of water quickening before a narrowing channel
When banks converge, and the wide river whitens;
Or when two rivers combine, the blue glacial torrent
And the yellowish-green from the mountainy upland,—
At first a swift rippling between rocks,
Then a long running over flat stones
Before descending to the alluvial plain,
To the clay banks, and the wild grapes hanging from the elmtrees.
The slightly trembling water
Dropping a fine yellow silt where the sun stays;
And the crabs bask near the edge,
The weedy edge, alive with small snakes and bloodsuckers,—
I have come to a still, but not a deep center,
A point outside the glittering current;
My eyes stare at the bottom of a river,
At the irregular stones, iridescent sandgrains,
My mind moves in more than one place,
In a country half-land, half-water.

I am renewed by death, thought of my death,
The dry scent of a dying garden in September,
The wind fanning the ash of a low fire.
What I love is near at hand,
Always, in earth and air.

IV

The lost self changes,
Turning toward the sea,
A sea-shape turning around,—
An old man with his feet before the fire,
In robes of green, in garments of adieu.

A man faced with his own immensity
Wakes all the waves, all their loose wandering fire.
The murmur of the absolute, the why
Of being born fails on his naked ears.
His spirit moves like monumental wind
That gentles on a sunny blue plateau.
He is the end of things, the final man.

All finite things reveal infinitude:
The mountain with its singular bright shade
Like the blue shine on freshly frozen snow,
The after-light upon ice-burdened pines;
Odor of basswood on a mountain-slope,
A scent beloved of bees;
Silence of water above a sunken tree:
The pure serene of memory in one man,—
A ripple widening from a single stone
Winding around the waters of the world.

In a Dark Time

In a dark time, the eye begins to see,
I meet my shadow in the deepening shade;
I hear my echo in the echoing wood—
A lord of nature weeping to a tree.
I live between the heron and the wren,
Beasts of the hill and serpents of the den.

What's madness but nobility of soul
At odds with circumstance? The day's on fire!
I know the purity of pure despair,
My shadow pinned against a sweating wall.
That place among the rocks—is it a cave,
Or winding path? The edge is what I have.

A steady storm of correspondences!
A night flowing with birds, a ragged moon,

And in broad day the midnight come again!
A man goes far to find out what he is—
Death of the self in a long, tearless night,
All natural shapes blazing unnatural light.

Dark, dark my light, and darker my desire.
My soul, like some heat-maddened summer fly,
Keeps buzzing at the sill. Which I is *I*?
A fallen man, I climb out of my fear.
The mind enters itself, and God the mind,
And one is One, free in the tearing wind.

Earle Birney

Vancouver Lights

About me the night   moonless   wimples the mountains
wraps ocean   land   air   and mounting
sucks at the stars   The city   throbbing below
webs the peninsula   Streaming   the golden
strands overleap the seajet   by bridge and buoy
vault the shears of the inlet   climb the woods
toward me   falter   and halt   Across to the firefly
haze of a ship on the gulf's erased horizon
roll the spokes of a restless lighthouse

Through the feckless years we have come to the time
when to look on this quilt of lamps is a troubling delight
Welling from Europe's bog   through Africa flowing
and Asia   drowning the lonely lumes on the oceans
tiding up over Halifax   now to this winking
outpost comes flooding the primal ink

On this mountain's brutish forehead with terror of space
I stir   of the changeless night and the stark ranges
of nothing   pulsing down from beyond and between
the fragile planets   We are a spark beleaguered
by darkness   this twinkle we make in a corner of emptiness
how shall we utter our fear that the black Experimentress
will never in the range of her microscope find it?   Our Phoebus
himself is a bubble that dries on Her slide   while the Nubian
wears for an evening's whim a necklace of nebulae

Yet we must speak   we the unique glowworms
Out of the waters and rocks of our little world
we cunningly conjured these flames   hooped these sparks
by our will   From blankness and cold we fashioned stars

to our size   and signalled Aldebaran   This must we say
whoever may be to hear us   if murk devour
and none weave again in gossamer:

                                        These rays were ours
we made and unmade them   Not the shudder of continents
doused us   the moon's passion   nor crash of comets
In the fathomless heat of our dwarfdom   our dream's combustion
we contrived the power   the blast that snuffed us
No one bound Prometheus   Himself he chained
and consumed his own bright liver   O stranger
Plutonian   descendant   or beast in the stretching night—
there was light

1941

Anglosaxon Street

Dawndrizzle ended   dampness steams from
blotching brick and   blank plasterwaste
Faded housepatterns   hoary and finicky
unfold stuttering   stick like a phonograph

Here is a ghetto   gotten for goyim
O with care denuded   of nigger and kike
No coonsmell rankles   reeks only cellarrot
ottar of carexhaust   catacorpse and cookinggrease
Imperial hearts   heave in this haven
Cracks across windows   are welded with slogans
There'll Always Be An England   enhances geraniums
and V's for a Victory   vanquish the housefly

Ho! with beaming sun   march the bleached beldames
festooned with shopping bags   farded   flatarched
bigthewed Saxonwives   stepping over buttrivers
waddling back wienerladen   to suckle smallfry

Hoy! with sunslope   shrieking over hydrants
flood from learninghall   the lean fingerlings
Nordic   nobblecheeked   not all clean of nose
leaping Commandowise   into leprous lanes

What! after whistleblow!   spewed from wheelboat
after daylong doughtiness   dire handplay
in sewertrench or sandpit   come Saxonthegns
Junebrown Jutekings   jawslack for meat

Sit after supper   on smeared doorsteps
not humbly swearing   hatedeeds on Huns
profiteers politicians   pacifists Jews

Then by twobit magic   to muse in movie
unlock picturehoard   or lope to alehall
soaking bleakly   in beer skittleless
Home again to hotbox   and humid husbandhood
in slumbertrough adding   sleepily to Anglekin

Alongside in lanenooks   carling and leman
caterwaul and clip   careless of Saxonry
with moonglow and haste   and a higher heartbeat

Slumbers now slumtrack   unstinks cooling
waiting brief for milkhind   mornstar and worldrise

Toronto 1942

From the Hazel Bough

He met a lady
    on a lazy street
hazel eyes
    and little plush feet

her legs swam by
    like lovely trout

eyes were trees
   where boys leant out

hands in the dark and
   a river side
round breasts rising
   with the finger's tide

she was plump as a finch
   and live as a salmon
gay as silk and
   proud as a Brahmin

they winked when they met
   and laughed when they parted
never took time
   to be brokenhearted

but no man sees
   where the trout lie now
or what leans out
   from the hazel bough

Toronto, 1945—Vancouver, 1947

Bushed

He invented a rainbow but lightning struck it
shattered it into the lake-lap of a mountain
so big his mind slowed when he looked at it

Yet he built a shack on the shore
learned to roast porcupine belly and
wore the quills on his hatband

At first he was out with the dawn
whether it yellowed bright as wood-columbine
or was only a fuzzed moth in a flannel of storm

But he found the mountain was clearly alive
sent messages whizzing down every hot morning
boomed proclamations at noon and spread out
a white guard of goat
before falling asleep on its feet at sundown

When he tried his eyes on the lake   ospreys
would fall like valkyries
choosing the cut-throat
He took then to waiting
till the night smoke rose from the boil of the sunset

But the moon carved unknown totems
out of the lakeshore
owls in the beardusky woods derided him
moosehorned cedars circled his swamps and tossed
their antlers up to the stars
Then he knew   though the mountain slept   the winds
were shaping its peak to an arrowhead
poised

And now he could only
bar himself in and wait
for the great flint to come singing into his heart

1951

A Walk in Kyoto

All week   the maid tells me   bowing
her doll's body at my mat   is Boys' Day
Also please Man's Day   and gravely
bends deeper   The magnolia sprig in my alcove
is it male?   The ancient discretions of Zen were not shaped
for my phallic western eye   There is so much discretion
in this small bowed body of an empire
the wild hair of waterfalls combed straight
in the ricefields   the inn-maid retreating
with the face of a shut flower   I stand hunched
and clueless like a castaway in the shoals of my room

When I slide my parchment door to stalk awkward
through Lilliput gardens framed and untouchable
as watercolors   the streets look much the same
the Men are being pulled past on the strings of their engines
the legs of the Boys are revolved by a thousand pedals
and all the faces as taut and unfestive as Moscow's
or Toronto's   or mine

Lord Buddha help us all there is vigor enough
in these islands and in all islands reefed and resounding
with cities   But the pitch is high as the ping
of cicadas   those small strained motors concealed
in the propped pines by the dying river   and only
male as the stretched falsetto of actors mincing
the women's roles in *kabuki*   or female only
as the lost heroes womanized in the Ladies' Opera
Where in these alleys jammed with competing waves
of signs in two tongues and three scripts
can the simple song of a man be heard?

By the shoguns' palace   the Important Cultural Property
stripped for tiptoeing schoolgirls   I stare at the staring
penned carp that flail on each other's backs
to the shrunk pool's edge for the crumb this non-fish
tossed   Is this the Day's one parable?
Or under that peeling pagoda the five hundred tons
of hermaphrodite Word?

At the inn I prepare to surrender again my defeated
shoes to the bending maid   But suddenly the closed
lotus opens to a smile and she points
over my shoulder   above the sagging tiles   to where
tall in the bare sky and huge as Gulliver
a carp is rising   golden and fighting
thrusting its paper body up from the fist
of a small boy on an empty roof   higher
and higher   into the endless winds of the world

1958

The Bear on the Delhi Road

Unreal   tall as a myth
by the road the Himalayan bear
is beating the brilliant air
with his crooked arms
About him two men   bare
spindly as locusts   leap

One pulls on a ring
in the great soft nose   His mate
flicks   flicks with a stick
up at the rolling eyes

They have not led him here
down from the fabulous hills
to this bald alien plain
and the clamorous world   to kill
but simply to teach him to dance

They are peaceful both   these spare
men of Kashmir   and the bear
alive is their living   too
If   far on the Delhi way
around him galvanic they dance
it is merely to wear   wear
from his shaggy body the tranced
wish forever to stay
only an ambling bear
four-footed in berries

It is no more joyous for them
In this hot dust to prance
out of reach of the praying claws
sharpened to paw for ants
in the shadows of deodars

It is not easy to free
myth from reality
or rear this fellow up
to lurch   lurch with them
in the tranced dancing of men

Srinagar, 1958—Île des Porquerolles, 1959

Twenty-Third Flight

Lo as I pause in the alien vale of the airport
fearing ahead the official ambush
a voice languorous and strange as these winds of Oahu
calleth my name and I turn to be quoited in orchids
and amazed with a kiss perfumed and soft as the *lei*
Straight from a travel poster thou steppest
thy arms like mangoes for smoothness
o implausible shepherdess for this one aging sheep
and leadest me through the righteous paths of the Customs
in a mist of my own wild hopes
Yea though I walk through the valley of Immigration
I fear no evil   for thou art a vision beside me
and my name is correctly spelled
and I shall dwell in the Hawaiian Village Hotel
where thy kindred prepareth a table before me
Thou restorest my baggage   and by limousine leadest me
to where I may lie on coral sands by a stream-lined pool

Nay but thou stayest not?
Thou anointest not my naked head with oil?
O shepherdess of Flight Number Twenty-three only
thou hastenest away on thy long brown legs to enchant
thy fellow-members in Local Five of the Greeters' Union
or that favored professor of Commerce mayhap
who leadeth thee into higher courses in Hotel Management

O nubile goddess of the Kaiser Training Programme
is it possible that tonight my cup runneth not over
and that I shall sit in the still pastures of the lobby
whilst thou leadest another old ram in garlands past me
and   bland as papaya   appearest not to remember me?
And that I shall lie by the waters of Waikiki   and want?

1958

Haiku for a Young Waitress

With dusk I am caught
peering over the holly
hedge at the dogwood

1960

Cartagena de Indias

'Ciudad triste, ayer reina de la mar.'—HEREDIA

Each face its own phantom
its own formula of breed and shade
but all the eyes accuse me back and say

> There are only two races here:
> we human citizens
> who are poor but have things to sell
> and you   from outer space
> unseasonable   our one tourist
> but plainly able to buy

This arthritic street
where Drake's men and Cole's ran
swung cutlasses   where wine and sweet blood
snaked in the cobble's joints
        leaps now in a sennet of taxi horns
        to betray my invasion
All watch my first retreat
to barbizans patched from Morgan's grapeshot
and they rush me
        three desperate tarantula youths
        waving Old Golds unexcised

By an altar blackened
where the Indian silver was scratched away
in sanctuary leaning   on lush cool marble
        I am hemmed by a Congo drum man in jeans
    He bares a brace of Swiss watches
        whispers in husky Texan

Where gems and indigo were sorted
        in shouting arcades
        I am deftly shortchanged
and slink to the trees that lean
and flower tall in the Plaza
        Nine shoeboys wham their boxes
        slap at my newshined feet

Only in the Indio market
mazed on the sodden quais
I am granted uneasy truce
Around the ritual braidings of hair
the magical arrangements of fish
the piled rainbows of rotting fruit
I cast a shadow of silence
        blue-dreaded eyes
        corpse face
        hidalgo clothes
        tall one   tall as a demon
        pass O pass us quickly

Behind me the bright blaze of patois
        leaps again

I step to the beautiful slave-built bridge
and a mestiza girl
        levels Christ's hands at me
        under a dangling goitre

Past the glazed-eyed screamers of *dulces*
swing to a pink lane
where a poxed and slit-eyed savage
        pouts an obscenity
        offering a sister
        as he would spit me
        a dart from a blowpipe

Somewhere there must be another bridge
from my stupid wish
to their human acceptance
but what can I offer—
my tongue half-locked in the cell
of its language—other than pesos
        to these old crones of thirty
        whose young sink in pellagra
        as I clump unmaimed
        in the bright shoes
        that keep me from hookworm
        lockjaw and snakebite

It's written in the cut of my glasses
I've a hotelroom all to myself
with a fan   and a box of Vitamin C
It can be measured
in my unnatural stride
that my life expectation
is more than forty
especially now that I'm close to sixty

older than ever bankrupt Bolívar was
who sits now in a frozen prance
high over the coconut trays
quivering on the heads
    of three gaunt mulatto ladies
    circling in a pavane of commerce
    down upon spotlit me

Out of the heaving womb of independence
Bolívar rode   and over the bloody afterbirth
into coffee and standard oil
    from inquisitional baroque
    to armed forces corbusier
He alone has nothing more   to sell me

I come routed now   scuffling
through dust in a nameless square
treeless   burning   deserted
come lost and guiltily wakeful
in the hour of siesta
    at last to a message

    to a pair of shoes
    in a circle of baked mud
    worn   out of shape   one on its side
For a second I am shaken by panic
heat? humidity? something has got me
    the shoes are concrete
    and ten feet long

    the sight of a plaque calms
    without telling me much

    En homenaje de la memoria de
        LUIS LOPEZ
    se erigió este monumento
      a los zapatos viejos
    el día 10 de febrero de 1957

Luis Lopez?   Monument to his old shoes?
What???   There was nothing else

Back through the huckster streets
the sad taxi men still awake and horn-happy

> *Si señor   Luis Lopez el poeta*
> Here is his book
> Unamuno praised it   *si si*
> You have seen *los zapatos*?   Ah?
> But they are us, *señor*
> It was about us he wrote
> about Cartagena where he was born
> and died.   See here this sonnet
> always he made hard words
> Said we were lazy except to make noise
> we only shout to get money
> ugly too, backward . . . why not?
> It is for a poet to write these things
> Also *plena*—how say it?—
> *plena de rancio desaliño*

Full of rancid disarray!

> *Si si* but look, at the end, when old
> he come to say one nice thing
> only one ever about us
> He say we inspire that love a man has
> for his old shoes—*Entonces*
> we give him a monument to the shoes

I bought the book   walked back
sat on the curb happier than Wordsworth
gazing away at his daffodils
Discarded queen   I thought   I love you too
Full of rancid disarray
city like any city
full of the stench of human indignity
and disarray of the human proportion
full of the noisy always poor

and the precocious dying
stinking with fear   the stale of ignorance
I love you first for giving birth
to Luis Lopez   suffering him
honouring him at last
in the grand laconic manner
he taught you

—and him I envy
I who am seldom read by my townsmen

Descendants of pirates   grandees
galleyslaves·and cannibals
I love the whole starved cheating
poetry-reading lot of you   most of all
for throwing me the shoes of deadman Luis
to walk me back into your brotherhood

Colombia, 1962—Greece, 1963

Alfred Purdy

The Cariboo Horses

At 100 Mile House the cowboys ride in rolling
stagey cigarettes with one hand reining
restive equine rebels on a morning grey as stone
—so much like riding dangerous women
                with whiskey coloured eyes—
such women as once fell dead with their lovers
with fire in their heads and slippery froth on thighs
—Beaver and Carrier women maybe or
                Blackfoot squaws far past the edge of this valley
on the other side of those two toy mountain ranges
                from the sunfierce plains beyond—

But only horses
                        waiting in stables
hitched at taverns
                        standing at dawn
pastured outside the town with
jeeps and fords and chevvys and
busy muttering stake trucks rushing
importantly over roads of man's devising
over the safe known roads of the ranchers
families and merchants of the town—
                On the high prairie
are only horse and rider
                        wind in dry grass
clopping in silence under the toy mountains
dropping sometimes and
                        lost in the dry grass
                        golden oranges of dung—
Only horses
                no stopwatch memories or palace ancestors

not Kiangs hauling undressed stone in the Nile Valley
and having stubborn Egyptian tantrums or
Onagers racing thru Hither Asia and
the last Quagga screaming in African highlands
              lost relatives of these
              whose hooves were thunder
the ghosts of horses battering thru the wind
whose names were the wind's common usage
whose life was the sun's
              arriving here at chilly noon
              in the gasoline smell of the
              dust and waiting 15 minutes
              at the grocer's—

Song of the Impermanent Husband

Oh I would
              I would in a minute
if the cusswords and bitter anger couldn't—
if the either/or quarrel didn't—
and the fat around my middle wasn't—
if I was young if
              I wasn't so damn sure
I couldn't find another maddening bitch
like you holding on for dear life to
all the different parts of me for
twenty or twenty
              thousand years
I'd leave in the night like
a disgraced caviar salesman
              descend the moonlight
stairs to Halifax
      (uh—no—not Halifax)
well then Toronto
             uh

I guess not Toronto either/or
nouveau riche Vancouver down
                              down
                                   down
the dark stairs to
the South Seas' sunlit milky reefs and
        the jungle's green
                    unending bank account with
all the brown girls being brown
                as they can be and all
the one piece behinds stretched tight tonight
in small sarongs not to be touched tho Oh
beautiful as an angel's ass without the genitals
and me
            in Paris like a smudged Canadian postcard and
(dear me)
        all the importuning white and lily girls
of Rue Pigalle
            and stroll
the sodden London streets and
            find a sullen foggy woman who
enjoyed my odd colonial ways and send
a postcard back to you about my faithfulness and
talk about the lovely lovely English weather
I'd be the slimiest most uxorious wife deserter
            my shrunk amoeba self absurd inside
a saffron girl's geography and
hating me between magnetic nipples
but
    fooling no one in all the sad
    and much emancipated world
Why then I'll stay at least for tea for
all the brownness is too brown and
all the whiteness too damned white
and I'm afraid
            afraid of being
any other woman's man who
might be me
            afraid

the unctuous and uneasy self I glimpse
sometimes might lose my faint and yapping cry for
being anything was never quite what I intended
And you you
                    bitch no irritating
questions re love and permanence only
                    an unrolling lifetime here
between your rocking thighs and
                    the semblance of motion

Eskimo Graveyard

Walking in glacial litter
frost boils and boulder pavements
of an old river delta
where angry living water
changes its mind every half century
and takes a new direction
to the blue fiord
The Public Works guy I'm with
says you always find good gravel
for concrete near a graveyard
where digging is easy maybe
a footnote on human character
But wrapped in blankets
above ground a dead old woman
(for the last few weeks I'm told)
without a grave marker
And a hundred yards away
the Anglican missionary's grave
with whitewashed cross
that means equally nothing
The river's soft roar
drifts to my ears and changes
tone when the wind changes
ice debris melts at low tide

& the Public Works guy is mildly pleased
with the good gravel we found
for work on the schoolhouse
which won't have to be shipped in
from Montreal
and mosquitoes join happily
in our conversation   Then
he stops to consult
with the construction foreman
I walk on
toward the tents of The People
half a mile away
at one corner of the picture
Mothers with children on their backs
in the clean white parkas
they take such pride in
buying groceries at H.B.C.
boys lounging under the store
in space where timber stilts
hold it above the permafrost
with two of them arm in arm
in the manner of Eskimo friends
After dinner
I walk down among the tents
and happen to think of the old woman
neither wholly among the dead
nor quite gone from the living
and wonder how often
a thought of hers enters the minds
of people she knew before
and what kind of flicker it is
as lights begin to come on
in nightlong twilight
and thoughts of me
occur to the mosquitoes
I keep walking
as if something ought to happen
(I don't know what)

with the sun stretching
a yellow band across the water
from headland to black headland
at high tide in the fiord
sealing in the settlement
as if there was no way out
and indeed there isn't
until the looping Cansos come
dropping thru the mountain doorway
That old woman?
it occurs to me
I might have been thinking
about human bookkeeping
debits and credits that is
or profit and loss
(and laugh at myself)
among the sealed white tents
like glowing swans
hoping
for a most improbable
birth

Arctic Rhododendrons

They are small purple surprises
in the river's white racket
and after you've seen them
a number of times
in water-places
where their silence seems
related to river-thunder
you think of them as 'noisy flowers'
Years ago
it may have been
that lovers came this way

stopped in the outdoor hotel
to watch the water floorshow
and lying prone together
where the purged green
boils to a white heart
and the shore trembles
like a stone song
with bodies touching
flowers were their conversation
and love the sound of a colour
that lasts two weeks in August
and then dies
except for the three or four
I pressed in a letter
and sent whispering to you

The Wine-Maker's Beat-Étude

I am picking wild grapes last year
in a field
              dragging down great lianas of vine
tearing at 20 feet of heavy infinite purple
having a veritable tug-o-war with Bacchus
who grins at me delightedly in the high branches
of one of those stepchild apple trees
unloved by anything but tent caterpillars
and ghosts of old settlers
become such strangers here—
I am thinking what the grapes are thinking
become part of their purple mentality
that is
              I am satisfied with the sun and
eventual fermenting bubble-talk together
then transformed and glinting with coloured lights in
              a GREAT JEROBOAM
that booms inside from the land beyond the world—

In fact
I am satisfied with my own shortcomings letting
myself happen then
                     I'm surrounded by Cows
black and white ones with tails—
At first I'm certain how to advise them
in mild protest or frank manly invective
then realize that the cows are right
it's *me* that's the trespasser—
                  Of course they are curious
perhaps wish to see me perform
               I moo off key
               I bark like a man
               laugh like a dog
               I talk like God
               hoping
they'll go away so Bacchus and I can get on with it—

Then I get logical thinking if there was ever a
feminine principle cows are it and why not but
what would so many females want?
I address them like Brigham Young hastily
           'No, that's out! I won't do it!
                Absolutely not!'
Contentment steals back among all this femininity
thinking cows are together so much they must be nearly
all lesbians fondling each other's dugs by moonlight why
Sappho's own star-reaching soul shines inward and outward
from the soft Aegean islands in these eyes and
I am dissolved like a salt lick instantly oh
              Sodium chloride!
              Prophylactic acid!
              Gamma particles (in suspension)!
              After shave lotion!
              Rubbing alcohol!
                    suddenly

I become the whole damn feminine principle so
happily noticing little tendrils of affection
steal out from each to each unshy honest encompassing
golden calves in Israel and slum babies in Canada and
a millionaire's brat left squalling on the toilet seat in
Rockefeller Center
                              O my sisters
                              I give purple milk!

Lament for the Dorsets

(Eskimos extinct in the 14th century A.D.*)*

Animal bones and some mossy tent rings
scrapers and spearheads   carved ivory swans
all that remains of the Dorset giants
who drove the Vikings back to their long ships
talked to spirits of earth and water
—a picture of terrifying old men
so large they broke the backs of bears
so small they lurk behind bone rafters
in the brain of modern hunters
among good thoughts and warm things
and come out at night
to spit on the stars

The big men with clever fingers
who had no dogs and hauled their sleds
over the frozen northern oceans

awkward giants
                    killers of seal
they couldn't compete with little men
who came from the west with dogs
Or else in a warm climatic cycle
the seals went back to cold waters
and the puzzled Dorsets scratched their heads
with hairy thumbs around 1350 A.D.
—couldn't figure it out
went around saying to each other
plaintively
            'What's wrong? What happened?
            Where are the seals gone?'
And died

Twentieth century people
apartment dwellers
executives of neon death
warmakers with things that explode
—they have never imagined us in their future
how could we imagine them in the past
squatting among the moving glaciers
six hundred years ago
with glowing lamps?
As remote or nearly
as the trilobites and swamps
when coal became
or the last great reptile hissed
at a mammal the size of a mouse
that squeaked and fled

Did they ever realize at all
what was happening to them?
Some old hunter with one lame leg
a bear had chewed

sitting in a caribou skin tent
—the last Dorset?
Let's say his name was Kudluk
carving 2-inch ivory swans
for a dead grand-daughter
taking them out of his mind
the places in his mind
where pictures are
He selects a sharp stone tool
to gouge a parallel pattern of lines
on both sides of the swan
holding it with his left hand
bearing down and transmitting
his body's weight
from brain to arm and right hand
and one of his thoughts
turns to ivory
The carving is laid aside
in beginning darkness
at the end of hunger
after a while wind
blows down the tent and snow
begins to cover him
After 600 years
the ivory thought
is still warm

The Runners

'It was when Leif was with King Olaf Tryggvason, and he bade him proclaim Christianity to Greenland, that the king gave him two Gaels; the
man's name was Haki, and the woman's Haekia. The king advised Leif to
have recourse to these people, if he should stand in need of fleetness, for
they were swifter than deer. Erick and Leif had tendered Karlsefni the
services of this couple. Now when they had sailed past Marvel-Strands (to
the New World) they put the Gaels ashore, and directed them to run to the
southward, and investigate the nature of the country, and return again
before the end of the third half-day.'

—From *Eric the Red's Saga.*

Brother, the wind of this place is cold,
and hills under our feet tremble,
the forests are making magic against us—
I think the land knows we are here,
I think the land knows we are strangers.
Let us stay close to our friend the sea,
or cunning dwarves at the roots of darkness
shall seize and drag us down—

Sister, we must share our strength between us,
until the heat of our bodies makes a single flame,
and one that we are is more than two that we were:
while the moon sees only one shadow,
and the sun knows only our double heartbeat,
and the rain does not come between—

Brother, I am afraid of this dark place,
I am hungry for the home islands,
and wind blowing the waves to coloured spray,
I am sick for the sun—

Sister, we must not think those thoughts again,
for three half days have gone by,
and we must return to the ship.
If we are away longer,
the Northmen will beat us with thongs,
until we cry for death—
Why do you stare at nothing?

Brother, a cold wind touched me,
tho I stand in your arms' circle:
perhaps the Northmen's runes have found us,
the runes they carve on wood and stone.
I am afraid of this dark land,
ground-mist that makes us half ghosts,
and another silence inside silence . . .
But there are berries and fish here,
and there are worse things than silence,
let us stay and not go back—

Sister, we should die slowly,
the beasts would gnaw at our bodies,
the rains whiten our bones.
The Northmen's runes are strong magic,
the runes would track us down,
tho we keep on running
past the Land of Flat Stones
over the Marvel-Strands
beyond the land of great trees . . .
Tho we ran to the edge of the world,
our masters would track us down—

Brother, take my hand in your hand,
this part of ourselves between us
while we run together,
over the stones of the sea-coast,
this much of ourselves is our own:
while rain cries out against us,
and darkness swallows the evening,
and morning moves into stillness,
and mist climbs to our throats,
while we are running,
while we are running—

Sister—

Poem

You are ill and so I lead you away
and put you to bed in the dark room
—you lie breathing softly and I hold your hand
feeling the fingertips relax as sleep comes

You will not sleep more than a few hours
and the illness is less serious than my anger or cruelty
and the dark bedroom is like a foretaste of other darknesses
to come later which all of us must endure alone
but here I am permitted to be with you

After a while in sleep your fingers clutch tightly
and I know that whatever may be happening
the fear coiled in dreams or the bright trespass of pain
there is nothing at all I can do except hold your hand
and not go away

Alive or Not

It's like a story
because it takes so long to happen:

a block away on an Ottawa street
I see this woman about to fall
and she collapses slowly
in sections the way you read about
and there just might be time
for me to reach her
running as fast as I can
before her head hits the sidewalk
Of course it's my wife

I am running toward her now
and there is a certain amount of horror
a time lag in which other things happen
I can almost see flowers break into blossom
while I am running toward the woman
my wife it seems
orchids in the Brazilian jungle
exist like unprovable ideas
until a man in a pith helmet
steps on one and yells Eureka or something
—and while I am thinking about this
her body splashes on the street
her glasses fall broken beside her
with a musical sound under the traffic
and she is probably dead too
Of course I cradle her in my arms
a doll perhaps without life
while someone I do not know
signals a taxi
as the bystanders stare
What this means years later
as I grow older and older
is that I am still running toward her:
the woman falls very slowly
she is giving me more and more time
to reach her and make the grab
and each time each fall she may die
or not die and this will go on forever
this will go on forever and ever
As I grow older and older
my speed afoot increases
each time I am running and reach
the place before she falls every time
I am running too fast to stop
I run past her farther and farther
it's almost like a story
as an orchid dies in the Brazilian jungle
and there is a certain amount of horror

Spinning

For Colleen Thibaudeau

'Can't see out of my left eye
nothing much happens on the left anyway'
—you have to spin around right quickly
then just catch a glimpse
of coat tails leaving the room
(lace doilies on the settee)
light foot rising and disappearing
the last shot fired at Batoche
or maybe it was Duck Lake
—thought I saw someone I knew
and turned faster and faster
said wait for me
it was my grandmother I never knew
before I was born she died
—sometimes I turned fast enough
and nearly caught up with the sun
it bounded like a big red ball
forward and then went backwards
over the mountains somewhere
—thought I saw someone I knew
she was young in an old summer
I tried to remember very carefully
balanced on one foot
and concentrated and concentrated
lightfoot white feet in the long grass
running to meet her lover
I couldn't stop turning then
wait for me wait for me

Robert Lowell

The Holy Innocents

Listen, the hay-bells tinkle as the cart
Wavers on rubber tires along the tar
And cindered ice below the burlap mill
And ale-wife run. The oxen drool and start
In wonder at the fenders of a car,
And blunder hugely up St Peter's hill.
These are the undefiled by woman—their
Sorrow is not the sorrow of this world:
King Herod shrieking vengeance at the curled
Up knees of Jesus choking in the air,

A king of speechless clods and infants. Still
The world out-Herods Herod; and the year,
The nineteen-hundred forty-fifth of grace,
Lumbers with losses up the clinkered hill
Of our purgation; and the oxen near
The worn foundations of their resting-place,
The holy manger where their bed is corn
And holly torn for Christmas. If they die,
As Jesus, in the harness, who will mourn?
Lamb of the shepherds, Child, how still you lie.

Christmas in Black Rock

Christ God's red shadow hangs upon the wall
The dead leaf's echo on these hours
Whose burden spindles to no breath at all;
Hard at our heels the huntress moonlight towers

And the green needles bristle at the glass
Tiers of defence-plants where the treadmill night
Churns up Long Island Sound with piston-fist.
Tonight, my child, the lifeless leaves will mass,
Heaving and heaping, as the swivelled light
Burns on the bell-spar in the fruitless mist.

Christ Child, your lips are lean and evergreen
Tonight in Black Rock, and the moon
Sidles outside into the needle-screen
And strikes the hand that feeds you with a spoon
Tonight, as drunken Polish night-shifts walk
Over the causeway and their juke-box booms
Hosannah in excelsis Domino.
Tonight, my child, the foot-loose hallows stalk
Us down in the blind alleys of our rooms;
By the mined root the leaves will overflow.

December, old leech, has leafed through Autumn's store
Where Poland has unleashed its dogs
To bay the moon upon the Black Rock shore:
Under our windows, on the rotten logs
The moonbeam, bobbing like an apple, snags
The undertow. O Christ, the spiralling years
Slither with child and manger to a ball
Of ice; and what is man? We tear our rags
To hang the Furies by their itching ears,
And the green needles nail us to the wall.

After the Surprising Conversions

September twenty-second, Sir: today
I answer. In the latter part of May,
Hard on our Lord's Ascension, it began
To be more sensible. A gentleman
Of more than common understanding, strict

In morals, pious in behaviour, kicked
Against our goad. A man of some renown,
An useful, honoured person in the town,
He came of melancholy parents; prone
To secret spells, for years they kept alone—
His uncle, I believe, was killed of it:
Good people, but of too much or little wit.
I preached one Sabbath on a text from Kings;
He showed concernment for his soul. Some things
In his experience were hopeful. He
Would sit and watch the wind knocking a tree
And praise this countryside our Lord has made.
Once when a poor man's heifer died, he laid
A shilling on the doorsill; though a thirst
For loving shook him like a snake, he durst
Not entertain much hope of his estate
In heaven. Once we saw him sitting late
Behind his attic window by a light
That guttered on his Bible; through that night
He meditated terror, and he seemed
Beyond advice or reason, for he dreamed
That he was called to trumpet Judgment Day
To Concord. In the latter part of May
He cut his throat. And though the coroner
Judged him delirious, soon a noisome stir
Palsied our village. At Jehovah's nod
Satan seemed more let loose amongst us: God
Abandoned us to Satan, and he pressed
Us hard, until we thought we could not rest
Till we had done with life. Content was gone.
All the good work was quashed. We were undone.
The breath of God had carried out a planned
And sensible withdrawal from this land;
The multitude, once unconcerned with doubt,
Once neither callous, curious nor devout,
Jumped at broadnoon, as though some peddler groaned
At it in its familiar twang: 'My friend,

Cut your own throat. Cut your own throat. Now! Now!'
September twenty-second, Sir, the bough
Cracks with the unpicked apples, and at dawn
The small-mouthed bass breaks water, gorged with spawn.

New Year's Day

Again and then again . . . the year is born
To ice and death, and it will never do
To skulk behind storm-windows by the stove
To hear the postgirl sounding her French horn
When the thin tidal ice is wearing through.
Here is the understanding not to love
Each other, or tomorrow that will sieve
Our resolutions. While we live, we live

To snuff the smoke of victims. In the snow
The kitten heaved its hindlegs, as if fouled,
And died. We bent it in a Christmas box
And scattered blazing weeds to scare the crow
Until the snake-tailed sea-winds coughed and howled
For alms outside the church whose double locks
Wait for St Peter, the distorted key.
Under St Peter's bell the parish sea

Swells with its smelt into the burlap shack
Where Joseph plucks his hand-lines like a harp,
And hears the fearful *Puer natus est*
Of Circumcision, and relives the wrack
And howls of Jesus whom he holds. How sharp
The burden of the Law before the beast:
Time and the grindstone and the knife of God.
The Child is born in blood, O child of blood.

The Quaker Graveyard in
Nantucket

(FOR WARREN WINSLOW, DEAD AT SEA)

*Let man have dominion over the fishes of the sea and the fowls of the air
and the beasts and the whole earth, and every creeping creature that moveth
upon the earth.*

I

A brackish reach of shoal off Madaket,—
The sea was still breaking violently and night
Had steamed into our North Atlantic Fleet,
When the drowned sailor clutched the drag-net. Light
Flashed from his matted head and marble feet,
He grappled at the net
With the coiled, hurdling muscles of his thighs:
The corpse was bloodless, a botch of reds and whites,
Its open, staring eyes
Were lustreless dead-lights
Or cabin-windows on a stranded hulk
Heavy with sand. We weight the body, close
Its eyes and heave it seaward whence it came,
Where the heel-headed dogfish barks its nose
On Ahab's void and forehead; and the name
Is blocked in yellow chalk.
Sailors, who pitch this portent at the sea
Where dreadnoughts shall confess
Its heel-bent deity,
When you are powerless
To sand-bag this Atlantic bulwark, faced
By the earth-shaker, green, unwearied, chaste
In his steel scales: ask for no Orphean lute
To pluck life back. The guns of the steeled fleet
Recoil and then repeat
The hoarse salute.

II

Whenever winds are moving and their breath
Heaves at the roped-in bulwarks of this pier,
The terns and sea-gulls tremble at your death
In these home waters. Sailor, can you hear
The Pequod's sea wings, beating landward, fall
Headlong and break on our Atlantic wall
Off 'Sconset, where the yawning S-boats splash
The bellbuoy, with ballooning spinnakers,
As the entangled, screeching mainsheet clears
The blocks: off Madaket, where lubbers lash
The heavy surf and throw their long lead squids
For blue-fish? Sea-gulls blink their heavy lids
Seaward. The winds' wings beat upon the stones,
Cousin, and scream for you and the claws rush
At the sea's throat and wring it in the slush
Of this old Quaker graveyard where the bones
Cry out in the long night for the hurt beast
Bobbing by Ahab's whaleboats in the East.

III

All you recovered from Poseidon died
With you, my cousin, and the harrowed brine
Is fruitless on the blue beard of the god,
Stretching beyond us to the castles in Spain,
Nantucket's westward haven. To Cape Cod
Guns, cradled on the tide,
Blast the eelgrass about a waterclock
Of bilge and backwash, roil the salt and sand
Lashing earth's scaffold, rock
Our warships in the hand
Of the great God, where time's contrition blues
Whatever it was these Quaker sailors lost
In the mad scramble of their lives. They died
When time was open-eyed,
Wooden and childish; only bones abide
There, in the nowhere, where their boats were tossed
Sky-high, where mariners had fabled news

Of IS, the whited monster. What it cost
Them is their secret. In the sperm-whale's slick
I see the Quakers drown and hear their cry:
'If God himself had not been on our side,
If God himself had not been on our side,
When the Atlantic rose against us, why,
Then it had swallowed us up quick.'

IV

This is the end of the whaleroad and the whale
Who spewed Nantucket bones on the thrashed swell
And stirred the troubled waters to whirlpools
To send the Pequod packing off to hell:
This is the end of them, three-quarters fools,
Snatching at straws to sail
Seaward and seaward on the turntail whale,
Spouting out blood and water as it rolls,
Sick as a dog to these Atlantic shoals:
Clamavimus, O depths. Let the sea-gulls wail

For water, for the deep where the high tide
Mutters to its hurt self, mutters and ebbs.
Waves wallow in their wash, go out and out,
Leave only the death-rattle of the crabs,
The beach increasing, its enormous snout
Sucking the ocean's side.
This is the end of running on the waves;
We are poured out like water. Who will dance
The mast-lashed master of Leviathans
Up from this field of Quakers in their unstoned graves?

V

When the whale's viscera go and the roll
Of its corruption overruns this world
Beyond tree-swept Nantucket and Wood's Hole
And Martha's Vineyard, Sailor, will your sword
Whistle and fall and sink into the fat?
In the great ash-pit of Jehoshaphat

The bones cry for the blood of the white whale,
The fat flukes arch and whack about its ears,
The death-lance churns into the sanctuary, tears
The gun-blue swingle, heaving like a flail,
And hacks the coiling life out: it works and drags
And rips the sperm-whale's midriff into rags,
Gobbets of blubber spill to wind and weather,
Sailor, and gulls go round the stoven timbers
Where the morning stars sing out together
And thunder shakes the white surf and dismembers
The red flag hammered in the mast-head. Hide,
Our steel, Jonas Messias, in Thy side.

VI

OUR LADY OF WALSINGHAM

There once the penitents took off their shoes
And then walked barefoot the remaining mile;
And the small trees, a stream, and hedgerows file
Slowly along the munching English lane,
Like cows to the old shrine, until you lose
Track of your dragging pain.
The stream flows down under the druid tree,
Shiloah's whirlpools gurgle and make glad
The castle of God. Sailor, you were glad
And whistled Sion by that stream. But see:

Our Lady, too small for her canopy,
Sits near the altar. There's no comeliness
At all or charm in that expressionless
Face with its heavy eyelids. As before,
This face, for centuries a memory,
Non est species, neque decor,
Expressionless, expresses God: it goes
Past castled Sion. She knows what God knows,
Not Calvary's Cross nor crib at Bethlehem
Now, and the world shall come to Walsingham.

VII

The empty winds are creaking and the oak
Splatters and splatters on the cenotaph,
The boughs are trembling and a gaff
Bobs on the untimely stroke
Of the greased wash exploding on a shoal-bell
In the old mouth of the Atlantic. It's well;
Atlantic, you are fouled with the blue sailors,
Sea-monsters, upward angel, downward fish:
Unmarried and corroding, spare of flesh
Mart once of supercilious, wing'd clippers,
Atlantic, where your bell-trap guts its spoil
You could cut the brackish winds with a knife
Here in Nantucket, and cast up the time
When the Lord God formed man from the sea's slime
And breathed into his face the breath of life,
And blue-lung'd combers lumbered to the kill.
The Lord survives the rainbow of His will.

Memories of West Street and Lepke

Only teaching on Tuesday, book-worming
in pajamas fresh from the washer each morning,
I hog a whole house on Boston's
'hardly passionate Marlborough Street',
where even the man
scavenging filth in the back alley trash cans,
has two children, a beach wagon, a helpmate,
and is a 'young Republican'.
I have a nine months' daughter,
young enough to be my granddaughter.
Like the sun she rises in her flame-flamingo infants' wear.

These are the tranquillized *Fifties*,
and I am forty. Ought I to regret my seedtime?
I was a fire-breathing Catholic C.O.,

and made my manic statement,
telling off the state and president, and then
sat waiting sentence in the bull pen
beside a Negro boy with curlicues
of marijuana in his hair.

Given a year,
I walked on the roof of the West Street Jail, a short
enclosure like my school soccer court,
and saw the Hudson River once a day
through sooty clothesline entanglements
and bleaching khaki tenements.
Strolling, I yammered metaphysics with Abramowitz,
a jaundice-yellow ('it's really tan')
and fly-weight pacifist,
so vegetarian,
he wore rope shoes and preferred fallen fruit.
He tried to convert Bioff and Brown,
the Hollywood pimps, to his diet.
Hairy, muscular, suburban,
wearing chocolate double-breasted suits,
they blew their tops and beat him black and blue.

I was so out of things, I'd never heard
of the Jehovah's Witnesses.
'Are you a C.O.?' I asked a fellow jailbird.
'No,' he answered. 'I'm a J.W.'
He taught me the 'hospital tuck',
and pointed out the T-shirted back
of *Murder Incorporated*'s Czar Lepke,
there piling towels on a rack,
or dawdling off to his little segregated cell full
of things forbidden the common man:
a portable radio, a dresser, two toy American
flags tied together with a ribbon of Easter palm.
Flabby, bald, lobotomized,
he drifted in a sheepish calm,

where no agonizing reappraisal
jarred his concentration on the electric chair—
hanging like an oasis in his air
of lost connections . . .

Skunk Hour

FOR ELIZABETH BISHOP

Nautilus Island's hermit
heiress still lives through winter in her Spartan cottage;
her sheep still graze above the sea.
Her son's a bishop. Her farmer
is first selectman in our village,
she's in her dotage.

Thirsting for
the hierarchic privacy
of Queen Victoria's century,
she buys up all
the eyesores facing her shore,
and lets them fall.

The season's ill—
we've lost our summer millionaire,
who seemed to leap from an L. L. Bean
catalogue. His nine-knot yawl
was auctioned off to lobstermen.
A red fox stain covers Blue Hill.

And now our fairy
decorator brightens his shop for fall,
his fishnet's filled with orange cork,
orange, his cobbler's bench and awl,
there is no money in his work,
he'd rather marry.

One dark night,
my Tudor Ford climbed the hill's skull,
I watched for love-cars. Lights turned down,
they lay together, hull to hull,
where the graveyard shelves on the town. . . .
My mind's not right.

A car radio bleats,
'Love, O careless Love . . .' I hear
my ill-spirit sob in each blood cell,
as if my hand were at its throat. . . .
I myself am hell,
nobody's here—

only skunks, that search
in the moonlight for a bite to eat.
They march on their soles up Main Street:
white stripes, moonstruck eyes' red fire
under the chalk-dry and spar spire
of the Trinitarian Church.

I stand on top
of our back steps and breathe the rich air—
a mother skunk with her column of kittens swills the garbage
    pail.
She jabs her wedge-head in a cup
of sour cream, drops her ostrich tail,
and will not scare.

For the Union Dead

'Relinquunt omnia servare rem publicam.'

The old South Boston Aquarium stands
in a Sahara of snow now. Its broken windows are boarded.
The bronze weathervane cod has lost half its scales.
The airy tanks are dry.

Once my nose crawled like a snail on the glass;
my hand tingled
to burst the bubbles
drifting from the noses of the cowed, compliant fish.

My hand draws back. I often sigh still
for the dark downward and vegetating kingdom
of the fish and reptile. One morning last March,
I pressed against the new barbed and galvanized

fence on the Boston Common. Behind their cage,
yellow dinosaur steamshovels were grunting
as they cropped up tons of mush and grass
to gouge their underworld garage.

Parking spaces luxuriate like civic
sandpiles in the heart of Boston.
A girdle of orange, Puritan-pumpkin colored girders
braces the tingling Statehouse,

shaking over the excavations, as it faces Colonel Shaw
and his bell-cheeked Negro infantry
on St Gaudens' shaking Civil War relief,
propped by a plank splint against the garage's earthquake.

Two months after marching through Boston,
half the regiment was dead;
at the dedication,
William James could almost hear the bronze Negroes breathe.

Their monument sticks like a fishbone
in the city's throat.
Its Colonel is as lean
as a compass-needle.

He has an angry wrenlike vigilance,
a greyhound's gentle tautness;
he seems to wince at pleasure,
and suffocate for privacy.

He is out of bounds now. He rejoices in man's lovely,
peculiar power to choose life and die—
when he leads his black soldiers to death,
he cannot bend his back.

On a thousand small town New England greens,
the old white churches hold their air
of sparse, sincere rebellion; frayed flags
quilt the graveyards of the Grand Army of the Republic.

The stone statues of the abstract Union Soldier
grow slimmer and younger each year—
wasp-waisted, they doze over muskets
and muse through their sideburns. . . .

Shaw's father wanted no monument
except the ditch,
where his son's body was thrown
and lost with his 'niggers'.

The ditch is nearer.
There are no statues for the last war here;
on Boylston Street, a commercial photograph
shows Hiroshima boiling

over a Mosler Safe, the 'Rock of Ages'
that survived the blast. Space is nearer.
When I crouch to my television set,
the drained faces of Negro school-children rise like balloons.

Colonel Shaw
is riding on his bubble,
he waits
for the blesséd break.

The Aquarium is gone. Everywhere,
giant finned cars nose forward like fish;
a savage servility
slides by on grease.

Mr Edwards and the Spider

I saw the spiders marching through the air,
Swimming from tree to tree that mildewed day
   In latter August when the hay
    Came creaking to the barn. But where
      The wind is westerly,
Where gnarled November makes the spiders fly
Into the apparitions of the sky,
They purpose nothing but their ease and die
Urgently beating east to sunrise and the sea;

What are we in the hands of the great God?
It was in vain you set up thorn and briar
   In battle array against the fire
    And treason crackling in your blood;
      For the wild thorns grow tame
And will do nothing to oppose the flame;
Your lacerations tell the losing game
You play against a sickness past your cure.
How will the hands be strong? How will the heart endure?

A very little thing, a little worm,
Or hourglass-blazoned spider, it is said,
   Can kill a tiger. Will the dead
    Hold up his mirror and affirm
      To the four winds the smell
And flash of his authority? It's well
If God who holds you to the pit of hell,
Much as one holds a spider, will destroy,
Baffle and dissipate your soul. As a small boy

On Windsor Marsh, I saw the spider die
When thrown into the bowels of fierce fire:
   There's no long struggle, no desire
    To get up on its feet and fly—
      It stretches out its feet
And dies. This is the sinner's last retreat;

Yes, and no strength exerted on the heat
Then sinews the abolished will, when sick
And full of burning, it will whistle on a brick.

But who can plumb the sinking of that soul?
Josiah Hawley, picture yourself cast
   Into a brick-kiln where the blast
   Fans your quick vitals to a coal—
     If measured by a glass,
How long would it seem burning! Let there pass
A minute, ten, ten trillion; but the blaze
Is infinite, eternal: this is death,
To die and know it. This is the Black Widow, death.

Philip Larkin

Lines on a Young Lady's Photograph Album

At last you yielded up the album, which,
Once open, sent me distracted. All your ages
Matt and glossy on the thick black pages!
Too much confectionery, too rich:
I choke on such nutritious images.

My swivel eye hungers from pose to pose—
In pigtails, clutching a reluctant cat;
Or furred yourself, a sweet girl-graduate;
Or lifting a heavy-headed rose
Beneath a trellis, or in a trilby hat

(Faintly disturbing, that, in several ways)—
From every side you strike at my control,
Not least through these disquieting chaps who loll
At ease about your earlier days:
Not quite your class, I'd say, dear, on the whole.

But o, photography! as no art is,
Faithful and disappointing! that records
Dull days as dull, and hold-it smiles as frauds,
And will not censor blemishes
Like washing-lines, and Hall's-Distemper boards,

But shows the cat as disinclined, and shades
A chin as doubled when it is, what grace
Your candour thus confers upon her face!
How overwhelmingly persuades
That this is a real girl in a real place,

In every sense empirically true!
Or is it just *the past*? Those flowers, that gate,
These misty parks and motors, lacerate
Simply by being over; you
Contract my heart by looking out of date.

Yes, true; but in the end, surely, we cry
Not only at exclusion, but because
It leaves us free to cry. We know *what was*
Won't call on us to justify
Our grief, however hard we yowl across

The gap from eye to page. So I am left
To mourn (without a chance of consequence)
You, balanced on a bike against a fence;
To wonder if you'd spot the theft
Of this one of you bathing; to condense,

In short, a past that no one now can share,
No matter whose your future; calm and dry,
It holds you like a heaven, and you lie
Unvariably lovely there,
Smaller and clearer as the years go by.

Wants

Beyond all this, the wish to be alone:
However the sky grows dark with invitation-cards
However we follow the printed directions of sex
However the family is photographed under the flagstaff—
Beyond all this, the wish to be alone.

Beneath it all, desire of oblivion runs:
Despite the artful tensions of the calendar,
The life insurance, the tabled fertility rites,
The costly aversion of the eyes from death—
Beneath it all, desire of oblivion runs.

Church Going

Once I am sure there's nothing going on
I step inside, letting the door thud shut.
Another church: matting, seats, and stone,
And little books; sprawlings of flowers, cut
For Sunday, brownish now; some brass and stuff
Up at the holy end; the small neat organ;
And a tense, musty, unignorable silence,
Brewed God knows how long. Hatless, I take off
My cycle-clips in awkward reverence,

Move forward, run my hand around the font.
From where I stand, the roof looks almost new—
Cleaned, or restored? Someone would know: I don't.
Mounting the lectern, I peruse a few
Hectoring large-scale verses, and pronounce
'Here endeth' much more loudly than I'd meant.
The echoes snigger briefly. Back at the door
I sign the book, donate an Irish sixpence,
Reflect the place was not worth stopping for.

Yet stop I did: in fact I often do,
And always end much at a loss like this,
Wondering what to look for; wondering, too,
When churches fall completely out of use
What we shall turn them into, if we shall keep
A few cathedrals chronically on show,
Their parchment, plate and pyx in locked cases,
And let the rest rent-free to rain and sheep.
Shall we avoid them as unlucky places?

Or, after dark, will dubious women come
To make their children touch a particular stone;
Pick simples for a cancer; or on some
Advised night see walking a dead one?
Power of some sort or other will go on
In games, in riddles, seemingly at random;

But superstition, like belief, must die,
And what remains when disbelief has gone?
Grass, weedy pavement, brambles, buttress, sky,

A shape less recognisable each week,
A purpose more obscure. I wonder who
Will be the last, the very last, to seek
This place for what it was; one of the crew
That tap and jot and know what rood-lofts were?
Some ruin-bibber, randy for antique,
Or Christmas-addict, counting on a whiff
Of gown-and-bands and organ-pipes and myrrh?
Or will he be my representative,

Bored, uninformed, knowing the ghostly silt
Dispersed, yet tending to this cross of ground
Through suburb scrub because it held unspilt
So long and equably what since is found
Only in separation—marriage, and birth,
And death, and thoughts of these—for which was built
This special shell? For, though I've no idea
What this accoutred frowsty barn is worth,
It pleases me to stand in silence here;

A serious house on serious earth it is,
In whose blent air all our compulsions meet,
Are recognised, and robed as destinies.
And that much never can be obsolete,
Since someone will forever be surprising
A hunger in himself to be more serious,
And gravitating with it to this ground,
Which, he once heard, was proper to grow wise in,
If only that so many dead lie round.

Toads

Why should I let the toad *work*
    Squat on my life?
Can't I use my wit as a pitchfork
    And drive the brute off?

Six days of the week it soils
    With its sickening poison—
Just for paying a few bills!
    That's out of proportion.

Lots of folk live on their wits:
    Lecturers, lispers,
Losels, loblolly-men, louts—
    They don't end as paupers;

Lots of folks live up lanes
    With fires in a bucket,
Eat windfalls and tinned sardines—
    They seem to like it.

Their nippers have got bare feet,
    Their unspeakable wives
Are skinny as whippets—and yet
    No one actually *starves.*

Ah, were I courageous enough
    To shout *Stuff your pension!*
But I know, all too well, that's the stuff
    That dreams are made on:

For something sufficiently toad-like
    Squats in me, too;
Its hunkers are heavy as hard luck,
    And cold as snow,

And will never allow me to blarney
  My way to getting
The fame and the girl and the money
  All at one sitting.

I don't say, one bodies the other
  One's spiritual truth;
But I do say it's hard to lose either,
  When you have both.

Poetry of Departures

Sometimes you hear, fifth-hand,
As epitaph:
He chucked up everything
And just cleared off,
And always the voice will sound
Certain you approve
This audacious, purifying,
Elemental move.

And they are right, I think.
We all hate home
And having to be there:
I detest my room,
Its specially-chosen junk,
The good books, the good bed,
And my life, in perfect order:
So to hear it said

He walked out on the whole crowd
Leaves me flushed and stirred,
Like *Then she undid her dress*
Or *Take that you bastard;*

Surely I can, if he did?
And that helps me stay
Sober and industrious.
But I'd go today,

Yes, swagger the nut-strewn roads,
Crouch in the fo'c'sle
Stubbly with goodness, if
It weren't so artificial,
Such a deliberate step backwards
To create an object:
Books; china; a life
Reprehensibly perfect.

If, My Darling

If my darling were once to decide
Not to stop at my eyes,
But to jump, like Alice, with floating skirt into my head,

She would find no tables and chairs,
No mahogany claw-footed sideboards,
No undisturbed embers;

The tantalus would not be filled, nor the fender-seat cosy,
Nor the shelves stuffed with small-printed books for the Sabbath,
Nor the butler bibulous, the housemaids lazy:

She would find herself looped with the creep of varying light,
Monkey-brown, fish-grey, a string of infected circles
Loitering like bullies, about to coagulate;

Delusions that shrink to the size of a woman's glove
Then sicken inclusively outwards. She would also remark
The unwholesome floor, as it might be the skin of a grave,

From which ascends an adhesive sense of betrayal,
A Grecian statue kicked in the privates, money,
A swill-tub of finer feelings. But most of all

She'd be stopping her ears against the incessant recital
Intoned by reality, larded with technical terms,
Each one   double-yolked with meaning and meaning's rebuttal:

For the skirl of that bulletin unpicks the world like a knot,
And to hear how the past is past and the future neuter
Might knock my darling off her unpriceable pivot.

Faith Healing

Slowly the women file to where he stands
Upright in rimless glasses, silver hair,
Dark suit, white collar. Stewards tirelessly
Persuade them onwards to his voice and hands,
Within whose warm spring rain of loving care
Each dwells some twenty seconds. *Now, dear child,
What's wrong,* the deep American voice demands,
And, scarcely pausing, goes into a prayer
Directing God about this eye, that knee.
Their heads are clasped abruptly; then, exiled

Like losing thoughts, they go in silence; some
Sheepishly stray, not back into their lives
Just yet; but some stay stiff, twitching and loud
With deep hoarse tears, as if a kind of dumb
And idiot child within them still survives
To re-awake at kindness, thinking a voice
At last calls them alone, that hands have come
To lift and lighten; and such joy arrives
Their thick tongues blort, their eyes squeeze grief, a crowd
Of huge unheard answers jam and rejoice—

What's wrong! Moustached in flowered frocks they shake:
By now, all's wrong. In everyone there sleeps
A sense of life lived according to love.
To some it means the difference they could make
By loving others, but across most it sweeps
As all they might have done had they been loved.
That nothing cures. An immense slackening ache,
As when, thawing, the rigid landscape weeps,
Spreads slowly through them—that, and the voice above
Saying *Dear child*, and all time has disproved.

An Arundel Tomb

Side by side, their faces blurred,
The earl and countess lie in stone,
Their proper habits vaguely shown
As jointed armour, stiffened pleat,
And that faint hint of the absurd—
The little dogs under their feet.

Such plainness of the pre-baroque
Hardly involves the eye, until
It meets his left-hand gauntlet, still
Clasped empty in the other; and
One sees, with a sharp tender shock,
His hand withdrawn, holding her hand.

They would not think to lie so long.
Such faithfulness in effigy

Was just a detail friends would see:
A sculptor's sweet commissioned grace
Thrown off in helping to prolong
The Latin names around the base.

They would not guess how early in
Their supine stationary voyage
The air would change to soundless damage,
Turn the old tenantry away;
How soon succeeding eyes begin
To look, not read. Rigidly they

Persisted, linked, through lengths and breadths
Of time. Snow fell, undated. Light
Each summer thronged the glass. A bright
Litter of birdcalls strewed the same
Bone-riddled ground. And up the paths
The endless altered people came,

Washing at their identity.
Now, helpless in the hollow of
An unarmorial age, a trough
Of smoke in slow suspended skeins
Above their scrap of history,
Only an attitude remains:

Time has transfigured them into
Untruth. The stone fidelity
They hardly meant has come to be
Their final blazon, and to prove
Our almost-instinct almost true:
What will survive of us is love.

Elizabeth Bishop

The Map

Land lies in water; it is shadowed green.
Shadows, or are they shallows, at its edges
showing the line of long sea-weeded ledges
where weeds hang to the simple blue from green.
Or does the land lean down to lift the sea from under,
drawing it unperturbed around itself?
Along the fine tan sandy shelf
is the land tugging at the sea from under?

The shadow of Newfoundland lies flat and still.
Labrador's yellow, where the moony Eskimo
has oiled it. We can stroke these lovely bays,
under a glass as if they were expected to blossom,
or as if to provide a clean cage for invisible fish.
The names of seashore towns run out to sea,
the names of cities cross the neighboring mountains
—the printer here experiencing the same excitement
as when emotion too far exceeds its cause.
These peninsulas take the water between thumb and finger
like women feeling for the smoothness of yard-goods.

Mapped waters are more quiet than the land is,
lending the land their waves' own conformation:
and Norway's hare runs south in agitation,
profiles investigate the sea, where land is.
Are they assigned, or can the countries pick their colors?
—What suits the character or the native waters best.
Topography displays no favorites; North's as near as West.
More delicate than the historians' are the map-makers' colors.

The Imaginary Iceberg

We'd rather have the iceberg than the ship,
although it meant the end of travel.
Although it stood stock-still like cloudy rock
and all the sea were moving marble.
We'd rather have the iceberg than the ship;
we'd rather own this breathing plain of snow
though the ship's sails were laid upon the sea
as the snow lies undissolved upon the water.
O solemn, floating field,
are you aware an iceberg takes repose
with you, and when it wakes may pasture on your snows?

This is a scene a sailor'd give his eyes for.
The ship's ignored. The iceberg rises
and sinks again; its glassy pinnacles
correct elliptics in the sky.
This is a scene where he who treads the boards
is artlessly rhetorical. The curtain
is light enough to rise on finest ropes
that airy twists of snow provide.
The wits of these white peaks
spar with the sun. Its weight the iceberg dares
upon a shifting stage and stands and stares.

This iceberg cuts its facets from within.
Like jewelry from a grave
it saves itself perpetually and adorns
only itself, perhaps the snows
which so surprise us lying on the sea.
Good-bye, we say, good-bye, the ship steers off
where waves give in to one another's waves
and clouds run in a warmer sky.
Icebergs behoove the soul
(both being self-made from elements least visible)
to see them so: fleshed, fair, erected indivisible.

At the Fishhouses

Although it is a cold evening,
down by one of the fishhouses
an old man sits netting,
his net, in the gloaming almost invisible,
a dark purple-brown,
and his shuttle worn and polished.
The air smells so strong of codfish
it makes one's nose run and one's eyes water.
The five fishhouses have steeply peaked roofs
and narrow, cleated gangplanks slant up
to storerooms in the gables
for the wheelbarrows to be pushed up and down on.
All is silver: the heavy surface of the sea,
swelling slowly as if considering spilling over,
is opaque, but the silver of the benches,
the lobster pots, and masts, scattered
among the wild jagged rocks,
is of an apparent translucence
like the small old buildings with an emerald moss
growing on their shoreward walls.
The big fish tubs are completely lined
with layers of beautiful herring scales
and the wheelbarrows are similarly plastered
with creamy iridescent coats of mail,
with small iridescent flies crawling on them.
Up on the little slope behind the houses,
set in the sparse bright sprinkle of grass,
is an ancient wooden capstan,
cracked, with two long bleached handles
and some melancholy stains, like dried blood,
where the ironwork has rusted.
The old man accepts a Lucky Strike.
He was a friend of my grandfather.
We talk of the decline in the population

and of codfish and herring
while he waits for a herring boat to come in.
There are sequins on his vest and on his thumb.
He has scraped the scales, the principal beauty,
from unnumbered fish with that black old knife,
the blade of which is almost worn away.

Down at the water's edge, at the place
where they haul up the boats, up the long ramp
descending into the water, thin silver
tree trunks are laid horizontally
across the gray stones, down and down
at intervals of four or five feet.

Cold dark deep and absolutely clear,
element bearable to no mortal,
to fish and to seals . . . One seal particularly
I have seen here evening after evening.
He was curious about me. He was interested in music;
like me a believer in total immersion,
so I used to sing him Baptist hymns.
I also sang 'A Mighty Fortress Is Our God.'
He stood up in the water and regarded me
steadily, moving his head a little.
Then he would disappear, then suddenly emerge
almost in the same spot, with a sort of shrug
as if it were against his better judgment.
Cold dark deep and absolutely clear,
the clear gray icy water . . . Back, behind us,
the dignified tall firs begin.
Bluish, associating with their shadows,
a million Christmas trees stand
waiting for Christmas. The water seems suspended
above the rounded gray and blue-gray stones.
I have seen it over and over, the same sea, the same,
slightly, indifferently swinging above the stones,

icily free above the stones,
above the stones and then the world.
If you should dip your hand in,
your wrist would ache immediately,
your bones would begin to ache and your hand would burn
as if the water were a transmutation of fire
that feeds on stones and burns with a dark gray flame.
If you tasted it, it would first taste bitter,
then briny, then surely burn your tongue.
It is like what we imagine knowledge to be:
dark, salt, clear, moving, utterly free,
drawn from the cold hard mouth
of the world, derived from the rocky breasts
forever, flowing and drawn, and since
our knowledge is historical, flowing, and flown.

Cape Breton

Out on the high 'bird islands', Ciboux and Hertford,
the razorbill auks and the silly-looking puffins all stand
with their backs to the mainland
in solemn, uneven lines along the cliff's brown grass-frayed edge,
while the few sheep pastured there go 'Baaa, baaa'.
(Sometimes, frightened by aeroplanes, they stampede
and fall over into the sea or onto the rocks.)
The silken water is weaving and weaving,
disappearing under the mist equally in all directions,
lifted and penetrated now and then
by one shag's dripping serpent-neck,
and somewhere the mist incorporates the pulse,
rapid but unurgent, of a motorboat.

The same mist hangs in thin layers
among the valleys and gorges of the mainland
like rotting snow-ice sucked away
almost to spirit; the ghosts of glaciers drift
among those folds and folds of fir: spruce and hackmatack—
dull, dead, deep peacock-colors,
each riser distinguished from the next
by an irregular nervous saw-tooth edge,
alike, but certain as a stereoscopic view.

The wild road clambers along the brink of the coast.
On it stand occasional small yellow bulldozers,
but without their drivers, because today is Sunday.
The little white churches have been dropped into the matted hills
like lost quartz arrowheads.
The road appears to have been abandoned.
Whatever the landscape had of meaning appears to have been
        abandoned,
unless the road is holding it back, in the interior,
where we cannot see,
where deep lakes are reputed to be,
and disused trails and mountains of rock
and miles of burnt forests standing in gray scratches
like the admirable scriptures made on stones by stones—
and these regions now have little to say for themselves
except in thousands of light song-sparrow songs floating upward
freely, dispassionately, through the mist, and meshing
in brown-wet, fine, torn fish-nets.

A small bus comes along, in up-and-down rushes,
packed with people, even to its step.
(On weekdays with groceries, spare automobile parts, and
        pump parts,
but today only two preachers extra, one carrying his frock coat
        on a hanger.)
It passes the closed roadside stand, the closed schoolhouse,

where today no flag is flying
from the rough-adzed pole topped with a white china doorknob.
It stops, and a man carrying a baby gets off,
climbs over a stile, and goes down through a small steep
        meadow,
which establishes its poverty in a snowfall of daisies,
to his invisible house beside the water.

The birds keep on singing, a calf bawls, the bus starts.
The thin mist follows
the white mutations of its dream;
an ancient chill is rippling the dark brooks.

Arrival at Santos

Here is a coast; here is a harbor;
here, after a meager diet of horizon, is some scenery:
impractically shaped and—who knows?—self-pitying
        mountains,
sad and harsh beneath their frivolous greenery,

with a little church on top of one. And warehouses,
some of them painted a feeble pink, or blue,
and some tall, uncertain palms. Oh, tourist,
is this how this country is going to answer you

and your immodest demands for a different world,
and a better life, and complete comprehension
of both at last, and immediately,
after eighteen days of suspension?

Finish your breakfast. The tender is coming,
a strange and ancient craft, flying a strange and brilliant rag.
So that's the flag. I never saw it before.
I somehow never thought of there *being* a flag,

but of course there was, all along. And coins, I presume,
and paper money; they remain to be seen.
And gingerly now we climb down the ladder backward,
myself and a fellow passenger named Miss Breen,

descending into the midst of twenty-six freighters
waiting to be loaded with green coffee beans.
Please, boy, do be more careful with that boat hook!
Watch out! Oh! It has caught Miss Breen's

skirt! There! Miss Breen is about seventy,
a retired police lieutenant, six feet tall,
with beautiful bright blue eyes and a kind expression.
Her home, when she is at home, is in Glens Fall

s, New York. There. We are settled.
The customs officials will speak English, we hope,
and leave us our bourbon and cigarettes.
Ports are necessities, like postage stamps, or soap,

but they seldom seem to care what impression they make,
or, like this, only attempt, since it does not matter,
the unassertive colors of soap, or postage stamps—
wasting away like the former, slipping the way the latter

do when we mail the letters we wrote on the boat,
either because the glue here is very inferior
or because of the heat. We leave Santos at once;
we are driving to the interior.

Questions of Travel

There are too many waterfalls here; the crowded streams
hurry too rapidly down to the sea,
and the pressure of so many clouds on the mountaintops
makes them spill over the sides in soft slow-motion,
turning to waterfalls under our very eyes.
—For if those streaks, those mile-long, shiny, tearstains,
aren't waterfalls yet,
in a quick age or so, as ages go here,
they probably will be.
But if the streams and clouds keep travelling, travelling,
the mountains look like the hulls of capsized ships,
slime-hung and barnacled.

Think of the long trip home.
Should we have stayed at home and thought of here?
Where should we be today?
Is it right to be watching strangers in a play
in this strangest of theatres?
What childishness is it that while there's a breath of life
in our bodies, we are determined to rush
to see the sun the other way around?
The tiniest green hummingbird in the world?
To stare at some inexplicable old stonework,
inexplicable and impenetrable,
at any view,
instantly seen and always, always delightful?
Oh, must we dream our dreams
and have them, too?
And have we room
for one more folded sunset, still quite warm?

But surely it would have been a pity
not to have seen the trees along this road,
really exaggerated in their beauty,

not to have seen them gesturing
like noble pantomimists, robed in pink.
—Not to have had to stop for gas and heard
the sad, two-noted, wooden tune
of disparate wooden clogs
carelessly clacking over
a grease-stained filling-station floor.
(In another country the clogs would all be tested.
Each pair there would have identical pitch.)
—A pity not to have heard
the other, less primitive music of the fat brown bird
who sings above the broken gasoline pump
in a bamboo church of Jesuit baroque:
three towers, five silver crosses.
—Yes, a pity not to have pondered,
blurr'dly and inconclusively,
on what connection can exist for centuries
between the crudest wooden footwear
and, careful and finicky,
the whittled fantasies of wooden cages.
—Never to have studied history in
the weak calligraphy of songbirds' cages.
—And never to have had to listen to rain
so much like politicians' speeches:
two hours of unrelenting oratory
and then a sudden golden silence
in which the traveller takes a notebook, writes:

'Is it lack of imagination that makes us come
to imagined places, not just stay at home?
Or could Pascal have been not entirely right
about just sitting quietly in one's room?

Continent, city, country, society:
the choice is never wide and never free.
And here, or there . . . No. Should we have stayed at home,
wherever that may be?'

Squatter's Children

On the unbreathing sides of hills
they play, a specklike girl and boy,
alone, but near a specklike house.
The sun's suspended eye
blinks casually, and then they wade
gigantic waves of light and shade.
A dancing yellow spot, a pup,
attends them. Clouds are piling up;

a storm piles up behind the house.
The children play at digging holes.
The ground is hard; they try to use
one of their father's tools,
a mattock with a broken haft
the two of them can scarcely lift.
It drops and clangs. Their laughter spreads
effulgence in the thunderheads,

weak flashes of inquiry
direct as is the puppy's bark.
But to their little, soluble,
unwarrantable ark,
apparently the rain's reply
consists of echolalia,
and Mother's voice, ugly as sin,
keeps calling to them to come in.

Children, the threshold of the storm
has slid beneath your muddy shoes;
wet and beguiled, you stand among
the mansions you may choose
out of a bigger house than yours,
whose lawfulness endures.
Its soggy documents retain
your rights in rooms of falling rain.

12 O'Clock News

gooseneck lamp

As you all know, tonight is the night of the full moon, half the world over. But here the moon seems to hang motionless in the sky. It gives very little light; it could be dead. Visibility is poor. Nevertheless, we shall try to give you some idea of the lay of the land and the present situation.

typewriter

The escarpment that rises abruptly from the central plain is in heavy shadow, but the elaborate terracing of its southern glacis gleams faintly in the dim light, like fish scales. What endless labor those small, peculiarly shaped terraces represent! And yet, on them the welfare of this tiny principality depends.

pile of mss.

A slight landslide occurred in the northwest about an hour ago. The exposed soil appears to be of poor quality: almost white, calcareous, and shaly. There are believed to have been no casualties.

typed sheet

Almost due north, our aerial reconnaissance reports the discovery of a large rectangular 'field', hitherto unknown to us, obviously man-made. It is dark-speckled. An airstrip? A cemetery?

envelopes

In this small, backward country, one of the most backward left in the world today, communications are crude and 'industrialization' and its products almost nonexistent. Strange to say, however, sign-boards are on a truly gigantic scale.

We have also received reports of a mysterious, oddly shaped, black structure, at an undisclosed distance to the east. Its presence was revealed only because its highly polished surface catches such feeble moonlight as prevails. The natural resources of the country being far from completely known to us, there is the possibility that this may be, or may contain, some powerful and terrifying 'secret weapon'. On the other hand, given what we *do* know, or have learned from our anthropologists and sociologists about this people, it may well be nothing more than a *numen*, or a great altar recently erected to one of their gods, to which, in their present historical state of superstition and helplessness, they attribute magical powers, and may even regard as a 'savior', one last hope of rescue from their grave difficulties.

ink-bottle

At last! One of the elusive natives has been spotted! He appears to be—rather, to have been —a unicyclist-courier, who may have met his end by falling from the height of the escarpment because of the deceptive illumination. Alive, he would have been small, but undoubtedly proud and erect, with the thick, bristling black hair typical of the indigenes.

typewriter eraser

From our superior vantage point, we can clearly see into a sort of dugout, possibly a shell crater, a 'nest' of soldiers. They lie heaped together, wearing the camouflage 'battle dress' intended for 'winter warfare'. They are in hideously con-

ashtray

torted positions, all dead. We can make out at
least eight bodies. These uniforms were designed
to be used in guerrilla warfare on the country's
one snow-covered mountain peak. The fact that
these poor soldiers are wearing them *here*, on
the plain, gives further proof, if proof were
necessary, either of the childishness and hopeless impracticality of this inscrutable people,
our opponents, or of the sad corruption of their
leaders.

Santarém

Of course I may be remembering it all wrong
after, after—how many years?

That golden evening I really wanted to go no farther;
more than anything else I wanted to stay awhile
in that conflux of two great rivers, Tapajós, Amazon,
grandly, silently flowing, flowing east.
Suddenly there'd been houses, people, and lots of mongrel
riverboats skittering back and forth
under a sky of gorgeous, under-lit clouds,
with everything gilded, burnished along one side,
and everything bright, cheerful, casual—or so it looked.
I liked the place; I liked the idea of the place.
Two rivers. Hadn't two rivers sprung
from the Garden of Eden? No, that was four
and they'd diverged. Here only two
and coming together. Even if one were tempted
to literary interpretations
such as: life/death, right/wrong, male/female
—such notions would have resolved, dissolved, straight off
in that watery, dazzling dialectic.

In front of the church, the Cathedral, rather
there was a modest promenade and a belvedere
about to fall into the river,
stubby palms, flamboyants like pans of embers,
buildings one story high, stucco, blue or yellow,
and one house faced with *azulejos*, buttercup yellow.
The street was deep in dark-gold river sand
damp from the ritual afternoon rain,
and teams of zebus plodded, gentle, proud,
and *blue*, with down-curved horns and hanging ears,
pulling carts with solid wheels.
The zebus' hooves, the people's feet
waded in golden sand,
dampered by golden sand,
so that almost the only sounds
were creaks and *shush, shush, shush.*

Two rivers full of crazy shipping—people
all apparently changing their minds, embarking,
disembarking, rowing clumsy dories.
(After the Civil War some Southern families
came here; here they could still own slaves.
They left occasional blue eyes, English names,
and *oars*. No other place, no one
on all the Amazon's four thousand miles
does anything but paddle.)
A dozen or so young nuns, white-habited,
waved gaily from an old stern-wheeler
getting up steam, already hung with hammocks
—off to their mission, days and days away
up God knows what lost tributary.
Side-wheelers, countless wobbling dugouts . . .
A cow stood up in one, quite calm,
chewing her cud while being ferried,
tipping, wobbling, somewhere, to be married.
A river schooner with raked masts
and violet-colored sails tacked in so close
her bowsprit seemed to touch the church

(Cathedral, rather!). A week or so before
there'd been a thunderstorm and the Cathedral'd
been struck by lightning. One tower had
a widening zigzag crack all the way down.
It was a miracle. The priest's house right next door
had been struck, too, and his brass bed
(the only one in town) galvanized black.
Graças a deus—he'd been in Belém.

In the blue pharmacy the pharmacist
had hung an empty wasps' nest from a shelf:
small, exquisite, clean matte white,
and hard as stucco. I admired it
so much he gave it to me.
Then—my ship's whistle blew. I couldn't stay.
Back on board, a fellow-passenger, Mr. Swan,
Dutch, the retiring head of Philips Electric,
really a very nice old man,
who wanted to see the Amazon before he died,
asked, 'What's that ugly thing?'

P. K. Page

Young Girls

Nothing, not even fear of punishment
can stop the giggle in a girl.
Oh mothers' trim
shapes on the chesterfield cannot dispel
their lolloping fatness.
Adolescence tumbles about in them
on cinder schoolyard or behind the expensive gates.

See them in class like porpoises
with smiles and tears
loosed from the same subterranean faucet; some
find individual adventure in
the obtuse angle, some in a phrase
that leaps like a smaller fish from a sea of words.
But most, deep in their daze, dawdle and roll,
their little breasts like wounds beneath their clothes.

A shoal of them in a room makes it a pool.
How can one teacher keep the water out,
or, being adult, find the springs and taps
of their tempers and tortures?
Who on a field filled with their female cries
can reel them in on a line of words
or land them neatly in a net?
On the dry ground they goggle, flounder, flap.

Too much weeping in them and unfamiliar blood
has set them perilously afloat.
Not divers these—but as if the waters rose in flood—

making them partially amphibious
and always drowning a little and hearing bells;
until the day the shore line wavers less,
and caught and swung on the bright hooks of their sex,
earth becomes home, their natural element.

T-Bar

Relentless, black on white, the cable runs
through metal arches up the mountain side.
At intervals giant pickaxes are hung
on long hydraulic springs. The skiers ride
propped by the axehead, twin automatons
supported by its handle, one each side.

In twos they move slow motion up the steep
incision in the mountain. Climb. Climb.
Somnambulists, bolt upright in their sleep
their phantom poles swung lazily behind,
while to the right, the empty T-bars keep
in mute descent, slow monstrous jigging time.

Captive the skiers now and innocent,
wards of eternity, each pair alone.
They mount the easy vertical ascent,
pass through successive arches, bride and groom,
as through successive naves, are newly wed
participants in some recurring dream.

So do they move forever. Clocks are broken.
In zones of silence they grow tall and slow,
inanimate dreamers, mild and gentle-spoken
blood-brothers of the haemophilic snow

until the summit breaks and they awaken
imagos from the stricture of the tow.

Jerked from her chrysalis the sleeping bride
suffers too sudden freedom like a pain.
The dreaming bridegroom severed from her side
singles her out, the old wound aches again.
Uncertain, lost, upon a wintry height
these two, not separate, but no longer one.

Now clocks begin to peck and sing. The slow
extended minute like a rubber band
contracts to catapult them through the snow
in tandem trajectory while behind
etching the sky-line, obdurate and slow
the spastic T-bars pivot and descend.

The Stenographers

After the brief bivouac of Sunday,
their eyes, in the forced march of Monday to Saturday,
hoist the white flag, flutter in the snow-storm of paper,
haul it down and crack in the mid-sun of temper.

In the pause between the first draft and the carbon
they glimpse the smooth hours when they were children—
the ride in the ice-cart, the ice-man's name,
the end of the route and the long walk home;

remember the sea where floats at high tide
were sea marrows growing on the scatter-green vine
or spools of grey toffee, or wasps' nests on water;
remember the sand and the leaves of the country.

Bell rings and they go and the voice draws their pencil
like a sled across snow; when its runners are frozen
rope snaps and the voice then is pulling no burden
but runs like a dog on the winter of paper.

Their climates are winter and summer—no wind
for the kites of their hearts—no wind for a flight;
a breeze at the most, to tumble them over
and leave them like rubbish—the boy-friends of blood.

In the inch of the noon as they move they are stagnant.
The terrible calm of the noon is their anguish;
the lip of the counter, the shapes of the straws
like icicles breaking their tongues, are invaders.

Their beds are their oceans—salt water of weeping
the waves that they know—the tide before sleep;
and fighting to drown they assemble their sheep
in columns and watch them leap desks for their fences
and stare at them with their own mirror-worn faces.

In the felt of the morning the calico-minded,
sufficiently starched, insert papers, hit keys,
efficient and sure as their adding machines;
yet they weep in the vault, they are taut as net curtains
stretched upon frames. In their eyes I have seen
the pin men of madness in marathon trim
race round the track of the stadium pupil.

The Landlady

Through sepia air the boarders come and go,
impersonal as trains. Pass silently
the craving silence swallowing her speech;
click doors like shutters on her camera eye.

Because of her their lives become exact:
their entrances and exits are designed;
phone calls are cryptic. Oh, her ticklish ears
advance and fall back stunned.

Nothing is unprepared. They hold the walls
about them as they weep or laugh. Each face
is dialled to zero publicly. She peers
stippled with curious flesh;

pads on the patient landing like a pulse,
unlocks their keyholes with the wire of sight,
searches their rooms for clues when they are out,
pricks when they come home late.

Wonders when they are quiet, jumps when they move,
dreams that they dope or drink, trembles to know
the traffic of their brains, jaywalks their street
in clumsy shoes.

Yet knows them better than their closest friends:
their cupboards and the secrets of their drawers,
their books, their private mail, their photographs
are theirs and hers.

Knows when they wash, how frequently their clothes
go to the cleaners, what they like to eat,
their curvature of health, but even so
is not content.

And like a lover must know all, all, all.
Prays she may catch them unprepared at last
and palm the dreadful riddle of their skulls—
hoping the worst.

Stories of Snow

Those in the vegetable rain retain
an area behind their sprouting eyes
held soft and rounded with the dream of snow
precious and reminiscent as those globes—
souvenir of some never-nether land—
which hold their snow-storms circular, complete,
high in a tall and teakwood cabinet.

In countries where the leaves are large as hands
where flowers protrude their fleshy chins
and call their colours,
an imaginary snow-storm sometimes falls
among the lilies.
And in the early morning one will waken
to think the glowing linen of his pillow
a northern drift, will find himself mistaken
and lie back weeping.
And there the story shifts from head to head,
of how in Holland, from their feather beds
hunters arise and part the flakes and go
forth to the frozen lakes in search of swans—
the snow-light falling white along their guns,
their breath in plumes.
While tethered in the wind like sleeping gulls
ice-boats wait the raising of their wings
to skim the electric ice at such a speed
they leap jet strips of naked water,
and how these flying, sailing hunters feel
air in their mouths as terrible as ether.
And on the story runs that even drinks
in that white landscape dare to be no colour;
how flasked and water clear, the liquor slips
silver against the hunters' moving hips.
And of the swan in death these dreamers tell

of its last flight and how it falls, a plummet,
pierced by the freezing bullet
and how three feathers, loosened by the shot,
descend like snow upon it.
While hunters plunge their fingers in its down
deep as a drift, and dive their hands
up to the neck of the wrist
in that warm metamorphosis of snow
as gentle as the sort that woodsmen know
who, lost in the white circle, fall at last
and dream their way to death.

And stories of this kind are often told
in countries where great flowers bar the roads
with reds and blues which seal the route to snow—
as if, in telling, raconteurs unlock
the colour with its complement and go
through to the area behind the eyes
where silent, unrefractive whiteness lies.

Photos of a Salt Mine

How innocent their lives look,
how like a child's
dream of caves and winter, both combined;
the steep descent to whiteness
and the stope
with its striated walls
their folds all leaning as if pointing to
the greater whiteness still,
that great white bank
with its decisive front,
that seam upon a slope,
salt's lovely ice.

And wonderful underfoot the snow of salt
the fine
particles a broom could sweep,
one thinks
muckers might make angels in its drifts
as children do in snow,
lovers in sheets,
lie down and leave imprinted where they lay
a feathered creature holier than they.

And in the outworked stopes
with lamps and ropes
up miniature matterhorns
the miners climb
probe with their lights
the ancient folds of rock—
syncline and anticline—
and scoop from darkness an Aladdin's cave:
rubies and opals glitter from its walls.

But hoses douse the brilliance of these jewels,
melt fire to brine.
Salt's bitter water trickles thin and forms,
slow fathoms down,
a lake within a cave,
lacquered with jet—
white's opposite.
There grey on black the boating miners float
to mend the stays and struts of that old stope
and deeply underground
their words resound,
are multiplied by echo, swell and grow
and make a climate of a miner's voice.

So all the photographs like children's wishes
are filled with caves or winter,
innocence

has acted as a filter,
selected only beauty from the mine.
Except in the last picture,
it is shot
from an acute high angle. In a pit
figures the size of pins are strangely lit
and might be dancing but you know they're not.
Like Dante's vision of the nether hell
men struggle with the bright cold fires of salt,
locked in the black inferno of the rock:
the filter here, not innocence but guilt.

The Permanent Tourists

Somnolent through landscapes and by trees
nondescript, almost anonymous,
they alter as they enter foreign cities—
the terrible tourists with their empty eyes
longing to be filled with monuments.

Verge upon statues in the public squares
remembering the promise of memorials
yet never enter the entire event
as dogs, abroad in any kind of weather,
move perfectly within their rainy climate.

Lock themselves into snapshots on the steps
of monolithic bronze as if suspecting
the subtle mourning of the photograph
might later conjure in the memory
all they are now incapable of feeling.

And search all heroes out: the boy who gave
his life to save a town; the stolid queen;
forgotten politicians minus names
and the plunging war dead, permanently brave,
forever and ever going down to death.

Look, you can see them nude in any café
reading their histories from the bill of fare,
creating futures from a foreign teacup.
Philosophies like ferns bloom from the fable
that travel is broadening at the café table.

Yet somehow beautiful, they stamp the plaza.
Classic in their anxiety they call
all sculptured immemorial stone
into their passive eyes, as rivers
draw ruined columns to their placid glass.

Cook's Mountains

By naming them he made them.
They were there
before he came
but they were not the same.
It was his gaze
that glazed each one.
He saw
the Glass House Mountains in his glass.
They shone.

And still they shine.
We saw them as we drove—
sudden, surrealist, conical
they rose
out of the rain forest.

The driver said,
'Those are the Glass House Mountains up ahead.'

And instantly they altered to become
the sum of shape and name.
Two strangenesses united into one
more strange than either.
Neither of us now
remembers how they looked before they broke
the light to fragments as the driver spoke.

Like mounds of mica,
hive-shaped hothouses,
mountains of mirror glimmering
they form
in diamond panes behind the tree ferns of
the dark imagination,
burn and shake
the lovely light of Queensland like a bell
reflecting Cook upon a deck
his tongue
silvered with paradox and metaphor.

Brazilian Fazenda

That day all the slaves were freed
their manacles, anklets
left on the window ledge to rust in the moist air

and all the coffee ripened
like beads on a bush or balls of fire
as merry as Christmas

and the cows all calved and the calves all lived
such a moo.

On the wide verandah where birds in cages
sang among the bell flowers
I in a bridal hammock
white and tasselled
whistled

and bits fell out of the sky near Nossa Senhora
who had walked all the way in bare feet from Bahia

and the chapel was lit by a child's
fistful of marigolds on the red velvet altar
thrown like a golden ball.

Oh let me come back on a day
when nothing extraordinary happens
so I can stare
at the sugar white pillars
and black lace grills
of this pink house.

Arras

Consider a new habit—classical,
and trees espaliered on the wall like candelabra.
How still upon that lawn our sandalled feet.

But a peacock rattling his rattan tail and screaming
has found a point of entry. Through whose eye
did it insinuate in furled disguise
to shake its jewels and silk upon that grass?

The peaches hang like lanterns. No one joins
those figures on the arras.
                              Who am I
or who am I become that walking here
I am observer, other, Gemini,
starred for a green garden of cinema?

I ask, what did they deal me in this pack?
The cards, all suits, are royal when I look.
My fingers slipping on a monarch's face
twitch and grow slack.
I want a hand to clutch, a heart to crack.

No one is moving now, the stillness is
infinite. If I should make a break. . . .
take to my springy heels. . . . ? But nothing moves.
The spinning world is stuck upon its poles,
the stillness points a bone at me. I fear
the future on this arras.
                                    I confess:

It was my eye.
Voluptuous it came.
Its head the ferrule and its lovely tail
folded so sweetly; it was strangely slim
to fit the retina. And then it shook
and was a peacock—living patina,
eye-bright, maculate!
Does no one care?

I thought their hands might hold me if I spoke.
I dreamed the bite of fingers in my flesh,
their poke smashed by an image, but they stand
as if within a treacle, motionless,
folding slow eyes on nothing. While they stare
another line has trolled the encircling air,
another bird assumes its furled disguise.

The Glass Air

I dreamed my most extraordinary darling
gangling, come to share
my hot and prairie childhood

the first day loosed the mare from her picket
and rode her bareback
over the little foothills towards the mountains.

And on the second, striding from his tent,
twisted a noose of butcher's string.
Ingenious to my eyes the knots he tied.

The third bright day he laid the slack noose over
the gopher's burrow,
unhurried by the chase,

and lolled a full week, lazy, in the sun
until the head popped, sleek, enquiring.
The noose pulled tight around its throat.

Then the small fur lashed, lit out, hurling
about only to turn
tame silk in his palm

as privy harness, tangled from his pocket
with leash of string
slipped simply on.

But the toy beast and the long rein and the paid out lengths
of our youth snapped
as the creature jibbed and bit

and the bright blood ran out, the bright blood trickled over,
slowed, grew dark
lay sticky on our skins.

And we two, dots upon that endless plain, Leviathan became
and filled and broke
the glass air like twin figures, vast, in stone.

Irving Layton

Against This Death

I have seen respectable
death
served up like bread and wine
in stores and offices,
in club and hostel,
and from the streetcorner
church
that faces
two-ways;
I have seen death
served up
like ice.

Against this death,
slow, certain:
the body,
this burly sun,
the exhalations
of your breath,
your cheeks
rose and lovely,
and the secret
life
of the imagination
scheming freedom
from labour
and stone.

The Birth of Tragedy

And me happiest when I compose poems.
      Love, power, the huzza of battle
      are something, are much;
yet a poem includes them like a pool
      water and reflection.
In me, nature's divided things—
      tree, mould on tree—
      have their fruition;
I am their core. Let them swap,
bandy, like a flame swerve
I am their mouth; as a mouth I serve.

And I observe how the sensual moths
      big with odour and sunshine
      dart into the perilous shrubbery;
or drop their visiting shadows
      upon the garden I one year made
of flowering stone to be a footstool
      for the perfect gods:
      who, friends to the ascending orders,
sustain all passionate meditations
and call down pardons
for the insurgent blood.

A quiet madman, never far from tears,
      I lie like a slain thing
      under the green air the trees
inhabit, or rest upon a chair
      towards which the inflammable air
tumbles on many robins' wings;
      noting how seasonably
      leaf and blossom uncurl
and living things arrange their death,
while someone from afar off
blows birthday candles for the world.

Look, the Lambs
Are All Around Us!

Your figure, love,
curves itself
into a man's memory;
or to put it the way
a junior prof
at Mount Allison might,
Helen with her thick
absconding limbs
about the waist
of Paris
did no better.

Hell, my back's sunburnt
from so much love-making
in the open air.
The Primate (somebody
made a monkey of him)
and the Sanhedrin
(long on the beard, short
on the brain)
send envoys to say
they don't approve.
You never see them, love.
You toss me in the air
with such abandon,
they take to their heels and run.
I tell you
each kiss of yours
is like a blow on the head!

What luck, what luck to be loved
by the one girl
in this Presbyterian
country
who knows how to give
a man pleasure.

The Cold Green Element

At the end of the garden walk
the wind and its satellite wait for me;
their meaning I will not know
            until I go there,
but the black-hatted undertaker

who, passing, saw my heart beating in the grass,
is also going there. Hi, I tell him,
a great squall in the Pacific blew a dead poet
            out of the water,
who now hangs from the city's gates.

Crowds depart daily to see it, and return
with grimaces and incomprehension;
if its limbs twitched in the air
            they would sit at its feet
peeling their oranges.

And turning over I embrace like a lover
the trunk of a tree, one of those
for whom the lightning was too much
            and grew a brilliant
hunchback with a crown of leaves.

The ailments escaped from the labels
of medicine bottles are all fled to the wind;
I've seen myself lately in the eyes
            of old women,
spent streams mourning my manhood,

in whose old pupils the sun became
a bloodsmear on broad catalpa leaves
and hanging from ancient twigs,
            my murdered selves
sparked the air like the muted collisions

of fruit. A black dog howls down my blood,
a black dog with yellow eyes;
he too by someone's inadvertence
            saw the bloodsmear
on the broad catalpa leaves.

But the furies clear a path for me to the worm
who sang for an hour in the throat of a robin,
and misled by the cries of young boys
            I am again
a breathless swimmer in that cold green element.

The Bull Calf

The thing could barely stand. Yet taken
from his mother and the barn smells
he still impressed with his pride,
with the promise of sovereignty in the way
his head moved to take us in.
The fierce sunlight tugging the maize from the ground
licked at his shapely flanks.
He was too young for all that pride.
I thought of the deposed Richard II.

'No money in bull calves,' Freeman had said.
The visiting clergyman rubbed the nostrils
now snuffing pathetically at the windless day.
'A pity,' he sighed.
My gaze slipped off his hat toward the empty sky
that circled over the black knot of men,
over us and the calf waiting for the first blow.

Struck,
the bull calf drew in his thin forelegs
as if gathering strength for a mad rush . . .
tottered . . . raised his darkening eyes to us,

and I saw we were at the far end
of his frightened look, growing smaller and smaller
till we were only the ponderous mallet
that flicked his bleeding ear
and pushed him over on his side, stiffly,
like a block of wood.

Below the hill's crest
the river snuffled on the improvised beach.
We dug a deep pit and threw the dead calf into it.
It made a wet sound, a sepulchral gurgle,
as the warm sides bulged and flattened.
Settled, the bull calf lay as if asleep,
one foreleg over the other,
bereft of pride and so beautiful now,
without movement, perfectly still in the cool pit,
I turned away and wept.

Sacrament by the Water

How shall I sing the accomplished waters
Whose teeming cells make green my hopes
How shall the Sun at daybreak marry us
Twirling these waters like a hoop.

Gift of the waters that sing
Their eternal passion for the sky,
Your cunning beauty in a wave of tumult
Drops an Eden about your thighs.

Green is the singing singing water
And green is every joyous leaf
White myrtle's in your hand and in the other
The hairy apple bringing life.

Whatever Else
Poetry is Freedom

Whatever else poetry is freedom.
Forget the rhetoric, the trick of lying
All poets pick up sooner or later. From the river,
Rising like the thin voice of grey castratos—the mist;
Poplars and pines grow straight but oaks are gnarled;
Old codgers must speak of death, boys break windows;
Women lie honestly by their men at last.

And I who gave my Kate a blackened eye
Did to its vivid changing colours
Make up an incredible musical scale;
And now I balance on wooden stilts and dance
And thereby sing to the loftiest casements.
See how with polish I bow from the waist.
Space for these stilts! More space or I fail!

And a crown I say for my buffoon's head.
Yet no more fool am I than King Canute,
Lord of our tribe, who scanned and scorned;
Who half-deceived, believed; and, poet, missed
The first white waves come nuzzling at his feet;
Then damned the courtiers and the foolish trial
With a most bewildering and unkingly jest.

It was the mist. It lies inside one like a destiny.
A real Jonah it lies rotting like a lung.
And I know myself undone who am a clown
And wear a wreath of mist for a crown;
Mist with the scent of dead apples,
Mist swirling from black oily waters at evening,
Mist from the fraternal graves of cemeteries.

It shall drive me to beg my food and at last
Hurl me broken I know and prostrate on the road;
Like a huge toad I saw, entire but dead,

That Time mordantly had blacked; O pressed
To the moist earth it pled for entry.
I shall be I say that stiff toad for sick with mist
And crazed I smell the odour of mortality.

And Time flames like a paraffin stove
And what it burns are the minutes I live.
At certain middays I have watched the cars
Bring me from afar their windshield suns;
What lay to my hand were blue fenders,
The suns extinguished, the drivers wearing sunglasses.
And it made me think I had touched a hearse.

So whatever else poetry is freedom. Let
Far off the impatient cadences reveal
A padding for my breathless stilts. Swivel,
O hero, in the fleshy groves, skin and glycerine,
And sing of lust, the sun's accompanying shadow
Like a vampire's wing, the stillness in dead feet—
Your stave brings resurrection. O aggrievèd king.

Berry Picking

Silently my wife walks on the still wet furze
Now darkgreen the leaves are full of metaphors
Now lit up is each tiny lamp of blueberry.
The white nails of rain have dropped and the sun is free.

And whether she bends or straightens to each bush
To find the children's laughter among the leaves
Her quiet hands seem to make the quiet summer hush—
Berries or children, patient she is with these.

I only vex and perplex her; madness, rage
Are endearing perhaps put down upon the page;
Even silence daylong and sullen can then
Enamour as restraint or classic discipline.

So I envy the berries she puts in her mouth,
The red and succulent juice that stains her lips;
I shall never taste that good to her, nor will they
Displease her with a thousand barbarous jests.

How they lie easily for her hand to take,
Part of the unoffending world that is hers;
Here beyond complexity she stands and stares
And leans her marvellous head as if for answers.

No more the easy soul my childish craft deceives
Nor the simpler one for whom yes is always yes;
No, now her voice comes to me from a far way off
Though her lips are redder than the raspberries.

Cain

Taking the air rifle from my son's hand,
I measured back five paces, the Hebrew
In me, narcissist, father of children,
Laid to rest. From there I took aim and fired.
The silent ball hit the frog's back an inch
Below the head. He jumped at the surprise
Of it, suddenly tickled or startled
(He must have thought) and leaped from the wet sand
Into the surrounding brown water. But
The ball had done its mischief. His next spring
Was a miserable flop, the thrust all gone
Out of his legs. He tried—like Bruce—again,
Throwing out his sensitive pianist's
Hands as a dwarf might or a helpless child.
His splash disturbed the quiet pondwater
And one old frog behind his weedy moat
Blinking, looking self-complacently on.
The lin's surface at once became closing
Eyelids and bubbles like notes of music

Liquid, luminous, dropping from the page
White, white-bearded, a rapid crescendo
Of inaudible sounds and a crone's whispering
Backstage among the reeds and bulrushes
As for an expiring Lear or Oedipus.

But Death makes us all look ridiculous.
Consider this frog (dog, hog, what you will)
Sprawling, his absurd corpse rocked by the tides
That his last vain spring had set in movement.
Like a retired oldster, I couldn't help sneer,
Living off the last of his insurance:
Billows—now crumbling—the premiums paid.
Absurd, how absurd. I wanted to kill
At the mockery of it, kill and kill
Again—the self-infatuate frog, dog, hog,
Anything with the stir of life in it,
Seeing the dead leaper, Chaplin-footed,
Rocked and cradled in this afternoon
Of tranquil water, reeds, and blazing sun,
The hole in his back clearly visible
And the torn skin a blob of shadow
Moving when the quiet poolwater moved.
O Egypt, marbled Greece, resplendent Rome,
Did you also finally perish from a small bore
In your back you could not scratch? And would
Your mouths open ghostily, gasping out
Among the murky reeds, the hidden frogs,
We climb with crushed spines toward the heavens?

When the next morning I came the same way
The frog was on his back, one delicate
Hand on his belly, and his white shirt front
Spotless. He looked as if he might have been
A comic; tapdancer apologizing
For a fall, or an Emcee, his wide grin
Coaxing a laugh from us for an aside
Or perhaps a joke we didn't quite hear.

Keine Lazarovitch
1870-1959

When I saw my mother's head on the cold pillow,
Her white waterfalling hair in the cheeks' hollows,
I thought, quietly circling my grief, of how
She had loved God but cursed extravagantly his creatures.

For her final mouth was not water but a curse,
A small black hole, a black rent in the universe,
Which damned the green earth, stars and trees in its stillness
And the inescapable lousiness of growing old.

And I record she was comfortless, vituperative,
Ignorant, glad, and much else besides; I believe
She endlessly praised her black eyebrows, their thick weave,
Till plagiarizing Death leaned down and took them for his mould.

And spoiled a dignity I shall not again find,
And the fury of her stubborn limited mind;
Now none will shake her amber beads and call God blind,
Or wear them upon a breast so radiantly.

O fierce she was, mean and unaccommodating;
But I think now of the toss of her gold earrings,
Their proud carnal assertion, and her youngest sings
While all the rivers of her red veins move into the sea.

A Tall Man Executes a Jig

I

So the man spread his blanket on the field
And watched the shafts of light between the tufts
And felt the sun push the grass towards him;
The noise he heard was that of whizzing flies,
The whistlings of some small imprudent birds,

And the ambiguous rumbles of cars
That made him look up at the sky, aware
Of the gnats that tilted against the wind
And in the sunlight turned to jigging motes.
Fruitflies he'd call them except there was no fruit
About, spoiling to hatch these glitterings,
These nervous dots for which the mind supplied
The closing sentences from Thucydides,
Or from Euclid having a savage nightmare.

II

Jig jig, jig jig. Like minuscule black links
Of a chain played with by some playful
Unapparent hand or the palpitant
Summer haze bored with the hour's stillness.
He felt the sting and tingle afterwards
Of those leaving their unorthodox unrest,
Leaving their undulant excitation
To drop upon his sleeveless arm. The grass,
Even the wildflowers become black hairs
And himself a maddened speck among them.
Still the assaults of the small flies made him
Glad at last, until he saw purest joy
In their frantic jiggings under a hair,
So changed from those in the unrestraining air.

III

He stood up and felt himself enormous.
Felt as might Donatello over stone,
Or Plato, or as a man who has held
A loved and lovely woman in his arms
And feels his forehead touch the emptied sky
Where all antinomies flood into light.
Yet jig jig jig, the haloing black jots
Meshed with the wheeling fire of the sun:
Motion without meaning, disquietude
Without sense or purpose, ephemerides
That mottled the resting summer air till
Gusts swept them from his sight like wisps of smoke.

Yet they returned, bringing a bee who, seeing
But a tall man, left him for a marigold.

IV

He doffed his aureole of gnats and moved
Out of the field as the sun sank down,
A dying god upon the blood-red hills.
Ambition, pride, the ecstasy of sex,
And all circumstance of delight and grief,
That blood upon the mountain's side, that flood
Washed into a clear incredible pool
Below the ruddied peaks that pierced the sun.
He stood still and waited. If ever
The hour of revelation was come
It was now, here on the transfigured steep.
The sky darkened. Some birds chirped. Nothing else.
He thought the dying god had gone to sleep:
An Indian fakir on his mat of nails.

V

And on the summit of the asphalt road
Which stretched towards the fiery town, the man
Saw one hill raised like a hairy arm, dark
With pines and cedars against the stricken sun
—The arm of Moses or of Joshua.
He dropped his head and let fall the halo
Of mountains, purpling and silent as time,
To see temptation coiled before his feet:
A violated grass snake that lugged
Its intestine like a small red valise.
A cold-eyed skinflint it now was, and not
The manifest of that joyful wisdom,
The mirth and arrogant green flame of life;
Or earth's vivid tongue that flicked in praise of earth.

VI

And the man wept because pity was useless.
'Your jig's up; the flies come like kites,' he said
And watched the grass snake crawl towards the hedge,

Convulsing and dragging into the dark
The satchel filled with curses for the earth,
For the odours of warm sedge, and the sun,
A blood-red organ in the dying sky.
Backwards it fell into a grassy ditch
Exposing its underside, white as milk,
And mocked by wisps of hay between its jaws;
And then it stiffened to its final length.
But though it opened its thin mouth to scream
A last silent scream that shook the black sky,
Adamant and fierce, the tall man did not curse.

VII

Beside the rigid snake the man stretched out
In fellowship of death; he lay silent
And stiff in the heavy grass with eyes shut,
Inhaling the moist odours of the night
Through which his mind tunnelled with flicking tongue
Backwards to caves, mounds, and sunken ledges
And desolate cliffs where come only kites,
And where of perished badgers and racoons
The claws alone remain, gripping the earth.
Meanwhile the green snake crept upon the sky,
Huge, his mailed coat glittering with stars that made
The night bright, and blowing thin wreaths of cloud
Athwart the moon; and as the weary man
Stood up, coiled above his head, transforming all.

The Curse

For David

Infinite stillness
by a Canadian lake
our rented cottage   plunked down

among maples and birches
my twelve-year-old son
on his cot   in troubled sleep
digesting *Der Gelbe Stern*

Documentary pictures
    Jews in talith and phylacteries
(the prescribed regalia
for angel-wrestling)
provoking   smiles and laughter
in the *Herrenvolk* soldiers
before they're shot
    Jewish children and their mothers
entering the death camps
    mass graves   huddled bodies
    the pallor and stillness
of death

On my lap   the *Globe and Mail*
gun-loving goons
civilized scum   in Belfast and Lebanon
the torturers of Chile
Uruguay   Soviet Russia   Iran

When he wakes up
how   shall I explain
human evil to him
without injecting   the weakening virus
of guilt and anxiety
how reach his mind   with the news
we belong   to an accursed species
and that greater disasters   more monstrous evils
are being readied for us
in the next century   his century

Minden, Ontario
August 16, 1976

Richard Wilbur

She

What was her beauty in our first estate
When Adam's will was whole, and the least thing
Appeared the gift and creature of his king,
How should we guess? Resemblance had to wait

For separation, and in such a place
She so partook of water, light, and trees
As not to look like any one of these.
He woke and gazed into her naked face.

But then she changed, and coming down amid
The flocks of Abel and the fields of Cain,
Clothed in their wish, her Eden graces hid,
A shape of plenty with a mop of grain,

She broke upon the world, in time took on
The look of every labor and its fruits.
Columnar in a robe of pleated lawn
She cupped her patient hand for attributes,

Was radiant captive of the farthest tower
And shed her honor on the fields of war,
Walked in her garden at the evening hour,
Her shadow like a dark ogival door,

Breasted the seas for all the westward ships
And, come to virgin country, changed again—
A moonlike being truest in eclipse,
And subject goddess of the dreams of men.

Tree, temple, valley, prow, gazelle, machine,
More named and nameless than the morning star,
Lovely in every shape, in all unseen,
We dare not wish to find you as you are,

Whose apparition, biding time until
Desire decay and bring the latter age,
Shall flourish in the ruins of our will
And deck the broken stones like saxifrage.

In the Smoking-Car

The eyelids meet. He'll catch a little nap.
The grizzled, crew-cut head drops to his chest.
It shakes above the briefcase on his lap.
Close voices breathe, 'Poor sweet, he did his best.'

'Poor sweet, poor sweet,' the bird-hushed glades repeat,
Through which in quiet pomp his litter goes,
Carried by native girls with naked feet.
A sighing stream concurs in his repose.

Could he but think, he might recall to mind
The righteous mutiny or sudden gale
That beached him here; the dear ones left behind . . .
So near the ending, he forgets the tale.

Were he to lift his eyelids now, he might
Behold his maiden porters, brown and bare.
But even here he has no appetite.
It is enough to know that they are there.

Enough that now a honeyed music swells ,
The gentle, mossed declivities begin,
And the whole air is full of flower-smells.
Failure, the longed-for valley, takes him in.

Love Calls Us to the Things
of This World

      The eyes open to a cry of pulleys,
And spirited from sleep, the astounded soul
Hangs for a moment bodiless and simple
As false dawn.
                  Outside the open window
The morning air is all awash with angels.

      Some are in bed-sheets, some are in blouses,
Some are in smocks: but truly there they are.
Now they are rising together in calm swells
Of halcyon feeling, filling whatever they wear
With the deep joy of their impersonal breathing;

      Now they are flying in place, conveying
The terrible speed of their omnipresence, moving
And staying like white water; and now of a sudden
They swoon down into so rapt a quiet
That nobody seems to be there.
                      The soul shrinks

      From all that it is about to remember,
From the punctual rape of every blessèd day,
And cries,
            'Oh, let there be nothing on earth but laundry,
Nothing but rosy hands in the rising steam
And clear dances done in the sight of heaven.'

      Yet, as the sun acknowledges
With a warm look the world's hunks and colors,
The soul descends once more in bitter love
To accept the waking body, saying now
In a changed voice as the man yawns and rises,

'Bring them down from their ruddy gallows;
Let there be clean linen for the backs of thieves;
Let lovers go fresh and sweet to be undone,
And the heaviest nuns walk in a pure floating
Of dark habits,
                    keeping their difficult balance.'

Beasts

             Beasts in their major freedom
        Slumber in peace tonight. The gull on his ledge
Dreams in the guts of himself the moon-plucked waves below,
        And the sunfish leans on a stone, slept
             By the lyric water,

             In which the spotless feet
        Of deer make dulcet splashes, and to which
The ripped mouse, safe in the owl's talon, cries
        Concordance. Here there is no such harm
             And no such darkness

             As the selfsame moon observes
        Where, warped in window-glass, it sponsors now
The werewolf's painful change. Turning his head away
        On the sweaty bolster, he tries to remember
             The mood of manhood,

             But lies at last, as always,
        Letting it happen, the fierce fur soft to his face,
Hearing with sharper ears the wind's exciting minors,
        The leaves' panic, and the degradation
             Of the heavy streams.

             Meantime, at high windows
        Far from thicket and pad-fall, suitors of excellence
Sigh and turn from their work to construe again the painful
        Beauty of heaven, the lucid moon
             And the risen hunter,

Making such dreams for men
As told will break their hearts as always, bringing
Monsters into the city, crows on the public statues,
Navies fed to the fish in the dark
Unbridled waters.

Exeunt

Piecemeal the summer dies;
At the field's edge a daisy lives alone;
A last shawl of burning lies
On the gray field-stone.

All cries are thin and terse;
The field has droned the summer's final mass;
A cricket like a dwindled hearse
Crawls from the dry grass.

A Glance from the Bridge

Letting the eye descend from reeking stack
And black façade to where the river goes,
You see the freeze has started in to crack
(As if the city squeezed it in a vice),
And here and there the limbering water shows,
And gulls colonial on the sullied ice.

Some rise and braid their glidings, white and spare,
Or sweep the hemmed-in river up and down,
Making a litheness in the barriered air,
And through the town the freshening water swirls
As if an ancient whore undid her gown
And showed a body almost like a girl's.

Giacometti

Rock insults us, hard and so boldly browed
Its scorn needs not to focus, and with fists
Which still unstirring strike:
Collected it resists
Until its buried glare begets a like
Anger in us, and finds our hardness. Proud,

Then, and armed, and with a patient rage
We carve cliff, shear stone to blocks,
And down to the image of man
Batter and shape the rock's
Fierce composure, closing its veins within
That ouside man, itself its captive cage.

So we can baffle rock, and in our will
Can clothe and keep it. But if our will, though locked
In stone it clutches, change,
Then are we much worse mocked
Than cliffs can do: then we ourselves are strange
To what we were, which lowers on us still.

High in the air those habitants of stone
Look heavenward, lean to a thought, or stride
Toward some concluded war,
While we on every side,
Random as shells the sea drops down ashore,
Are walking, walking, many and alone.

What stony shape could hold us now, what hard
Bent can we bulk in air, where shall our feet
Come to a common stand?
Follow along this street
(Where rock recovers carven eye and hand),
Open the gate, and cross the narrow yard

And look where Giacometti in a room
Dim as a cave of the sea, has built the man
We are, and made him walk:
Towering like a thin
Coral, out of a reef of plaster chalk,
This is the single form we can assume.

We are this man unspeakably alone
Yet stripped of the singular utterly, shaved and scraped
Of all but being there,
Whose fullness is escaped
Like a burst balloon's: no nakedness so bare
As flesh gone in inquiring of the bone.

He is pruned of every gesture, saving only
The habit of coming and going. Every pace
Shuffles a million feet.
The faces in this face
Are all forgotten faces of the street
Gathered to one anonymous and lonely.

No prince and no Leviathan, he is made
Of infinite farewells. Oh never more
Diminished, nonetheless
Embodied here, we are
This starless walker, one who cannot guess
His will, his keel his nose's bony blade.

And volumes hover round like future shades
This least of man, in whom we join and take
A pilgrim's step behind,
And in whose guise we make
Our grim departures now, walking to find
What railleries of rock, what palisades?

Place Pigalle

Now homing tradesmen scatter through the streets
Toward suppers, thinking on improved conditions,
While evening, with a million simple fissions,
Takes up its warehouse watches, storefront beats,
By nursery windows its assigned positions.

Now at the corners of the Place Pigalle
Bright bars explode against the dark's embraces;
The soldiers come, the boys with ancient faces,
Seeking their ancient friends, who stroll and loll
Amid the glares and glass: electric graces.

The puppies are asleep, and snore the hounds;
But here wry hares, the soldier and the whore,
Mark off their refuge with a gaudy door,
Brazen at bay, and boldly out of bounds:
The puppies dream, the hounds superbly snore.

Ionized innocence: this pair reclines,
She on the table, he in a tilting chair,
With Arden ease; her eyes as pale as air
Travel his priestgoat face; his hand's thick tines
Touch the gold whorls of her Corinthian hair.

'Girl, if I love thee not, then let me die;
Do I not scorn to change my state with kings?
Your muchtouched flesh, incalculable, which wrings
Me so, now shall I gently seize in my
Desperate soldier's hands which kill all things.'

Charles Olson

The Kingfishers

I

What does not change / is the will to change

He woke, fully clothed, in his bed. He
remembered only one thing, the birds, how
when he came in, he had gone around the rooms
and got them back in their cage, the green one first,
she with the bad leg, and then the blue,
the one they had hoped was a male

Otherwise? Yes, Fernand, who had talked lispingly of Albers &
    Angkor Vat.
He had left the party without a word. How he got up, got into his
    coat,
I do not know. When I saw him, he was at the door, but it did
    not matter,
he was already sliding along the wall of the night, losing himself
in some crack of the ruins. That it should have been he who said,
    'The kingfishers!
who cares
for their feathers
now?'

His last words had been, 'The pool is slime.' Suddenly everyone,
ceasing their talk, sat in a row around him, watched
they did not so much hear, or pay attention, they
wondered, looked at each other, smirked, but listened,
he repeated and repeated, could not go beyond his thought

'The pool   the kingfishers' feathers were wealth   why
did the export stop?'

It was then he left

II

I thought of the E on the stone, and of what Mao said
la lumiere'
            but the kingfisher
de l'aurore'
            but the kingfisher flew west
est devant nous!
            he got the color of his breast
            from the heat of the setting sun!

The features are, the feebleness of the feet (syndactylism of the
        3rd & 4th digit)
the bill, serrated, sometimes a pronounced beak, the wings
where the color is, short and round, the tail
inconspicuous.

But not these things were the factors. Not the birds.
The legends are
legends. Dead, hung up indoors, the kingfisher
will not indicate a favoring wind,
or avert the thunderbolt. Nor, by its nesting,
still the waters, with the new year, for seven days.
It is true, it does nest with the opening year, but not on the
        waters.
It nests at the end of a tunnel bored by itself in a bank. There,
six or eight white and translucent eggs are laid, on fishbones
not on bare clay, on bones thrown up in pellets by the birds.

                        On these rejectamenta
(as they accumulate they form a cup-shaped structure) the young
        are born.
And, as they are fed and grow, this nest of excrement and de-
        cayed fish becomes
                        a dripping, fetid mass

Mao concluded:
                    nous devons
                              nous lever
                                        et agir!

III

When the attentions change / the jungle
leaps in
              even the stones are split
                              they rive

Or,
enter
that other conqueror we more naturally recognize
he so resembles ourselves

But the E
cut so rudely on that oldest stone
sounded otherwise,
was differently heard

as, in another time, were treasures used:

(and, later, much later, a fine ear thought
a scarlet coat)

              'of green feathers   feet, beaks and eyes
              of gold

              'animals likewise,
              resembling snails

              'a large wheel, gold, with figures of unknown four-
                    foots,
              and worked with tufts of leaves, weight
              3800 ounces

              'last, two birds, of thread and featherwork, the quills
              gold, the feet

gold, the two birds perched on two reeds
gold, the reeds arising from two embroidered mounds,
one yellow, the other
white.

            'And from each reed hung
            seven feathered tassels.

In this instance, the priests
(in dark cotton robes, and dirty,
their dishevelled hair matted with blood, and flowing wildly
over their shoulders)
rush in among the people, calling on them
to protect their gods

And all now is war
where so lately there was peace,
and the sweet brotherhood, the use
of tilled fields.

IV

Not one death but many,
not accumulation but change, the feed-back proves, the feed-
      back is the law
           Into the same river no man steps twice
           When fire dies air dies
           No one remains, nor is, one

Around an appearance, one common model, we grow up
many. Else how is it,
if we remain the same,
we take pleasure now
in what we did not take pleasure before? love
contrary objects? admire and/or find fault? use
other words, feel other passions, have
nor figure, appearance, disposition, tissue
the same?
           To be in different states without a change
           is not a possibility

We can be precise. The factors are
in the animal and/or the machine the factors are
communication and/or control, both involve
the message. And what is the message? The message is
a discrete or continuous sequence of measurable events
      distributed in time

is the birth of air, is
the birth of water, is
a state between
the origin and
the end, between
birth and the beginning of
another fetid nest

is change, presents
no more than itself

And the too strong grasping of it,
when it is pressed together and condensed,
loses it

This very thing you are

                ii

                They buried their dead in a sitting posture
                serpent   came   razor   ray of the sun

                And she sprinkled water on the head of the child, crying
                'Cioa-coatl! Cioa-coatl!'
                with her face to the west

                Where the bones are found, in each personal heap
                with what each enjoyed, there is always
                the Mongolian louse

The light is in the east. Yes. And we must rise, act. Yet
in the west, despite the apparent darkness (the whiteness

which covers all), if you look, if you can bear, if you can, long
    enough
            as long as it was necessary for him, my guide
            to look into the yellow of that longest-lasting rose

so you must, and, in that whiteness, into that face, with what
    candor, look

and, considering the dryness of the place
    the long absence of an adequate race

        (of the two who first came, each a conquistador, one
            healed, the other
        tore the eastern idols down, toppled
        the temple walls, which, says the excuser
        were black from human gore)

hear
hear, where the dry blood talks
    where the old appetite walks

                la piu saporita et migliore
                che si possa truovar al mondo

where it hides, look
in the eye how it runs
in the flesh / chalk

        but under these petals
        in the emptiness
        regard the light, contemplate
        the flower

whence it arose

        with what violence benevolence is bought
        what cost in gesture justice brings
        what wrongs domestic rights involve
        what stalks
        this silence

what pudor pejorocracy affronts
how awe, night-rest and neighborhood can rot
what breeds where dirtiness is law
what crawls
below

    iii

I am no Greek, hath not th'advantage.
And of course, no Roman:
he can take no risk that matters,
the risk of beauty least of all.

But I have my kin, if for no other reason than
(as he said, next of kin) I commit myself, and,
given my freedom, I'd be a cad
if I didn't. Which is most true.

It works out this way, despite the disadvantage.
I offer, in explanation, a quote:
si j'ai du goût, ce n'est guères
que pour la terre et les pierres

Despite the discrepancy (an ocean   courage   age)
this is also true: if I have any taste
it is only because I have interested myself
in what was slain in the sun

    I pose you your question:

shall you uncover honey / where maggots are?

    I hunt among stones

As the Dead Prey upon Us

I

As the dead prey upon us,
they are the dead in ourselves,
awake, my sleeping ones, I cry out to you,
disentangle the nets of being!

I pushed my car, it had been sitting so long unused.
I thought the tires looked as though they only needed air.
But suddenly the huge underbody was above me,
                                        and the rear tires
were masses of rubber and thread variously clinging together

as were the dead souls in the living room, gathered
about my mother, some of them taking care to pass
beneath the beam of the movie projector, some record
playing on the victrola, and all of them
desperate with the tawdriness of their life in hell

I turned to the young man on my right and asked, 'How is it,
there?' And he begged me protestingly don't ask, we are poor
poor. And the whole room was suddenly posters
                                        and presentations
of brake linings and other automotive accessories, cardboard
displays, the dead roaming from one to another
as bored back in life as they are in hell, poor and doomed
to mere equipments

            my mother, as alive as ever she was, asleep
when I entered the house as I often found her in a rocker
under the lamp, and awaking, as I came up to her,
                                        as she ever had
I found out she returns to the house once a week, and with her
the throng of the unknown young who center on her
                                        as much in death
as other like suited and dressed people did in life

O the dead!

>and the Indian woman and I
>enabled the blue deer
>to walk

>and the blue deer talked,
>in the next room,
>a Negro talk

>it was like walking a jackass,
>and its talk
>was the pressing gabber of gammers
>of old women

>and we helped walk it around the room
>because it was seeking socks
>or shoes for its hooves
>now that it was acquiring

>human possibilities

In the five hindrances men and angels
stay caught in the net, in the immense nets
which spread out across each plane of being, the multiple nets
which hamper at each step of the ladders as the angels
and the demons
and men
go up and down

>Walk the jackass
>Hear the victrola
>Let the automobile
>be tucked into a corner of the white fence
>when it is a white chair. Purity

is only an instant of being, the trammels

recur

In the five hindrances, perfection
is hidden

             I shall get
             to the place
             10 minutes late.

             It will be 20 minutes
             of 9. And I don't know,

             without the car,

             how I shall get there

O peace, my mother, I do not know
how differently I could have done
what I did or did not do.

             That you are back each week
             that you fall asleep
             with your face to the right

             that you are as present there
             when I come in as you were
             when you were alive

             that you are as solid, and your flesh
             is as I knew it, that you have the company
             I am used to your having
             but o, that you all find it
             such a cheapness!

o peace, mother, for the mammothness
of the comings and goings
of the ladders of life

The nets we are entangled in. Awake,
my soul, let the power into the last wrinkle
of being, let none of the threads and rubber of the tires

be left upon the earth. Let even your mother
go. Let there be only paradise

The desperateness is, that the instant
which is also paradise (paradise
is happiness) dissolves
into the next instant, and power
flows to meet the next occurrence

       Is it any wonder
       my mother comes back?
       Do not that throng
       rightly seek the room
       where they might expect
       happiness? They did not complain
       of life, they obviously wanted
       the movie, each other, merely to pass
       among each other there,
       where the real is, even to the display cards,
       to be out of hell

       The poverty
       of hell

O souls, in life and in death,
awake, even as you sleep, even in sleep
know what wind
even under the crankcase of the ugly automobile
lifts it away, clears the sodden weights of goods,
equipment, entertainment, the foods the Indian woman,
the filthy blue deer, the 4 by 3 foot 'Viewbook,'
the heaviness of the old house, the stuffed inner room
lifts the sodden nets

       and they disappear as ghosts do,
       as spider webs, nothing
       before the hand of man

The vent! You must have the vent,
or you shall die. Which means
never to die, the ghastliness

of going, and forever
coming back, returning
to the instants which were not lived

O mother, this I could not have done,
I could not have lived what you didn't,
I am myself netted in my own being

I want to die. I want to make that instant, too,
perfect

O my soul, slip
the cog

II

The death in life (death itself)
is endless, eternity
is the false cause

The knot is otherwise, each topological corner
presents itself, and no sword
cuts it, each knot is itself its fire

each knot of which the net is made
is for the hands to untake
the knot's making. And touch alone

can turn the knot into its own flame

    (o mother, if you had once touched me

    o mother, if I had once touched you)

The car did not burn. Its underside

was not presented to me
a grotesque corpse. The old man

merely removed it as I looked up at it,
and put it in a corner of the picket fence
like was it my mother's white dog?

or a child's chair

            The woman,
            playing on the grass,
            with her son (the woman next door)

            was angry with me whatever it was
            slipped across the playpen or whatever
            she had out there on the grass

            And I was quite flip in reply
            that anyone who used plastic
            had to expect things to skid

            and break, that I couldn't worry
            that her son might have been hurt
            by whatever it was I sent skidding

            down on them.

            It was just then I went into my house
            and to my utter astonishment
            found my mother sitting there

            as she always had sat, as must she always
            forever sit there her head lolling
            into sleep? Awake, awake my mother

            what wind will lift you too
            forever from the tawdriness
            make you rich as all those souls

crave crave crave

to be rich?

They are right. We must have
what we want. We cannot afford
not to. We have only one course:

the nets which entangle us are flames

> O souls, burn
> alive, burn now
>
> that you may forever
> have peace, have
>
> what you crave
>
> O souls,
> go into everything,
> let not one knot pass
> through your fingers
>
> let not any they tell you
> you must sleep as the net
> comes through your authentic hands
>
> What passes
> is what is, what shall be, what has
> been, what hell and heaven is
> is earth to be rent, to shoot you
> through the screen of flame which each knot
> hides as all knots are a wall ready
> to be shot open by you
>
>   the nets of being
> are only eternal if you sleep as your hands
> ought to be busy. Method, method

> I too call on you to come
> to the aid of all men, to women most
> who know most, to woman to tell
> men to awake. Awake, men,
> awake

I ask my mother
to sleep. I ask her
to stay in the chair.
My chair
is in the corner of the fence.
She sits by the fireplace made of paving stones. The blue deer
need not trouble either of us.

And if she sits in happiness the souls
who trouble her and me
will also rest. The automobile

has been hauled away.

Variations Done for
Gerald Van de Wiele

I. LE BONHEUR

dogwood flakes
what is green

the petals
from the apple
blow on the road

mourning doves
mark the sway
of the afternoon, bees
dig the plum blossoms

the morning
stands up straight, the night
is blue from the full of the April moon

iris and lilac, birds
birds, yellow flowers
white flowers, the Diesel
does not let up dragging
the plow

        as the whippoorwill,
the night's tractor, grinds
his song

        and no other birds but us
are as busy (O saisons, o chateaux!

Délires!

        What soul
is without fault?

Nobody studies
happiness

Every time the cock crows
I salute him

I have no longer any excuse
for envy. My life

has been given its orders: the seasons
seize

the soul and the body, and make mock
of any dispersed effort. The hour of death

is the only trespass

II. THE CHARGE

dogwood flakes
the green

the petals from the apple-trees
fall for the feet to walk on

the birds are so many they are
loud, in the afternoon

they distract, as so many bees do
suddenly all over the place

With spring one knows today to see
that in the morning each thing

is separate but by noon
they have melted into each other

and by night only crazy things
like the full moon and the whippoorwill

and us, are busy. We are busy
if we can get by that whiskered bird,

that nightjar, and get across, the moon
is our conversation, she will say

what soul
isn't in default?

can you afford not to make
the magical study

which happiness is? do you hear
the cock when he crows? do you know the charge,

that you shall have no envy, that your life
has its orders, that the seasons

seize you too, that no body and soul are one
if they are not wrought

in this retort? that otherwise efforts
are efforts? And that the hour of your flight

will be the hour of your death?

III. SPRING

The dogwood
lights up the day.

The April moon
flakes the night.

Birds, suddenly,
are a multitude

The flowers are ravined
by bees, the fruit blossoms

are thrown to the ground, the wind
the rain forces everything. Noise—

even the night is drummed
by whippoorwills, and we get

as busy, we plow, we move,
we break out, we love. The secret

which got lost neither hides
nor reveals itself, it shows forth

tokens. And we rush
to catch up. The body

whips the soul. In its great desire
it demands the elixir

In the roar of spring,
transmutations. Envy

drags herself off. The fault of the body and the soul
—that they are not one—

the matutinal cock clangs
and singleness: we salute you

season of no bungling

Maximus, to Himself

I

I have had to learn the simplest things
last. Which made for difficulties.
Even at sea I was slow, to get the hand out, or to cross
a wet deck.
        The sea was not, finally, my trade.
But even my trade, at it, I stood estranged
from that which was most familiar. Was delayed,
and not content with the man's argument
that such postponement
is now the nature of
obedience,
        that we are all late
        in a slow time,
        that we grow up many
        And the single
        is not easily
        known

It could be, though the sharpness (the *achiote*)
I note in others,
makes more sense
than my own distances. The agilities

> they show daily
> who do the world's
> businesses
> and who do nature's
> as I have no sense
> I have done either

I have made dialogues,
have discussed ancient texts,
have thrown what light I could, offered
what pleasures
doceat allows

> But the known?
This, I have had to be given,
a life, love, and from one man
the world.

> Tokens.
> But sitting here
> I look out as a wind
> and water man, testing
> And missing
> Some proof

I know the quarters
of the weather, where it comes from,
where it goes. But the stem of me,
this I took from their welcome,
or their rejection, of me

And my arrogance
was neither diminished
nor increased,
by the communication

II

it is undone business
I speak of, this morning,
with the sea
stretching out
from my feet

John Berryman

The Dispossessed

'and something that . . that is theirs—no longer ours'
stammered to me the Italian page. A wood
seeded & towered suddenly. I understood.—

The Leading Man's especially, and the Juvenile Lead's,
and the Leading Lady's thigh that switches & warms
and their grimaces, and their flying arms:

our arms, our story. Every seat was sold.
A crone met in a clearing sprouts a beard
and has a tirade. Not a word we heard.

Movement of stone within a woman's heart,
abrupt & dominant. They gesture how
fings really are. Rarely a child sings now.

My harpsichord weird as a koto drums
adagio for twilight, for the storm-worn dove
no more de-iced, and the spidery business of love.

The Juvenile Lead's the Leader's arm, one arm
running the whole bole, branches, roots, (O watch)
and the faceless fellow waving from her crotch,

Stalin-unanimous! who procured a vote
and care not use it, who have kept an eye
and care not use it, percussive vote, clear eye.

That which a captain and a weaponeer
one day and one more day did, we did, *ach*
we did not, *They* did . . cam slid, the great lock

lodged, and no soul of us all was near was near,—
an evil sky (where the umbrella bloomed)
twirled its mustaches, hissed, the ingenue fumed,

poor virgin, and no hero rides. The race
is done. Drifts through, between the cold black trunks,
the peachblow glory of the perishing sun

in empty houses where old things take place.

A Professor's Song

(. . rabid or dog-dull.) Let me tell you how
The Eighteenth Century couplet ended. Now
Tell me. Troll me the sources of that Song—
Assigned last week—by Blake. Come, come along,
Gentlemen. (Fidget and huddle, do. Squint soon.)
I want to end these fellows all by noon.

'That deep romantic chasm'—an early use;
The word is from the French, by our abuse
Fished out a bit. (Red all your eyes. O when?)
'A poet is a man speaking to men':
But I am then a poet, am I not?—
Ha ha. The radiator, please. Well, what?

Alive now—no—Blake would have written prose,
But movement following movement crisply flows,
So much the better, better the much so,
As burbleth Mozart. Twelve. The class can go.
Until I meet you, then, in Upper Hell
Convulsed, foaming immortal blood: farewell.

From *Homage to Mistress Bradstreet*

2

Outside the New World winters in grand dark
white air lashing high thro' the virgin stands
foxes down foxholes sigh,
surely the English heart quails, stunned.
I doubt if Simon than this blast, that sea,
spares from his rigour for your poetry
more. We are on each other's hands
who care. Both of our worlds unhanded us. Lie stark,

3

thy eyes look to me mild. Out of maize & air
your body's made, and moves. I summon, see,
from the centuries it.
I think you won't stay. How do we
linger, diminished, in our lovers' air,
implausibly visible, to whom, a year,
years, over interims; or not;
to a long stranger; or not; shimmer and disappear.

4

Jaw-ript, rot with its wisdom, rending then;
then not. When the mouth dies, who misses you?
Your master never died,
Simon ah thirty years past you—
Pockmarkt & westward staring on a haggard deck
it seems I find you, young. I come to check,
I come to stay with you,
and the Governor, & Father, & Simon, & the huddled men.

5

By the week we landed we were, most, used up.
Strange ships across us, after a fortnight's winds
unfavouring, frightened us;
bone-sad cold, sleet, scurvy; so were ill
many as one day we could have no sermons;
broils, quelled; a fatherless child unkennelled; vermin
crowding & waiting: waiting
And the day itself he leapt ashore young Henry Winthrop

6

(delivered from the waves; because he found
off their wigwams, sharp-eyed, a lone canoe
across a tidal river,
that water glittered fair & blue
& narrow, none of the other men could swim
and the plantation's prime theft up to him,
shouldered on a glad day
hard on the glorious feasting of thanksgiving) drowned.

9

Winter than summer worse, that first, like a file
on a quick, or the poison suck of a thrilled tooth;
and still we may unpack.
Wolves & storms among, uncouth
board-pieces, boxes, barrels vanish, grow
houses, rise. Motes that hop in sunlight slow
indoors, and I am Ruth
away: open my mouth, my eyes wet: I wóuld smile:

10

vellum I palm, and dream. Their forest dies
to greensward, privets, elms & towers, whence
a nightingale is throbbing.

Women sleep sound. I was happy once . .
(Something keeps on not happening; I shrink?)
These minutes all their passions & powers sink
and I am not one chance
for an unknown cry or a flicker of unknown eyes.

11

Chapped souls ours, by the day Spring's strong winds swelled,
Jack's pulpits arched, more glad. The shawl I pinned
flaps like a shooting soul
might in such weather Heaven send.
Succumbing half, in spirit, to a salmon sash
I prod the nerveless novel succotash—
I must be disciplined,
in arms, against that one, and our dissidents, and myself.

19

So squeezed, wince you I scream? I love you & hate
off with you. Ages! *Useless*. Below my waist
he has me in Hell's vise.
Stalling. He let go. Come back: brace
me somewhere. No. No. Yes! everything down
hardens I press with horrible joy down
my back cracks like a wrist
shame I am voiding oh behind it is too late.

20

hide me forever I work thrust I must free
now I all muscles & bones concentrate
what is living from dying?
Simon I must leave you so untidy
Monster you are killing me Be sure
I'll have you later Women do endure
I can *can* no longer
and it passes the wretched trap whelming and I am me

21

drencht & powerful, I did it with my body!
One proud tug greens Heaven. Marvellous,
unforbidding Majesty.
Swell, imperious bells. I fly
Mountainous, woman not breaks and will bend:
sways God nearby: anguish comes to an end.
Blossomed Sarah, and I
blossom. It that thing alive? I hear a famisht howl.

37

I fear Hell's hammer-wind. But fear does wane.
Death's blossoms grain my hair; I cannot live.
A black joy clashes
joy, in twilight. The Devil said
'I will deal toward her softly, and her enchanting cries
will fool the horns of Adam.' Father of lies,
a male great pestle smashes
small women swarming towards the mortar's rim in vain.

NOTES

Stanzas   The poem is about the woman, but this exordium is spoken by
1-4   the poet, his voice modulating in stanza 4, line 8 [4.8] into hers.

5.4,5   Many details are from quotations in Helen Campbell's biography,
          the Winthrop papers, narratives, town histories.

37.7,8   After an engraving somewhere in Fuchs's collections. *Bray*, above
          (36.4), puns.

From 77 *Dream Songs*

1

Huffy Henry hid   the day,
unappeasable Henry sulked.
I see his point,—a trying to put things over.
It was the thought that they thought
they could *do* it made Henry wicked & away.
But he should have come out and talked.

All the world like a woolen lover
once did seem on Henry's side.
Then came a departure.
Thereafter nothing fell out as it might or ought.
I don't see how Henry, pried
open for all the world to see, survived.

What he has now to say is a long
wonder the world can bear & be.
Once in a sycamore I was glad
all at the top, and I sang.
Hard on the land wears the strong sea
and empty grows every bed.

8

The weather was fine. They took away his teeth,
white & helpful; bothered his backhand;
halved his green hair.
They blew out his loves, his interests. 'Underneath,'
(they called in iron voices) 'understand,
is nothing. So there.'

The weather was very fine. They lifted off
his covers till he showed, and cringed & pled
to see himself less.

They installed mirrors till he flowed. 'Enough'
(murmured they) 'if you will watch Us instead,
yet you may saved be. Yes.'

The weather fleured. They weakened all his eyes,
and burning thumbs into his ears, and shook
his hand like a notch.
They flung long silent speeches. (Off the hook!)
They sandpapered his plumpest hope. (So capsize.)
They took away his crotch.

14

Life, friends, is boring. We must not say so.
After all, the sky flashes, the great sea yearns,
we ourselves flash and yearn,
and moreover my mother told me as a boy
(repeatingly) 'Ever to confess you're bored
means you have no

Inner Resources.' I conclude now I have no
inner resources, because I am heavy bored.
Peoples bore me,
literature bores me, especially great literature,
Henry bores me, with his plights & gripes
as bad as achilles,

who loves people and valiant art, which bores me.
And the tranquil hills, & gin, look like a drag
and somehow a dog
has taken itself & its tail considerably away
into mountains or sea or sky, leaving
behind: me, wag.

26

The glories of the world struck me, made me aria, once.
—What happen then, Mr Bones?
if be you cares to say.
—Henry. Henry became interested in women's bodies,
his loins were & were the   scene of stupendous achievement.
Stupor. Knees, dear. Pray.

All the knobs & softnesses of, my God,
the ducking & trouble it swarm on Henry,
at one time.
—What happen then, Mr Bones?
you seems excited-like.
—Fell Henry back into   the original crime: art, rime

besides a sense of others, my God, my God,
and a jealousy for the honour (alive) of his country,
what can get more odd?
and discontent with the thriving gangs & pride.
—What happen then, Mr Bones?
—I had a most marvellous   piece of luck. I died.

29

There sat down, once, a thing on Henry's heart
só heavy, if he had a hundred years
& more, & weeping, sleepless, in all them time
Henry could not make good.
Starts again always in Henry's ears
the little cough somewhere, an odour, a chime.

And there is another thing he has in mind
like a grave Sienese face a thousand years
would fail to blur the still profiled reproach of. Ghastly,
with open eyes, he attends, blind.

All the bells say: too late. This is not for tears;
thinking.

But never did Henry, as he thought he did,
end anyone and hacks her body up
and hide the pieces, where they may be found.
He knows: he went over everyone, & nobody's missing.
Often he reckons, in the dawn, them up.
Nobody is ever missing.

40

I'm scared a lonely. Never see my son,
easy be not to see anyone,
combers out to sea
know they're goin somewhere but not me.
Got a little poison, got a little gun,
I'm scared a lonely.

I'm scared a only one thing, which is me,
from othering I don't take nothin, see,
for any hound dog's sake.
But this is where I livin, where I rake
my leaves and cop my promise, this' where we
cry oursel's awake.

Wishin was dyin but I gotta make
it all this way to that bed on these feet
where peoples said to meet.
Maybe but even if I see my son
forever never, get back on the take,
free, black & forty-one.

49

Blind

Old Pussy-cat if he won't eat, he don't
feel good into his tum', old Pussy-cat.
He *wants* to have eaten.
Tremor, heaves, he sweaterings. He can't.
A dizzy swims of where is Henry at;
. . . somewhere streng verboten.

How come he sleeps & sleeps and sleeps, waking like death:
locate the restorations of which we hear
as of profound sleep.
From daylight he got maintrackt, from friends' breath,
wishes, his hopings. Dreams make crawl with fear
Henry but not get up.

The course his mind his body steer, poor Pussy-cat,
in weakness & disorder, will see him down
whiskers & tail.
'Wastethrift': Oh one of cunning wives know that
he hoardy-squander, where is nor downtown
neither suburba. Braille.

50

In a motion of night they massed nearer my post.
I hummed a short blues. When the stars went out
I studied my weapons system.
Grenades, the portable rack, the yellow spout
of the anthrax-ray: in order. Yet, and most
of my pencils were sharp.

This edge of the galaxy has often seen
a defence so stiff, but it could only go
one way.

—Mr Bones, your troubles give me vertigo,
& backache. Somehow, when I make your scene,
I cave to feel as if

de roses of dawns & pearls of dusks, made up
by some ol' writer-man, got right forgot
& the greennesses of ours.
Springwater grow so thick it gonna clot
and the pleasing ladies cease. I figure, yup,
you is bad powers.

52

Silent Song

Bright-eyed & bushy-tailed woke not Henry up.
Bright though upon his workshop shone a vise
central, moved in
while he was doing time down hospital
and growing wise.
He gave it the worst look he had left.

Alone. They all abandoned   Henry—wonder! all,
when most he—under the sun.
That was all right.
He can't work well with it here, or think.
A bilocation, yellow like catastrophe.
The name of this was freedom.

Will Henry again ever be on the lookout for women & milk,
honour & love again,
have a buck or three?
He felt like shrieking but he shuddered as
(spring mist, warm, rain) an handful with quietness
vanisht & the thing took hold.

Adrienne Rich

At a Bach Concert

Coming by evening through the wintry city
We said that art is out of love with life.
Here we approach a love that is not pity.

This antique discipline, tenderly severe,
Renews belief in love yet masters feeling,
Asking of us a grace in what we bear.

Form is the ultimate gift that love can offer—
The vital union of necessity
With all that we desire, all that we suffer.

A too-compassionate art is half an art.
Only such proud restraining purity
Restores the else-betrayed, too-human heart.

Snapshots of a Daughter-in-Law

1

You, once a belle in Shreveport,
with henna-colored hair, skin like a peachbud,
still have your dresses copied from that time,
and play a Chopin prelude
called by Cortot: *'Delicious recollections
float like perfume through the memory.'*

Your mind now, moldering like wedding-cake,
heavy with useless experience, rich
with suspicion, rumor, fantasy,
crumbling to pieces under the knife-edge
of mere fact. In the prime of your life.

Nervy, glowering, your daughter
wipes the teaspoons, grows another way.

2

Banging the coffee-pot into the sink
she hears the angels chiding, and looks out
past the raked gardens to the sloppy sky.
Only a week since They said: *Have no patience.*

The next time it was: *Be insatiable.*
Then: *Save yourself; others you cannot save.*
Sometimes she's let the tapstream scald her arm,
a match burn to her thumbnail,

or held her hand above the kettle's snout
right in the woolly steam. They are probably angels,
since nothing hurts her anymore, except
each morning's grit blowing into her eyes.

3

A thinking woman sleeps with monsters.
The beak that grips her, she becomes. And Nature,
that sprung-lidded, still commodious
steamer-trunk of *tempora* and *mores*
gets stuffed with it all: the mildewed orange-flowers,
the female pills, the terrible breasts
of Boadicea beneath flat foxes' heads and orchids.

Two handsome women, gripped in argument,
each proud, acute, subtle, I hear scream
across the cut glass and majolica

like Furies cornered from their prey:
The argument *ad feminam,* all the old knives
that have rusted in my back, I drive in yours,
ma semblable, ma soeur!

4

Knowing themselves too well in one another:
their gifts no pure fruition, but a thorn,
the prick filed sharp against a hint of scorn . . .
Reading while waiting
for the iron to heat,
writing, *My Life had stood—a Loaded Gun—*
in that Amherst pantry while the jellies boil and scum,
or, more often,
iron-eyed and beaked and purposed as a bird,
dusting everything on the whatnot every day of life.

5

Dulce ridens, dulce loquens,
she shaves her legs until they gleam
like petrified mammoth-tusk.

6

When to her lute Corinna sings
neither words nor music are her own;
only the long hair dipping
over her cheek, only the song
of silk against her knees
and these
adjusted in reflections of an eye.

Poised, trembling and unsatisfied, before
an unlocked door, that cage of cages,
tell us, you bird, you tragical machine—
is this *fertilisante douleur?* Pinned down

by love, for you the only natural action,
are you edged more keen
to prise the secrets of the vault? has Nature shown
her household books to you, daughter-in-law,
that her sons never saw?

7

'To have in this uncertain world some stay
which cannot be undermined, is
of the utmost consequence.'
                              Thus wrote
a woman, partly brave and partly good,
who fought with what she partly understood.
Few men about her would or could do more,
hence she was labeled harpy, shrew and whore.

8

'You all die at fifteen,' said Diderot,
and turn part legend, part convention.
Still, eyes inaccurately dream
behind closed windows blankening with steam.
Deliciously, all that we might have been,
all that we were—fire, tears,
wit, taste, martyred ambition—
stirs like the memory of refused adultery
the drained and flagging bosom of our middle years.

9

Not that it is done well, but
that it is done at all? Yes, think
of the odds! or shrug them off forever.
This luxury of the precocious child,
Time's precious chronic invalid,—
would we, darlings, resign it if we could?

Our blight has been our sinecure:
mere talent was enough for us—
glitter in fragments and rough drafts.

Sigh no more, ladies.
                              Time is male
and in his cups drinks to the fair.
Bemused by gallantry, we hear
our mediocrities over-praised,
indolence read as abnegation,
slattern thought styled intuition,
every lapse forgiven, our crime
only to cast too bold a shadow
or smash the mold straight off.

For that, solitary confinement,
tear gas, attrition shelling.
Few applicants for that honor.

10

                              Well,
she's long about her coming, who must be
more merciless to herself than history.
Her mind full to the wind, I see her plunge
breasted and glancing through the currents,
taking the light upon her
at least as beautiful as any boy
or helicopter,
                    poised, still coming,
her fine blades making the air wince

but her cargo
no promise then:
delivered
palpable
ours.

Necessities of Life

Piece by piece I seem
to re-enter the world: I first began

a small, fixed dot, still see
that old myself, a dark-blue thumbtack

pushed into the scene,
a hard little head protruding

from the pointillist's buzz and bloom.
After a time the dot

begins to ooze. Certain heats
melt it.
Now I was hurriedly

blurring into ranges
of burnt red, burning green,

whole biographies swam up and
swallowed me like Jonah.

Jonah! I was Wittgenstein,
Mary Wollstonecraft, the soul

of Louis Jouvet, dead
in a blown-up photograph.

Till, wolfed almost to shreds,
I learned to make myself

unappetizing. Scaly as a dry bulb
thrown into a cellar

I used myself, let nothing use me.
Like being on a private dole,

sometimes more like kneading bricks in Egypt.
What life was there, was mine,

now and again to lay
one hand on a warm brick

and touch the sun's ghost
with economical joy,

now and again to name
over the bare necessities.

So much for those days. Soon
practice may make me middling-perfect, I'll

dare inhabit the world
trenchant in motion as an eel, solid

as a cabbage-head. I have invitations:
a curl of mist steams upward

from a field, visible as my breath,
houses along a road stand waiting

like old women knitting, breathless
to tell their tales.

The Burning of Paper Instead of Children

> *I was in danger of*
> *verbalizing my moral*
> *impulses out of existence.*
> —Daniel Berrigan,
> on trial in Baltimore.

1. My neighbor, a scientist and art-collector, telephones me in a
state of violent emotion. He tells me that my son and his, aged
eleven and twelve, have on the last day of school burned a
mathematics textbook in the backyard. He has forbidden my
son to come to his house for a week, and has forbidden his own
son to leave the house during that time. 'The burning of a
book,' he says, 'arouses terrible sensations in me, memories of
Hitler; there are few things that upset me so much as the idea
of burning a book.'

Back there: the library, walled
with green Britannicas
Looking again
in Dürer's *Complete Works*
for MELANCOLIA, the baffled woman

the crocodiles in Herodotus
the Book of the Dead
the *Trial of Jeanne d'Arc,* so blue
I think, It is her color

and they take the book away
because I dream of her too often

love and fear in a house
knowledge of the oppressor
I know it hurts to burn

2. To imagine a time of silence
or few words
a time of chemistry and music

the hollows above your buttocks
traced by my hand
or, *hair is like flesh*, you said

an age of long silence

relief

from this tongue   this slab of limestone
or reinforced concrete
fanatics and traders
dumped on this coast wildgreen clayred
that breathed once
in signals of smoke
sweep of the wind

knowledge of the oppressor
this is the oppressor's language

yet I need it to talk to you

*3. People suffer highly in poverty and it takes dignity and in-
telligence to overcome this suffering. Some of the suffering are:
a child did not had dinner last night: a child steal because he
did not have money to buy it: to hear a mother say she do not
have money to buy food for her children and to see a child
without cloth it will make tears in your eyes.*

(the fracture of order
the repair of speech
to overcome this suffering)

4. We lie under the sheet
after making love, speaking
of loneliness
relieved in a book
relived in a book

so on that page
the clot and fissure
of it appears
words of a man
in pain
a naked word
entering the clot
a hand grasping
through bars:

deliverance

What happens between us
has happened for centuries
we know it from literature

still it happens

sexual jealousy
outflung hand
beating bed

dryness of mouth
after panting

there are books that describe all this
and they are useless

You walk into the woods behind a house
there in that country
you find a temple
built eighteen hundred years ago
you enter without knowing
what it is you enter

so it is with us

no one knows what may happen
though the books tell everything

burn the texts   said Artaud

5. *I am composing on the typewriter late at night, thinking of today. How well we all spoke. A language is a map of our failures. Frederick Douglass wrote an English purer than Milton's. People suffer highly in poverty. There are methods but we do not use them. Joan, who could not read, spoke some peasant form of French. Some of the suffering are: it is hard to tell the truth; this is America; I cannot touch you now. In America we have only the present tense. I am in danger. You are in danger. The burning of a book arouses no sensation in me. I know it hurts to burn. There are flames of napalm in Catonsville, Maryland. I know it hurts to burn. The typewriter is overheated, my mouth is burning, I cannot touch you and this is the oppressor's language.*

A Valediction Forbidding Mourning

My swirling wants. Your frozen lips.
The grammar turned and attacked me.
Themes, written under duress.
Emptiness of the notations.

They gave me a drug that slowed the healing of wounds.

I want you to see this before I leave:
the experience of repetition as death
the failure of criticism to locate the pain
the poster in the bus that said:
my bleeding is under control.

A red plant in a cemetery of plastic wreaths.

A last attempt: the language is a dialect called metaphor.
These images go unglossed: hair, glacier, flashlight.
When I think of a landscape I am thinking of a time.
When I talk of taking a trip I mean forever.
I could say: those mountains have a meaning
but further than that I could not say.

To do something very common, in my own way.

Diving into the Wreck

First having read the book of myths,
and loaded the camera,
and checked the edge of the knife-blade,
I put on
the body-armor of black rubber
the absurd flippers
the grave and awkward mask.
I am having to do this
not like Cousteau with his
assiduous team
aboard the sun-flooded schooner
but here alone.

There is a ladder.
The ladder is always there
hanging innocently
close to the side of the schooner.
We know what it is for,
we who have used it.
Otherwise
it's a piece of maritime floss
some sundry equipment.

I go down.
Rung after rung and still
the oxygen immerses me
the blue light
the clear atoms
of our human air.
I go down.
My flippers cripple me,
I crawl like an insect down the ladder
and there is no one
to tell me when the ocean
will begin.

First the air is blue and then
it is bluer and then green and then
black I am blacking out and yet
my mask is powerful
it pumps my blood with power
the sea is another story
the sea is not a question of power
I have to learn alone
to turn my body without force
in the deep element.

And now: it is easy to forget
what I came for
among so many who have always
lived here
swaying their crenellated fans
between the reefs
and besides
you breathe differently down here.

I came to explore the wreck.
The words are purposes.
The words are maps.

I came to see the damage that was done
and the treasures that prevail.
I stroke the beam of my lamp
slowly along the flank
of something more permanent
than fish or weed

the thing I came for:
the wreck and not the story of the wreck
the thing itself and not the myth
the drowned face always staring
toward the sun
the evidence of damage
worn by salt and sway into this threadbare beauty
the ribs of the disaster
curving their assertion
among the tentative haunters.

This is the place.
And I am here, the mermaid whose dark hair
streams black, the merman in his armored body
We circle silently
about the wreck
we dive into the hold.
I am she: I am he

whose drowned face sleeps with open eyes
whose breasts still bear the stress
whose silver, copper, vermeil cargo lies
obscurely inside barrels
half-wedged and left to rot
we are the half-destroyed instruments
that once held to a course
the water-eaten log
the fouled compass

We are, I am, you are
by cowardice or courage
the one who find our way
back to this scene
carrying a knife, a camera
a book of myths
in which
our names do not appear.

The Phenomenology of Anger

1. The freedom of the wholly mad
to smear & play with her madness
write with her fingers dipped in it
the length of a room

which is not, of course, the freedom
you have, walking on Broadway
to stop & turn back or go on
10 blocks; 20 blocks

but feels enviable maybe
to the compromised

curled in the placenta of the real
which was to feed & which is strangling her.

2. Trying to light a log that's lain in the damp
as long as this house has stood:
even with dry sticks I can't get started
even with thorns.
I twist last year into a knot of old headlines
—this rose won't bloom.

How does a pile of rags the machinist wiped his hands on
feel in its cupboard, hour upon hour?
Each day during the heat-wave
they took the temperature of the haymow.
I huddled fugitive
in the warm sweet simmer of the hay

muttering: *Come.*

3. Flat heartland of winter.
The moonmen come back from the moon
the firemen come out of the fire.
Time without a taste: time without decisions.

Self-hatred, a monotone in the mind.
The shallowness of a life lived in exile
even in the hot countries.
Cleaver, staring into a window full of knives.

4. White light splits the room.
Table.   Window.   Lampshade.   You.

Integrity

the quality or state of being complete; unbroken condition; entirety
                                                    —Webster

A wild patience has taken me this far

as if I had to bring to shore
a boat with a spasmodic outboard motor
old sweaters, nets, spray-mottled books
tossed in the prow

some kind of sun burning my shoulder-blades.
Splashing the oarlocks. Burning through.
Your fore-arms can get scalded, licked with pain
in a sun blotted like unspoken anger
behind a casual mist.

The length of daylight
this far north, in this
forty-ninth year of my life
is critical.

The light is critical: of me, of this
long-dreamed, involuntary landing
on the arm of an inland sea.
The glitter of the shoal
depleting into shadow
I recognize: the stand of pines
violet-black really, green in the old postcard
but really I have nothing but myself
to go by; nothing
stands in the realm of pure necessity
except what my hands can hold.

Nothing but myself? . . . My selves.
After so long, this answer.
As if I had always known
I steer the boat in, simply.
The motor dying on the pebbles
cicadas taking up the hum
dropped in the silence.

Anger and tenderness: my selves.
And now I can believe they breathe in me
as angels, not polarities.
Anger and tenderness: the spider's genius
to spin and weave in the same action
from her own body, anywhere—
even from a broken web.

The cabin in the stand of pines
is still for sale. I know this. Know the print
of the last foot, the hand that slammed and locked that door,
then stopped to wreathe the rain-smashed clematis
back on the trellis
for no one's sake except its own.
I know the chart nailed to the wallboards
the icy kettle squatting on the burner.
The hands that hammered in those nails
emptied that kettle one last time
are these two hands
and they have caught the baby leaping
from between trembling legs
and they have worked the vacuum aspirator
and stroked the sweated temples
and steered the boat here through this hot
misblotted sunlight, critical light
imperceptibly scalding
the skin these hands will also salve.

Frame

Winter twilight. She comes out of the laboratory, last class of the day
a pile of notebooks slung in her knapsack, coat
zipped high against the already swirling
evening sleet. The wind is wicked and the
busses slower than usual. On her mind
is organic chemistry and the issue
of next month's rent and will it be possible to
bypass the professor with the coldest eyes
to get a reference for graduate school,
and whether any of them, even those who smile

can see, looking at her, a biochemist
or a marine biologist, which of the faces
can she trust to see her at all, either today
or in any future. The busses are worm-slow in the
quickly gathering dark. *I don't know her. I am*
standing though somewhere just outside the frame
of all this, trying to see. At her back
the newly finished building suddenly looks
like shelter, it has glass doors, lighted halls
presumably heat. The wind is wicked. She throws a
glance down the street, sees no bus coming and runs
up the newly constructed steps into the newly
constructed hallway. *I am standing all this time*
just beyond the frame, trying to see. She runs
her hand through the crystals of sleet about to melt
on her hair. She shifts the weight of the books
on her back. It isn't warm here exactly but it's
out of that wind. Through the glass
door panels she can watch for the bus through the thickening
weather. Watching so, she is not
watching for the white man who watches the building
who has been watching her. This is Boston 1979.
I am standing somewhere at the edge of the frame
watching the man, we are both white, who watches the building
telling her to move on, get out of the hallway.
I can hear nothing because I am not supposed to be
present but I can see her gesturing
out toward the street at the wind-raked curb
I see her drawing her small body up
against the implied charges. The man
goes away. Her body is different now.
It is holding together with more than a hint of fury
and more than a hint of fear. She is smaller, thinner
more fragile-looking than I am. *But I am not supposed to be*
there. I am just outside the frame
of this action when the anonymous white man
returns with a white police officer. Then she starts

to leave into the windraked night but already
the policeman is going to work, the handcuffs are on her
wrists he is throwing her down his knee has gone into
her breast he is dragging her down the stairs *I am unable*
to hear a sound of all this all that I know is what
I can see from this position there is no soundtrack
to go with this and I understand at once
it is meant to be in silence that this happens
in silence that he pushes her into the car
banging her head in silence that she cries out
in silence that she tries to explain she was only
waiting for a bus
in silence that he twists the flesh of her thigh
with his nails in silence that her tears begin to flow
that she pleads with the other policeman as if
he could be trusted to see her at all
in silence that in the precinct she refuses to give her name
in silence that they throw her into the cell
in silence that she stares him
straight in the face in silence that he sprays her
in her eyes with Mace in silence that she sinks her teeth
into his hand in silence that she is charged
with trespass assault and battery in
silence that at the sleet-swept corner her bus
passes without stopping and goes on
in silence. *What I am telling you*
is told by a white woman who they will say
was never there. I say I am there.

Robert Creeley

The Immoral Proposition

If you never do anything for anyone else
you are spared the tragedy of human relation-

ships. If quietly and like another time
there is the passage of an unexpected thing:

to look at it is more
than it was. God knows

nothing is competent nothing is
all there is. The unsure

egoist is not
good for himself.

The Way

My love's manners in bed
are not to be discussed by me,
as mine by her
I would not credit comment upon gracefully.

Yet I ride by the margin of that lake in
the wood, the castle,
and the excitement of strongholds;
and have a small boy's notion of doing good.

Oh well, I will say here,
knowing each man,
let you find a good wife too,
and love her as hard as you can.

The Awakening

FOR CHARLES OLSON

He feels small as he awakens,
but in the stream's sudden mirror,
a pool of darkening water,
sees his size with his own two eyes.

The trees are taller here,
fall off to no field or clearing,
and depend on the inswept air
for the place in which he finds himself thus lost.

I was going on to tell you
when the door bell rang it was
another story as I know
previously had happened, had occurred.

That was a woman's impression
of the wonders of the morning, the same place,
whiter air now, and strong breezes
move the birds off in that first freshening.

O wisest of gods! Unnatural prerogatives
would err to concur, would fall deafened
between the seen, the green green,
and the ring of a far off telephone.

God is no bone of whitened contention.
God is not air, nor hair, is not
a conclusive concluding
to remote yearnings. He moves

only as I move, you also move to
the awakening, across long rows, of beds,
stumble breathlessly, on leg pins and crutch,
moving at all as all men, because you must.

The Rain

All night the sound had
come back again,
and again falls
this quiet, persistent rain.

What am I to myself
that must be remembered,
insisted upon
so often? Is it

that never the ease,
even the hardness,
of rain falling
will have for me

something other than this,
something not so insistent—
am I to be locked in this
final uneasiness.

Love, if you love me,
lie next to me.
Be for me, like rain,
the getting out

of the tiredness, the fatuousness, the semi-
lust of intentional indifference.
Be wet
with a decent happiness.

For Love

FOR BOBBIE

Yesterday I wanted to
speak of it, that sense above
the others to me
important because all

that I know derives
from what it teaches me.
Today, what is it that
is finally so helpless,

different, despairs of its own
statement, wants to
turn away, endlessly
to turn away.

If the moon did not . . .
no, if you did not
I wouldn't either, but
what would I not

do, what prevention, what
thing so quickly stopped.
That is love yesterday
or tomorrow, not

now. Can I eat
what you give me. I
have not earned it. Must
I think of everything

as earned. Now love also
becomes a reward so
remote from me I have
only made it with my mind.

Here is tedium,
despair, a painful
sense of isolation and
whimsical if pompous

self-regard. But that image
is only of the mind's
vague structure, vague to me
because it is my own.

Love, what do I think
to say. I cannot say it.
What have you become to ask,
what have I made you into,

companion, good company,
crossed legs with skirt, or
soft body under
the bones of the bed.

Nothing says anything
but that which it wishes
Would come true, fears
what else might happen in

some other place, some
other time not this one.
A voice in my place, an
echo of that only in yours.

Let me stumble into
not the confession but
the obsession I begin with
now. For you

also (also)
some time beyond place, or
place beyond time, no
mind left to

say anything at all,
that face gone, now.
Into the company of love
it all returns.

The Rhythm

It is all a rhythm,
from the shutting
door, to the window
opening,

the seasons, the sun's
light, the moon,
the oceans, the
growing of things,

the mind in men
personal, recurring
in them again,
thinking the end

is not the end, the
time returning,
themselves dead but
someone else coming.

If in death I am dead,
then in life also
dying, dying . . .
And the women cry and die.

The little children
grow only to old men.
The grass dries,
the force goes.

But is met by another
returning, oh not mine,
not mine, and
in turn dies.

The rhythm which projects
from itself continuity
bending all to its force
from window to door,
from ceiling to floor,
light at the opening,
dark at the closing.

I keep to myself
such measures

I keep to myself such
measures as I care for,
daily the rocks
accumulate position.

There is nothing
but what thinking makes
it less tangible. The mind,
fast as it goes, loses

pace, puts in place of it
like rocks simple markers,
for a way only to
hopefully come back to

where it cannot. All
forgets. My mind sinks.
I hold in both hands such weight
it is my only description.

A Place

The wetness of that street, the light,
the way the clouds were heavy is
not description. But in the memory I fear

the distortion. I do not feel
what it was I was feeling. I am impatient to begin again, open

whatever door it was, find the weather
is out there, grey, the rain then and
now falling from the sky to the wet ground.

Thom Gunn

The Wound

The huge wound in my head began to heal
About the beginning of the seventh week.
Its valleys darkened, its villages became still:
For joy I did not move and dared not speak;
Not doctors would cure it, but time, its patient skill.

And constantly my mind returned to Troy.
After I sailed the seas I fought in turn
On both sides, sharing even Helen's joy
Of place, and growing up—to see Troy burn—
As Neoptolemus, that stubborn boy.

I lay and rested as prescription said.
Manoeuvred with the Greeks, or sallied out
Each day with Hector. Finally my bed
Became Achilles' tent, to which the lout
Thersites came reporting numbers dead.

I was myself: subject to no man's breath:
My own commander was my enemy.
And while my belt hung up, sword in the sheath,
Thersites shambled in and breathlessly
Cackled about my friend Patroclus' death.

I called for armour, rose, and did not reel.
But, when I thought, rage at his noble pain
Flew to my head, and turning I could feel
My wound break open wide. Over again
I had to let those storm-lit valleys heal.

The Beach Head

Now that a letter gives me ground at last
For starting from, I see my enterprise
Is more than application by a blast
Upon a trumpet slung beside a gate,
Security a fraud, and how unwise
Was disembarking on your Welfare State.

What should they see in you but what I see,
These friends you mention whom I do not know?
—You unsuspecting that a refugee
Might want the land complete, write in a tone
Too matter-of-fact, of small affairs below
Some minister's seduction of the Crown.

And even if they could be innocent,
They still applaud you, keep you satisfied
And occupy your time, which I resent.
Their werewolf lust and cunning are afraid
Of night-exposure in the hair, so hide
Distant as possible from my palisade.

I have my ground. A brain-sick enemy
Pacing the beach head he so plotted for
Which now seems trivial to his jealousy
And ignorance of the great important part,
I almost wish I had no narrow shore.
I seek a pathway to the country's heart.

Shall I be John a Gaunt and with my band
Of mad bloods pass in one spectacular dash,
Fighting before and after, through your land,
To issue out unharmed the farther side,
With little object other than panache
And showing what great odds may be defied?

That way achievement would at once be history:
Living inside, I would not know, the danger:

Hurry is blind and so does not brave mystery;
I should be led to underrate, by haste,
Your natural beauties: while I, hare-brained stranger,
Would not be much distinguished from the rest.

Or shall I wait and calculate my chances,
Consolidating this my inch-square base,
Picking off rival spies that tread your glances:
Then plan when you have least supplies or clothing
A pincer-move to end in an embrace,
And risk that your mild liking turn to loathing?

On the Move

'Man, you gotta Go.'

The blue jay scuffling in the bushes follows
Some hidden purpose, and the gust of birds
That spurts across the field, the wheeling swallows,
Have nested in the trees and undergrowth.
Seeking their instinct, or their poise, or both,
One moves with an uncertain violence
Under the dust thrown by a baffled sense
Or the dull thunder of approximate words.

On motorcycles, up the road, they come:
Small, black, as flies hanging in heat, the Boys,
Until the distance throws them forth, their hum
Bulges to thunder held by calf and thigh.
In goggles, donned impersonality,
In gleaming jackets trophied with the dust,
They strap in doubt—by hiding it, robust—
And almost hear a meaning in their noise.

Exact conclusion of their hardiness
Has no shape yet, but from known whereabouts

They ride, direction where the tires press.
They scare a flight of birds across the field:
Much that is natural, to the will must yield.
Men manufacture both machine and soul,
And use what they imperfectly control
To dare a future from the taken routes.

It is a part solution, after all.
One is not necessarily discord.
On earth; or damned because, half animal,
One lacks direct instinct, because one wakes
Afloat on movement that divides and breaks.
One joins the movement in a valueless world,
Choosing it, till, both hurler and the hurled,
One moves as well, always toward, toward.

A minute holds them, who have come to go:
The self-defined, astride the created will
They burst away; the towns they travel through
Are home for neither bird nor holiness,
For birds and saints complete their purposes.
At worst, one is in motion; and at best,
Reaching no absolute, in which to rest,
One is always nearer by not keeping still.

California

Lines for a Book

I think of all the toughs through history
And thank heaven they lived, continually.
I praise the overdogs from Alexander
To those who would not play with Stephen Spender.
Their pride exalted some, some overthrew,
But was not vanity at last: they knew
That though the mind has also got a place
It's not in marvelling at its mirrored face

And evident sensibility. It's better
To go and see your friend than write a letter;
To be a soldier than to be a cripple;
To take an early weaning from the nipple
Than think your mother is the only girl;
To be insensitive, to steel the will,
Than sit irresolute all day at stool
Inside the heart; and to despise the fool,
Who may not help himself and may not choose,
Than give him pity which he cannot use.
I think of those exclusive by their action,
For whom mere thought could be no satisfaction—
The athletes lying under tons of dirt
Or standing gelded so they cannot hurt
The pale curators and the families
By calling up disturbing images.
I think of all the toughs through history
And thank heaven they lived, continually.

Thoughts on Unpacking

Unpacking in the raw new rooms, I clear,
Or try to clear, a space for us, that we
May cultivate an ease of moving here
    With no encumbrance near,
In amplitude. But something hinders me:

Where do these go, these knick-knacks I forgot?
—Gadgets we bought and kept, thinking perhaps
They might be useful some day, and a lot
    Of others that were not:
Bent keys, Italian grammars, Mickey Mouse caps.

And there are worse grotesques that, out of sight,
Unpacked, unlabelled, somehow followed too:
The urgencies we did not share, the spite

Of such and such a night,
Poses, mistakes—an unclean residue—

That drift, one after other, till I find
They have filled the space I carefully prepared;
The sagging shapes I thought we left behind
    Crawl out within the mind
Seeming to sneer 'This is the past you shared.'

I take a broom to them; but when I thrust
Round the diminished luggage, some roll back,
Surviving from my outbreak of disgust
    As balls of hair and dust
Made buoyant with a kind of fictive lack.

I need your help with these. They rest unseen
In furniture we know, and plot a changing
To grey confusion of the space between.
    Now, as I sweep it clean,
I realise that love is an arranging.

In Santa Maria Del Popolo

Waiting for when the sun an hour or less
Conveniently oblique makes visible
The painting on one wall of this recess
By Caravaggio, of the Roman School,
I see how shadow in the painting brims
With a real shadow, drowning all shapes out
But a dim horse's haunch and various limbs,
Until the very subject is in doubt.

But evening gives the act, beneath the horse
And one indifferent groom, I see him sprawl,
Foreshortened from the head, with hidden face,
Where he has fallen, Saul becoming Paul.

O wily painter, limiting the scene
From a cacophony of dusty forms
To the one convulsion, what is it you mean
In that wide gesture of the lifting arms?

No Ananias croons a mystery yet,
Casting the pain out under name of sin.
The painter saw what was, an alternate
Candour and secrecy inside the skin.
He painted, elsewhere, that firm insolent
Young whore in Venus' clothes, those pudgy cheats,
Those sharpers; and was strangled, as things went,
For money, by one such picked off the streets.

I turn, hardly enlightened, from the chapel
To the dim interior of the church instead,
In which there kneel already several people,
Mostly old women: each head closeted
In tiny fists holds comfort as it can.
Their poor arms are too tired for more than this
—For the large gesture of solitary man,
Resisting, by embracing, nothingness.

Innocence

TO TONY WHITE

He ran the course and as he ran he grew,
And smelt his fragrance in the field. Already,
Running he knew the most he ever knew,
The egotism of a healthy body.

Ran into manhood, ignorant of the past:
Culture of guilt and guilt's vague heritage,
Self-pity and the soul; what he possessed
Was rich, potential, like the bud's tipped rage.

The Corps developed, it was plain to see,
Courage, endurance, loyalty, and skill
To a morale firm as morality,
Hardening him to an instrument, until

The finitude of virtues that were there
Bodied within the swarthy uniform
A compact innocence, child-like and clear,
No doubt could penetrate, no act could harm.

When he stood near the Russian partisan
Being burned alive, he therefore could behold
The ribs wear gently through the darkening skin
And sicken only at the Northern cold,

Could watch the fat burn with a violent flame
And feel disgusted only at the smell,
And judge that all pain finishes the same
As melting quietly by his boots it fell.

In the Tank

A man sat in the felon's tank, alone,
Fearful, ungrateful, in a cell for two.
And from his metal bunk, the lower one,
He studied where he was, as felons do.

The cell was clean and cornered, and contained
A bowl, grey gritty soap, and paper towels,
A mattress lumpy and not over-stained,
Also a toilet, for the felon's bowels.

He could see clearly all there was to see,
And later when the lights flicked off at nine
He saw as clearly all there was to see:
An order without colour, bulk, or line.

And then he knew exactly where he sat.
For though the total riches could not fail
—Red weathered brick, fountains, wisteria—yet
Still they contained the silence of a jail,

The jail contained a tank, the tank contained
A box, a mere suspension, at the centre,
Where there was nothing left to understand,
And where he must re-enter and re-enter.

Lawrence Ferlinghetti

In Goya's greatest scenes we seem to see

In Goya's greatest scenes we seem to see
                              the people of the world
      exactly at the moment when
            they first attained the title of
                              'suffering humanity'
      They writhe upon the page
                        in a veritable rage
                              of adversity
         Heaped up
               groaning with babies and bayonets
                              under cement skies
            in an abstract landscape of blasted trees
            bent statues bats wings and beaks
                  slippery gibbets
            cadavers and carnivorous cocks
            and all the final hollering monsters
                  of the
                  'imagination of disaster'
            they are so bloody real
                        it is as if they really still existed

   And they do

            Only the landscape is changed

   They still are ranged along the roads
         plagued by legionaires
                        false windmills and demented roosters

They are the same people
                              only further from home
        on freeways fifty lanes wide
                    on a concrete continent
                              spaced with bland billboards
                    illustrating imbecile illusions of happiness
        The scene shows fewer tumbrils
                    but more maimed citizens
                                        in painted cars
        and they have strange license plates
        and engines
                    that devour America

Don't let that horse eat that violin

Don't let that horse
                    eat that violin

    cried Chagall's mother

                              But he
                    kept right on
                              painting

And became famous

And kept on painting
                    The Horse With Violin In Mouth

And when he finally finished it
he jumped up upon the horse
                              and rode away
            waving the violin

And then with a low bow gave it
to the first naked nude he ran across

And there were no strings
                    attached

Constantly risking absurdity and death

Constantly risking absurdity
                              and death
        whenever he performs
                        above the heads
                                    of his audience
    the poet like an acrobat
                        climbs on rime
                              to a high wire of his own making
and balancing on eyebeams
                        above a sea of faces
        paces his way
                    to the other side of day
    performing entrechats
                        and sleight-of-foot tricks
and other high theatrics
                        and all without mistaking
            any thing
                    for what it may not be

    For he's the super realist
                        who must perforce perceive
            taut truth
                        before the taking of each stance or step
    in his supposed advance
                            toward that still higher perch
where Beauty stands and waits
                            with gravity
                                    to start her death-defying leap

    And he
        a little charleychaplin man
                        who may or may not catch
            her fair eternal form
                            spreadeagled in the empty air
            of existence

The pennycandystore beyond the El

The pennycandystore beyond the El
is where I first
                fell in love
                        with unreality
Jellybeans glowed in the semi-gloom
of that september afternoon
A cat upon the counter moved among
                                the licorice sticks
                    and tootsie rolls
        and Oh Boy Gum

Outside the leaves were falling as they died

A wind had blown away the sun

A girl ran in
Her hair was rainy
Her breasts were breathless in the little room

Outside the leaves were falling
                        and they cried
                                Too soon! too soon!

Dog

The dog trots freely in the street
and sees reality
and the things he sees
are bigger than himself
and the things he sees
are his reality
Drunks in doorways
Moons on trees
The dog trots freely thru the street

and the things he sees
are smaller than himself
Fish on newsprint
Ants in holes
Chickens in Chinatown windows
their heads a block away
The dog trots freely in the street
and the things he smells
smell something like himself
The dog trots freely in the street
past puddles and babies
cats and cigars
poolrooms and policemen
He doesn't hate cops
He merely has no use for them
and he goes past them
and past the dead cows hung up whole
in front of the San Francisco Meat Market
He would rather eat a tender cow
than a tough policeman
though either might do
And he goes past the Romeo Ravioli Factory
and past Coit's Tower
and past Congressman Doyle
He's afraid of Coit's Tower
but he's not afraid of Congressman Doyle
although what he hears is very discouraging
very depressing
very absurd
to a sad young dog like himself
to a serious dog like himself
But he has his own free world to live in
His own fleas to eat
He will not be muzzled
Congressman Doyle is just another
fire hydrant
to him
The dog trots freely in the street

and has his own dog's life to live
and to think about
and to reflect upon
touching and tasting and testing everything
investigating everything
without benefit of perjury
a real realist
with a real tale to tell
and a real tail to tell it with
a real live
            barking
                    democratic dog
engaged in real
                free enterprise
with something to say
                    about ontology
something to say
                about reality
                        and how to see it
                            and how to hear it
with his head cocked sideways
                        at streetcorners
as if he is just about to have
                        his picture taken
                            for Victor Records
                    listening for
                        His Master's Voice
            and looking
                    like a living questionmark
                            into the
                            great gramaphone
                            of puzzling existence
        with its wondrous hollow horn
                which always seems
            just about to spout forth
                            some Victorious answer
                                to everything

Junkman's Obbligato

Let's go
Come on
Let's go
Empty out our pockets
and disappear.
Missing all our appointments
and turning up unshaven
years later
old cigarette papers
stuck to our pants
leaves in our hair.
Let us not
worry about the payments
anymore.
Let them come
and take it away
whatever it was
we were paying for.
And us with it.

Let us arise and go now
to where dogs do it
Over the Hill
where they keep the earthquakes
behind the city dumps
lost among gasmains and garbage.
Let us see the City Dumps
for what they are.
My country tears of thee.
Let us disappear
in automobile graveyards
and reappear years later
picking rags and newspapers
drying our drawers
on garbage fires
patches on our ass.
Do not bother

to say goodbye
to anyone.
Your missus will not miss us.

Let's go
smelling of sterno
where the benches are filled
with discarded Bowling Green statues
in the interior dark night
of the flowery bowery
our eyes watery
with the contemplation
of empty bottles of muscatel.
Let us recite from broken bibles
on streetcorners
Follow dogs on docks
Speak wild songs
Throw stones
Say anything
Blink at the sun and scratch
and stumble into silence
Diddle in doorways
Know whores thirdhand
after everyone else is finished
Stagger befuddled into East River sunsets
Sleep in phone booths
Puke in pawnshops
wailing for a winter overcoat.

Let us arise and go now
under the city
where ashcans roll
and reappear in putrid clothes
as the uncrowned underground kings
of subway men's rooms.
Let us feed the pigeons
at the City Hall
urging them to do their duty
in the Mayor's office.

Hurry up please it's time.
The end is coming.
Flash floods
Disasters in the sun
Dogs unleashed
Sister in the street
her brassiere backwards.

Let us arise and go now
into the interior dark night
of the soul's still bowery
and find ourselves anew
where subways stall and wait
under the River.
Cross over
into full puzzlement.
South Ferry will not run forever.
They are cutting out the Bay ferries
but it is still not too late
to get lost in Oakland.
Washington has not yet toppled
from his horse.
There is still time to goose him
and go
leaving our income tax form behind
and our waterproof wristwatch with it
staggering blind after alleycats
under Brooklyn's Bridge
blown statues in baggy pants
our tincan cries and garbage voices
trailing.
Junk for sale!

Let's cut out let's go
into the real interior of the country
where hockshops reign
mere unblind anarchy upon us.
The end is here

but golf goes on at Burning Tree.
It's raining it's pouring
The Ole Man is snoring.
Another flood is coming
though not the kind you think.
There is still time to sink
and think.
I wish to descend in society.
I wish to make like free.
Swing low sweet chariot.
Let us not wait for the cadillacs
to carry us triumphant
into the interior
waving at the natives
like roman senators in the provinces
wearing poet's laurels
on lighted brows.
Let us not wait for the write-up
on page one
of The New York Times Book Review
images of insane success
smiling from the photo.
By the time they print your picture
in Life Magazine
you will have become a negative anyway
a print with a glossy finish.
They will have come and gotten you
to be famous
and you still will not be free.
Goodbye I'm going.
I'm selling everything
and giving away the rest
to the Good Will Industries.
It will be dark out there
with the Salvation Army Band.
And the mind its own illumination.
Goodbye I'm walking out on the whole scene.
Close down the joint.

The system is all loused up.
Rome was never like this.
I'm tired of waiting for Godot.
I am going where turtles win
I am going
where conmen puke and die
Down the sad esplanades
of the official world.
Junk for sale!
My country tears of thee.

Let us go then you and I
leaving our neckties behind on lampposts
Take up the full beard
of walking anarchy
looking like Walt Whitman
a homemade bomb in the pocket.
I wish to descend in the social scale.
High society is low society.
I am a social climber
climbing downward
And the descent is difficult.
The Upper Middle Class Ideal
is for the birds
but the birds have no use for it
having their own kind of pecking order
based upon birdsong.
Pigeons on the grass alas.

Let us arise and go now
to the Isle of Manisfree.
Let loose the hogs of peace.
Hurry up please it's time.
Let us arise and go now
into the interior
of Foster's Cafeteria.
So long Emily Post.
So long

Lowell Thomas.
Goodbye Broadway.
Goodbye Herald Square.
Turn it off.
Confound the system.
Cancel all our leases.
Lose the War
without killing anybody.
Let horses scream
and ladies run
to flushless powderrooms.
The end has just begun.
I want to announce it.
Run don't walk
to the nearest exit.
The real earthquake is coming.
I can feel the building shake.
I am the refined type.
I cannot stand it.
I am going
where asses lie down
with customs collectors who call themselves
literary critics.
My tool is dusty.
My body hung up too long
in strange suspenders.

Get me a bright bandana
for a jockstrap.
Turn loose and we'll be off
where sports cars collapse
and the world begins again.
Hurry up please it's time.
It's time and a half
and there's the rub.
The thinkpad makes homeboys of us all.
Let us cut out
into stray eternity.

Somewhere the fields are full of larks.
Somewhere the land is swinging.
My country 'tis of thee
I'm singing.

Let us arise and go now
to the Isle of Manisfree
and live the true blue simple life
of wisdom and wonderment
where all things grow
straight up
aslant and singing
in the yellow sun
poppies out of cowpods
thinking angels out of turds.
I must arise and go now
to the Isle of Manisfree
way up behind the broken words
and woods of Arcady.

Leonard Cohen

Elegy

Do not look for him
In brittle mountain streams:
They are too cold for any god;
And do not examine the angry rivers
For shreds of his soft body
Or turn the shore stones for his blood;
But in the warm salt ocean
He is descending through cliffs
Of slow green water
And the hovering coloured fish
Kiss his snow-bruised body
And build their secret nests
In his fluttering winding-sheet.

Story

She tells me a child built her house
one Spring afternoon,
but that the child was killed
crossing the street.

She says she read it in the newspaper,
that at the corner of this and this avenue
a child was run down by an automobile.

Of course I do not believe her.
She has built the house herself,
hung the oranges and coloured beads in the doorways,
crayoned flowers on the walls.

She has made the paper things for the wind,
collected crooked stones for their shadows in the sun,
fastened yellow and dark balloons to the ceiling.

Each time I visit her
she repeats the story of the child to me,
I never question her. It is important
to understand one's part in a legend.

I take my place
among the paper fish and make-believe clocks,
naming the flowers she has drawn,
smiling while she paints my head on large clay coins,
and making a sort of courtly love to her
when she contemplates her own traffic death.

You have the lovers

You have the lovers,
they are nameless, their histories only for each other,
and you have the room, the bed, and the windows.
Pretend it is a ritual.
Unfurl the bed, bury the lovers, blacken the windows,
let them live in that house for a generation or two.
No one dares disturb them.
Visitors in the corridor tip-toe past the long closed door,
they listen for sounds, for a moan, for a song:
nothing is heard, not even breathing.
You know they are not dead,
you can feel the presence of their intense love.
Your children grow up, they leave you,
they have become soldiers and riders.
Your mate dies after a life of service.
Who knows you? Who remembers you?
But in your house a ritual is in progress:
it is not finished: it needs more people.

One day the door is opened to the lover's chamber.
The room has become a dense garden,
full of colours, smells, sounds you have never known.
The bed is smooth as a wafer of sunlight,
in the midst of the garden it stands alone.
In the bed the lovers, slowly and deliberately and silently,
perform the act of love.
Their eyes are closed,
as tightly as if heavy coins of flesh lay on them.
Their lips are bruised with new and old bruises.
Her hair and his beard are hopelessly tangled.
When he puts his mouth against her shoulder
she is uncertain whether her shoulder
has given or received the kiss.
All her flesh is like a mouth.
He carries his fingers along her waist
and feels his own waist caressed.
She holds him closer and his own arms tighten around her.
She kisses the hand beside her mouth.
It is his hand or her hand, it hardly matters,
there are so many more kisses.
You stand beside the bed, weeping with happiness,
you carefully peel away the sheets
from the slow-moving bodies.
Your eyes are filled with tears, you barely make out the lovers,
As you undress you sing out, and your voice is magnificent
because now you believe it is the first human voice
heard in that room.
The garments you let fall grow into vines.
You climb into bed and recover the flesh.
You close your eyes and allow them to be sewn shut.
You create an embrace and fall into it.
There is only one moment of pain or doubt
as you wonder how many multitudes are lying beside your body,
but a mouth kisses and a hand soothes the moment away.

As the mist leaves no scar

As the mist leaves no scar
On the dark green hill,
So my body leaves no scar
On you, nor ever will.

When wind and hawk encounter,
What remains to keep?
So you and I encounter,
Then turn, then fall to sleep.

As many nights endure
Without a moon or star,
So will we endure
When one is gone and far.

Now of Sleeping

Under her grandmother's patchwork quilt
a calico bird's-eye view
of crops and boundaries
naming dimly the districts of her body
sleeps my Annie like a perfect lady

Like ages of weightless snow
on tiny oceans filled with light
her eyelids enclose deeply
a shade tree of birthday candles
one for every morning
until the now of sleeping

The small banner of blood
kept and flown by Brother Wind
long after the pierced bird fell down
is like her red mouth
among the squalls of pillow

Bearers of evil fancy
of dark intention and corrupting fashion
who come to rend the quilt
plough the eye and ground the mouth
will contend with mighty Mother Goose
and Farmer Brown and all good stories
of invincible belief
which surround her sleep
like the golden weather of a halo

Well-wishers and her true lover
may stay to watch my Annie
sleeping like a perfect lady
under her grandmother's patchwork quilt
but they must promise to whisper
and to vanish by morning—
all but her one true lover.

The Genius

For you
I will be a ghetto jew
and dance
and put white stockings
on my twisted limbs
and poison wells
across the town

For you
I will be an apostate jew
and tell the Spanish priest
of the blood vow
in the Talmud
and where the bones
of the child are hid

For you
I will be a banker jew

and bring to ruin
a proud old hunting king
and end his line

For you
I will be a Broadway jew
and cry in theatres
for my mother
and sell bargain goods
beneath the counter

For you
I will be a doctor jew
and search
in all the garbage cans
for foreskins
to sew back again

For you
I will be a Dachau jew
and lie down in lime
with twisted limbs
and bloated pain
no mind can understand

Style

I don't believe the radio stations
of Russia and America
but I like the music and I like
the solemn European voices announcing jazz
I don't believe opium or money
though they're hard to get
and punished with long sentences
I don't believe love
in the midst of my slavery I
do not believe

I am a man sitting in a house
on a treeless Argolic island
I will forget the grass of my mother's lawn
I know I will
I will forget the old telephone number
Fitzroy seven eight two oh
I will forget my style
I will have no style
I hear a thousand miles of hungry static
and the old clear water eating rocks
I hear the bells of mules eating
I hear the flowers eating the night
under their folds
Now a rooster with a razor
plants the haemophilia gash across
the soft black sky
and now I know for certain
I will forget my style
Perhaps a mind will open in this world
perhaps a heart will catch rain
Nothing will heal and nothing will freeze
but perhaps a heart will catch rain
America will have no style
Russia will have no style
It is happening in the twenty-eighth year
of my attention
I don't know what will become
of the mules with their lady eyes
or the old clear water
or the giant rooster
The early morning greedy radio eats
the governments one by one the languages
the poppy fields one by one
Beyond the numbered band
a silence develops for every style
for the style I laboured on
an external silence like the space
between insects in a swarm
electric unremembering

and it is aimed at us
(I am sleepy and frightened)
it makes toward me brothers

The Bus

I was the last passenger of the day,
I was alone on the bus,
I was glad they were spending all that money
just getting me up Eighth Avenue.
Driver! I shouted, it's you and me tonight,
let's run away from this big city
to a smaller city more suitable to the heart,
let's drive past the swimming pools of Miami Beach,
you in the driver's seat, me several seats back,
but in the racial cities we'll change places
so as to show how well you've done up North,
and let us find ourselves some tiny American fishing village
in unknown Florida
and park right at the edge of the sand,
a huge bus pointing out,
metallic, painted, solitary,
with New York plates.

The Music Crept by Us

I would-like to remind
the management
that the drinks are watered
and the hat-check girl
has syphilis
and the band is composed
of former ss monsters
However since it is

New Year's Eve
and I have lip cancer
I will place my
paper hat on my
concussion and dance

Disguises

I am sorry that the rich man must go
and his house become a hospital.
I loved his wine, his contemptuous servants,
his ten-year-old ceremonies.
I loved his car which he wore like a snail's shell
everywhere, and I loved his wife,
the hours she put into her skin,
the milk, the lust, the industries
that served her complexion.
I loved his son who looked British
but had American ambitions
and let the word aristocrat comfort him
like a reprieve while Kennedy reigned.
I loved the rich man: I hate to see
his season ticket for the Opera
fall into a pool for opera-lovers.

I am sorry that the old worker must go
who called me mister when I was twelve
and sir when I was twenty
who studied against me in obscure socialist
clubs which met in restaurants.
I loved the machine he knew like a wife's body.
I loved his wife who trained bankers
in an underground pantry
and never wasted her ambition in ceramics.
I loved his children who debate
and come first at McGill University.

Goodbye old gold-watch winner
all your complex loyalties
must now be borne by one-faced patriots.

Goodbye dope fiends of North Eastern Lunch
circa 1948, your spoons which were not
Swedish Stainless, were the same colour
as the hoarded clasps and hooks
of discarded soiled therapeutic corsets.
I loved your puns about snow
even if they lasted the full seven-month
Montreal winter. Go write your memoirs
for the Psychedelic Review.

Goodbye sex fiends of Beaver Pond
who dreamed of being jacked-off
by electric milking machines.
You had no Canada Council.
You had to open little boys
with a pen-knife.
I loved your statement to the press:
'I didn't think he'd mind.'
Goodbye articulate monsters
Abbot and Costello have met Frankenstein.

I am sorry that the conspirators must go
the ones who scared me by showing me
a list of all the members of my family.
I loved the way they reserved judgement
about Genghis Khan. They loved me because
I told them their little beards
made them dead-ringers for Lenin.
The bombs went off in Westmount
and now they are ashamed
like a successful outspoken Schopenhauerian
whose room-mate has committed suicide.
Suddenly they are all making movies.
I have no one to buy coffee for.

Allen Ginsberg

Howl (I & II)

FOR CARL SOLOMON

I

I saw the best minds of my generation destroyed by madness, starving hysterical naked,

dragging themselves through the negro streets at dawn looking for an angry fix,

angelheaded hipsters burning for the ancient heavenly connection to the starry dynamo in the machinery of night,

who poverty and tatters and hollow-eyed and high sat up smoking in the supernatural darkness of cold-water flats floating across the tops of cities contemplating jazz,

who bared their brains to Heaven under the El and saw Mohammedan angels staggering on tenement roofs illuminated,

who passed through universities with radiant cool eyes hallucinating Arkansas and Blake-light tragedy among the scholars of war,

who were expelled from the academies for crazy & publishing obscene odes on the windows of the skull,

who cowered in unshaven rooms in underwear, burning their money in wastebaskets and listening to the Terror through the wall,

who got busted in their pubic beards returning through Laredo with a belt of marijuana for New York,

who ate fire in paint hotels or drank turpentine in Paradise Alley, death, or purgatoried their torsos night after night

with dreams, with drugs, with waking nightmares, alcohol and cock and endless balls,

incomparable blind streets of shuddering cloud and lightning in the mind leaping toward poles of Canada & Paterson, illuminating all the motionless world of Time between,

Peyote solidities of halls, backyard green tree cemetery dawns, wine drunkenness over the rooftops, storefront boroughs of teahead joyride neon blinking traffic light, sun and moon and tree vibrations in the roaring winter dusks of Brooklyn, ashcan rantings and kind king light of mind,

who chained themselves to subways for the endless ride from Battery to holy Bronx on benzedrine until the noise of wheels and children brought them down shuddering mouth-wracked and battered bleak of brain all drained of brilliance in the drear light of Zoo,

who sank all night in submarine light of Bickford's floated out and sat through the stale beer afternoon in desolate Fugazzi's, listening to the crack of doom on the hydrogen jukebox,

who talked continuously seventy hours from park to pad to bar to Bellevue to museum to the Brooklyn Bridge,

a lost battalion of platonic conversationalists jumping down the stoops off fire escapes off windowsills off Empire State out of the moon,

yacketayakking screaming vomiting whispering facts and memories and anecdotes and eyeball kicks and shocks of hospitals and jails and wars,

whole intellects disgorged in total recall for seven days and nights with brilliant eyes, meat for the Synagogue cast on the pavement,

who vanished into nowhere Zen New Jersey leaving a trail of ambiguous picture postcards of Atlantic City Hall,

suffering Eastern sweats and Tangerian bone-grindings and migraines of China under junk-withdrawal in Newark's bleak furnished room,

who wandered around and around at midnight in the railroad yard wondering where to go, and went, leaving no broken hearts,

who lit cigarettes in boxcars boxcars boxcars racketing through snow toward lonesome farms in grandfather night,

who studied Plotinus Poe St John of the Cross telepathy and bop kaballa because the cosmos instinctively vibrated at their feet in Kansas,

who loned it through the streets of Idaho seeking visionary indian
    angels who were visionary indian angels,

who thought they were only mad when Baltimore gleamed in
    supernatural ecstasy,

who jumped in limousines with the Chinaman of Oklahoma on
    the impulse of winter midnight streetlight smalltown rain,

who lounged hungry and lonesome through Houston seeking
    jazz or sex or soup, and followed the brilliant Spaniard to
    converse about America and Eternity, a hopeless task, and
    so took ship to Africa,

who disappeared into the volcanoes of Mexico leaving behind
    nothing but the shadow of dungarees and the lava and ash
    of poetry scattered in fireplace Chicago,

who reappeared on the West Coast investigating the FBI in beards
    and shorts with big pacifist eyes sexy in their dark skin
    passing out incomprehensible leaflets,

who burned cigarette holes in their arms protesting the narcotic
    tobacco haze of Capitalism,

who distributed Supercommunist pamphlets in Union Square
    weeping and undressing while the sirens of Los Alamos
    wailed them down, and wailed down Wall, and the Staten
    Island ferry also wailed,

who broke down crying in white gymnasiums naked and trem-
    bling before the machinery of other skeletons,

who bit detectives in the neck and shrieked with delight in
    policecars for committing no crime but their own wild
    cooking pederasty and intoxication,

who howled on their knees in the subway and were dragged off
    the roof waving genitals and manuscripts,

who let themselves be fucked in the ass by saintly motorcyclists,
    and screamed with joy,

who blew and were blown by those human seraphim, the sailors,
    caresses of Atlantic and Caribbean love,

who balled in the morning in the evenings in rosegardens and the
    grass of public parks and cemeteries scattering their semen
    freely to whomever come who may,

who hiccupped endlessly trying to giggle but wound up with a
    sob behind a partition in a Turkish Bath when the blonde &
    naked angel came to pierce them with a sword,

who lost their loveboys to the three old shrews of fate the one
    eyed shrew of the heterosexual dollar the one eyed shrew
    that winks out of the womb and the one eyed shrew that
    does nothing but sit on her ass and snip the intellectual
    golden threads of the craftsman's loom,

who copulated ecstatic and insatiate with a bottle of beer a
    sweetheart a package of cigarettes a candle and fell off the
    bed, and continued along the floor and down the hall and
    ended fainting on the wall with a vision of ultimate cunt
    and come eluding the last gyzym of consciousness,

who sweetened the snatches of a million girls trembling in the
    sunset, and were red eyed in the morning but prepared to
    sweeten the snatch of the sunrise, flashing buttocks under
    barns and naked in the lake,

who went out whoring through Colorado in myriad stolen night-
    cars, N.C., secret hero of these poems, cocksman and Adonis
    of Denver—joy to the memory of his innumerable lays of
    girls in empty lots & diner backyards, moviehouses' rickety
    rows, on mountaintops in caves or with gaunt waitresses in
    familiar roadside lonely petticoat upliftings & especially
    secret gas-station solipisisms of johns, & hometown alleys
    too,

who faded out in vast sordid movies, were shifted in dreams,
    woke on a sudden Manhattan, and picked themselves up out
    of basements hungover with heartless Tokay and horrors of
    Third Avenue iron dreams & stumbled to unemployment
    offices,

who walked all night with their shoes full of blood on the snow-
    bank docks waiting for a door in the East River to open to
    a room full of steamheat and opium,

who created great suicidal dramas on the apartment cliff-banks of
    the Hudson under the wartime blue floodlight of the moon
    & their heads shall be crowned with laurel in oblivion,

who ate the lamb stew of the imagination or digested the crab at
    the muddy bottom of the rivers of Bowery,

who wept at the romance of the streets with their pushcarts full
    of onions and bad music,

who sat in boxes breathing in the darkness under the bridge, and
    rose up to build harpsichords in their lofts,

who coughed on the sixth floor of Harlem crowned with flame
under the tubercular sky surrounded by orange crates of
theology,

who scribbled all night rocking and rolling over lofty incan-
tations which in the yellow morning were stanzas of gibberish,

who cooked rotten animals lung heart feet tail borsht & tortillas
dreaming of the pure vegetable kingdom,

who plunged themselves under meat trucks looking for an egg,

who threw their watches off the roof to cast their ballot for
Eternity outside of Time, & alarm clocks fell on their heads
every day for the next decade,

who cut their wrists three times successively unsuccessfully, gave
up and were forced to open antique stores where they
thought they were growing old and cried,

who were burned alive in their innocent flannel suits on Madison
Avenue amid blasts of leaden verse & the tanked-up clatter
of the iron regiments of fashion & the nitroglycerine shrieks
of the fairies of advertising & the mustard gas of sinister
intelligent editors, or were run down by the drunken taxi-
cabs of Absolute Reality,

who jumped off the Brooklyn Bridge this actually happened and
walked away unknown and forgotten into the ghostly daze
of Chinatown soup alleyways & firetrucks, not even one
free beer,

who sang out of their windows in despair, fell out of the subway
window, jumped in the filthy Passaic, leaped on negroes,
cried all over the street, danced on broken wineglasses
barefoot smashed phonograph records of nostalgic European
1930s German jazz finished the whiskey and threw up
groaning into the bloody toilet, moans in their ears and the
blast of colossal steamwhistles,

who barreled down the highways of the past journeying to each
other's hotrod-Golgotha jail-solitude watch or Birmingham
jazz incarnation,

who drove crosscountry seventytwo hours to find out if I had a
vision or you had a vision or he had a vision to find out
Eternity,

who journeyed to Denver, who died in Denver, who came back
to Denver & waited in vain, who watched over Denver &
brooded & loned in Denver and finally went away to find
out the Time, & now Denver is lonesome for her heroes,

who fell on their knees in hopeless cathedrals praying for each
other's salvation and light and breasts, until the soul illuminated its hair for a second,

who crashed through their minds in jail waiting for impossible
criminals with golden heads and the charm of reality in
their hearts who sang sweet blues to Alcatraz,

who retired to Mexico to cultivate a habit, or Rocky Mount to
tender Buddha or Tangiers to boys or Southern Pacific to
the black locomotive or Harvard to Narcissus to Woodlawn
to the daisychain or grave,

who demanded sanity trials accusing the radio of hypnotism &
were left with their insanity & their hands & a hung jury,

who threw potato salad at CCNY lectures on Dadaism and sub-
sequently presented themselves on the granite steps of the
madhouse with shaven heads and harlequin speech of suicide, demanding instantaneous lobotomy,

and who were given instead the concrete void of insulin metrasol
electricity hydrotherapy psychotherapy occupational ther-
apy pingpong & amnesia,

who in humorless protest overturned only one symbolic pingpong table, resting briefly in catatonia,

returning years later truly bald except for a wig of blood, and
tears and fingers, to the visible madman doom of the wards
of the madtowns of the East,

Pilgrim State's Rockland's and Greystone's foetid halls, bicker-
ing with the echoes of the soul, rocking and rolling in the
midnight solitude-bench dolmen-realms of love, dream of
life a nightmare, bodies turned to stone as heavy as the
moon,

with mother finally ******, and the last fantastic book flung out
of the tenement window, and the last door closed at 4 a.m.
and the last telephone slammed at the wall in reply and the
last furnished room emptied down to the last piece of
mental furniture, a yellow paper rose twisted on a wire

hanger in the closet, and even that imaginary, nothing but a hopeful little bit of hallucination—

ah, Carl, while you are not safe I am not safe, and now you're really in the total animal soup of time—

and who therefore ran through the icy streets obsessed with a sudden flash of the alchemy of the use of the ellipse the catalog the meter & the vibrating plane,

who dreamt and made incarnate gaps in Time & Space through images juxtaposed, and trapped the archangel of the soul between 2 visual images and joined the elemental verbs and set the noun and dash of consciousness together jumping with sensation of Pater Omnipotens Aeterna Deus

to recreate the syntax and measure of poor human prose and stand before you speechless and intelligent and shaking with shame, rejected yet confessing out the soul to conform to the rhythm of thought in his naked and endless head,

the madman bum and angel beat in Time, unknown, yet putting down here what might be left to say in time come after death,

and rose reincarnate in the ghostly clothes of jazz in the goldhorn shadow of the band and blew the suffering of America's naked mind for love into an eli eli lamma lamma sabacthani saxophone cry that shivered the cities down to the last radio

with the absolute heart of the poem of life butchered out of their own bodies good to eat a thousand years.

II

What sphinx of cement and aluminum bashed open their skulls and ate up their brains and imagination?

Moloch! Solitude! Filth! Ugliness! Ashcans and unobtainable dollars! Children screaming under the stairways! Boys sobbing in armies! Old men weeping in the parks!

Moloch! Moloch! Nightmare of Moloch! Moloch the loveless! Mental Moloch! Moloch the heavy judger of men!

Moloch the incomprehensible prison! Moloch the crossbone soulless jailhouse and Congress of sorrows! Moloch whose buildings are judgement! Moloch the vast stone of war! Moloch the stunned goverments!

Moloch whose mind is pure machinery! Moloch whose blood is running money! Moloch whose fingers are ten armies! Moloch whose breast is a cannibal dynamo! Moloch whose ear is a smoking tomb!

Moloch whose eyes are a thousand blind windows! Moloch whose skyscrapers stand in the long streets like endless Jehovahs! Moloch whose factories dream and croak in the fog! Moloch whose smokestacks and antennae crown the cities!

Moloch whose love is endless oil and stone! Moloch whose soul is electricity and banks! Moloch whose poverty is the specter of genius! Moloch whose fate is a cloud of sexless hydrogen! Moloch whose name is the Mind!

Moloch in whom I sit lonely! Moloch in whom I dream Angels! Crazy in Moloch! Cocksucker in Moloch! Lacklove and manless in Moloch!

Moloch who entered my soul early! Moloch in whom I am a consciousness without a body! Moloch who frightened me out of my natural ecstasy! Moloch whom I abandon! Wake up in Moloch! Light streaming out of the sky!

Moloch! Moloch! Robot apartments! invisible suburbs! skeleton treasuries! blind capitals! demonic industries! spectral nations! invincible madhouses! granite cocks! monstrous bombs!

They broke their backs lifting Moloch to Heaven! Pavements, trees, radios, tons! lifting the city to Heaven which exists and is everywhere about us!

Visions! omens! hallucinations! miracles! ecstasies! gone down the American river!

Dreams! adorations! illuminations! religions! the whole boatload of sensitive bullshit!

Breakthroughs! over the river! flips and crucifixions! gone down the flood! Highs! Epiphanies! Despairs! Ten years' animal screams and suicides! Minds! New loves! Mad generation! down on the rocks of Time!

Real holy laughter in the river! They saw it all! the wild eyes! the holy yells! They bade farewell! They jumped off the roof! to solitude! waving! carrying flowers! Down to the river! into the street!

A Supermarket in California

What thoughts I have of you tonight, Walt Whitman, for I walked down the sidestreets under the trees with a headache self-conscious looking at the full moon.

In my hungry fatigue, and shopping for images, I went into the neon fruit supermarket, dreaming of your enumerations!

What peaches and what penumbras! Whole familes shopping at night! Aisles full of husbands! Wives in the avocados, babies in the tomatoes!—and you, Garcia Lorca, what were you doing down by the watermelons?

I saw you, Walt Whitman, childless, lonely old grubber, poking among the meats in the refrigerator and eyeing the grocery boys.

I heard you asking questions of each: Who killed the pork chops? What price bananas? Are you my Angel?

I wandered in and out of the brilliant stacks of cans following you, and followed in my imagination by the store detective.

We strode down the open corridors together in our solitary fancy tasting artichokes, possessing every frozen delicacy, and never passing the cashier.

Where are we going, Walt Whitman? The doors close in an hour. Which way does your beard point tonight?

(I touch your book and dream of our odyssey in the supermarket and feel absurd.)

Will we walk all night through solitary streets? The trees add shade to shade, lights out in the houses, we'll both be lonely.

Will we stroll dreaming of the lost America of love past blue automobiles in driveways, home to our silent cottage?

Ah, dear father, graybeard, lonely old courage-teacher, what America did you have when Charon quit poling his ferry and you got out on a smoking bank and stood watching the boat disappear on the black waters of Lethe?

Sunflower Sutra

I walked on the banks of the tincan banana dock and sat down
    under the huge shade of a Southern Pacific locomotive to
    look at the sunset over the box house hills and cry.
Jack Kerouac sat beside me on a busted rusty iron pole, compan-
    ion, we thought the same thoughts of the soul, bleak and
    blue and sad-eyed, surrounded by the gnarled steel roots
    of trees of machinery.
The oily water on the river mirrored the red sky, sun sank on top
    of final Frisco peaks, no fish in that stream, no hermit in
    those mounts, just ourselves rheumy-eyed and hungover
    like old bums on the riverbank, tired and wily.
Look at the Sunflower, he said, there was a dead gray shadow
    against the sky, big as a man, sitting dry on top of a pile of
    ancient sawdust—
—I rushed up enchanted—it was my first sunflower, memories of
    Blake—my visions—Harlem
and Hells of the Eastern rivers, bridges clanking Joes Greasy
    Sandwiches, dead baby carriages, black treadless tires for-
    gotten and unretreaded, the poem of the riverbank, con-
    doms & pots, steel knives, nothing stainless, only the dank
    muck and the razor sharp artifacts passing into the past—
and the gray Sunflower poised against the sunset, crackly bleak
    and dusty with the smut and smog and smoke of olden
    locomotives in its eye—
corolla of bleary spikes pushed down and broken like a battered
    crown, seeds fallen out of its face, soon-to-be-toothless
    mouth of sunny air, sunrays obliterated on its hairy head
    like a dried wire spiderweb,
leaves stuck out like arms out of the stem, gestures from the
    sawdust root, broke pieces of plaster fallen out of the black
    twigs, a dead fly in its ear,
Unholy battered old thing you were, my sunflower O my soul,
    I loved you then!
The grime was no man's grime but death and human locomotives,

all that dress of dust, that veil of darkened railroad skin, that
   smog of cheek, that eyelid of black mis'ry, that sooty hand
   or phallus or protuberance of artificial worse-than-dirt—
   industrial—modern—all that civilization spotting your crazy
   golden crown—

and those blear thoughts of death and dusty loveless eyes and
   ends and withered roots below, in the home-pile of sand and
   sawdust, rubber dollar bills, skin of machinery, the guts and
   innards of the weeping coughing car, the empty lonely tin-
   cans with their rusty tongues alack, what more could I
   name, the smoked ashes of some cock cigar, the cunts of
   wheelbarrows and the milky breasts of cars, wornout asses
   out of chairs & sphincters of dynamos—all these

entangled in your mummied roots—and you there standing before me in the sunset, all your glory in your form!

A perfect beauty of a sunflower! a perfect excellent lovely sunflower existence! a sweet natural eye to the new hip moon,
   woke up alive and excited grasping in the sunset shadow
   sunrise golden monthly breeze!

How many flies buzzed round you innocent of your grime, while
   you cursed the heavens of the railroad and your flower soul?

Poor dead flower? When did you forget you were a flower? when
   did you look at your skin and decide you were an impotent
   dirty old locomotive? the ghost of a locomotive? the specter
   and shade of a once powerful mad American locomotive?

You were never no locomotive, Sunflower, you were a sunflower!

And you Locomotive, you are a locomotive, forget me not!

So I grabbed up the skeleton thick sunflower and stuck it at my
   side like a scepter,

and deliver my sermon to my soul, and Jack's soul too, and anyone who'll listen,

—We're not our skin of grime, we're not our dread bleak dusty
   imageless locomotive, we're all beautiful golden sunflowers
   inside, we're blessed by our own seed & golden hairy naked
   accomplishment-bodies growing into mad black formal sunflowers in the sunset, spied on by our eyes under the shadow
   of the mad locomotive riverbank sunset Frisco hilly tincan
   evening sitdown vision.

America

America I've given you all and now I'm nothing.
America two dollars and twentyseven cents January 17, 1956.
I can't stand my own mind.
America when will we end the human war?
Go fuck yourself with your atom bomb.
I don't feel good don't bother me.
I won't write my poem till I'm in my right mind.
America when will you be angelic?
When will you take off your clothes?
When will you look at yourself through the grave?
When will you be worthy of your million Trotskyites?
America why are your libraries full of tears?
America when will you send your eggs to India?
I'm sick of your insane demands.
When can I go into the supermarket and buy what I need with
    my good looks?
America after all it is you and I who are perfect not the next
    world.
Your machinery is too much for me.
You made me want to be a saint.
There must be some other way to settle this argument.
Burroughs is in Tangiers I don't think he'll come back it's sinister.
Are you being sinister or is this some form of practical joke?
I'm trying to come to the point.
I refuse to give up my obsession.
America stop pushing I know what I'm doing.
America the plum blossoms are falling.
I haven't read the newspapers for months, everyday somebody
    goes on trial for murder.
America I feel sentimental about the Wobblies.
America I used to be a communist when I was a kid I'm not sorry.
I smoke marijuana every chance I get.
I sit in my house for days on end and stare at the roses in the
    closet.
When I go to Chinatown I get drunk and never get laid.

My mind is made up there's going to be trouble.

You should have seen me reading Marx.

My psychoanalyst thinks I'm perfectly right.

I won't say the Lord's Prayer.

I have mystical visions and cosmic vibrations.

America I still haven't told you what you did to Uncle Max after
he came over from Russia.

I'm addressing you.

Are you going to let your emotional life be run by Time Magazine?

I'm obsessed by Time Magazine.

I read it every week.

Its cover stares at me everytime I slink past the corner candy-
store.

I read it in the basement of the Berkeley Public Library.

It's always telling me about responsibility. Businessmen are serious. Movie producers are serious. Everybody's serious but me.

It occurs to me that I am America.

I am talking to myself again.

Asia is rising against me.

I haven't got a chinaman's chance.

I'd better consider my national resources.

My national resources consist of two joints of marijuana millions
of genitals an unpublishable private literature that goes 1400
miles an hour and twentyfive-thousand mental institutions.

I say nothing about my prisons nor the millions of underprivileged who live in my flowerpots under the light of five
hundred suns.

I have abolished the whorehouses of France, Tangiers is the next
to go.

My ambition is to be President despite the fact that I'm a Catholic.

America how can I write a holy litany in your silly mood?

I will continue like Henry Ford my strophes are as individual as his automobiles more so they're all different sexes.

America I will sell you strophes $2500 apiece $500 down on your old strophe

America free Tom Mooney

America save the Spanish Loyalists

America Sacco & Vanzetti must not die

America I am the Scottsboro boys.

America when I was seven momma took me to Communist Cell meetings they sold us garbanzos a handful per ticket a ticket costs a nickel and the speeches were free everybody was angelic and sentimental about the workers it was all so sincere you have no idea what a good thing the party was in 1835 Scott Nearing was a grand old man a real mensch Mother Bloor made me cry I once saw Israel Amter plain. Everybody must have been a spy.

America you don't really want to go to war.

America it's them bad Russians.

Them Russians them Russians and them Chinamen. And them Russians.

The Russia wants to eat us alive. The Russia's power mad. She wants to take our cars from out our garages.

Her wants to grab Chicago. Her needs a Red Readers' Digest. Her wants our auto plants in Siberia. Him big bureaucracy running our fillingstations.

That no good. Ugh. Him make Indians learn read. Him need big black niggers. Hah. Her make us all work sixteen hours a day. Help.

America this is quite serious.

America this is the impression I get from looking in the television set.

America is this correct?

I'd better get right down to the job.

It's true I don't want to join the Army or turn lathes in precision parts factories, I'm nearsighted and psychopathic anyway.

America I'm putting my queer shoulder to the wheel.

Phyllis Webb

A Tall Tale

The whale, improbable as lust,
carved out a cave
for the seagirl's rest;
with rest the seagirl, sweet as dust, devised
a manner for the whale
to lie between her thighs.
Like this they lay
within the shadowed cave
under the waters, under the waters wise,
and nested there, and nested there and stayed,
this coldest whale aslant the seagirl's thighs.

Two hundred years perhaps swam by them there
before the cunning waters so distilled the pair
they turned to brutal artifacts of stone
polished, O petrified prisoners of their lair.
And thus, with quiet, submerged in deathly calm,
the two disclosed a future geologic long,
lying cold, whale to thigh revealed
the secret of their comfort
to the marine weeds,
to fish, to shell, sand, sediment and wave,
to the broken, dying sun
which probed their ocean grave.
These, whale and seagirl, stone gods,
stone lust, stone grief,
interred on the sedimented sand
amongst the orange starfish,
these cold and stony mariners
invoked the moral snail
and in sepulchral voice intoned a moral tale:

'Under the waters, under the waters wise,
all loving flesh will quickly meet demise,
the cave, the shadow cave is nowhere wholly safe
and even the oddest couple can scarcely find relief:
appear then to submit to this tide and timing sea,
but secrete a skillful shell and stone and perfect be.'

Love Story

It was easy to see what he was up to,
the grey, bundled ape,
as he sidled half-playfully
up to the baby
and with a sly look behind
put his hands onto the crib
and leapt in.

The child's pink, beginning face
stared up as the hair-handed monkey
explored the flesh, so soft, of our infant race.
The belly spread like plush to the monkey's haunch,
he settled, heavy and gay, his nuzzling
mouth at the baby's neck.

But, no answer accurate to a smile,
he bit, tasted time, maddened,
and his nails rooted sudden fire in the ribs of Adam,
towered, carnivorous, for aim
and baby face, ears, arm
were torn and taken in his ravaging.

And so the killing, too-late parents came,
hysteric, after their child's
futile pulse had stopped its beating.

Only the half-pathetic, half-triumphant
monkey peered out from the crib,
bobbed nervously on the dead infant's belly,
then stopped, suddenly paralyzed on that soft tomb.

Was it the donkey Death brayed out at him
from the human mother's eyes,
or did his love for her in that pause
consume him?

The jealous ape's death was swift
and of natural cause. 'Died of shame,'
some said, others, 'of shock.'
But his death was Othello's death,
as great, as picayune,
he died of envy, lacking the knack of wisdom.

To Friends Who Have Also Considered Suicide

It's still a good idea.
Its exercise is discipline:
to remember to cross the street without looking,
to remember not to jump when the cars side-swipe,
to remember not to bother to have clothes cleaned,
to remember not to eat or want to eat,
to consider the numerous methods of killing oneself,
that is surely the finest exercise of the imagination:
death by drowning, sleeping pills, slashed wrists,
kitchen fumes, bullets through the brain or through
the stomach, hanging by the neck in attic or basement,
a clean frozen death—the ways are endless.
And consider the drama! It's better than a whole season
at Stratford when you think of the emotion of your
family on hearing the news and when you imagine
how embarrassed some will be when the body is found.

One could furnish a whole chorus in a Greek play
with expletives and feel sneaky and omniscient
at the same time. But there's no shame
in this concept of suicide.
It has concerned our best philosophers
and inspired some of the most popular
of our politicians and financiers.
Some people swim lakes, others climb flagpoles,
some join monasteries, but we, my friends,
who have considered suicide take our daily walk
with death and are not lonely.
In the end it brings more honesty and care
than all the democratic parliaments of tricks.
It is the 'sickness unto death'; it is death;
it is not death; it is the sand from the beaches
of a hundred civilizations, the sand in the teeth
of death and barnacles our singing tongue:
and this is 'life' and we owe at least this much
contemplation to our western fact: to Rise,
Decline, Fall, to futility and larks,
to the bright crustaceans of the oversky.

Poetics Against the Angel of Death

I am sorry to speak of death again
(some say I'll have a long life)
but last night Wordsworth's 'Prelude'
suddenly made sense—I mean the measure,
the elevated tone, the attitude
of private Man speaking to public men.
Last night I thought I would not wake again
but now with this June morning I run ragged to elude
The Great Iambic Pentameter
who is the Hound of Heaven in our stress
because I want to die

writing Haiku
or, better,
long lines, clean and syllabic as knotted bamboo. Yes!

Occasions of Desire

Occasions of desire with their attendant envies,
the white heat of the cold swan dying,
create their gestures, obscene or most beautiful.
Oh, the clear shell of a swan's fluted wings!

And as the old swan calls clarity from dark waters,
sailing triumphant into the forgotten,
desire in its moving is that rapacious cry,
gorgeous as the torrent Lethe, and as wise.

And if the curl of cygnets on the Avon,
so freshly broken from their perfect shells,
take from a dying bird not moral or enticement,
but float with their own white mother, that is just.
Oh, imperious innocence to envy
only the water bearing such beauty!

For Fyodor

I am a beetle in the cabbage soup they serve up for geniuses
in the House of the Dead.

I am a black beetle and loll seductively at the bottom of the
warm slop.

Someday, Fyodor, by mistake you'll swallow me down and I'll
         become
a part of your valuable gutworks.

In the next incarnation I hope to imitate that idiot and saint,
Prince Myshkin, drop off my wings for his moronic glory.

Or, if I miss out on the Prince, Sonya or Dunya might do.

I'm not joking. I am not the result of bad sanitation in the
kitchen, as you think.

Up here in Omsk in Siberia beetles are not accidents but
        destinies.

I'm drowning fast, but even in this condition I realize your bad
tempered haughtiness is part of your strategy.

You are about to turn this freezing hell into an ecstatic emblem.
A ferocious shrine.

Ah, what delicious revenge. But take care! A fit is coming!
Now, now I'll leap into your foaming mouth and jump your
        tongue.
Now I stamp on this not quite famous tongue

shouting: Remember Fyodor, you may hate men but it's here in
Omsk you came to love mankind.

But you don't hear, do you: there you are writing in epileptic
        visions.

Hold your tongue! You can't speak yet. You are mine,
        Dostoevsky.

I aim to slip down your gullet and improve myself.
I can almost hear what you'll say:

    Crime and Punishment
    Suffering and Grace

and of the dying

   pass by and forgive
   us our happiness

Rilke

Rilke, I speak your name I throw it away
with your angels, your angels, your statues
and virgins, and a horse in a field held
at the hoof by wood. I cannot take so much
tenderness, tenderness, snow falling like lace
over your eyes year after year as the poems
receded, roses, the roses, sinking in snow
in the distant mountains.

Go away with your women to Russia or take them
to France, and take them or don't the poet is
in you, the spirit, they love that.
(I met one in Paris, her death leaning outward,
death in all forms. The letters you'd sent her,
she said, stolen from a taxi.)

Rilke.
Clowns and angels held your compassion.
You could sit in a room saying nothing,
nothing. Your admirers thought you were there,
a presence, a wisdom. But you had to leave
everyone once, once at least. That was your
hardness.

This page is a shadowed hall in Duino Castle.
Echoes. The echoes.
I don't know why I'm here.

Treblinka Gas Chamber

Klostermayer ordered another count of the children.
Then their stars were snipped off and thrown into
the center of the courtyard. It looked like a field of
buttercups.—Joseph Hyams, *A Field of Buttercups*

fallingstars
          'a field of
                    buttercups'

          yellow stars
                    of David
                              falling

the prisoners
              the children
                        falling

              in heaps
                    on one another
                              they go down

Thanatos
        showers
                his dirty breath
                          they must breathe
                                    him in

              they see stars
                        behind their
                                    eyes

David's
        'a field of
                buttercups'

          a metaphor
                  where all that's
                            left lies down

Prison Report

The eye of Jacobo Timerman looks through the hole and sees
another eye looking through a hole.

These holes are cut into steel doors in prison cells in Argentina.

Both eyes are wary.
They disappear.

Timerman rests his cheek on the icy door,
amazed at the sense of space he feels—the joy.

He looks again: the other's eye is there,
then vanishes like a spider.

Comes back, goes, comes back.

This is a game of hide-and-seek.
This is intelligence with a sense of humour.
Timerman joins the game.

Sometimes two eyes meet at exactly the same moment.

This is music. This is love
playing in the middle of a dark night
in a prison in Argentina.

My name is Jacobo one eye says.
Other eye says something, but Jacobo can't quite catch it.

Now a nose appears in the vision-field
of Timerman. It rubs cold edges of the hole,
a love-rub for Jacobo.

This is a kiss, he decides, a caress,
an emanation of solitude's tenderness.

In this prison everything is powered electrically
for efficiency and pain. But tenderness is also
a light and a shock.

An eye, a nose, a cheek resting against a steel door
in the middle of a dark night.
These are parts of bodies, parts of speech,
saying,
I am with you.

Messages

> 'They are always projecting themselves.
> Cats play to cats we cannot see.
> This is confidential.'
> —Letter from E. D. Blodgett

The young psychic comes back from halfway down the hall
to tell me to write about the cat on the postcard
tacked to the wall above my typewriter.

There is an understanding between us, and I show her
a photo in the *Journal* where the cat appears behind
my shoulder—

A piece of politics. A creature of state.

Out of Ptolemy's reign, cast in bronze (earrings restored)
far from Egypt now in its northern home.
Probable use: to hold the bones of a kitten.
Representative on this earth of the Goddess Bastet.

She prances toward me down the ramp of the poem
sent to me by the young psychic who is writing
an historical novel.

She moves toward me through an aura composed
of new light and the golden dust of Ptolemy.
Halfway down the ramp her high ears turn against
the task of the poem toward allurements
of stockmarket and monopoly.

Cats play to cats we cannot see.

Now it is night. I have locked her in this pyramid
of my own free will. She toys with the unwinding
sheet of a mummified king, paws at royal jewels
and sighs.
As I sleep at the 5 a.m. poem's edge she sniffs my skin
for news of her old lost world.
She names the Princes as they pass
heading for Bay Street in the winter blight.

They are always projecting themselves.
This is confidential.

Now it is morning in North Nineteen Hundred and Eighty.
The message clear: price of gold slumps,
war cracks at the border.
The Queen's cold mouth sends warning:

Beware.

How to get out of the poem without a scratch?
Each cast of the line seductive and minimal.
The ramp of the poem folding against
the power of the cat.
Possible use: to hold the bones of little ones
who cannot speak for themselves
or the Goddess Bastet.

Possible worth: treasure beyond speech
out of the old tomb, out of the mind's
sarcophagus. Wanting to touch
wanting to stare at her agate eyes
in the dark night of a museum postcard.

Bastet!
She moves toward me. She is here—
HISS HISS
With one paw raised
she scratches the final hieroglyphs
at the end of a bronze poem
I cannot see.

Ted Hughes

Macaw and Little Miss

In a cage of wire-ribs
The size of a man's head, the macaw bristles in a staring
Combustion, suffers the stoking devils of his eyes.
In the old lady's parlour, where an aspidistra succumbs
To the musk of faded velvet, he hangs as in clear flames,
  Like a torturer's iron instrument preparing
    With dense slow shudderings of greens, yellows, blues,
      Crimsoning into the barbs:

Or like the smouldering head that hung
In Killdevil's brass kitchen, in irons, who had been
Volcano swearing to vomit the world away in black ash,
And would, one day; or a fugitive aristocrat
From some thunderous mythological hierarchy, caught
  By a little boy with a crust and a bent pin,
    Or snare of horsehair set for a song-thrush,
      And put in a cage to sing.

The old lady who feeds him seeds
Has a grand-daughter. The girl calls him 'Poor Polly,' pokes
      fun.
'Jolly Mop.' But lies under every full moon,
The spun glass of her body bared and so gleam-still
Her brimming eyes do not tremble or spill
  The dream where the warrior comes, lightning and iron,
    Smashing and burning and rending towards her loin:
      Deep into her pillow her silence pleads.

All day he stares at his furnace
With eyes red-raw, but when she comes they close.
'Polly, Pretty Poll,' she cajoles, and rocks him gently.

She caresses, whispers kisses. The blue lids stay shut.
She strikes the cage in a tantrum and swirls out:
   Instantly beak, wings, talons crash
   The bars in conflagration and frenzy,
     And his shriek shakes the house.

The Thought-Fox

I imagine this midnight moment's forest:
Something else is alive
Beside the clock's loneliness
And this blank page where my fingers move.

Through the window I see no star:
Something more near
Though deeper within darkness
Is entering the loneliness:

Cold, delicately as the dark snow,
A fox's nose touches twig, leaf;
Two eyes serve a movement, that now
And again now, and now, and now

Sets neat prints into the snow,
Between trees, and warily a lame
Shadow lags by stump and in hollow
Of a body that is bold to come

Across clearings, an eye,
A widening deepening greenness,
Brilliantly, concentratedly,
Coming about its own business

Till, with a sudden sharp hot stink of fox
It enters the dark hole of the head.
The window is starless still; the clock ticks,
The page is printed.

Invitation to the Dance

The condemned prisoner stirred, but could not stir:
Cold had shackled the blood-prints of the knout.
The light of his death's dawn put the dark out.
He lay, his lips numb to the frozen floor.
He dreamed some other prisoner was dragged out—
Nightmare of command in the dawn, and a shot.
The bestial gaoler's boot was at his ear.

Upon his sinews torturers had grown strong,
The inquisitor old against a tongue that could not,
Being torn out, plead even for death.
All bones were shattered, the whole body unstrung.
Horses, plunging apart towards North and South,
Tore his heart up by the shrieking root.
He was flung to the blow-fly and the dog's fang.

Pitched onto his mouth in a black ditch
All spring he heard the lovers rustle and sigh.
The sun stank. Rats worked at him secretly.
Rot and maggot stripped him stich by stich.
Yet still this dream engaged his vanity:
That could he get upright he would dance and cry
Shame on every shy or idle wretch.

Six Young Men

The celluloid of a photograph holds them well,—
Six young men, familiar to their friends.
Four decades that have faded and ochre-tinged
This photograph have not wrinkled the faces or the hands.
Though their cocked hats are not now fashionable,
Their shoes shine. One imparts an intimate smile,
One chews a grass, one lowers his eyes, bashful,
One is ridiculous with cocky pride—
Six months after this picture they were all dead.

All are trimmed for a Sunday jaunt. I know
That bilberried bank, that thick tree, that black wall,
Which are there yet and not changed. From where these sit
You hear the water of seven streams fall
To the roarer in the bottom, and through all
The leafy valley a rumouring of air go.
Pictured here, their expressions listen yet,
And still that valley has not changed its sound
Though their faces are four decades under the ground.

This one was shot in an attack and lay
Calling in the wire, then this one, his best friend,
Went out to bring him in and was shot too;
And this one, the very moment he was warned
From potting at tin-cans in no-man's-land,
Fell back dead with his rifle-sights shot away.
The rest, nobody knows what they came to,
But come to the worst they must have done, and held it
Closer than their hope; all were killed.

Here see a man's photograph,
The locket of a smile, turned overnight
Into the hospital of his mangled last
Agony and hours; see bundled in it
His mightier-than-a-man dead bulk and weight:
And on this one place which keeps him alive
(In his Sunday best) see fall war's worst
Thinkable flash and rending, onto his smile
Forty years rotting into soil.

That man's not more alive whom you confront
And shake by the hand, see hale, hear speak loud,
Than any of these six celluloid smiles are,
Nor prehistoric or fabulous beast more dead;
No thought so vivid as their smoking blood:
To regard this photograph might well dement,
Such contradictory permanent horrors here
Smile from the single exposure and shoulder out
One's own body from its instant and heat.

Hawk Roosting

I sit in the top of the wood, my eyes closed.
Inaction, no falsifying dream
Between my hooked head and hooked feet:
Or in sleep rehearse perfect kills and eat.

The convenience of the high trees!
The air's buoyancy and the sun's ray
Are of advantage to me;
And the earth's face upward for my inspection.

My feet are locked upon the rough bark.
It took the whole of Creation
To produce my foot, my each feather:
Now I hold Creation in my foot

Or fly up, and revolve it all slowly—
I kill where I please because it is all mine.
There is no sophistry in my body:
My manners are tearing off heads—

The allotment of death.
For the one path of my flight is direct
Through the bones of the living.
No arguments assert my right:

The sun is behind me.
Nothing has changed since I began.
My eye has permitted no change.
I am going to keep things like this.

Pike

Pike, three inches long, perfect
Pike in all parts, green tigering the gold.
Killers from the egg: the malevolent aged grin.
They dance on the surface among the flies.

Or move, stunned by their own grandeur,
Over a bed of emerald, silhouette
Of submarine delicacy and horror.
A hundred feet long in their world.

In ponds, under the heat-struck lily pads—
Gloom of their stillness:
Logged on last year's black leaves, watching upwards.
Or hung in an amber cavern of weeds

The jaw's hooked clamp and fangs
Not to be changed at this date;
A life subdued to its instrument;
The gills kneading quietly, and the pectorals.

Three we kept behind glass,
Jungled in weed: three inches, four,
And four and a half: fed fry to them—
Suddenly there were two. Finally one

With a sag belly and the grin it was born with.
And indeed they spare nobody.
Two, six pounds each, over two feet long,
High and dry and dead in the willow-herb—

One jammed past its gills down the other's gullet:
The ouside eye stared: as a vice locks—
The same iron in this eye
Though its film shrank in death.

A pond I fished, fifty yards across,
Whose lilies and muscular tench
Had outlasted every visible stone
Of the monastery that planted them—

Stilled legendary depth:
It was as deep as England. It held
Pike too immense to stir, so immense and old
That past nightfall I dared not cast

But silently cast and fished
With the hair frozen on my head
For what might move, for what eye might move.
The still splashes on the dark pond,

Owls hushing the floating woods
Frail on my ear against the dream
Darkness beneath night's darkness had freed,
That rose slowly towards me, watching.

A Childish Prank

Man's and woman's bodies lay without souls,
Dully gaping, foolishly staring, inert
On the flowers of Eden.
God pondered.

The problem was so great, it dragged him asleep.

Crow laughed.
He bit the Worm, God's only son,
Into two writhing halves.

He stuffed into man the tail half
With the wounded end hanging out.
He stuffed the head half headfirst into woman
And it crept in deeper and up
To peer out through her eyes
Calling its tail-half to join up quickly, quickly
Because O it was painful.

Man awoke being dragged across the grass.
Woman awoke to see him coming.
Neither knew what had happened.

God went on sleeping.

Crow went on laughing.

Crow's First Lesson

God tried to teach Crow how to talk.
'Love,' said God. 'Say, Love.'
Crow gaped, and the white shark crashed into the sea
And went rolling downwards, discovering its own depth.

'No, no,' said God, 'Say Love. Now try it. LOVE.'
Crow gaped, and a bluefly, a tsetse, a mosquito
Zoomed out and down
To their sundry flesh-pots.

'A final try,' said God. 'Now, LOVE.'
Crow convulsed, gaped, retched and
Man's bodiless prodigious head
Bulbed out onto the earth, with swivelling eyes,
Jabbering protest—

And Crow retched again, before God could stop him.
And woman's vulva dropped over man's neck and tightened.
The two struggled together on the grass.
God struggled to part them, cursed, wept—

Crow flew guiltily off.

A Disaster

There came news of a word.
Crow saw it killing men. He ate well.
He saw it bulldozing
Whole cities to rubble. Again he ate well.
He saw its excreta poisoning seas.
He became watchful.
He saw its breath burning whole lands
To dusty char.
He flew clear and peered.

The word oozed its way, all mouth,
Earless, eyeless.
He saw it sucking the cities
Like the nipples of a sow
Drinking out all the people
Till there were none left,
All digested inside the word.

Ravenous, the word tried its great lips
On the earth's bulge, like a giant lamprey—
There it started to suck.

But its effort weakened.
It could digest nothing but people.
So there it shrank, wrinkling weaker,
Puddling
Like a collapsing mushroom.
Finally, a drying salty lake.
Its era was over.
All that remained of it a brittle desert
Dazzling with the bones of earth's people

Where Crow walked and mused.

Dehorning

Bad-tempered bullying bunch, the horned cows
Among the unhorned. Feared, spoilt.
Cantankerous at the hay, at assemblies, at crowded
Yard operations. Knowing their horntips' position
To a fraction, every other cow knowing it too,
Like their own tenderness. Horning of bellies, hair-tufting
Of horntips. Handy levers. But
Off with the horns.
So there they all are in the yard—
The pick of the bullies, churning each other
Like thick fish in a bucket, churning their mud.
One by one, into the cage of the crush: the needle,
A roar not like a cow—more like a tiger,
Blast of air down a cavern, and long, long,
Beginning in pain and ending in terror—then the next.
The needle between the horn and the eye, so deep
Your gut squirms for the eyeball twisting
In its pink-white fastenings of tissue. This side and that.
Then the first one anesthetized, back in the crush.
The bulldog pincers in the septum, stretched full strength,
The horn levered right over, the chin pulled round
With the pincers, the mouth drooling, the eye
Like a live eye caught in a pan, like the eye of a fish
Imprisoned in air. Then the cheese cutter
Of braided wire, and stainless-steel peg handles,
Aligned on the hair-bedded root of the horn, then leaning
Backward full weight, pull-punching backwards,
Left right left right and the blood leaks
Down over the cheekbone, the wire bites
And buzzes, the ammonia horn-burn smokes
And the cow groans, roars shapelessly, hurls
Its half-ton commotion in the tight cage. Our faces
Grimace like faces in the dentist's chair. The horn
Rocks from its roots, the wire pulls through
The last hinge of hair, the horn is heavy and free,

And a water-pistol jet of blood
Rains over the one who holds it—a needle jet
From the white-rasped and bloody skull crater. Then tweezers
Twiddle the artery nozzle, knotting it enough,
And purple antiseptic squirts a cuttlefish cloud over it.
Then the other side the same. We collect
A heap of horns. The floor of the crush
Is a trampled puddle of scarlet. The purple-crowned cattle,
The bullies, with suddenly no horns to fear,
Start ramming and wrestling. Maybe their heads
Are still anesthetized. A new order
Among the hornless. The bitchy high-headed
Straight-back brindle, with her Spanish bull trot,
And her head-shaking snorting advance and her crazy spirit,
Will have to get maternal. What she's lost
In weapons, she'll have to make up for in tits.
But they've all lost one third of their beauty.

Gary Snyder

Piute Creek

One granite ridge
A tree, would be enough
Or even a rock, a small creek,
A bark shred in a pool.
Hill beyond hill, folded and twisted
Tough trees crammed
In thin stone fractures
A huge moon on it all, is too much.
The mind wanders. A million
Summers, night air still and the rocks
Warm. Sky over endless mountains.
All the junk that goes with being human
Drops away, hard rock wavers
Even the heavy present seems to fail
This bubble of a heart.
Words and books
Like a small creek off a high ledge
Gone in the dry air.

A clear, attentive mind
Has no meaning but that
Which sees is truly seen.
No one loves rock, yet we are here.
Night chills. A flick
In the moonlight
Slips into Juniper shadow:
Back there unseen
Cold proud eyes
Of Cougar or Coyote
Watch me rise and go.

Riprap

Lay down these words
Before your mind like rocks.
                    placed solid, by hands
In choice of place, set
Before the body of the mind
                    in space and time:
Solidity of bark, leaf, or wall
                    riprap of things:
Cobble of milky way,
                    straying planets,
These poems, people,
                    lost ponies with
Dragging saddles—
                    and rocky sure-foot trails.
The worlds like an endless
                    four-dimensional
Game of *Go*.
                    ants and pebbles
In the thin loam, each rock a word
                    a creek-washed stone
Granite: ingrained
                    with torment of fire and weight
Crystal and sediment linked hot
                    all change, in thoughts,
As well as things.

Journeys

SECTION SIX

1

Genji caught a gray bird, fluttering. It
was wounded, so I hit it with a coal shovel.
It stiffened, grew straight and symmetrical,
and began to increase in size. I took it by

the head with both hands and held it as it
swelled, turning the head from side to side.
It turned into a woman, and I was embracing
her. We walked down a dim-lighted stairway
holding hands, walking more and more swiftly
through an enormous maze, all underground.
Occasionally we touched surface, and redescended.
As we walked I kept a chart of our route in
mind—but it became increasingly complex—and
just when we reached the point where I was
about to lose my grasp of it, the woman transferred a piece of fresh-tasting apple from her
mouth to mine. Then I woke.

2

Through deep forests to the coast,
and stood on a white sandspit looking in:
over lowland swamps and prairies
where no man had ever been
to a chill view of the Olympics, in a chill clear wind.

3

We moved across dark stony ground to the great
wall: hundreds of feet high. What was beyond
it, cows?—then a thing began to rise
up from behind.
I shot my arrows, shot arrows at it, but it came —
until we turned and ran, 'It's too big to
fight'—the rising thing a quarter mile across—
it was the flaming, pulsing sun. We fled and
stumbled on the bright lit plain.

4

Where were we—
A girl in a red skirt, high heels,
going up the stairs before me in a made-over barn.
White-wash peeling, we lived together in the loft,
on cool bare boards.˙
—lemme tell you something kid—
        back in 1910.

5

Walking a dusty road through plowed-up fields
at forest-fire time—the fir tree hills dry,
smoke of the far fires blurred the air—
& passed on into woods, along a pond,
beneath a big red cedar,
to a bank of blinding blue wild flowers
and thick green grass on levelled ground
of hillside where our old house used to stand.
I saw the footings damp and tangled,
and thought my father was in jail,
and wondered why my mother never died,
and thought I ought to bring my sister back.

6

High up in a yellow-gold
dry range of mountains—
brushy, rocky, cactussy hills
slowly hiking down—finally can see below,
a sea of clouds.

Lower down, always moving slowly over the
dry ground descending, can see through breaks
in the clouds: flat land.
Damp green level ricefields, farm houses,
at last to feel the heat and damp.

Descending to this humid, clouded, level world:
now I have come to the LOWLANDS.

7

Underground building chambers clogged with refuse heaps
discarded furniture, slag, old nails,
rotting plaster, faint wisps—antique newspapers
rattle in the winds that come forever down the hall.
ladders
passing, climbing, and stopping, on from door to door.
one tiny light bulb left still burning
                    —now the last—
locked *inside* is hell.
Movies going, men milling round the posters
                in shreds
                the movie always running
—we all head in here somewhere;

—years just looking for the bathrooms.
Huge and filthy, with strange-shaped toilets full of shit.
Dried shit all around, smeared across the walls of the
adjoining room,
and a vast hat rack.

8

With Lew rode in a bus over the mountains—
rutted roads along the coast of Washington
through groves of redwoods. Sitting in the
back of an almost-empty bus,
talking and riding through.
Yellow leaves fluttering down. Passing
through tiny towns at times. Damp cabins
set in dark groves of trees.
Beaches with estuaries and sandbars. I brought
a woman here once long ago,
but passed on through too quick.

9

We were following a long river into the mountains.
Finally we rounded a ridge and could see deeper in—

the farther peaks stony and barren, a few alpine
trees.
Ko-san and I stood on a point by a cliff, over a
rock-walled canyon. Ko said, 'Now we have come to
where we die.' I asked him, what's that up there,
then—meaning the further mountains.
'That's the world after death.' I thought it looked
just like the land we'd been travelling, and couldn't
see why we should have to die.
Ko grabbed me and pulled me over the cliff—
both of us falling. I hit and I was dead. I saw
my body for a while, then it was gone. Ko was
there too. We were at the bottom of the gorge.
We started drifting up the canyon. 'This is the
way to the back country.'

Song of the Taste

Eating the living germs of grasses
Eating the ova of large birds

    the fleshy sweetness packed
    around the sperm of swaying trees

The muscles of the flanks and thighs of
          soft-voiced cows
    the bounce in the lamb's leap
    the swish in the ox's tail

Eating roots grown swoll
        inside the soil

Drawing on life of living
    clustered points of light spun
        out of space
hidden in the grape.

Eating each other's seed
        eating
  ah, each other.

Kissing the lover in the mouth of bread:
        lip to lip.

Kai, Today

A teen-age boy in training pants
        stretching by the river
A girl child weeping, climbing
      up her elder sister;
The Kawaramachi Beggar's steady look and
       searching reach of gritty hand
     in plastic sidewalk pail
        with lip of grease

      these fates.

    before Masa and I met
What's your from-the-beginning face?
    Kai
    born again
To the Mother's hoarse bear-down
     groan and dark red mask:
     spiralling, glistening, blue-white, up

And out from her
        (dolphins leaping in threes
        through blinding silver inter-
        faces, Persian
        Gulf tanker's wave-slip
        opening, boundless
          whap

       as they fall back,
       arcing
       into her—)

          sea.

Anasazi

Anasazi,
Anasazi,

tucked up in clefts in the cliffs
growing strict fields of corn and beans
sinking deeper and deeper in earth
up to your hips in Gods
       your head all turned to eagle-down
       & lightning for knees and elbows
your eyes full of pollen

       the smell of bats.
       the flavor of sandstone
       grit on the tongue.

       women
       birthing
at the foot of ladders in the dark.

trickling streams in hidden canyons
under the cold rolling desert

corn-basket   wide-eyed
       red baby
       rock lip home,

Anasazi

Front Lines

The edge of the cancer
Swells against the hill—we feel
                    a foul breeze—
And it sinks back down.
The deer winter here
A chainsaw growls in the gorge.

Ten wet days and the log trucks stop,
The trees breathe.
Sunday the 4-wheel jeep of the
Realty Company brings in
Landseekers, lookers, they say
To the land,
Spread your legs.

The jets crack sound overhead, it's OK here;
Every pulse of the rot at the heart
In the sick fat veins of Amerika
Pushes the edge up closer—

A bulldozer grinding and slobbering
Sideslipping and belching on top of
The skinned-up bodies of still-live bushes
In the pay of a man
From town.

Behind is a forest that goes to the Arctic
And a desert that still belongs to the Piute
And here we must draw
Our line.

Margaret Avison

The World Still Needs

Frivolity is out of season.
Yet, in this poetry, let it be admitted
The world still needs piano-tuners
And has fewer, and more of these
Gray fellows prone to liquor
On an unlikely Tuesday, gritty with wind,
When somewhere, behind windows,
A housewife stays for him until the
   Hour of the uneasy bridge-club cocktails
   And the office rush at the groceteria
   And the vesper-bell and lit-up buses passing
   And the supper trays along the hospital corridor,
Suffering from
Sore throat and dusty curtains.

Not all alone on the deserted boathouse
Or even on the prairie freight
(The engineer leaned out, watchful and blank
And had no Christmas worries
Mainly because it was the eve of April),
Is like the moment
When the piano in the concert-hall
Finds texture absolute, a single solitude
For those hundreds in rows, half out of overcoats,
Their eyes swimming with sleep.

From this communal cramp of understanding
Springs up suburbia, where every man would build
A clapboard in a well of Russian forest
With yard enough for a high clothesline strung
To a small balcony . . .

A woman whose eyes shine like evening's star
Takes in the freshblown linen
While sky a lonely wash of pink is still
reflected in brown mud
Where lettuces will grow, another spring.

To Professor X, Year Y

The square for civic receptions
Is jammed, static, black with people in topcoats
Although November
Is mean, and day grows late.

The newspapermen, who couldn't
Force their way home, after the council meeting
&c., move between windows and pressroom
In ugly humour. They do not know
What everybody is waiting for
At this hour
To stand massed and unmoving
When there should be—well—nothing to expect
Except the usual hubbub
Of city five o'clock.

Winter pigeons walk the cement ledges
Urbane, discriminating.

Down in the silent crowd few can see anything.
It is disgusting, this uniformity
Of stature.
If only someone climbed in pyramid
As circus families can . . .
Strictly, each knows
Downtown buildings block all view anyway
Except, to tease them,
Four narrow passages, and ah

One clear towards open water
(If 'clear'
Suits with the prune and mottled plumes of
Madam night).

Nobody gapes skyward
Although the notion of
Commerce by air is utterly
familiar.

Many citizens at this hour
Are of course miles away, under
Rumpus-room lamps, dining-room chandeliers,
Or bound elsewhere.
One girl who waits in a lit drugstore doorway
North 48 blocks for the next bus
Carries a history, an ethics, a Russian grammar,
And a pair of gym shoes.

But the few thousand inexplicably here
Generate funny currents, zigzag
Across the leaden miles, and all suburbia
Suffers, uneasily.

You, historian, looking back at us,
Do you think I'm not trying to be helpful?
If I fabricated cause-and-effect
You'd listen? I've been dead too long for fancies.
Ignore us, hunched in these dark streets
If in a minute now the explosive
Meaning fails to disperse us and provide resonance
Appropriate to your chronicle.

But if you do, I have a hunch
You've missed a portent.
('Twenty of six.' 'Snow?—I wouldn't wonder.')

The Swimmer's Moment

For everyone
The swimmer's moment at the whirlpool comes,
But many at that moment will not say
'This is the whirlpool, then.'
By their refusal they are saved
From the black pit, and also from contesting
The deadly rapids, and emerging in
The mysterious, and more ample, further waters.
And so their bland-blank faces turn and turn
Pale and forever on the rim of suction
They will not recognize.
Of those who dare the knowledge
Many are whirled into the ominous centre
That, gaping vertical, seals up
For them an eternal boon of privacy,
So that we turn away from their defeat
With a despair, not for their deaths, but for
Ourselves, who cannot penetrate their secret
Nor even guess at the anonymous breadth
Where one or two have won:
(The silver reaches of the estuary).

Voluptuaries and Others

That Eureka of Archimedes out of his bath
Is the kind of story that kills what it conveys;
Yet the banality is right for that story, since it is not a
    communicable one
But just a particular instance of
The kind of lighting up of the terrain
That leaves aside the whole terrain, really,
But signalizes, and compels, an advance in it.
Such an advance through a be-it-what-it-may but take-it-not-
    quite-as-given locale:

Probably that is the core of being alive.
The speculation is not a concession
To limited imaginations. Neither is it
A constrained voiding of the quality of immanent death.
Such near values cannot be measured in values
Just because the measuring
Consists in that other kind of lighting up
That shows the terrain comprehended, as also its containing
     space,
And wipes out adjectives, and all shadows
     (or, perhaps, all but shadows).

The Russians made a movie of a dog's head
Kept alive by blood controlled by physics, chemistry, equip-
     ment, and
Russian women scientists in cotton gowns with writing tablets.
The heart lay on a slab midway in the apparatus
And went phluff, phluff.
Like the first kind of illumination, that successful experiment
Can not be assessed either as conquest or as defeat.
But it is living, creating the chasm of creation,
Contriving to cast only man to brood in it, further.

History makes the spontaneous jubilation at such moments
     less and less likely though,
And that story about Archimedes does get into public school
     textbooks.

Pace

'Plump raindrops in these
faintly clicking groves,
the pedestrians' place, July's
violet and albumen
close?'

'No. No. It is perhaps the conversational side-effect
among the pigeons; behold
the path-dust is nutmeg powdered and
bird-foot embroidered.'

> The silk-fringed hideaway
> permits the beechnut-cracking
> squirrrels to plumply
> pick and click and
> not listen.

Pedestrians linger
striped stippled sunfloating
> at the rim of the
> > thin-wearing groves

letting the ear experience this
discrete, delicate
clicking.

Black-White Under Green:
May 18, 1965

This day of the leafing-out
speaks with blue power—
among the buttery grassblades
white, tiny-spraying spokes on the end of a weed-stem
and in the formal beds, tulips
and invisible birds inaudibly hallooing,
enormous, their beaks out wide, throats bulging, aflutter,
eyes weeping with speed
where the ultraviolets play and the scythe of the jets
flashes, carrying
the mind-wounded heartpale person, still a boy, a pianist, dying
> not
of the mind's wounds (as they read the x-rays) but

dying, fibres separated, parents ruddy and
American, strong, sheathed in the cold of
years of his differentness, clustered by two at
the nether arc of flight.

This day of the leafing-out is one to remember
        how the ice crackled among
            stiff twigs. Glittering strongly
                the old trees sagged. Boughs
            abruptly unsocketed. Dry, orange gashes
the dawn's fine snowing discovered and powdered over.

. . . to remember the leaves ripped loose
the thudding of the dark sky-beams
and the pillared plunging sea
shelterless. Down the centuries
a flinching speck
    in the white fury found of itself—and another—
the rich blood spilling, mother to child, threading
the perilous combers, marbling
the surges, flung
out, and ten-fingered, feeling for
the lollop, the fine-wired
music, dying skyhigh
still between carpets and the
cabin-pressuring windows
on the day of the leafing.

Faces fanned by
rubberized, cool air
are opened; eyes wisely
smile.
The tulips, weeds, new leaves
neither smile nor are scorning to smile nor uncertain,
dwelling in light.
A flick of ice, fire, flood,
far off from
the day of the leafing-out I knew

when knee-wagon small, or from my
father's once at a horse-tail silk-shiny
fence-corner or this
day when the runways wait
white in the sun, and a new leaf is
metal, torn out of that blue
afloat in the dayshine.

July Man

Old, rain-wrinkled, time-soiled, city-wise, morning man
whose weeping is for the dust of the elm-flowers
and the hurting motes of time,
rotted with rotting grape,
sweet with the fumes,
puzzled for good by fermented potato-
peel out of the vat of the times,
turned out and left
in this grass-patch, this city-gardener's place
under the buzzing populace's
square shadows, and the green shadows
of elm and ginkgo and lime
(planted for Sunday strollers and summer evening
families, and for those
bird-cranks with bread-crumbs
and crumpled umbrellas who come
while the dew is wet on the park, and beauty
is fan-tailed, gray and dove-gray, aslant, folding in
from the white fury of day).

In the sound of the fountain
you rest, at the cinder-rim, on your bench.

The rushing river of cars
makes you a stillness, a pivot, a heart-stopping
blurt, in the sorrow

of the last rubbydub swig, the searing, and
stone-jar solitude lost, and yet,
and still—wonder (for good now) and
trembling:

> The too much none of us knows
> is weight, sudden sunlight, falling
> on your hands and arms, in your lap,
> all, all, in time.

The Absorbed

The sun has not absorbed
this icy day, and this day's industry—in
behind glass—hasn't the blue and gold, cold
outside. Though not absorbing, this
sought that:

> sheeted, steely, vaulted,
> all gleam, this morning;
> bright blue with one stained wing in the
>   northeast, at lunch hour;
> in early afternoon
> abruptly a dust-flurry,
>   all but this private coign of place
>   deafened, all winding in one cloth of moth.
> Then space breathed, hollowing twilight
>   on ice and the pale-gray, pale-blue,
>   and far fur-colored wooden trees
>   and ornamental trees.

Towards sundown
a boy came with an aluminum toboggan.
He worked his way, absorbed,
past footmark pocks, on crust,
up ice-ridge, sometimes bumping

down to the Japanese yews, sometimes
scooter-shoving athwart the hill,
then, with a stake,
kneeling,
he paddles, thrusting, speed-wise, then
stabbing, uphill; then
dangling the rope and poring on
slope-sheen, standing, he stashes
the aluminum, upright, in a frost-lumpy shoal
and beside coasting motorcars and parked cars
listens . . . and off again, toque to the eyebrows,
alone still in the engulfing dark.

The inside breathing here
closes down all the window but a visor-slit
on the night glare.
                    New cold is
in dry-thorn nostrils.

Alone, he plays, still there. We
struggle, our animal fires
pitted against those
several grape-white stars,
their silence.

In a Season of Unemployment

These green painted park benches are
all new. The Park Commissioner had them
planted.
Sparrows go on
having dust baths at the edge of
the park maple's shadow, just where
the bench is cemented down, planted
and then cemented.

Not a breath moves
this newspaper.
I'd rather read it by the Lapland sun at midnight. Here we're
bricked in early by a
stifling dark.

On that bench a man in a
pencil-striped white shirt
keeps his head up and steady.

The newspaper-astronaut says
  'I feel excellent under the condition of weightlessness.'
And from his bench a
scatter of black bands in the hollow-air
ray out—too quick for the eye—
and cease.

  'Ground observers watching him on a TV circuit said
  At the time of this report he
  was smiling,' Moscow radio reported.
I glance across at him, and mark that
he is feeling
excellent too, I guess, and
weightless and
'smiling.'

A Nameless One

Hot in June a narrow winged
long-elbowed-thread-legged
living insect lived
and died within
the lodgers' second-floor bathroom here.

At six a.m.
wafting ceilingward,
no breeze but what it living made there;

at noon standing
still as a constellation of spruce needles
before the moment of
making it, whirling;

at four a
wilted flotsam, cornsilk, on the linoleum:

now that it is
over, I
look with new eyes
upon this room
adequate for one to
be, in.

Its insect-day
has threaded a needle
for me for my eyes dimming
over rips and tears and
thin places.

Sylvia Plath

Two Views of a Cadaver Room

I

The day she visited the dissecting room
They had four men laid out, black as burnt turkey,
Already half unstrung. A vinegary fume
Of the death vats clung to them;
The white-smocked boys started working.
The head of his cadaver had caved in,
And she could scarcely make out anything
In that rubble of skull plates and old leather.
A sallow piece of string held it together.

In their jars the snail-nosed babies moon and glow.
He hands her the cut-out heart like a cracked heirloom.

II

In Brueghel's panorama of smoke and slaughter
Two people only are blind to the carrion army:
He, afloat in the sea of her blue satin
Skirts, sings in the direction
Of her bare shoulder, while she bends,
Fingering a leaflet of music, over him,
Both of them deaf to the fiddle in the hands
Of the death's-head shadowing their song.
These Flemish lovers flourish; not for long.

Yet desolation, stalled in paint, spares the little country
Foolish, delicate, in the lower right hand corner.

The Colossus

I shall never get you put together entirely,
Pieced, glued, and properly jointed.
Mule-bray, pig-grunt, and bawdy cackles
Proceed from your great lips.
It's worse than a barnyard.

Perhaps you consider yourself an oracle,
Mouthpiece of the dead, or of some god or other.
Thirty years now I have laboured
To dredge the silt from your throat.
I am none the wiser.

Scaling little ladders with gluepots and pails of lysol
I crawl like an ant in mourning
Over the weedy acres of your brow
To mend the immense skull-plates and clear
The bald, white tumuli of your eyes.

A blue sky out of the Oresteia
Arches above us. O father, all by yourself
You are pithy and historical as the Roman Forum.
I open my lunch on a hill of black cypress.
Your fluted bones and acanthine hair are littered

In their old anarchy to the horizon-line.
It would take more than a lightning-stroke
To create such a ruin.
Nights, I squat in the cornucopia
Of your left ear, out of the wind,

Counting the red stars and those of plum-colour.
The sun rises under the pillar of your tongue.
My hours are married to shadow.
No longer do I listen for the scrape of a keel
On the blank stones of the landing.

Black Rook in Rainy Weather

On the stiff twig up there
Hunches a wet black rook
Arranging and rearranging its feathers in the rain.
I do not expect miracle
Or an accident

To set the sight on fire
In my eye, nor seek
Any more in the desultory weather some design,
But let spotted leaves fall as they fall,
Without ceremony, or portent.

Although, I admit, I desire,
Occasionally, some backtalk
From the mute sky, I can't honestly complain:
A certain minor light may still
Leap incandescent

Out of kitchen table or chair
As if a celestial burning took
Possession of the most obtuse objects now and then—
Thus hallowing an interval
Otherwise inconsequent

By bestowing largesse, honour,
One might say love. At any rate, I now walk
Wary (for it could happen
Even in this dull, ruinous landscape); sceptical,
Yet politic; ignorant

Of whatever angel may choose to flare
Suddenly at my elbow. I only know that a rook
Ordering its black feathers can so shine
As to seize my senses, haul
My eyelids up, and grant

A brief respite from fear
Of total neutrality. With luck,
Trekking stubborn through this season
Of fatigue, I shall
Patch together a content

Of sorts. Miracles occur,
If you care to call those spasmodic
Tricks of radiance miracles. The wait's begun again,
The long wait for the angel,
For that rare, random descent.

Blue Moles

I

They're out of the dark's ragbag, these two
Moles dead in the pebbled rut,
Shapeless as flung gloves, a few feet apart—
Blue suede a dog or fox has chewed.
One, by himself, seemed pitiable enough,
Little victim unearthed by some large creature
From his orbit under the elm root.
The second carcase makes a duel of the affair:
Blind twins bitten by bad nature.

The sky's far dome is sane and clear.
Leaves, undoing their yellow caves
Between the road and the lake water,
Bare no sinister spaces. Already
The moles look neutral as the stones.
Their corkscrew noses, their white hands
Uplifted; stiffen in a family pose.
Difficult to imagine how fury struck—
Dissolved now, smoke of an old war.

II

Nightly the battle-shouts start up
In the ear of the veteran, and again
I enter the soft pelt of the mole.
Light's death to them: they shrivel in it.
They move through their mute rooms while I sleep,
Palming the earth aside, grubbers
After the fat children of root and rock.
By day, only the topsoil heaves.
Down there one is alone.

Outsize hands prepare a path,
They go before: opening the veins,
Delving for the appendages
Of beetles, sweetbreads, shards—to be eaten
Over and over. And still the heaven
Of final surfeit is just as far
From the door as ever. What happens between us
Happens in darkness, vanishes
Easy and often as each breath.

The Disquieting Muses

Mother, mother, what illbred aunt
Or what disfigured and unsightly
Cousin did you so unwisely keep
Unasked to my christening, that she
Sent these ladies in her stead
With heads like darning-eggs to nod
And nod and nod at foot and head
And at the left side of my crib?

Mother, who made to order stories
Of Mixie Blackshort the heroic bear,
Mother, whose witches always, always

Got baked into gingerbread, I wonder
Whether you saw them, whether you said
Words to rid me of those three ladies
Nodding by night around my bed,
Mouthless, eyeless, with stitched bald head.

In the hurricane, when father's twelve
Study windows bellied in
Like bubbles about to break, you fed
My brother and me cookies and ovaltine
And helped the two of us to choir:
'Thor is angry: boom boom boom!
Thor is angry: we don't care!'
But those ladies broke the panes.

When on tiptoe the schoolgirls danced,
Blinking flashlights like fireflies
And singing the glowworm song, I could
Not lift a foot in the twinkle-dress
But, heavy-footed, stood aside
In the shadow cast by my dismal-headed
Godmothers, and you cried and cried:
And the shadow stretched, the lights went out.

Mother, you sent me to piano lessons
And praised my arabesques and trills
Although each teacher found my touch
Oddly wooden in spite of scales
And the hours of practising, my ear
Tone-deaf and yes, unteachable.
I learned, I learned, I learned elsewhere,
From muses unhired by you, dear mother.

I woke one day to see you, mother,
Floating above me in bluest air
On a green balloon bright with a million
Flowers and bluebirds that never were
Never, never, found anywhere.

But the little planet bobbed away
Like a soap-bubble as you called: Come here!
And I faced my travelling companions.

Day now, night now, at head, side, feet,
They stand their vigil in gowns of stone,
Faces blank as the day I was born,
Their shadows long in the setting sun
That never brightens or goes down.

And this is the kingdom you bore me to,
Mother, mother. But no frown of mine
Will betray the company I keep.

Lady Lazarus

I have done it again.
One year in every ten
I manage it——

A sort of walking miracle, my skin
Bright as a Nazi lampshade,
My right foot

A paperweight,
My face a featureless, fine
Jew linen.

Peel off the napkin
O my enemy.
Do I terrify?——

The nose, the eye pits, the full set of teeth?
The sour breath
Will vanish in a day.

Soon, soon the flesh
The grave cave ate will be
At home on me

And I a smiling woman.
I am only thirty.
And like the cat I have nine times to die.

This is Number Three.
What a trash
To annihilate each decade.

What a million filaments.
The peanut-crunching crowd
Shoves in to see

Them unwrap me hand and foot——
The big strip tease.
Gentlemen, ladies

These are my hands
My knees.
I may be skin and bone,

Nevertheless, I am the same, identical woman.
The first time it happened I was ten.
It was an accident.

The second time I meant
To last it out and not come back at all.
I rocked shut

As a seashell.
They had to call and call
And pick the worms off me like sticky pearls.

Dying
Is an art, like everything else.
I do it exceptionally well.

I do it so it feels like hell.
I do it so it feels real.
I guess you could say I've a call.

It's easy enough to do it in a cell.
It's easy enough to do it and stay put.
It's the theatrical

Comeback in broad day
To the same place, the same face, the same brute
Amused shout:

'A miracle!'
That knocks me out.
There is a charge

For the eyeing of my scars, there is a charge
For the hearing of my heart——
It really goes.

And there is a charge, a very large charge
For a word or a touch
Or a bit of blood

Or a piece of my hair or my clothes.
So, so, Herr Doktor.
So, Herr Enemy.

I am your opus,
I am your valuable,
The pure gold baby

That melts to a shriek.
I turn and burn.
Do not think I underestimate your great concern.

Ash, ash—
You poke and stir.
Flesh, bone, there is nothing there——

A cake of soap,
A wedding ring,
A gold filling.

Herr God, Herr Lucifer
Beware
Beware.

Out of the ash
I rise with my red hair
And I eat men like air.

Tulips

The tulips are too excitable, it is winter here.
Look how white everything is, how quiet, how snowed-in.
I am learning peacefulness, lying by myself quietly
As the light lies on these white walls, this bed, these hands.
I am nobody; I have nothing to do with explosions.
I have given my name and my day-clothes up to the nurses
And my history to the anaesthetist and my body to surgeons.

They have propped my head between the pillow and the
        sheet-cuff
Like an eye between two white lids that will not shut.
Stupid pupil, it has to take everything in.
The nurses pass and pass, they are no trouble,
They pass the way gulls pass inland in their white caps,
Doing things with their hands, one just the same as another,
So it is impossible to tell how many there are.

My body is a pebble to them, they tend it as water
Tends to the pebbles it must run over, smoothing them gently.
They bring me numbness in their bright needles, they bring
        me sleep.
Now I have lost myself I am sick of baggage——

My patent leather overnight case like a black pillbox,
My husband and child smiling out of the family photo;
Their smiles catch onto my skin, little smiling hooks.

I have let things slip, a thirty-year-old cargo boat
Stubbornly hanging on to my name and address.
They have swabbed me clear of my loving associations.
Scared and bare on the green plastic-pillowed trolley
I watched my teaset, my bureaus of linen, my books
Sink out of sight, and the water went over my head.
I am a nun now, I have never been so pure.

I didn't want any flowers, I only wanted
To lie with my hands turned up and be utterly empty.
How free it is, you have no idea how free——
The peacefulness is so big it dazes you,
And it asks nothing, a name tag, a few trinkets.
It is what the dead close on, finally; I imagine them
Shutting their mouths on it, like a Communion tablet.

The tulips are too red in the first place, they hurt me.
Even through the gift paper I could hear them breathe
Lightly, through their white swaddlings, like an awful baby.
Their redness talks to my wound, it corresponds.
They are subtle: they seem to float, though they weigh me
     down,
Upsetting me with their sudden tongues and their colour,
A dozen red lead sinkers round my neck.

Nobody watched me before, now I am watched.
The tulips turn to me, and the window behind me
Where once a day the light slowly widens and slowly thins,
And I see myself, flat, ridiculous, a cut-paper shadow
Between the eye of the sun and the eyes of the tulips,
And I have no face, I have wanted to efface myself.
The vivid tulips eat my oxygen.

Before they came the air was calm enough,
Coming and going, breath by breath, without any fuss.
Then the tulips filled it up like a loud noise.
Now the air snags and eddies round them the way a river
Snags and eddies round a sunken rust-red engine.
They concentrate my attention, that was happy
Playing and resting without committing itself.

The walls, also, seem to be warming themselves.
The tulips should be behind bars like dangerous animals;
They are opening like the mouth of some great African cat,
And I am aware of my heart: it opens and closes
Its bowl of red blooms out of sheer love of me.
The water I taste is warm and salt, like the sea,
And comes from a country far away as health.

Ariel

Stasis in darkness.
Then the substanceless blue
Pour of tor and distances.

God's lioness,
How one we grow,
Pivot of heels and knees!—The furrow

Splits and passes, sister to
The brown arc
Of the neck I cannot catch,

Nigger-eye
Berries cast dark
Hooks——

Black sweet blood mouthfuls,
Shadows.
Something else

Hauls me through air——
Thighs, hair;
Flakes from my heels.

White
Godiva, I unpeel——
Dead hands, dead stringencies.

And now I
Foam to wheat, a glitter of seas.
The child's cry

Melts in the wall.
And I
Am the arrow,

The dew that flies
Suicidal, at one with the drive
Into the red

Eye, the cauldron of morning.

Getting There

How far is it?
How far is it now?
The gigantic gorilla interior
Of the wheels move, they appal me——
The terrible brains
Of Krupp, black muzzles
Revolving, the sound
Punching out Absence! like cannon.
It is Russia I have to get across, it is some war or other.
I am dragging my body
Quietly through the straw of the boxcars.
Now is the time for bribery.

What do wheels eat, these wheels
Fixed to their arcs like gods,
The silver leash of the will——
Inexorable. And their pride!
All the gods know is destinations.
I am a letter in this slot——
I fly to a name, two eyes.
Will there be fire, will there be bread?
Here there is such mud.
It is a trainstop, the nurses
Undergoing the faucet water, its veils, veils in a nunnery,
Touching their wounded,
The men the blood still pumps forward,
Legs, arms piled outside
The tent of unending cries——
A hospital of dolls.
And the men, what is left of the men
Pumped ahead by these pistons, this blood
Into the next mile,
The next hour——
Dynasty of broken arrows!
How far is it?
There is mud on my feet,
Thick, red and slipping. It is Adam's side,
This earth I rise from, and I in agony.
I cannot undo myself, and the train is steaming.
Steaming and breathing, its teeth
Ready to roll, like a devil's.
There is a minute at the end of it
A minute, a dewdrop.
How far is it?
It is so small
The place I am getting to, why are there these obstacles——
The body of this woman,
Charred skirts and deathmask
Mourned by religious figures, by garlanded children.
And now detonations——
Thunder and guns.

The fire's between us.
Is there no still place
Turning and turning in the middle air,
Untouched and untouchable.
The train is dragging itself, it is screaming——
An animal
Insane for the destination,
The bloodspot,
The face at the end of the flare.
I shall bury the wounded like pupas,
I shall count and bury the dead.
Let their souls writhe in a dew,
Incense in my track.
The carriages rock, they are cradles.
And I, stepping from this skin
Of old bandages, boredoms, old faces

Step to you from the black car of Lethe,
Pure as a baby.

Daddy

You do not do, you do not do
Any more, black shoe
In which I have lived like a foot
For thirty years, poor and white,
Barely daring to breathe or Achoo.

Daddy, I have had to kill you.
You died before I had time——
Marble-heavy, a bag full of God,
Ghastly statue with one grey toe
Big as a Frisco seal

And a head in the freakish Atlantic
Where it pours bean green over blue

In the waters off beautiful Nauset.
I used to pray to recover you.
Ach, du.

In the German tongue, in the Polish town
Scraped flat by the roller
Of wars, wars, wars.
But the name of the town is common.
My Polack friend

Says there are a dozen or two.
So I never could tell where you
Put your foot, your root,
I never could talk to you.
The tongue stuck in my jaw.

It stuck in a barb wire snare.
Ich, ich, ich, ich,
I could hardly speak.
I thought every German was you.
And the language obscene

An engine, an engine
Chuffing me off like a Jew.
A Jew to Dachau, Auschwitz, Belsen.
I began to talk like a Jew.
I think I may well be a Jew.

The snows of the Tyrol, the clear beer of Vienna
Are not very pure or true.
With my gypsy ancestress and my weird luck
And my Taroc pack and my Taroc pack
I may be a bit of a Jew.

I have always been scared of *you*,
With your Luftwaffe, your gobbledygoo.
And your neat moustache
And your Aryan eye, bright blue.
Panzer-man, panzer-man, O You——

Not God but a swastika
So black no sky could squeak through.
Every woman adores a Fascist,
The boot in the face, the brute
Brute heart of a brute like you.

You stand at the blackboard, daddy,
In the picture I have of you,
A cleft in your chin instead of your foot
But no less a devil for that, no not
Any less the black man who

Bit my pretty red heart in two.
I was ten when they buried you.
At twenty I tried to die
And get back, back, back to you.
I thought even the bones would do.

But they pulled me out of the sack,
And they stuck me together with glue.
And then I knew what to do.
I made a model of you,
A man in black with a Meinkampf look

And a love of the rack and the screw.
And I said I do, I do.
So daddy, I'm finally through.
The black telephone's off at the root,
The voices just can't worm through.

If I've killed one man, I've killed two——
The vampire who said he was you
And drank my blood for a year,
Seven years, if you want to know.
Daddy, you can lie back now.

There's a stake in your fat black heart
And the villagers never liked you.
They are dancing and stamping on you.
They always *knew* it was you.
Daddy, daddy, you bastard, I'm through.

Two Campers in Cloud Country

(Rock Lake, Canada)

In this country there is neither measure nor balance
To redress the dominance of rocks and woods,
The passage, say, of these man-shaming clouds.

No gesture of yours or mine could catch their attention,
No word make them carry water or fire the kindling
Like local trolls in the spell of a superior being.

Well, one wearies of the Public Gardens: one wants a vacation
Where trees and clouds and animals pay no notice;
Away from the labelled elms, the tame tea-roses.

It took three days driving north to find a cloud
The polite skies over Boston couldn't possibly accommodate.
Here on the last frontier of the big, brash spirit

The horizons are too far off to be chummy as uncles;
The colours assert themselves with a sort of vengeance.
Each day concludes in a huge splurge of vermilions

And night arrives in one gigantic step.
It is comfortable, for a change, to mean so little.
These rocks offer no purchase to herbage or people:

They are conceiving a dynasty of perfect cold.
In a month we'll wonder what plates and forks are for.
I lean to you, numb as a fossil. Tell me I'm here.

The Pilgrims and Indians might never have happened.
Planets pulse in the lake like bright amoebas;
The pines blot our voices up in their lightest sighs.

Around our tent the old simplicities sough
Sleepily as Lethe, trying to get in.
We'll wake blank-brained as water in the dawn.

Margaret Atwood

It Is Dangerous to Read Newspapers

While I was building neat
castles in the sandbox,
the hasty pits were
filling with bulldozed corpses

and as I walked to the school
washed and combed, my feet
stepping on the cracks in the cement
detonated red bombs.

Now I am grownup
and literate, and I sit in my chair
as quietly as a fuse

and the jungles are flaming, the underbrush is charged with soldiers,
the names on the difficult
maps go up in smoke.

I am the cause, I am a stockpile of chemical
toys, my body
is a deadly gadget,
I reach out in love, my hands are guns,
my good intentions are completely lethal.

Even my
passive eyes transmute
everything I look at to the pocked
black and white of a war photo,
how
can I stop myself

It is dangerous to read newspapers.

Each time I hit a key
on my electric typewriter,
speaking of peaceful trees

another village explodes.

Progressive Insanities of a Pioneer

I

He stood, a point
on a sheet of green paper
proclaiming himself the centre,

with no walls, no borders
anywhere; the sky no height
above him, totally un-
enclosed
and shouted:

Let me out!

II

He dug the soil in rows,
imposed himself with shovels.
He asserted
into the furrows, I
am not random.

The ground
replied with aphorisms:

a tree-sprout, a nameless
weed, words
he couldn't understand.

III

The house pitched
the plot staked
in the middle of nowhere.

At night the mind
inside, in the middle
of nowhere.

The idea of an animal
patters across the roof.

In the darkness the fields
defend themselves with fences
in vain:
      everything
      is getting in.

IV

By daylight he resisted.
He said, disgusted
with the swamp's clamourings and the outbursts
of rocks,

      This is not order
      but the absence
      of order.

He was wrong, the unanswering
forest implied:

      It was
      an ordered absence

V

For many years
he fished for a great vision,
dangling the hooks of sown

roots under the surface
of the shallow earth.

It was like
enticing whales with a bent
pin. Besides he thought

in that country
only the worms were biting.

VI

If he had known unstructured
space is a deluge
and stocked his log house-
boat with all the animals

even the wolves,

he might have floated.

But obstinate he
stated, The land is solid
and stamped,

watching his foot sink
down through stone
up to the knee.

VII

Things
refused to name themselves; refused
to let him name them.

The wolves hunted
outside.

On his beaches, his clearings,
by the surf of under-
growth breaking

at his feet, he foresaw
disintegration
                and in the end
through eyes
made ragged by his
effort, the tension
between subject and object,

the green
vision, the unnamed
whale invaded.

Backdrop Addresses Cowboy

Starspangled cowboy
sauntering out of the almost-
silly West, on your face
a porcelain grin,
tugging a papier-mâché cactus
on wheels behind you with a string,

you are innocent as a bathtub
full of bullets.

Your righteous eyes, your laconic
trigger-fingers
people the streets with villains:
as you move, the air in front of you
blossoms with targets

and you leave behind you a heroic
trail of desolation:
beer bottles
slaughtered by the side
of the road, bird-
skulls bleaching in the sunset.

I ought to be watching
from behind a cliff or a cardboard storefront
when the shooting starts, hands clasped
in admiration,

but I am elsewhere.

Then what about me

what about the I
confronting you on that border
you are always trying to cross?

I am the horizon
you ride towards, the thing you can never lasso

I am also what surrounds you:
my brain
scattered with your
tincans, bones, empty shells,
the litter of your invasions.

I am the space you desecrate
as you pass through.

Death of a Young Son by Drowning

He, who navigated with success
the dangerous river of his own birth
once more set forth

on a voyage of discovery
into the land I floated on
but could not touch to claim.

His feet slid on the bank,
the currents took him;
he swirled with ice and trees in the swollen water

and plunged into distant regions,
his head a bathysphere;
through his eyes' thin glass bubbles

he looked out, reckless adventurer
on a landscape stranger than Uranus
we have all been to and some remember.

There was an accident; the air locked,
he was hung in the river like a heart.
They retrieved the swamped body,

cairn of my plans and future charts,
with poles and hooks
from among the nudging logs.

It was spring, the sun kept shining, the new grass
lept to solidity;
my hands glistened with details.

After the long trip I was tired of waves.
My foot hit rock. The dreamed sails
collapsed, ragged.

> I planted him in this country
> like a flag.

You Take my Hand

You take my hand and
I'm suddenly in a bad movie,
it goes on and on and
why am I fascinated

We waltz in slow motion
through an air stale with aphorisms
we meet behind endless potted palms
you climb through the wrong windows

Other people are leaving
but I always stay till the end
I paid my money, I
want to see what happens.

In chance bathtubs I have to
peel you off me
in the form of smoke and melted
celluloid

       Have to face it I'm
finally an addict,
the smell of popcorn and worn plush
lingers for weeks

Variation on the Word Sleep

I would like to watch you sleeping,
which may not happen.
I would like to watch you,
sleeping. I would like to sleep
with you, to enter
your sleep as its smooth dark wave
slides over my head

and walk with you through that lucent
wavering forest of bluegreen leaves
with its watery sun & three moons
towards the cave where you must descend,
towards your worst fear

I would like to give you the silver
branch, the small white flower, the one
word that will protect you
from the grief at the center
of your dream, from the grief
at the center. I would like to follow
you up the long stairway
again & become
the boat that would row you back
carefully, a flame
in two cupped hands
to where your body lies
beside me, and you enter
it as easily as breathing in

I would like to be the air
that inhabits you for a moment
only. I would like to be that unnoticed
& that necessary.

Marrying the Hangman

She has been condemned to death by hanging. A man may escape this death by becoming the hangman, a woman by marrying
the hangman. But at the present time there is no hangman;
thus there is no escape. There is only a death, indefinitely postponed. This is not fantasy, it is history.

*

To live in prison is to live without mirrors. To live without mirrors is to live without the self. She is living selflessly, she finds
a hole in the stone wall and on the the other side of the wall, a
voice. The voice comes through darkness and has no face. This
voice becomes her mirror.

*

In order to avoid her death, her particular death, with wrung neck and swollen tongue, she must marry the hangman. But there is no hangman, first she must create him, she must persuade this man at the end of the voice, this voice she has never seen and which has never seen her, this darkness, she must persuade him to renounce his face, exchange it for the impersonal mask of death, of official death which has eyes but no mouth, this mask of a dark leper. She must transform his hands so they will be willing to twist the rope around throats that have been singled out as hers was, throats other than hers. She must marry the hangman or no one, but that is not so bad. Who else is there to marry?

*

You wonder about her crime. She was condemned to death for stealing clothes from her employer, from the wife of her employer. She wished to make herself more beautiful. This desire in servants was not legal.

*

She uses her voice like a hand, her voice reaches through the wall, stroking and touching. What could she possibly have said that would have convinced him? He was not condemned to death, freedom awaited him. What was the temptation, the one that worked? Perhaps he wanted to live with a woman whose life he had saved, who had seen down into the earth but had nevertheless followed him back up to life. It was his only chance to be a hero, to one person at least, for if he became the hangman the others would despise him. He was in prison for wounding another man, on one finger of the right hand, with a sword. This too is history.

*

My friends, who are both women, tell me their stories, which cannot be believed and which are true. They are horror stories and they have not happened to me, they have not yet happened to me, they have happened to me but we are detached, we watch our unbelief with horror. Such things cannot happen to us, it is afternoon and these things do not happen in the afternoon. The trouble was, she said, I didn't have time to put my glasses on and without them I'm blind as a bat, I couldn't even see who it was. These things happen and we sit at a table and tell stories about them so we can finally believe. This is not fantasy, it is history, there is more than one hangman and because of this some of them are unemployed.

*

He said: the end of walls, the end of ropes, the opening of doors, a field, the wind, a house, the sun, a table, an apple.

She said: nipple, arms, lips, wine, belly, hair, bread, thighs, eyes, eyes.

They both kept their promises.

*

The hangman is not such a bad fellow. Afterwards he goes to the refrigerator and cleans up the leftovers, though he does not wipe up what he accidentally spills. He wants only the simple things: a chair, someone to pull off his shoes, someone to watch him while he talks, with admiration and fear, gratitude if possible, someone in whom to plunge himself for rest and renewal. These things can best be had by marrying a woman who has been condemned to death by other men for wishing to be beautiful. There is a wide choice.

*

Everyone said he was a fool.
Everyone said she was a clever woman.
They used the word *ensnare*.

*

What did they say the first time they were alone together in the same room? What did he say when she had removed her veil and he could see that she was not a voice but a body and therefore finite? What did she say when she discovered that she had left one locked room for another? They talked of love, naturally, though that did not keep them busy forever.

*

The fact is there are no stories I can tell my friends that will make them feel better. History cannot be erased, although we can soothe ourselves by speculating about it. At that time there were no female hangmen. Perhaps there have never been any, and thus no man could save his life by marriage. Though a woman could, according to the law.

*

He said: foot, boot, order, city, fist, roads, time, knife.

She said: water, night, willow, rope hair, earth belly, cave, meat, shroud, open, blood.

They both kept their promises.

In eighteenth-century Quebec the only way for someone under sentence of death to escape hanging was, for a man, to become a hangman, or, for a woman, to marry one. Françoise Laurent, sentenced to hang for stealing, persuaded Jean Corolère, in the next cell, to apply for the vacant post of executioner, and also to marry her.

Notes Towards a Poem
That Can Never Be Written

For Carolyn Forché

I

This is the place
you would rather not know about,
this is the place that will inhabit you,
this is the place you cannot imagine,
this is the place that will finally defeat you

where the word *why* shrivels and empties
itself. This is famine.

II

There is no poem you can write
about it, the sandpits
where so many were buried
& unearthed, the unendurable
pain still traced on their skins.

This did not happen last year
or forty years ago but last week.
This has been happening,
this happens.

We make wreaths of adjectives for them,
we count them like beads,
we turn them into statistics & litanies
and into poems like this one.

Nothing works.
They remain what they are.

III

The woman lies on the wet cement floor
under the unending light,
needle marks on her arms put there
to kill the brain
and wonders why she is dying.

She is dying because she said.
She is dying for the sake of the word.
It is her body, silent
and fingerless, writing this poem.

IV

It resembles an operation
but it is not one

nor despite the spread legs, grunts
& blood, is it a birth.

Partly it's a job
partly it's a display of skill
like a concerto.

It can be done badly
or well, they tell themselves.

Partly it's an art.

V

The facts of this world seen clearly
are seen through tears;
why tell me then
there is something wrong with my eyes?

To see clearly and without flinching,
without turning away,
this is agony, the eyes taped open
two inches from the sun.

What is it you see then?
Is it a bad dream, a hallucination?
Is it a vision?
What is it you hear?

The razor across the eyeball
is a detail from an old film.
It is also a truth.
Witness is what you must bear.

VI

In this country you can say what you like
because no one will listen to you anyway,
it's safe enough, in this country you can try to write
the poem that can never be written,
the poem that invents
nothing and excuses nothing,
because you invent and excuse yourself each day.

Elsewhere, this poem is not invention.
Elsewhere, this poem takes courage.
Elsewhere, this poem must be written
because the poets are already dead.

Elsewhere, this poem must be written
as if you are already dead,
as if nothing more can be done
or said to save you.

Elsewhere you must write this poem
because there is nothing more to do.

Seamus Heaney

Digging

Between my finger and my thumb
The squat pen rests; snug as a gun.
Under my window, a clean rasping sound
When the spade sinks into gravelly ground:
My father, digging. I look down

Till his straining rump among the flowerbeds
Bends low, comes up twenty years away
Stooping in rhythm through potato drills
Where he was digging.

The coarse boot nestled on the lug, the shaft
Against the inside knee was levered firmly.
He rooted out tall tops, buried the bright edge deep
To scatter new potatoes that we picked
Loving their cool hardness in our hands.

By God, the old man could handle a spade.
Just like his old man.

My grandfather cut more turf in a day
Than any other man on Toner's bog.
Once I carried him milk in a bottle
Corked sloppily with paper. He straightened up
To drink it, then fell to right away

Nicking and slicing neatly, heaving sods
Over his shoulder, going down and down
For the good turf. Digging.

The cold smell of potato mould, the squelch and slap
Of soggy peat, the curt cuts of an edge
Through living roots awaken in my head.
But I've no spade to follow men like them.

Between my finger and my thumb
The squat pen rests.
I'll dig with it.

Death of a Naturalist

All year the flax-dam festered in the heart
Of the townland; green and heavy headed
Flax had rotted there, weighted down by huge sods.
Daily it sweltered in the punishing sun.
Bubbles gargled delicately, bluebottles
Wove a strong gauze of sound around the smell.
There were dragon-flies, spotted butterflies,
But best of all was the warm thick slobber
Of frogspawn that grew like clotted water
In the shade of the banks. Here, every spring
I would fill jampotfuls of the jellied
Specks to range on window-sills at home,
On shelves at school, and wait and watch until
The fattening dots burst into nimble-
Swimming tadpoles. Miss Walls would tell us how
The daddy frog was called a bullfrog
And how he croaked and how the mammy frog
Laid hundreds of little eggs and this was
Frogspawn. You could tell the weather by frogs too
For they were yellow in the sun and brown
In rain.

Then one hot day when fields were rank
With cowdung in the grass the angry frogs
Invaded the flax-dam; I ducked through hedges
To a coarse croaking that I had not heard
Before. The air was thick with a bass chorus.
Right down the dam gross-bellied frogs were cocked
On sods; their loose necks pulsed like sails. Some hopped:
The slap and plop were obscene threats. Some sat
Poised like mud grenades, their blunt heads farting.
I sickened, turned, and ran. The great slime kings
Were gathered there for vengeance and I knew
That if I dipped my hand the spawn would clutch it.

Mid-Term Break

I sat all morning in the college sick bay
Counting bells knelling classes to a close.
At two o'clock our neighbours drove me home.

In the porch I met my father crying—
He had always taken funerals in his stride—
And Big Jim Evans saying it was a hard blow.

The baby cooed and laughed and rocked the pram
When I came in, and I was embarrassed
By old men standing up to shake my hand

And tell me they were 'sorry for my trouble';
Whispers informed strangers I was the eldest,
Away at school, as my mother held my hand

In hers and coughed out angry tearless sighs.
At ten o'clock the ambulance arrived
With the corpse, stanched and bandaged by the nurses.

Next morning I went up into the room. Snowdrops
And candles soothed the bedside; I saw him
For the first time in six weeks. Paler now,

Wearing a poppy bruise on his left temple,
He lay in the four foot box as in his cot.
No gaudy scars, the bumper knocked him clear.

A four foot box, a foot for every year.

Personal Helicon

For Michael Longley

As a child, they could not keep me from wells
And old pumps with buckets and windlasses.
I loved the dark drop, the trapped sky, the smells
Of waterweed, fungus and dank moss.

One, in a brickyard, with a rotted board top.
I savoured the rich crash when a bucket
Plummeted down at the end of a rope.
So deep you saw no reflection in it.

A shallow one under a dry stone ditch
Fructified like any aquarium.
When you dragged out long roots from the soft mulch
A white face hovered over the bottom.

Others had echoes, gave back your own call
With a clean new music in it. And one
Was scaresome for there, out of ferns and tall
Foxgloves, a rat slapped across my reflection.

Now, to pry into roots, to finger slime,
To stare, big-eyed Narcissus, into some spring
Is beneath all adult dignity. I rhyme
To see myself, to set the darkness echoing.

Requiem for the Croppies

The pockets of our great coats full of barley—
No kitchens on the run, no striking camp—
We moved quick and sudden in our own country.
The priest lay behind ditches with the tramp.
A people, hardly marching—on the hike—
We found new tactics happening each day:
We'd cut through reins and rider with the pike
And stampede cattle into infantry,
Then retreat through hedges where cavalry must be thrown.
Until, on Vinegar Hill, the fatal conclave.
Terraced thousands died, shaking scythes at cannon.
The hillside blushed, soaked in our broken wave.
They buried us without shroud or coffin
And in August the barley grew up out of the grave.

Bogland

For T. P. Flanagan

We have no prairies
To slice a big sun at evening—
Everywhere the eye concedes to
Encroaching horizon,

Is wooed into the cyclops' eye
Of a tarn. Our unfenced country
Is bog that keeps crusting
Between the sights of the sun.

They've taken the skeleton
Of the Great Irish Elk
Out of the peat, set it up
An astounding crate full of air.

Butter sunk under
More than a hundred years
Was recovered salty and white.
The ground itself is kind, black butter

Melting and opening underfoot,
Missing its last definition
By millions of years.
They'll never dig coal here,

Only the waterlogged trunks
Of great firs, soft as pulp.
Our pioneers keep striking
Inwards and downwards,

Every layer they strip
Seems camped on before.
The bogholes might be Atlantic seepage.
The wet centre is bottomless.

The Tollund Man

I

Some day I will go to Aarhus
To see his peat-brown head,
The mild pods of his eye-lids,
His pointed skin cap.

In the flat country nearby
Where they dug him out,
His last gruel of winter seeds
Caked in his stomach,

Naked except for
The cap, noose and girdle,
I will stand a long time.
Bridegroom to the goddess,

She tightened her torc on him
And opened her fen,
Those dark juices working
Him to a saint's kept body,

Trove of the turfcutters'
Honeycombed workings.
Now his stained face
Reposes at Aarhus.

II

I could risk blasphemy,
Consecrate the cauldron bog
Our holy ground and pray
Him to make germinate

The scattered, ambushed
Flesh of labourers,

Stockinged corpses
Laid out in the farmyards,

Tell-tale skin and teeth
Flecking the sleepers
Of four young brothers, trailed
For miles along the lines.

III

Something of his sad freedom
As he rode the tumbril
Should come to me, driving,
Saying the names

Tollund, Grauballe, Nebelgard,
Watching the pointing hands
Of country people,
Now knowing their tongue.

Out there in Jutland
In the old man-killing parishes
I will feel lost,
Unhappy and at home.

Summer Home

I

Was it wind off the dumps
or something in heat

dogging us, the summer gone sour,
a fouled nest incubating somewhere?

Whose fault, I wondered, inquisitor
of the possessed air.

To realize suddenly,
whip off the mat

that was larval, moving—
and scald, scald, scald.

II

Bushing the door, my arms full
of wild cherry and rhododendron,
I hear her small lost weeping
through the hall, that bells and hoarsens
on my name, my name.

O love, here is the blame.

The loosened flowers between us
gather in, compose
for a May altar of sorts.
These frank and falling blooms
soon taint to a sweet chrism.

Attend. Anoint the wound.

III

O we tented our wound all right
under the homely sheet

and lay as if the cold flat of a blade
had winded us.

More and more I postulate
thick healings, like now

as you bend in the shower
water lives down the tilting stoups of your breasts.

IV

With a final
unmusical drive
long grains begin
to open and split

ahead and once more
we sap
the white, trodden
path to the heart.

V

My children weep out the hot foreign night.
We walk the floor, my foul mouth takes it out
On you and we lie stiff till dawn
Attends the pillow, and the maize, and vine

That holds its filling burden to the light.
Yesterday rocks sang when we tapped
Stalactites in the cave's old, dripping dark—
Our love calls tiny as a tuning fork.

Bog Queen

I lay waiting
between turf-face and demesne wall,
between heathery levels
and glass-toothed stone.

My body was braille
for the creeping influences:
dawn suns groped over my head
and cooled at my feet,

through my fabrics and skins
the seeps of winter
digested me,
the illiterate roots

pondered and died
in the cavings
of stomach and socket.
I lay waiting

on the gravel bottom,
my brain darkening,
a jar of spawn
fermenting underground

dreams of Baltic amber.
Bruised berries under my nails,
the vital hoard reducing
in the crock of the pelvis.

My diadem grew carious,
gemstones dropped
in the peat floe
like the bearings of history.

My sash was a black glacier
wrinkling, dyed weaves
and phoenician stitchwork
retted on my breasts'

soft moraines.
I knew winter cold
like the nuzzle of fjords
at my thighs—

the soaked fledge, the heavy
swaddle of hides.

My skull hibernated
in the wet nest of my hair.

Which they robbed.
I was barbered
and stripped
by a turfcutter's spade

who veiled me again
and packed coomb softly
between the stone jambs
at my head and my feet.

Till a peer's wife bribed him.
The plait of my hair,
a slimy birth-cord
of bog, had been cut

and I rose from the dark,
hacked bone, skull-ware,
frayed stitches, tufts,
small gleams on the bank.

Act of Union

I

To-night, a first movement, a pulse,
As if the rain in bogland gathered head
To slip and flood: a bog-burst,
A gash breaking open the ferny bed.
Your back is a firm line of eastern coast
And arms and legs are thrown
Beyond your gradual hills. I caress

The heaving province where our past has grown.
I am the tall kingdom over your shoulder
That you would neither cajole nor ignore.
Conquest is a lie. I grow older
Conceding your half-independent shore
Within whose borders now my legacy
Culminates inexorably.

II

And I am still imperially
Male, leaving you with the pain,
The rending process in the colony,
The battering ram, the boom burst from within.
The act sprouted an obstinate fifth column
Whose stance is growing unilateral.
His heart beneath your heart is a wardrum
Mustering force. His parasitical
And ignorant little fists already
Beat at your borders and I know they're cocked
At me across the water. No treaty
I foresee will salve completely your tracked
And stretchmarked body, the big pain
That leaves you raw, like opened ground, again.

Michael Ondaatje

Signature

The car carried him
racing the obvious moon
beating in the trees like a white bird.

Difficult to make words sing
around your appendix.
The obvious upsets me,
everyone has scars which crawl
into the mystery of swimming trunks.

I was the first appendix in my family.
My brother who was given the stigma
of a rare blood type
proved to have ulcers instead.

The rain fell like applause as I approached the hospital.

It takes seven seconds she said,
strapped my feet,
entered my arm.
I stretched all senses
on *five*
the room closed on me like an eyelid.

At night the harmonica plays,
a whistler joins in respect.
I am a sweating marble saint
full of demerol and sleeping pills.

A man in the armour of shining plaster
walks to my door, then past.
Imagine the rain
falling like white bees on the sidewalk
imagine Snyder
high on poetry and mountains

Three floors down
my appendix
swims in a jar

O world, I shall be buried all over Ontario

Elizabeth

Catch, my Uncle Jack said
and oh I caught this huge apple
red as Mrs Kelly's bum.
It's as red as Mrs Kelly's bum, I said
and Daddy roared
and swung me on his stomach with a heave.
Then I hid the apple in my room
till it shrunk like a face
growing eyes and teeth ribs.

Then Daddy took me to the zoo
he knew the man there
they put a snake around my neck
and it crawled down the front of my dress.
I felt its flicking tongue
dripping onto me like a shower.
Daddy laughed and said Smart Snake
and Mrs Kelly with us scowled.

In the pond where they kept the goldfish
Philip and I broke the ice with spades
and tried to spear the fishes;
we killed one and Philip ate it,
then he kissed me
with raw saltless fish in his mouth.

My sister Mary's got bad teeth
and said I was lucky, then she said
I had big teeth, but Philip said I was pretty.
He had big hands that smelled.

I would speak of Tom, soft laughing,
who danced in the mornings round the sundial
teaching me the steps from France, turning
with the rhythm of the sun on the warped branches,
who'd hold my breast and watch it move like a snail
leaving his quick urgent love in my palm.
And I kept his love in my palm till it blistered.

When they axed his shoulders and neck
the blood moved like a branch into the crowd.
And he staggered with his hanging shoulder
cursing their thrilled cry, wheeling,
waltzing in the French style to his knees
holding his head with the ground,
blood settling on his clothes like a blush;
this way
when they aimed the thud into his back.

And I find cool entertainment now
with white young Essex, and my nimble rhymes.

Peter

I

That spring Peter was discovered, freezing
the maze of bones from a dead cow,
skull and hooves glazed
with a skin of ice.
The warmth in his hands
carved hollows of muscle,
his fingers threading veins on its flank.

In the attempt to capture him
he bit, to defend himself,
three throats and a wrist;
that night villagers found the cow
frozen in red, and Peter
eating a meal beside it.

II

They snared him in evening light,
his body a pendulum
between the walls of the yard,
rearing from shrinking flashes of steel
until they, with a new science,
stretched his heels and limbs,
scarred through the back of his knees
leaving his veins unpinned,
and him singing in the evening air.

Till he fainted, and a brown bitch
nosed his pain, stared in interest,
and he froze into consciousness
to drag his feet to the fountain,
to numb wounds.

III

In the first months of his capture
words were growls, meaningless;
disgust in his tone burned everyone.
At meals, in bed, you heard Peter's howl
in the depths of the castle like a bell.
After the first year they cut out his tongue;

difficult
to unpin a fish's mouth
without the eventual jerk
to empty throat of pin and matter.

There followed months of silence,
then the eventual grunting;
he began to speak with the air of his body,
torturing breath into tones; it was despicable,
they had made a dead animal of his throat.

He was little more than a marred stone,
a baited gargoyle, escaped
from the fountain in the courtyard:
his throat swollen like an arm muscle,
his walk stuttered with limp, his knees straight,
his feet arcing like a compass.

IV

They made a hive for him in the court,
Jason throwing him bones from the table,
the daughter Tara tousling in detail
the hair that collapsed like a nest
over his weaving eyes.
She, bored with innocence,
would pet him like a flower,
place vast kisses on his wrists,
thrilled at scowls and obscenities,

delighted at sudden grins
that opened his face like a dawn.

He ate, bouldered at their feet,
vast hands shaping rice,
and he walked with them on grit drives—
his legs dragged like a suitcase behind him.

v

All this while Peter formed violent beauty.
He carved death on chalices,
made spoons of yawning golden fishes;
forks stemmed from the tongues of reptiles,
candle holders bent like the ribs of men.

He made fragments of people: breasts
in the midst of a girl's stride,
a head burrowed in love,
an arm swimming—fingers heaved
to nose barricades of water.

His squat form, the rippled arms
of seaweeded hair,
the fingers black, bent from moulding silver,
poured all his strength
into the bare reflection of eyes

vi

Then Tara grew.

When he first saw her, tall,
ungainly as trees,
her fat knees dangled his shoulders
as her hips rode him,
the court monster, she
swaying from side to side, held

only by the grip of her thighs
on his obtuse neck—
she bending over him,
muttering giggles at his eyes,
covering his creased face with her hair.

And he made golden spiders for her
and silver frogs, with opal glares.

And as she grew, her body
burned its awkwardness.
The full bones roamed
in brown warm skin.
The ridge in her back broadened,
her dress hid seas of thighs,
arms trailed to adjust hair that paused
like a long bird at her shoulder;
and vast brown breasts
restless at each gesture
clung to her body like new sea beasts.

And she smiled cool at Peter now,
a quiet hand received gifts from him,
and her fingers, poised,
touched
to generate expressions.

VII

An arm held her, splayed
its fingers like a cross at her neck
till he could feel fear thrashing at her throat,
while his bent hands tore the sheet of skirt,
lifted her, buttock and neck to the table.
Then laying arm above her breasts
he shaped her body like a mould,
the stub of tongue sharp as a cat, cold,
dry as a cat, rasping neck and breasts

till he poured loathing of fifteen years on her,
a vat of lush oil, staining,
the large soft body like a whale.

Then he lay there breathing at her neck
his face wet from her tears
that glued him to her pain.

Letters & Other Worlds

> 'for there was no more darkness for him and, no doubt
> like Adam before the fall, he could see in the dark'

My father's body was a globe of fear
His body was a town we never knew
He hid that he had been where we were going
His letters were a room he seldom lived in
In them the logic of his love could grow

My father's body was a town of fear
He was the only witness to its fear dance
He hid where he had been that we might lose him
His letters were a room his body scared

He came to death with his mind drowning.
On the last day he enclosed himself
in a room with two bottles of gin, later
fell the length of his body
so that brain blood moved
to new compartments
that never knew the wash of fluid
and he died in minutes of a new equilibrium.

His early life was a terrifying comedy
and my mother divorced him again and again.

He would rush into tunnels magnetized
by the white eye of trains
and once, gaining instant fame,
managed to stop a Perahara in Ceylon
—the whole procession of elephants dancers
local dignitaries—by falling
dead drunk onto the street.

As a semi-official, and semi-white at that,
the act was seen as a crucial
turning point in the Home Rule Movement
and led to Ceylon's independence in 1948.

(My mother had done her share too—
her driving so bad
she was stoned by villagers
whenever her car was recognized)

For 14 years of marriage
each of them claimed he or she
was the injured party.
Once on the Colombo docks
saying goodbye to a recently married couple
my father, jealous
at my mother's articulate emotion,
dove into the waters of the harbour
and swam after the ship waving farewell.
My mother pretending no affiliation
mingled with the crowd back to the hotel.

Once again he made the papers
though this time my mother
with a note to the editor
corrected the report—saying he was drunk
rather than broken hearted at the parting of friends.
The married couple received both editions
of *The Ceylon Times* when their ship reached Aden.

And then in his last years
he was the silent drinker,
the man who once a week
disappeared into his room with bottles
and stayed there until he was drunk
and until he was sober.

There speeches, head dreams, apologies,
the gentle letters, were composed.
With the clarity of architects
he would write of the row of blue flowers
his new wife had planted,
the plans for electricity in the house,
how my half-sister fell near a snake
and it had awakened and not touched her.
Letters in a clear hand of the most complete empathy
his heart widening and widening and widening
to all manner of change in his children and friends
while he himself edged
into the terrible acute hatred
of his own privacy
till he balanced and fell
the length of his body
the blood screaming in
the empty reservoir of bones
the blood searching in his head without metaphor

White Dwarfs

This is for people who disappear
for those who descend into the code
and make their room a fridge for Superman
—who exhaust costume and bones that could perform flight,
who shave their moral so raw
they can tear themselves through the eye of a needle

this is for those people
that hover and hover
and die in the ether peripheries

There is my fear
of no words   of
falling without words
over and over   of
mouthing the silence
Why do I love most
among my heroes those
who sail to that perfect edge
where there is no social fuel
Release of sandbags
to understand their altitude—

       that silence of the third cross
       3rd man hung so high and lonely
       we don't hear him say
       say his pain, say his unbrotherhood
       What has he to do with the smell of ladies
       can they eat off his skeleton of pain?

The Gurkhas in Malaya
cut the tongues of mules
so they were silent beasts of burden
in enemy territories
after such cruelty what could they speak of anyway
And Dashiell Hammett in success
suffered conversation and moved
to the perfect white between the words

This white that can grow
is fridge, bed,
is an egg—most beautiful
when unbroken, where
what we cannot see is growing
in all the colours we cannot see

there are those burned out stars
who implode into silence
after parading in the sky
after such choreography what would they wish to
speak of   anyway

Bearhug

Griffin calls to come and and kiss him goodnight
I yell ok. Finish something I'm doing,
then something else, walk slowly round
the corner to my son's room.
He is standing arms outstretched
waiting for a bearhug. Grinning.

Why do I give my emotion an animal's name,
give it that dark squeeze of death?
This is the hug which collects
all his small bones and his warm neck against me.
The thin tough body under the pyjamas
locks to me like a magnet of blood.

How long was he standing there
like that, before I came?

Light

For Doris Gratiaen

Midnight storm. Trees walking off across the fields in fury
naked in the spark of lightning.
I sit on the white porch on the brown hanging cane chair
coffee in my hand midnight storm midsummer night.

The past, friends and family, drift into the rain shower.
Those relatives in my favourite slides
re-shot from old minute photographs so they now stand
complex ambiguous grainy on my wall.

This is my Uncle who turned up to his marriage
on an elephant. He was a chaplain.
This shy looking man in the light jacket and tie was infamous,
when he went drinking he took the long blonde beautiful hair
of his wife and put one end in the cupboard and locked it
leaving her tethered in an armchair.
He was terrified of her possible adultery
and this way died peaceful happy to the end.
My Grandmother, who went to a dance in a muslin dress
with fireflies captured and embedded in the cloth, shining
and witty. This calm beautiful face
organised wild acts in the tropics.
She hid the mailman in her house
after he had committed murder and at the trial
was thrown out of court for making jokes at the judge.
Her son became a Q.C.
This is my brother at 6. With his cousin and his sister
and Pam de Voss who fell on a pen-knife and lost her eye.
My Aunt Christie. She knew Harold MacMillan was a spy
communicating with her through pictures in the newspapers.
Every picture she believed asked her to forgive him,
his hound eyes pleading.
Her husband Uncle Fitzroy a doctor in Ceylon had a memory
sharp as scalpels into his 80's
though I never bothered to ask him about anything
—interested then more in the latest recordings of Bobby Darin.

And this is my Mother with her brother Noel in fancy dress.
They are 7 and 8 years old, a hand-coloured photograph,
it is the earliest picture I have. The one I love most.
A picture of my kids at Halloween
has the same contact and laughter.
My Uncle dying at 68, and my Mother a year later dying at 68.

She told me about his death and the day he died
his eyes clearing out of illness as if seeing
right through the room the hospital and she said
he saw something so clear and good his whole body
for a moment became youthful and she remembered
when she sewed badges on his trackshirts.
Her voice joyous in telling me this, her face light and clear.
(My firefly Grandmother also dying at 68).

These are the fragments I have of them, tonight
in this storm, the dogs restless on the porch.
They were all laughing, crazy, and vivid in their prime.
At a party my drunk Father
tried to explain a complex operation on chickens
and managed to kill them all in the process, the guests
having dinner an hour later while my Father slept
and the kids watched the servants clean up the litter
of beaks and feathers on the lawn.

These are their fragments, all I remember,
wanting more knowledge of them. In the mirror and in my kids
I see them in my flesh. Wherever we are
they parade in my brain and the expanding stories
connect to the grey grainy pictures on the wall,
as they hold their drinks or 20 years later
hold grandchildren, pose with favourite dogs,
coming through the light, the electricity, which the storm
destroyed an hour ago, a tree going down by the highway
so that now inside the kids play dominoes by candlelight
and out here the thick rain static the spark of my match
        to a cigarette
and the trees across the fields leaving me, distinct
lonely in their own knife scars and cow-chewed bark
frozen in the jagged light as if snapped in their run
the branch arms waving to what was a second ago the dark sky
when in truth like me they haven't moved.
Haven't moved an inch from me.

From Billy the Kid

After shooting Gregory
this is what happened

I'd shot him well and careful
made it explode under his heart
so it wouldnt last long and
was about to walk away
when this chicken paddles out to him
and as he was falling hops on his neck
digs the beak into his throat
straightens legs and heaves
a red and blue vein out

Meanwhile he fell
and the chicken walked away

still tugging at the vein
till it was 12 yards long
as if it held that body like a kite
Gregory's last words being

get away from me yer stupid chicken

.   .   .

The barn I stayed in for a week then was at the edge of a farm
and had been deserted it seemed for several years, though built
of stone and good wood. The cold dark grey of the place made
my eyes become used to soft light and I burned out my fever
there. It was twenty yards long, about ten yards wide. Above
me was another similar sized room but the floors were unsafe
for me to walk on. However I heard birds and the odd animal
scrape their feet, the rotten wood magnifying the sound so they
entered my dreams and nightmares.

But it was the colour and light of the place that made me stay there, not my fever. It became a calm week. It was the colour and the light. The colour a grey with remnants of brown—for instance those rust brown pipes and metal objects that before had held bridles or pails, that slid to machine uses; the thirty or so grey cans in one corner of the room, their ellipses, from where I sat, setting up patterns in the dark.

When I had arrived I opened two windows and a door and the sun poured blocks and angles in, lighting up the floor's skin of feathers and dust and old grain. The windows looked out onto fields and plants grew at the door, me killing them gradually with my urine. Wind came in wet and brought in birds who flew to the other end of the room to get their aim to fly out again. An old tap hung from the roof, the same colour as the walls, so once I knocked myself out on it.

For that week then I made a bed of the table there and lay out my fever, whatever it was. I began to block my mind of all thought. Just sensed the room and learnt what my body could do, what it could survive, what colours it liked best, what songs I sang best. There were animals who did not move out and accepted me as a larger breed. I ate the old grain with them, drank from a constant puddle about twenty yards away from the barn. I saw no human and heard no human voice, learned to squat the best way when shitting, used leaves for wiping, never ate flesh or touched another animal's flesh, never entered his boundary. We were all aware and allowed each other. The fly who sat on my arm, after his inquiry, just went away, ate his disease and kept it in him. When I walked I avoided the cobwebs who had places to grow to, who had stories to finish. The flies caught in those acrobat nets were the only murder I saw.

And in the barn next to us there was another granary, separated by just a thick wood door. In it a hundred or so rats, thick rats, eating and eating the foot deep pile of grain abandoned now and fermenting so that at the end of my week, after a heavy rain storm burst the power in those seeds and brought drunkenness into the minds of those rats, they abandoned the sanity of eating the food before them and turned on each other and grotesque and awkwardly because of their size they went for each other's eyes and ribs so the yellow stomachs slid out and they came through that door and killed a chipmunk—about ten of them onto that one striped thing and the ten eating each other before they realised the chipmunk was long gone so that I, sitting on the open window with its thick sill where they couldnt reach me, filled my gun and fired again and again into their slow wheel across the room at each boommm, and reloaded and fired again and again till I went through the whole bag of bullet supplies—the noise breaking out the seal of silence in my ears, the smoke sucked out of the window as it emerged from my fist and the long twenty yard space between me and them empty but for the floating bullet lonely as an emissary across and between the wooden posts that never returned, so the rats continued to wheel and stop in the silences and eat each other, some even the bullet. Till my hand was black and the gun was hot and no other animal of any kind remained in that room but for the boy in the blue shirt sitting there coughing at the dust, rubbing the sweat of his upper lip with his left forearm.

The Cinnamon Peeler

If I were a cinnamon peeler
I would ride your bed
and leave the yellow bark dust
on your pillow.

Your breasts and shoulders would reek
you could never walk through markets
without the profession of my fingers

floating over you. The blind would
stumble certain of whom they approached
though you might bathe
under rain gutters, monsoon.

Here on the upper thigh
at this smooth pasture
neighbour to your hair
or the crease
that cuts your back. This ankle.
You will be known among strangers
as the cinnamon peeler's wife.

I could hardly glance at you
before marriage
never touch you
—your keen nosed mother, your rough brothers.
I buried my hands
in saffron, disguised them
over smoking tar,
helped the honey gatherers . . .

                    *

When we swam once
I touched you in water
and our bodies remained free,
you could hold me and be blind of smell.
You climbed the bank and said

                this is how you touch other women
the grass cutter's wife, the lime burner's daughter.
And you searched your arms
for the missing perfume
                        and knew

      what good is it
to be the lime burner's daughter
left with no trace
as if not spoken to in the act of love
as if wounded without the pleasure of a scar.

You touched
your belly to my hands
in the dry air and said
I am the cinnamon
peeler's wife. Smell me.

To a Sad Daughter

All night long the hockey pictures
gaze down at you
sleeping in your tracksuit.
Belligerent goalies are your ideal.
Threats of being traded
cuts and wounds
—all this pleases you.
O my god! you say at breakfast
reading the sports page over the Alpen
as another player breaks his ankle
or assaults the coach.

When I thought of daughters
I wasn't expecting this
but I like this more.
I like all your faults
even your purple moods
when you retreat from everyone
to sit in bed under a quilt.

And when I say 'like'
I mean of course 'love'
but that embarrasses you.
You who feel superior to black and white movies
(coaxed for hours to see *Casablanca*)
though you were moved
by *Creature from the Black Lagoon*.

One day I'll come swimming
beside your ship or someone will
and if you hear the siren
listen to it. For if you close your ears
only nothing happens. You will never change.

I don't care if you risk
your life to angry goalies
creatures with webbed feet.
You can enter their caves and castles
their glass laboratories. Just
don't be fooled by anyone but yourself.

This is the first lecture I've given you.
You're 'sweet sixteen' you said.
I'd rather be your closest friend
than your father. I'm not good at advice
you know that, but ride
the ceremonies
until they grow dark.

Sometimes you are so busy
discovering your friends
I ache with a loss
—but that is greed.
And sometimes I've gone
into *my* purple world
and lost you.

One afternoon I stepped
into your room. You were sitting
at the desk where I now write this.
Forsythia outside the window
and sun spilled over you
like a thick yellow miracle
as if another planet
was coaxing you out of the house
—all those possible worlds!—
and you, meanwhile, busy with mathematics.

I cannot look at forsythia now
without loss, or joy for you.
You step delicately
into the wild world
and your real prize will be
the frantic search.
Want everything. If you break
break going out not in.
How you live your life I don't care
but I'll sell my arms for you,
hold your secrets forever.

If I speak of death
which you fear now, greatly,
it is without answers,
except that each
one we know is
in our blood.
Don't recall graves.
Memory is permanent.
Remember the afternoon's
yellow suburban annunciation.
Your goalie
in his frightening mask
dreams perhaps
of gentleness.

In a Yellow Room

There was another reason for Fats Waller to record, on May 8th, 1935, 'I'm gonna sit right down and write myself a letter.' It is for this moment, driving down from Goderich and past Blyth, avoiding Blyth by taking the gravel concessions, four adults and a child, who have just swum in a very cold Lake Huron. His piano drips from the cassette player and we all recognize the piece but are mute. We cannot sing before he does, before he eases himself into the lyrics as if into a chair, this large man who is to die in 1943 sitting in a train in Kansas City, finally still.

He was always moving, grand on the street or the midnight taxi rides with Andy Razaf during which it is rumoured he wrote most of his songs. I have always loved him but I love him most in the company of friends. Because his body was a crowd and we desire to imitate such community. His voice staggers or is gentle behind a whimsical piano, the melody ornamental and cool as vichyssoise in that hot studio in this hot car on a late June Ontario summer day. What else of importance happened on May 8th, 1935?

The only creature I've ever met who disliked him was a nervous foxhound I had for three years. As soon as I put on Mr. Waller the dog would dart from the room and hide under a bed. The dog recognised the anarchy, the unfolding of musical order, the growls and muttering, the fact that Fats Waller was talking to someone over your shoulder as well as to you. What my dog did not notice was the serenity he should have learned from. The notes as fresh as creek washed clothes.

The windows are open as we drive under dark maples that sniff up a rumour of Lake Huron. The piano energizes the hay bound into wheels, a white field of turkeys, various tributaries of the Maitland River. Does he, drunk and carrying his tin of tomatoes—'it feeds the body and cuts the hangover'—does he, in the midnight taxi with Razaf, imagine where the music disappears? Where it will recur? Music and lyrics they wrote then sold to false composers for ready cash and only later admitting they had written 'Sunny side of the street' and 'I can't give you anything but love' and so many of the best songs of their time. The hidden authors on their two hour taxi ride out of Harlem to Brooklyn and back again to Harlem, the night heat and smells yells overheard from the streets they passed through which they incorporated into what they were making every texture entering this large man, a classical organist in his youth, who strode into most experiences, hid from his ex-wife Edith Hatchett, visiting two kinds of women, 'ladies who had pianos and ladies who did not', and died of bronchial pneumonia on the Acheson-Topeka and Santa Fe, a song he did not write.

He and the orchestra of his voice have now entered the car with us. This is his first visit to the country, though he saw it from a train window the day before he died. Saw the heartland where the music could disappear, the diaspora of notes, a rewinding, a backward movement of the formation of the world, the invention of his waltz.

Poetics

W. H. AUDEN

From *The Poet and the City**

Before the phenomenon of the Public appeared in society, there existed naive art and sophisticated art which were different from each other but only in the way that two brothers are different. The Athenian court may smile at the mechanics' play of Pyramus and Thisbe, but they recognize it as a play. Court poetry and Folk poetry were bound by the common tie that both were made by hand and both were intended to last; the crudest ballad was as custom-built as the most esoteric sonnet. The appearance of the Public and the mass media which cater to it have destroyed naive popular art. The sophisticated 'highbrow' artist survives and can still work as he did a thousand years ago, because his audience is too small to interest the mass media. But the audience of the popular artist is the majority and this the mass media must steal from him if they are not to go bankrupt. Consequently, aside from a few comedians, the only art today is 'highbrow'. What the mass media offer is not popular art, but entertainment which is intended to be consumed like food, forgotten, and replaced by a new dish. This is bad for everyone; the majority lose all genuine taste of their own, and the minority become cultural snobs.

The two characteristics of art which make it possible for an art historian to divide the history of art into periods, are, firstly, a common style of expression over a certain period and, secondly, a common notion, explicit or implicit, of the hero, the kind of human being who most deserves to be celebrated, remembered, and, if possible, imitated. The characteristic style of 'Modern' poetry is an intimate tone of voice, the speech of one person

---

* From *The Dyer's Hand* by W. H. Auden.

addressing one person, not a large audience; whenever a modern poet raises his voice he sounds phony. And its characteristic hero is neither the 'Great Man' nor the romantic rebel, both doers of extraordinary deeds, but the man or woman in any walk of life who, despite all the impersonal pressures of modern society, manages to acquire and preserve a face of his own.

Poets are, by the nature of their interests and the nature of artistic fabrication, singularly ill-equipped to understand politics or economics. Their natural interest is in singular individuals and personal relations, while politics and economics are concerned with large numbers of people, hence with the human average (the poet is bored to death by the idea of the Common Man), and with impersonal, to a great extent involuntary, relations. The poet cannot understand the function of money in modern society because for him there is no relation between subjective value and market value; he may be paid ten pounds for a poem which he believes is very good and took him months to write, and a hundred pounds for a piece of journalism which costs him but a day's work. If he is a successful poet—though few poets make enough money to be called successful in the way that a novelist or playwright can—he is a member of the Manchester school and believes in absolute *laissez-faire;* if he is unsuccessful and embittered, he is liable to combine aggressive fantasies about the annihilation of the present order with impractical daydreams of Utopia. Society has always to beware of the utopias being planned by artists *manqués* over cafeteria tables late at night.

All poets adore explosions, thunderstorms, tornadoes, conflagrations, ruins, scenes of spectacular carnage. The poetic imagination is not at all a desirable quality in a statesman.

In a war or a revolution a poet may do very well as a guerilla fighter or a spy, but it is unlikely that he will make a good regular soldier, or in peacetime, a conscientious member of a parliamentary committee.

All political theories which, like Plato's, are based on analogies drawn from artistic fabrication are bound, if put into practice, to turn into tyrannies. The whole aim of a poet, or any other kind of artist, is to produce something which is complete and will endure without change. A poetic city would always contain exactly the same number of inhabitants doing exactly the same jobs for ever.

Moreover, in the process of arriving at the finished work, the artist has continually to employ violence. A poet writes:

> The mast-high anchor dives through a cleft

changes it to

> The anchor dives through closing paths

changes it again to

> The anchor dives among hayricks

and finally to

> The anchor dives through the floors of a church.

A *cleft* and *closing paths* have been liquidated, and hayricks deported to another stanza.

A society which was really like a good poem, embodying the aesthetic virtues of beauty, order, economy, and subordination of detail to the whole, would be a nightmare of horror for, given the historical reality of actual men, such a society could only come into being through selective breeding, extermination of the physically and mentally unfit, absolute obedience to its Director, and a large slave class kept out of sight in cellars.

Vice versa, a poem which was really like a political democracy—examples, unfortunately, exist—would be formless, windy, banal, and utterly boring.

There are two kinds of political issues, Party issues and Revolutionary issues. In a party issue, all parties are agreed as to the nature and justice of the social goal to be reached, but differ in their policies for reaching it. The existence of different parties is justified, firstly, because no party can offer irrefutable proof that its policy is the only one which will achieve the commonly desired goal and, secondly, because no social goal can be achieved without some sacrifice of individual or group interest and it is natural for each individual and social group to seek a policy which will keep its sacrifice to a minimum, to hope that, if sacrifices must be made, it would be more just if someone else made them. In a party issue, each party seeks to convince the members of its society, primarily by appealing to their reason; it marshals facts and arguments to convince others that its policy is more likely to achieve the desired goal than that of its opponents. On a party issue it is essential that passions be kept at a low temperature: effective oratory requires, of course, some appeal to the emotions of the audience, but in party politics orators should display the mock-passion of prosecuting and defending attorneys, not really lose their tempers. Outside the Chamber, the rival deputies should be able to dine in each other's houses; fanatics have no place in party politics.

A revolutionary issue is one in which different groups within a society hold different views as to what is just. When this is the case, argument and compromise are out of the question; each group is bound to regard the other as wicked or mad or both. Every revolutionary issue is potentially a *casus belli*. On a revolutionary issue, an orator cannot convince his audience by appealing to their reason; he may convert some of them by awakening and appealing to their conscience, but his principal function, whether he represent the revolutionary or the counter-revolutionary group, is to arouse its passion to the point where it will give all its energies to achieving total victory for itself and total defeat for its opponents. When an issue is revolutionary, fanatics are essential.

Today, there is only one genuine world-wide revolutionary issue, racial equality. The debate between capitalism, socialism, and communism is really a party issue, because the goal which all seek is really the same, a goal which is summed up in Brecht's well-known line:

Erst kommt das Fressen, dann kommt die Moral.

I.e., Grub first, then Ethics. In all the technologically advanced countries today, whatever political label they give themselves, their policies have, essentially, the same goal: to guarantee to every member of society, as a psychophysical organism, the right to physical and mental health. The positive symbolic figure of this goal is a naked anonymous baby, the negative symbol, a mass of anonymous concentration camp corpses.

What is so terrifying and immeasurably depressing about most contemporary politics is the refusal—mainly but not, alas, only by the communists—to admit that this is a party issue to be settled by appeal to facts and reason, the insistence that there is a revolutionary issue between us. If an African gives his life for the cause of racial equality, his death is meaningful to him; but what is utterly absurd, is that people should be deprived every day of their liberties and their lives, and that the human race may quite possibly destroy itself over what is really a matter of practical policy like asking whether, given its particular historical circumstances, the health of a community is more or less likely to be secured by Private Practice or by Socialized Medicine.

What is peculiar and novel to our age is that the principal goal of politics in every advanced society is not, strictly speaking, a political one, that is to say, it is not concerned with human beings as persons and citizens but with human bodies, with the precultural, prepolitical human creature. It is, perhaps, inevitable that respect for the liberty of the individual should have so greatly diminished and the authoritarian powers of the State have so greatly increased from what they were fifty years ago, for the main political issue today is concerned not with human liberties but with human necessities.

As creatures we are all equally slaves to natural necessity; we are not free to vote how much food, sleep, light, and air we need to keep in good health; we all need a certain quantity, and we all need the same quantity.

Every age is one-sided in its political and social preoccupation and in seeking to realize the particular value it esteems most highly, it neglects and even sacrifices other values. The relation of a poet, or any artist, to society and politics is, except in Africa or still backward semifeudal countries, more difficult than it has ever been because, while he cannot but approve of the importance of *everybody* getting enough food to eat and enough leisure, this problem has nothing whatever to do with art, which is concerned with *singular persons*, as they are alone and as they are in their personal relations. Since these interests are not the predominant ones in his society; indeed, in so far as it thinks about them at all, it is with suspicion and latent hostility—it secretly or openly thinks that the claim that one is a singular person, or a demand for privacy, is putting on airs, a claim to be superior to other folk—every artist feels himself at odds with modern civilization.

In our age, the mere making of a work of art is itself a political act. So long as artists exist, making what they please and think they ought to make, even if it is not terribly good, even if it appeals to only a handful of people, they remind the Management of something managers need to be reminded of, namely, that the managed are people with faces, not anonymous members, that *Homo Laborans* is also *Homo Ludens*.

If a poet meets an illiterate peasant, they may not be able to say much to each other, but if they both meet a public official, they share the same feeling of suspicion; neither will trust one further than he can throw a grand piano. If they enter a government building, both share the same feeling of apprehension; perhaps they will never get out again. Whatever the cultural differences between them, they both sniff in any official world the smell of an unreality in which persons are treated as statistics. The peasant may play cards in the evening while the poet writes verses, but there is one political principle to which they both subscribe, namely, that among the half-dozen or so things for which a man of honour should be prepared, if necessary, to die, the right to play, the right to frivolity, is not the least.

From *The Virgin and the Dynamo**

The subject matter of a poem is comprised of a crowd of recollected occasions of feeling, among which the most important are recollections of encounters with sacred beings or events. This crowd the poet attempts to transform into a community by embodying it in a verbal society. Such a society, like any society in nature, has its own laws; its laws of prosody and syntax are analogous to the laws of physics and chemistry. Every poem must presuppose—sometimes mistakenly—that the history of the language is at an end.

One should say, rather, that a poem is a natural organism, not an inorganic thing. For example, it is rhythmical. The temporal recurrences of rhythm are never identical, as the metrical notation would seem to suggest. Rhythm is to time what symmetry is

---

* From *The Dyer's Hand* by W. H. Auden.

to space. Seen from a certain distance, the features of a human face seem symmetrically arranged, so that a face with a nose a foot long or a left eye situated two inches away from the nose would appear monstrous. Close up, however, the exact symmetry disappears; the size and position of the features vary slightly from face to face and, indeed, if a face could exist in which the symmetry were mathematically perfect, it would look, not like a face, but like a lifeless mask. So with rhythm. A poem may be described as being written in iambic pentameters, but if every foot in every line were identical, the poem would sound intolerable to the ear. I am sometimes inclined to think that the aversion of many modern poets and their readers to formal verse may be due to their association of regular repetition and formal restrictions with all that is most boring and lifeless in modern life, road drills, time-clock punching, bureaucratic regulations.

It has been said that a poem should not mean but be. This is not quite accurate. In a poem, as distinct from many other kinds of verbal societies, meaning and being are identical. A poem might be called a pseudo-person. Like a person, it is unique and addresses the reader personally. On the other hand, like a natural being and unlike a historical person, it cannot lie. We may be and frequently are mistaken as to the meaning or the value of a poem, but the cause of our mistake lies in our own ignorance or self-deception, not in the poem itself.

The nature of the final poetic order is the outcome of a dialectical struggle between the recollected occasions of feeling and the verbal system. As a society the verbal system is actively coercive upon the occasions it is attempting to embody; what it cannot embody truthfully it excludes. As a potential community the occasions are passively resistant to all claims of the system to embody them which they do not recognize as just; they decline all unjust persuasions. As members of crowds, every occasion competes with every other, demanding inclusion and a dominant position to which they are not necessarily entitled, and every word demands that the system shall modify itself in its case, that a special exception shall be made for it and it only.

In a successful poem, society and community are one order and the system may love itself because the feelings which it embodies are all members of the same community, loving each other and it. A poem may fail in two ways; it may exclude too much (banality), or attempt to embody more than one community at once (disorder).

In writing a poem, the poet can work in two ways. Starting from an intuitive idea of the kind of community he desires to call into being, he may work backwards in search of the system which will most justly incarnate that idea, or, starting with a certain system, he may work forward in search of the community which it is capable of incarnating most truthfully. In practice he nearly always works simultaneously in both directions, modifying his conception of the ultimate nature of the community at the immediate suggestions of the system, and modifying the system in response to his growing intuition of the future needs of the community.

A system cannot be selected completely arbitrarily nor can one say that any given system is absolutely necessary. The poet searches for one which imposes just obligations on the feelings. 'Ought' always implies 'can' so that a system whose claims cannot be met must be scrapped. But the poet has to beware of accusing the system of injustice when what is at fault is the laxness and self-love of the feelings upon which it is making its demands.

Every poet, consciously or unconsciously, holds the following absolute presuppositions, as the dogmas of his art:

(1) A historical world exists, a world of unique events and unique persons, related by analogy, not identity. The number of events and analogical relations is potentially infi-

nite. The existence of such a world is a good, and every addition to the number of events, persons, and relations is an additional good.

(2) The historical world is a fallen world, i.e., though it is good that it exists, the way in which it exists is evil, being full of unfreedom and disorder.

(3) The historical world is a redeemable world. The unfreedom and disorder of the past can be reconciled in the future.

It follows from the first presupposition that the poet's activity in creating a poem is analogous to God's activity in creating man after his own image. It is not an imitation, for were it so, the poet would be able to create like God *ex nihilo*; instead, he requires pre-existing occasions of feeling and a pre-existing language out of which to create. It is analogous in that the poet creates not necessarily according to a law of nature but voluntarily according to provocation.

It is untrue, strictly speaking, to say that a poet should not write poems unless he must; strictly speaking it can only be said that he should not write them unless he can. The phrase is sound in practice, because only in those who can and when they can is the motive genuinely compulsive.

In those who profess a desire to write poetry, yet exhibit an incapacity to do so, it is often the case that their desire is not for creation but for self-perpetuation, that they refuse to accept their own mortality, just as there are parents who desire children, not as new persons analogous to themselves, but to prolong their own existence in time. The sterility of this substitution of identity for analogy is expressed in the myth of Narcissus. When the poet speaks, as he sometimes does of achieving immortality through his poem, he does not mean that he hopes, like Faust, to live for ever, but that he hopes to rise from the dead. In poetry as in other matters the law holds good that he who would save his life must lose it; unless the poet sacrifices his feelings completely to the poem so that they are no longer his but the poem's, he fails.

It follows from the second presupposition, that a poem is a witness to man's knowledge of evil as well as good. It is not the duty of a witness to pass moral judgement on the evidence he has to give, but to give it clearly and accurately; the only crime of which a witness can be guilty is perjury. When we say that poetry is beyond good and evil, we simply mean that a poet can no more change the facts of what he has felt than, in the natural order, parents can change the inherited physical characteristics which they pass on to their children. The judgement good-or-evil applies only to the intentional movements of the will. Of our feelings in a given situation which are the joint product of our intention and the response to the external factors in that situation it can only be said that, given an intention and the response, they are appropriate or inappropriate. Of a recollected feeling it cannot be said that it is appropriate or inappropriate because the historical situation in which it arose no longer exists.

Every poem, therefore, is an attempt to present an analogy to that paradisal state in which Freedom and Law, System and Order are united in harmony. Every good poem is very nearly a Utopia. Again, an analogy, not an imitation; the harmony is possible and verbal only.

It follows from the third presupposition that a poem is beautiful or ugly to the degree that it succeeds or fails in reconciling contradictory feelings in an order of mutual propriety. Every beautiful poem presents an analogy to the forgiveness of sins; an analogy, not an imitation, because it is not evil intentions which are repented of and pardoned but contradictory feelings which the poet surrenders to the poem in which they are reconciled.

The effect of beauty, therefore, is good to the degree that, through its analogies, the goodness of created existence, the historical fall into unfreedom and disorder, and the possibility of regaining paradise through repentance and forgiveness are recognized. Its effect is evil to the degree that beauty is taken, not

as analogous to, but identical with goodness, so that the artist
regards himself or is regarded by others as God, the pleasure of
beauty taken for the joy of Paradise, and the conclusion drawn
that, since all is well in the work of art, all is well in history. But
all is not well there.

E. E. CUMMINGS

Three Statements

1*

On the assumption that my technique is either complicated or original or both, the publishers have politely requested me to write an introduction to this book.

At least my theory of technique, if I have one, is very far from original; nor is it complicated. I can express it in fifteen words, by quoting The Eternal Question And Immortal Answer of burlesk, viz., 'Would you hit a woman with a child?—No, I'd hit her with a brick.' Like the burlesk comedian, I am abnormally fond of that precision which creates movement.

If a poet is anybody, he is somebody to whom things made matter very little—somebody who is obsessed by Making. Like all obsessions, the Making obsession has disadvantages; for instance, my only interest in making money would be to make it. Fortunately, however, I should prefer to make almost anything else, including locomotives and roses. It is with roses and locomotives (not to mention acrobats Spring electricity Coney Island the 4th of July the eyes of mice and Niagara Falls) that my 'poems' are competing.

They are also competing with each other, with elephants, and with El Greco.

Ineluctable preoccupation with The Verb gives a poet one priceless advantage: whereas nonmakers must content themselves with the merely undeniable fact that two times two is four, he rejoices in a purely irresistible truth (to be found, in abbreviated costume, upon the title page of the present volume).

---

* Foreword from *is 5* by e. e. cummings.

2*

The poems to come are for you and for me and are not for mostpeople

—it's no use trying to pretend that mostpeople and ourselves are alike. Mostpeople have less in common with ourselves than the squarerootofminusone. You and I are human beings:mostpeople are snobs.

Take the matter of being born. What does being born mean to mostpeople? Catastrophe unmitigated. Socialrevolution. The cultured aristocrat yanked out of his hyperexclusively ultravoluptuous superpalazzo,and dumped into an incredibly vulgar detentioncamp swarming with every conceivable species of undesirable organism. Mostpeople fancy a guaranteed birthproof safetysuit of nondestructible selflessness. If mostpeople were to be born twice they'd improbably call it dying—

you and I are not snobs. We can never be born enough. We are human beings;for whom birth is a supremely welcome mystery,the mystery of growing:the mystery which happens only and whenever we are faithful to ourselves. You and I wear the dangerous looseness of doom and find it becoming. Life,for eternal us,is now;and now is much too busy being a little more than everything to seem anything,catastrophic included.

Life,for mostpeople,simply isn't. Take the socalled standardofliving. What do mostpeople mean by 'living'? They don't mean living. They mean the latest and closest plural approximation to singular prenatal passivity which science,in its finite but unbounded wisdom,has succeeded in selling their wives. If science could fail,a mountain's a mammal. Mostpeople's wives can spot a genuine delusion of embryonic omnipotence immediately and will accept no substitutes.

—luckily for us,a mountain is a mammal. The plusorminus movie to end moving,the strictly scientific parlourgame of real

---

* Introduction from *Collected Poems* by e. e. cummings.

unreality,the tyranny conceived in misconception and dedicated to the proposition that every man is a woman and any woman a king,hasn't a wheel to stand on. What their most synthetic not to mention transparent majesty,mrsadmr collective foetus,would improbably call a ghost is walking. He isn't an undream of anaesthetized impersons,or a cosmic comfortstation,or a transcendentally sterilized lookiesoundiefeelietastiesmellie. He is a healthily complex,a naturally homogeneous,citizen of immortality. The now of his each pitying free imperfect gesture,his any birth or breathing,insults perfected inframortally millenniums of slavishness. He is a little more than everything,he is democracy; he is alive:he is ourselves.

Miracles are to come. With you I leave a remembrance of miracles: they are by somebody who can love and who shall be continually reborn,a human being;somebody who said to those near him,when his fingers would not hold a brush 'tie it into my hand'—

nothing proving or sick or partial. Nothing false,nothing difficult or easy or small or colossal. Nothing ordinary or extraordinary,nothing emptied or filled,real or unreal;nothing feeble and known or clumsy and guessed. Everywhere tints childrening, innocent spontaneous,true. Nowhere possibly what flesh and impossibly such a garden,but actually flowers which breasts are among the very mouths of light. Nothing believed or doubted; brain over heart, surface:nowhere hating or to fear;shadow, mind without soul. Only how measureless cool flames of making;only each other building always distinct selves of mutual entirely opening;only alive. Never the murdered finalities of wherewhen and yesno,impotent nongames of wrongright and rightwrong;never to gain or pause,never the soft adventure of undoom,greedy anguishes and cringing ecstasies of inexistence; never to rest and never to have:only to grow.

Always the beautiful answer who asks a more beautiful question.

3*

A poet is somebody who feels, and who expresses his feeling through words.

This may sound easy. It isn't.

A lot of people think or believe or know they feel—but that's thinking or believing or knowing; not feeling. And poetry is feeling—not knowing or believing or thinking.

Almost anybody can learn to think or believe or know, but not a single human being can be taught to feel. Why? Because whenever you think or you believe or you know, you're a lot of other people: but the moment you feel, you're nobody-but-yourself.

To be nobody-but-yourself—in a world which is doing its best, night and day, to make you everybody else—means to fight the hardest battle which any human being can fight; and never stop fighting.

As for expressing nobody-but-yourself in words, that means working just a little harder than anybody who isn't a poet can possibly imagine. Why? Because nothing is quite as easy as using words like somebody else. We all of us do exactly this nearly all of the time—and whenever we do it, we're not poets.

If, at the end of your first ten or fifteen years of fighting and working and feeling, you find you've written one line of one poem, you'll be very lucky indeed.

And so my advice to all young people who wish to become poets is: do something easy, like learning how to blow up the world—unless you're not only willing, but glad, to feel and work and fight till you die.

Does this sound dismal? It isn't.

It's the most wonderful life on earth.

Or so I feel.

---

* 'A Poet's Advice to Students' appeared originally in the Ottawa Hills *Spectator*. From *e.e. cummings: A Miscellany Revised* ed. by George J. Firmage.

T. S. ELIOT

Tradition and the Individual Talent*

I

In English writing we seldom speak of tradition, though we occasionally apply its name in deploring its absence. We cannot refer to 'the tradition' or to 'a tradition'; at most, we employ the adjective in saying that the poetry of So-and-so is 'traditional' or even 'too traditional'. Seldom, perhaps, does the word appear except in a phrase of censure. If otherwise, it is vaguely approbative, with the implication, as to the work approved, of some pleasing archæological reconstruction. You can hardly make the word agreeable to English ears without this comfortable reference to the reassuring science of archæology.

Certainly the word is not likely to appear in our appreciations of living or dead writers. Every nation, every race, has not only its own creative, but its own critical turn of mind; and is even more oblivious of the shortcomings and limitations of its critical habits than of those of its creative genius. We know, or think we know, from the enormous mass of critical writing that has appeared in the French language the critical method or habit of the French; we only conclude (we are such unconscious people) that the French are 'more critical' than we, and sometimes even plume ourselves a little with the fact, as if the French were the less spontaneous. Perhaps they are; but we might remind ourselves that criticism is as inevitable as breathing, and that we should be none the worse for articulating what passes in our minds when we read a book and feel an emotion about it, for criticizing our own minds in their work of criticism. One of the facts that might come to light in this process is our tendency to insist, when we praise a poet, upon those aspects of his work in

---

* From *Selected Essays*, new edition, by T. S. Eliot.

which he least resembles anyone else. In these aspects or parts of his work we pretend to find what is individual, what is the peculiar essence of the man. We dwell with satisfaction upon the poet's difference from his predecessors, especially his immediate predecessors; we endeavour to find something that can be isolated in order to be enjoyed. Whereas if we approach a poet without this prejudice we shall often find that not only the best, but the most individual parts of his work may be those in which the dead poets, his ancestors, assert their immortality most vigorously. And I do not mean the impressionable period of adolescence, but the period of full maturity.

Yet if the only form of tradition, of handing down, consisted in following the ways of the immediate generation before us in a blind or timid adherence to its successes, 'tradition' should positively be discouraged. We have seen many such simple currents soon lost in the sand; and novelty is better than repetition. Tradition is a matter of much wider significance. It cannot be inherited, and if you want it you must obtain it by great labour. It involves, in the first place, the historical sense, which we may call nearly indispensable to anyone who would continue to be a poet beyond his twenty-fifth year; and the historical sense involves a perception, not only of the pastness of the past, but of its presence; the historical sense compels a man to write not merely with his own generation in his bones, but with a feeling that the whole of the literature of Europe from Homer and within it the whole of the literature of his own country has a simultaneous existence and composes a simultaneous order. This historical sense, which is a sense of the timeless as well as of the temporal and of the timeless and of the temporal together, is what makes a writer traditional. And it is at the same time what makes a writer most acutely conscious of his place in time, of his contemporaneity.

No poet, no artist of any art, has his complete meaning alone. His significance, his appreciation is the appreciation of his relation to the dead poets and artists. You cannot value him alone;

you must set him, for contrast and comparison, among the dead. I mean this as a principle of æsthetic, not merely historical, criticism. The necessity that he shall conform, that he shall cohere, is not one-sided; what happens when a new work of art is created is something that happens simultaneously to all the works of art which preceded it. The existing monuments form an ideal order among themselves, which is modified by the introduction of the new (the really new) work of art among them. The existing order is complete before the new work arrives; for order to persist after the supervention of novelty, the *whole* existing order must be, if ever so slightly, altered; and so the relations, proportions, values of each work of art toward the whole are readjusted; and this is conformity between the old and the new. Whoever has approved this idea of order, of the form of European, of English literature, will not find it preposterous that the past should be altered by the present as much as the present is directed by the past. And the poet who is aware of this will be aware of great difficulties and responsibilities.

In a peculiar sense he will be aware also that he must inevitably be judged by the standards of the past. I say judged, not amputated, by them; not judged to be as good as, or worse or better than, the dead; and certainly not judged by the canons of dead critics. It is a judgement, a comparison, in which two things are measured by each other. To conform merely would be for the new work not really to conform at all; it would not be new, and would therefore not be a work of art. And we do not quite say that the new is more valuable because it fits in; but its fitting in is a test of its value—a test, it is true, which can only be slowly and cautiously applied, for we are none of us infallible judges of conformity. We say: it appears to conform, and is perhaps individual, or it appears individual, and may conform; but we are hardly likely to find that it is one and not the other.

To proceed to a more intelligible exposition of the relation of the poet to the past: he can neither take the past as a lump, an indiscriminate bolus, nor can he form himself wholly on one or two private admirations, nor can he form himself wholly upon one preferred period. The first course is inadmissible, the second is an important experience of youth, and the third is a pleasant and highly desirable supplement. The poet must be very conscious of the main current, which does not at all flow invariably through the most distinguished reputations. He must be quite aware of the obvious fact that art never improves, but that the material of art is never quite the same. He must be aware that the mind of Europe—the mind of his own country—a mind which he learns in time to be much more important than his own private mind—is a mind which changes, and that this change is a development which abandons nothing *en route*, which does not superannuate either Shakespeare, or Homer, or the rock drawing of the Magdalenian draughtsmen. That this development, refinement perhaps, complication certainly, is not, from the point of view of the artist, any improvement. Perhaps not even an improvement from the point of view of the psychologist or not to the extent which we imagine; perhaps only in the end based upon a complication in economics and machinery. But the difference between the present and the past is that the conscious present is an awareness of the past in a way and to an extent which the past's awareness of itself cannot show.

Someone said: 'The dead writers are remote from us because we *know* so much more than they did.' Precisely, and they are that which we know.

I am alive to a usual objection to what is clearly part of my program for the *métier* of poetry. The objection is that the doctrine requires a ridiculous amount of erudition (pedantry), a claim which can be rejected by appeal to the lives of poets in any pantheon. It will even be affirmed that much learning deadens or perverts poetic sensibility. While, however, we persist in believing that a poet ought to know as much as will not encroach upon his necessary receptivity and necessary laziness, it is not desirable to confine knowledge to whatever can be put into a useful shape for examinations, drawing-rooms, or the still more pretentious modes of publicity. Some can absorb knowledge, the more tardy must sweat for it. Shakespeare acquired more essential history from Plutarch than most men could from the whole British Museum. What is to be insisted upon is that the poet must develop or procure the consciousness of the past and that he should continue to develop this consciousness throughout his career.

What happens is a continual surrender of himself as he is at the moment to something which is more valuable. The progress of an artist is a continual self-sacrifice, a continual extinction of personality.

There remains to define this process of depersonalization and its relation to the sense of tradition. It is in this depersonalization that art may be said to approach the condition of science. I shall, therefore, invite you to consider, as a suggestive analogy, the action which takes place when a bit of finely filiated platinum is introduced into a chamber containing oxygen and sulphur dioxide.

II

Honest criticism and sensitive appreciation is directed not upon the poet but upon the poetry. If we attend to the confused cries of the newspaper critics and the susurrus of popular repetition that follows, we shall hear the names of poets in great numbers; if we seek not Blue-book knowledge but the enjoyment of poetry, and ask for a poem, we shall seldom find it. In the last article I tried to point out the importance of the relation of the poem to other poems by other authors, and suggested the conception of poetry as a living whole of all the poetry that has ever been written. The other aspect of this Impersonal theory of poetry is the relation of the poem to its author. And I hinted, by an analogy, that the mind of the mature poet differs from that of the immature one not precisely in any valuation of 'personality', not being necessarily more interesting, or having 'more to say', but rather by being a more finely perfected medium in which special, or very varied, feelings are at liberty to enter into new combinations.

The analogy was that of the catalyst. When the two gases previously mentioned are mixed in the presence of a filament of platinum, they form sulphurous acid. This combination takes place only if the platinum is present; nevertheless the newly formed acid contains no trace of platinum, and the platinum itself is apparently unaffected; has remained inert, neutral, and unchanged. The mind of the poet is the shred of platinum. It may partly or exclusively operate upon the experience of the man himself; but, the more perfect the artist, the more completely separate in him will be the man who suffers and the mind which creates; the more perfectly will the mind digest and transmute the passions which are its material.

The experience, you will notice, the elements which enter the presence of the transforming catalyst, are of two kinds: emotions and feelings. The effect of a work of art upon the person who enjoys it is an experience different in kind from any experience not of art. It may be formed out of one emotion, or may be a combination of several; and various feelings, inhering for the writer in particular words or phrases or images, may be added to compose the final result. Or great poetry may be made without the direct use of any emotion whatever: composed out of feelings solely. Canto xv of the *Inferno* (Brunetto Latini) is a working up of the emotion evident in the situation; but the effect, though single as that of any work of art, is obtained by considerable complexity of detail. The last quatrain gives an image, a feeling attaching to an image, which 'came', which did not develop simply out of what precedes, but which was probably in suspension in the poet's mind until the proper combination arrived for it to add itself to. The poet's mind is in fact a receptacle for seizing and storing up numberless feelings, phrases, images, which remain there until the particles which can unite to form a new compound are present together.

If you compare several representative passages of the greatest poetry you see how great is the variety of types of combination, and also how completely any semi-ethical criterion of 'sublimity' misses the mark. For it is not the 'greatness', the intensity, of the emotions, the components, but the intensity of the artistic process, the pressure, so to speak, under which the fusion takes place, that counts. The episode of Paolo and Francesca employs a definite emotion, but the intensity of the poetry is something quite different from whatever intensity in the supposed experience it may give the impression of. It is no more intense, furthermore, than Canto xxvi, the voyage of Ulysses, which has not the direct dependence upon an emotion. Great variety is possible in the process of transmutation of emotion: the murder of Agamemnon, or the agony of Othello, gives an artistic effect apparently closer to a possible original than the scenes from Dante. In the *Agamemnon*, the artistic emotion approximates to the emotion of an actual spectator; in *Othello* to the emotion of the protagonist himself. But the difference between art and the event is always absolute; the combination which is the murder of Agamemnon is probably as complex as that which is the voyage of Ulysses. In either case there has been a fusion of elements. The ode of Keats contains a number of feelings which have nothing particular to do with the nightingale, but which the nightingale, partly, perhaps, because of its attractive name, and partly because of its reputation, served to bring together.

The point of view which I am struggling to attack is perhaps related to the metaphysical theory of the substantial unity of the soul: for my meaning is, that the poet has, not a 'personality' to express, but a particular medium, which is only a medium and not a personality, in which impressions and experiences combine in peculiar and unexpected ways. Impressions and experiences which are important for the man may take no place in the poetry, and those which become important in the poetry may play quite a negligible part in the man, the personality.

I will quote a passage which is unfamiliar enough to be re-

garded with fresh attention in the light—or darkness—of these
observations:

> And now methinks I could e'en chide myself
> For doating on her beauty, though her death
> Shall be revenged after no common action.
> Does the silkworm expend her yellow labours
> For thee? For thee does she undo herself?
> Are lordships sold to maintain ladyships
> For the poor benefit of a bewildering minute?
> Why does yon fellow falsify highways,
> And put his life between the judge's lips,
> To refine such a thing—keeps horse and men
> To beat their valours for her? . . .

In this passage (as is evident if it is taken in its context) there is
a combination of positive and negative emotions: an intensely
strong attraction toward beauty and an equally intense fascination by the ugliness which is contrasted with it and which destroys it. This balance of contrasted emotion is in the dramatic
situation to which the speech is pertinent, but that situation
alone is inadequate to it. This is, so to speak, the structural
emotion, provided by the drama. But the whole effect, the dominant tone, is due to the fact that a number of floating feelings,
having an affinity to this emotion by no means superficially evident, have combined with it to give us a new art emotion.

It is not in his personal emotions, the emotions provoked by
particular events in his life, that the poet is in any way remarkable or interesting. His particular emotions may be simple, or
crude, or flat. The emotion in his poetry will be a very complex
thing, but not with the complexity of the emotions of people
who have very complex or unusual emotions in life. One error,
in fact, of eccentricity in poetry is to seek for new human emotions to express; and in this search for novelty in the wrong
place it discovers the perverse. The business of the poet is not to
find new emotions, but to use the ordinary ones and, in working
them up into poetry, to express feelings which are not in actual
emotions at all. And emotions which he has never experienced
will serve his turn as well as those familiar to him. Conse-

quently, we must believe that 'emotion recollected in tranquillity' is an inexact formula. For it is neither emotion, nor recollection, nor, without distortion of meaning, tranquillity. It is a concentration, and a new thing resulting from the concentration, of a very great number of experiences which to the practical and active person would not seem to be experiences at all; it is a concentration which does not happen consciously or of deliberation. These experiences are not 'recollected', and they finally unite in an atmosphere which is 'tranquil' only in that it is a passive attending upon the event. Of course this is not quite the whole story. There is a great deal, in the writing of poetry, which must be conscious and deliberate. In fact, the bad poet is usually unconscious where he ought to be conscious, and conscious where he ought to be unconscious. Both errors tend to make him 'personal'. Poetry is not a turning loose of emotion, but an escape from emotion; it is not the expression of personality, but an escape from personality. But, of course, only those who have personality and emotions know what it means to want to escape from these things.

III

ὁ δὲ νοῦς ἴσως θειότερόν τι καὶ ἀπαθές ἐστιν[1]

This essay proposes to halt at the frontier of metaphysics or mysticism, and confine itself to such practical conclusions as can be applied by the responsible person interested in poetry. To divert interest from the poet to the poetry is a laudable aim: for it would conduce to a juster estimation of actual poetry, good and bad. There are many people who appreciate the expression of sincere emotion in verse, and there is a smaller number of people who can appreciate technical excellence. But very few know when there is expression of *significant* emotion, emotion which has its life in the poem and not in the history of the poet. The emotion of art is impersonal. And the poet cannot reach

---

[1] ['The mind is undoubtedly something more divine and unimpressionable.' From Aristotle's *De Anima*, I, 4.]

this impersonality without surrendering himself wholly to the work to be done. And he is not likely to know what is to be done unless he lives in what is not merely the present, but the present moment of the past, unless he is conscious, not of what is dead, but of what is already living.

From *The Music of Poetry**

It may appear strange, that when I profess to be talking about the 'music' of poetry, I put such emphasis upon conversation. But I would remind you, first, that the music of poetry is not something which exists apart from the meaning. Otherwise, we could have poetry of great musical beauty which made no sense, and I have never come across such poetry. The apparent exceptions only show a difference of degree: there are poems in which we are moved by the music and take the sense for granted, just as there are poems in which we attend to the sense and are moved by the music without noticing it. Take an apparently extreme example—the nonsense verse of Edward Lear. His nonsense is not vacuity of sense: it is a parody of sense, and that is the sense of it. 'The Jumblies' is a poem of adventure, and of nostalgia for the romance of foreign voyage and exploration; 'The Yongy-Bongy Bo' and 'The Dong with a Luminous Nose' are poems of unrequited passion—'blues' in fact. We enjoy the music, which is of a high order, and we enjoy the feeling of irresponsibility towards the sense. Or take a poem of another type, the 'Blue Closet' of William Morris. It is a delightful poem, though I cannot explain what it means and I doubt whether the

---

* The third W. P. Ker Memorial Lecture, delivered at Glasgow University in 1942, and published by Glasgow University Press in the same year. From *On Poetry and Poets* by T. S. Eliot.

author could have explained it. It has an effect somewhat like that of a rune or charm, but runes and charms are very practical formulae designed to produce definite results, such as getting a cow out of a bog. But its obvious intention (and I think the author succeeds) is to produce the effect of a dream. It is not necessary, in order to enjoy the poem, to know what the dream means; but human beings have an unshakeable belief that dreams mean something: they used to believe—and many still believe—that dreams disclose the secrets of the future; the orthodox modern faith is that they reveal the secrets—or at least the more horrid secrets—of the past. It is a commonplace to observe that the meaning of a poem may wholly escape paraphrase. It is not quite so commonplace to observe that the meaning of a poem may be something larger than its author's conscious purpose, and something remote from its origins. One of the more obscure of modern poets was the French writer Stéphane Mallarmé, of whom the French sometimes say that his language is so peculiar that it can be understood only by foreigners. The late Roger Fry, and his friend Charles Mauron, published an English translation with notes to unriddle the meanings: when I learn that a difficult sonnet was inspired by seeing a painting on the ceiling reflected on the polished top of a table, or by seeing the light reflected from the foam on a glass of beer, I can only say that this may be a correct embryology, but it is not the meaning. If we are moved by a poem, it has meant something, perhaps something important, to us; if we are not moved, then it is, as poetry, meaningless. We can be deeply stirred by hearing the recitation of a poem in a language of which we understand no word; but if we are then told that the poem is gibberish and has no meaning, we shall consider that we have been deluded—this was no poem, it was merely an imitation of instrumental music. If, as we are aware, only a part of the meaning can be conveyed by paraphrase, that is because the poet is occupied with frontiers of consciousness beyond which words fail, though meanings still exist. A poem may appear to mean very different things to different readers, and all of these meanings may be different from what the author thought he meant. For instance, the author may have been writing some peculiar personal experience, which he saw quite unrelated to anything outside; yet for the reader the poem may become the expression of a general situation, as well as of some private experience of his own. The reader's interpretation may differ from the author's and be equally valid—it may even be better. There may be much more in a poem than the author was aware of. The different interpretations may all be partial formulations of one thing; the ambiguities may be due to the fact that the poem means more, not less, than ordinary speech can communicate.

So, while poetry attempts to convey something beyond what can be conveyed in prose rhythms, it remains, all the same, one person talking to another; and this is just as true if you sing it, for singing is another way of talking. The immediacy of poetry to conversation is not a matter on which we can lay down exact laws. Every revolution in poetry is apt to be, and sometimes to announce itself to be, a return to common speech. That is the revolution which Wordsworth announced in his prefaces, and he was right: but the same revolution had been carried out a century before by Oldham, Waller, Denham, and Dryden; and the same revolution was due again something over a century later. The followers of a revolution develop the new poetic idiom in one direction or another; they polish or perfect it; meanwhile the spoken language goes on changing, and the poetic idiom goes out of date. Perhaps we do not realize how natural the speech of Dryden must have sounded to the most sensitive of his contemporaries. No poetry, of course, is ever exactly the same speech that the poet talks and hears: but it has to be in such a relation to the speech of his time that the listener or reader can say, 'that is how I should talk if I could talk poetry.' This is the reason why the best contemporary poetry can give us a feeling of excitement and a sense of fulfilment different from any sentiment aroused by even very much greater poetry of a past age.

The music of poetry, then, must be a music latent in the common speech of its time. And that means also that it must be latent in the common speech of the poet's *place*. It would not be to my present purpose to inveigh against the ubiquity of standardized, or 'BBC' English. If we all came to talk alike there would no longer be any point in our not writing alike: but until that time comes—and I hope it may be long postponed—it is the poet's business to use the speech which he finds about him, that with which he is most familiar. I shall always remember the impression of W. B. Yeats reading poetry aloud. To hear him read his own works was to be made to recognize how much the Irish way of speech is needed to bring out the beauties of Irish poetry: to hear Yeats reading William Blake was an experience of a different kind, more astonishing than satisfying. Of course, we do not want the poet merely to reproduce exactly the conversational idiom of himself, his family, his friends, and his particular district: but what he finds there is the material out of which he must make his poetry. He must, like the sculptor, be faithful to the material in which he works; it is out of sounds that he has heard that he must make his melody and harmony.

It would be a mistake, however, to assume that all poetry ought to be melodious, or that melody is more than one of the components of the music of words. Some poetry is meant to be sung; most poetry, in modern times, is meant to be spoken—and there are many other things to be spoken of besides the murmur of innumerable bees or the moan of doves in immemorial elms. Dissonance, even cacophony, has its place: just as, in a poem of any length, there must be transitions between passages of greater and less intensity, to give a rhythm of fluctuating emotion essential to the musical structure of the whole; and the passages of less intensity will be, in relation to the level on which the total poem operates, prosaic—so that, in the sense implied by that context, it may be said that no poet can write a poem of amplitude unless he is a master of the prosaic.[1]

What matters, in short, is the whole poem: and if the whole poem need not be, and often should not be, wholly melodious, it follows that a poem is not made only out of 'beautiful words'. I doubt whether, from the point of view of *sound* alone, any word is more or less beautiful than another—within its own language, for the question whether some languages are not more beautiful than others is quite another question. The ugly words are the words not fitted for the company in which they find themselves; there are words which are ugly because of rawness or because of antiquation; there are words which are ugly because of foreignness or ill-breeding (e.g., *television*): but I do not believe that any word well-established in its own language is either beautiful or ugly. The music of a word is, so to speak, at a point of intersection: it arises from its relation first to the words immediately preceding and following it, and indefinitely to the rest of its context; and from another relation, that of its immediate meaning in that context to all the other meanings which it has had in other contexts, to its greater or less wealth of association. Not all words, obviously, are equally rich and well-connected: it is part of the business of the poet to dispose the richer among the poorer, at the right points, and we cannot afford to load a poem too heavily with the former—for it is only at certain moments that a word can be made to insinuate the whole history of a language and a civilization. This is an 'allusiveness' which is not the fashion or eccentricity of a peculiar type of poetry; but an allusiveness which is in the nature of words, and which is equally the concern of every kind of poet. My purpose here is to insist that a 'musical poem' is a poem which has a musical pattern of sound and a musical pattern of the secondary meanings of the words which compose it, and that these two patterns

---

[1] This is the complementary doctrine to that of the 'touchstone' line or passage of Matthew Arnold: this test of the greatness of a poet is the way he writes his less intense, but structurally vital, matter. (T.S.E.)

are indissoluble and one. And if you object that it is only the pure sound, apart from the sense, to which the adjective 'musical' can be rightly applied, I can only reaffirm my previous assertion that the sound of a poem is as much an abstraction from the poem as is the sense.

·   ·   ·

So far, I have spoken only of versification and not of poetic structure; and it is time for a reminder that the music of verse is not a line by line matter, but a question of the whole poem. Only with this in mind can we approach the vexed question of formal pattern and free verse. In the plays of Shakespeare a musical design can be discovered in particular scenes, and in his more perfect plays as wholes. It is a music of imagery as well as sound: Mr Wilson Knight has shown in his examination of several of the plays, how much the use of recurrent imagery and dominant imagery, throughout one play, has to do with the total effect. A play of Shakespeare is a very complex musical structure; the more easily grasped structure is that of forms such as the sonnet, the formal ode, the ballade, the villanelle, rondeau, or sestina. It is sometimes assumed that modern poetry has done away with forms like these. I have seen signs of a return to them; and indeed I believe that the tendency to return to set, and even elaborate patterns is permanent, as permanent as the need for a refrain or a chorus to a popular song. Some forms are more appropriate to some languages than to others, and any form may be more appropriate to some periods than to others. At one stage the stanza is a right and natural formalization of speech into pattern. But the stanza—and the more elaborate it is, the more rules to be observed in its proper execution, the more surely this happens—tends to become fixed to the idiom of the moment of its perfection. It quickly loses contact with the changing colloquial speech, being possessed by the mental outlook of a past generation; it becomes discredited when employed solely by those writers who, having no impulse to form within them, have recourse to pouring their liquid sentiment into a ready-made mould in which they vainly hope that it will set. In a perfect sonnet, what you admire is not so much the author's skill in adapting himself to the pattern as the skill and power with which he makes the pattern comply with what he has to say. Without this fitness, which is contingent upon period as well as individual genius, the rest is at best virtuosity: and where the musical element is the only element, that also vanishes. Elaborate forms return: but there have to be periods during which they are laid aside.

As for 'free verse', I expressed my view twenty-five years ago by saying that no verse is free for the man who wants to do a good job. No one has better cause to know than I, that a great deal of bad prose has been written under the name of free verse; though whether its authors wrote bad prose or bad verse, or bad verse in one style or in another, seems to me a matter of indifference. But only a bad poet could welcome free verse as a liberation from form. It was a revolt against dead form, and a preparation for new form or for the renewal of the old; it was an insistence upon the inner unity which is unique to every poem, against the outer unity which is typical. The poem comes before the form, in the sense that a form grows out of the attempt of somebody to say something; just as a system of prosody is only a formulation of the identities in the rhythms of a succession of poets influenced by each other.

Forms have to be broken and remade: but I believe that any language, so long as it remains the same language, imposes its laws and restrictions and permits its own licence, dictates its own speech rhythms and sound patterns. And a language is always changing; its developments in vocabulary, in syntax, pronunciation, and intonation—even, in the long run, its deterioration— must be accepted by the poet and made the best of. He in turn has the privilege of contributing to the development and maintaining the quality, the capacity of the language to express a wide range, and subtle gradation, of feeling and emotion; his task is both to respond to change and make it conscious, and to battle against degradation below the standards which he has learnt from the past. The liberties that he may take are for the sake of order.

At what stage contemporary verse now finds itself, I must leave you to judge for yourselves. I suppose that it will be agreed that if the work of the last twenty years is worthy of being classified at all, it is as belonging to a period of search for a proper modern colloquial idiom. We have still a good way to go in the invention of a verse medium for the theatre, a medium in which we shall be able to hear the speech of contemporary human beings, in which dramatic characters can express the purest poetry without high-falutin and in which they can convey the most commonplace message without absurdity. But when we reach a point at which the poetic idiom can be stabilized, then a period of musical elaboration can follow. I think that a poet may gain much from the study of music: how much technical knowledge of musical form is desirable I do not know, for I have not that technical knowledge myself. But I believe that the properties in which music concerns the poet most nearly, are the sense of rhythm and the sense of structure. I think that it might be possible for a poet to work too closely to musical analogies: the result might be an effect of artificiality; but I know that a poem, or a passage of a poem, may tend to realize itself first as a particular rhythm before it reaches expression in words, and that this rhythm may bring to birth the idea and the image; and I do not believe that this is an experience peculiar to myself. The use of recurrent themes is as natural to poetry as to music. There are possibilities for verse which bear some analogy to the development of a theme by different groups of instruments; there are possibilities of transitions in a poem comparable to the different movements of a symphony or a quartet; there are possibilities of contrapuntal arrangement of subject-matter. It is in the concert room, rather than in the opera house, that the germ of a poem may be quickened. More than this I cannot say, but must leave the matter here to those who have had a musical education. But I would remind you again of the two tasks of poetry, the two directions in which language must at different times be worked: so that however far it may go in musical elaboration, we must expect a time to come when poetry will have again to be recalled to speech. The same problems arise, and always in new forms; and poetry has always before it, as F. S. Oliver said of politics, an 'endless adventure'.

From *Hamlet and his Problems**

The grounds of *Hamlet*'s failure are not immediately obvious. Mr Robertson is undoubtedly correct in concluding that the essential emotion of the play is the feeling of a son towards a guilty mother:

'[Hamlet's] tone is that of one who has suffered tortures on the score of his mother's degradation. . . . The guilt of a mother is an almost intolerable motive for drama, but it had to be maintained and emphasized to supply a psychological solution, or rather a hint of one.'

This, however, is by no means the whole story. It is not merely the 'guilt of a mother' that cannot be handled as Shakespeare handled the suspicion of Othello, the infatuation of Antony, or the pride of Coriolanus. The subject might conceivably have expanded into a tragedy like these, intelligible, self-complete, in the sunlight. *Hamlet*, like the sonnets, is full of some stuff that the writer could not drag to light, contemplate, or manipulate into art. And when we search for this feeling, we find it, as in the sonnets, very difficult to localize. You cannot point to it in the speeches; indeed, if you examine the two famous

---

* From *Selected Essays*, new edition, by T. S. Eliot.

soliloquies you see the versification of Shakespeare, but a content which might be claimed by another, perhaps by the author of the *Revenge of Bussy d'Ambois*, Act v, sc. i. We find Shakespeare's Hamlet not in the action, not in any quotations that we might select, so much as in an unmistakable tone which is unmistakably not in the earlier play.

The only way of expressing emotion in the form of art is by finding an 'objective correlative'; in other words, a set of objects, a situation, a chain of events which shall be the formula of that *particular* emotion; such that when the external facts, which must terminate in sensory experience, are given, the emotion is immediately evoked. If you examine any of Shakespeare's more successful tragedies, you will find this exact equivalence; you will find that the state of mind of Lady Macbeth walking in her sleep has been communicated to you by a skilful accumulation of imagined sensory impressions; the words of Macbeth on hearing of his wife's death strike us as if, given the sequence of events, these words were automatically released by the last event in the series. The artistic 'inevitability' lies in this complete adequacy of the external to the emotion; and this is precisely what is deficient in *Hamlet*. Hamlet (the man) is dominated by an emotion which is inexpressible, because it is in *excess* of the facts as they appear. And the supposed identity of Hamlet with his author is genuine to this point: that Hamlet's bafflement at the absence of objective equivalent to his feelings is a prolongation of the bafflement of his creator in the face of his artistic problem. Hamlet is up against the difficulty that his disgust is occasioned by his mother, but that his mother is not an adequate equivalent for it; his disgust envelops and exceeds her. It is thus a feeling which he cannot understand; he cannot objectify it, and it therefore remains to poison life and obstruct action. None of the possible actions can satisfy it; and nothing that Shakespeare can do with the plot can express Hamlet for him. And it must be noticed that the very nature of the *données* of the problem precludes objective equivalence. To have heightened the criminality of Gertrude would have been to provide the formula for a totally different emotion in Hamlet; it is just *because* her character is so negative and insignificant that she arouses in Hamlet the feeling which she is incapable of representing.

The 'madness' of Hamlet lay to Shakespeare's hand; in the earlier play a simple ruse, and to the end, we may presume, understood as a ruse by the audience. For Shakespeare it is less than madness and more than feigned. The levity of Hamlet, his repetition of phrase, his puns, are not part of a deliberate plan of dissimulation, but a form of emotional relief. In the character Hamlet it is the buffoonery of an emotion which can find no outlet in action; in the dramatist it is the buffoonery of an emotion which he cannot express in art. The intense feeling, ecstatic or terrible, without an object or exceeding its object, is something which every person of sensibility has known; it is doubtless a subject of study for pathologists. It often occurs in adolescence: the ordinary person puts these feelings to sleep, or trims down his feelings to fit the business world; the artist keeps them alive by his ability to intensify the world to his emotions. The Hamlet of Laforgue is an adolescent; the Hamlet of Shakespeare is not, he has not that explanation and excuse. We must simply admit that here Shakespeare tackled a problem which proved too much for him. Why he attempted it at all is an insoluble puzzle; under compulsion of what experience he attempted to express the inexpressibly horrible, we cannot ever know. We need a great many facts in his biography; and we should like to know whether, and when, and after or at the same time as what personal experience, he read Montaigne, II. xii, *Apologie de Raimond Sebond*. We should have, finally, to know something which is by hypothesis unknowable, for we assume it to be an experience which, in the manner indicated, exceeded the facts. We should have to understand things which Shakespeare did not understand himself.

ROBERT FROST

*The Figure a Poem Makes**

Abstraction is an old story with the philosophers, but it has been like a new toy in the hands of the artists of our day. Why can't we have any one quality of poetry we choose by itself? We can have in thought. Then it will go hard if we can't in practice. Our lives for it.

Granted no one but a humanist much cares how sound a poem is if it is only *a* sound. The sound is the gold in the ore. Then we will have the sound out alone and dispense with the inessential. We do till we make the discovery that the object in writing poetry is to make all poems sound as different as possible from each other, and the resources for that of vowels, consonants, punctuation, syntax, words, sentences, metre are not enough. We need the help of context—meaning—subject matter. That is the greatest help towards variety. All that can be done with words is soon told. So also with metres—particularly in our language where there are virtually but two, strict iambic and loose iambic. The ancients with many were still poor if they depended on metres for all tune. It is painful to watch our sprung-rhythmists straining at the point of omitting one short from a foot for relief from monotony. The possibilities for tune from the dramatic tones of meaning struck across the rigidity of a limited metre are endless. And we are back in poetry as merely one more art of having something to say, sound or unsound. Probably better if sound, because deeper and from wider experience.

Then there is this wildness whereof it is spoken. Granted again that it has an equal claim with sound to being a poem's

---

* From *Complete Poems of Robert Frost*.

better half. If it is a wild tune, it is a poem. Our problem then is, as modern abstractionists, to have the wildness pure; to be wild with nothing to be wild about. We bring up as aberrationists, giving way to undirected associations and kicking ourselves from one chance suggestion to another in all directions as of a hot afternoon in the life of a grasshopper. Theme alone can steady us down. Just as the first mystery was how a poem could have a tune in such a straightness as metre, so the second mystery is how a poem can have wildness and at the same time a subject that shall be fulfilled.

It should be of the pleasure of a poem itself to tell how it can. The figure a poem makes. It begins in delight and ends in wisdom. The figure is the same as for love. No one can really hold that the ecstasy should be static and stand still in one place. It begins in delight, it inclines to the impulse, it assumes direction with the first line laid down, it runs a course of lucky events, and ends in a clarification of life—not necessarily a great clarification, such as sects and cults are founded on, but in a momentary stay against confusion. It has denouement. It has an outcome that though unforeseen was predestined from the first image of the original mood—and indeed from the very mood. It is but a trick poem and no poem at all if the best of it was thought of first and saved for the last. It finds its own name as it goes and discovers the best waiting for it in some final phrase at once wise and sad—the happy-sad blend of the drinking song.

No tears in the writer, no tears in the reader. No surprise for the writer, no surprise for the reader. For me the initial delight is in the surprise of remembering something I didn't know I knew. I am in a place, in a situation, as if I had materialized from cloud or risen out of the ground. There is a glad recognition of the long lost and the rest follows. Step by step the wonder of unexpected supply keeps growing. The impressions most useful to my purpose seem always those I was unaware of and so made no note of at the time when taken, and the conclusion is come to that like giants we are always hurling experience ahead of us to pave the future with against the day when we may want to strike a line of purpose across it for somewhere. The line will have the more charm for not being mechanically straight. We enjoy the straight crookedness of a good walking stick. Modern instruments of precision are being used to make things crooked as if by eye and hand in the old days.

I tell how there may be a better wildness of logic than of inconsequence. But the logic is backward, in retrospect, after the act. It must be more felt than seen ahead like prophecy. It must be a revelation, or a series of revelations, as much for the poet as for the reader. For it to be that there must have been the greatest freedom of the material to move about in it and to establish relations in it regardless of time and space, previous relation, and everything but affinity. We prate of freedom. We call our schools free because we are not free to stay away from them till we are sixteen years of age. I have given up my democratic prejudices and now willingly set the lower classes free to be completely taken care of by the upper classes. Political freedom is nothing to me. I bestow it right and left. All I would keep for myself is the freedom of my material—the condition of body and mind now and then to summons aptly from the vast chaos of all I have lived through.

Scholars and artists thrown together are often annoyed at the puzzle of where they differ. Both work from knowledge; but I suspect they differ most importantly in the way their knowledge is come by. Scholars get theirs with conscientious thoroughness along projected lines of logic; poets theirs cavalierly and as it happens in and out of books. They stick to nothing deliberately, but let what will stick to them like burrs where they walk in the fields. No acquirement is on assignment, or even self-assignment. Knowledge of the second kind is much more available in the wild free ways of wit and art. A schoolboy may be defined as one who can tell you what he knows in the order in which he learned it. The artist must value himself as he snatches a thing from some previous order in time and space into a new order with not so much as a ligature clinging to it of the old place where it was organic.

More than once I should have lost my soul to radicalism if it had been the originality it was mistaken for by its young converts. Originality and initiative are what I ask for my country. For myself the originality need be no more than the freshness of a poem run in the way I have described: from delight to wisdom. The figure is the same as for love. Like a piece of ice on a hot stove the poem must ride on its own melting. A poem may be worked over once it is in being, but may not be worried into being. Its most previous quality will remain its having run itself and carried away the poet with it. Read it a hundred times: it will forever keep its freshness as a petal keeps its fragrance. It can never lose its sense of a meaning that once unfolded by surprise as it went.

ALLEN GINSBERG

*Notes for Howl and Other Poems**

By 1955 I wrote poetry adapted from prose seeds, journals, scratchings, arranged by phrasing or breath groups into little short-line patterns according to ideas of measure of American speech I'd picked up from W. C. Williams's imagist preoccupations. I suddenly turned aside in San Francisco, unemployment compensation leisure, to follow my romantic inspiration—Hebraic-Melvillian bardic breath. I thought I wouldn't write a *poem*, but just write what I wanted to without fear, let my imagination go, open secrecy, and scribble magic lines from my real mind—sum up my life—something I wouldn't be able to show anybody, write for my own soul's ear and a few other golden ears. So the first line of 'Howl', 'I saw the best minds', etc. the whole first section typed out madly in one afternoon, a huge sad comedy of wild phrasing, meaningless images for the beauty of abstract poetry of mind running along making awkward combinations like Charlie Chaplin's walk, long saxophone-like chorus lines I knew Kerouac woud hear *sound* of—taking off from his own inspired prose line really a new poetry.

I depended on the word 'who' to keep the beat, a base to keep measure, return to and take off from again onto another streak of invention: 'who lit cigarettes in boxcars boxcars boxcars', continuing to prophesy what I really knew despite the drear consciousness of the world: 'who were visionary indian angels'. Have I really been attacked for this sort of joy? So the poem got serious, I went on to what my imagination believed true to Eternity (for I'd had a beatific illumination years before during which I'd heard Blake's ancient voice & saw the universe unfold

---

* From *Fantasy* LP recording 7006 (1959).

in my brain), & what my memory could reconstitute of the data of celestial experience.

But how sustain a long line in poetry (lest it lapse into prosaic)? It's natural inspiration of the moment that keeps it moving, disparate thinks put down together, shorthand notations of visual imagery, juxtapositions of hydrogen juke-box—abstract haikus sustain the mystery & put iron poetry back into the line: the last line of 'Sunflower Sutra' is the extreme, one stream of single word associations, summing up. Mind is shapely, Art is shapely. Meaning Mind practised in spontaneity invents forms in its own image & gets to Last Thoughts. Loose ghosts wailing for body try to invade the bodies of living men. I hear ghostly Academics in Limbo screeching about form.

Ideally each line of 'Howl' is a single breath unit. Tho in this recording it's not pronounced so, I was exhausted at climax of 3 hour Chicago reading with Corso & Orlovsky. My breath is long—that's the Measure, one physical—mental inspiration of thought contained in the elastic of a breath. It probably bugs Williams now, but it's a natural consequence, my own heightened conversation, not cooler average-dailytalk short breath. I got to mouth more madly this way.

So these poems are a series of experiments with the formal organization of the long line. Explanations follow. I realized at the time that Whitman's form had rarely been further explored (improved on even) in the U.S. Whitman always a mountain too vast to be seen. Everybody assumes (with Pound?) (except Jeffers) that his line is a big freakish uncontrollable necessary prosaic goof. No attempt's been made to use it in the light of early xx Century organization of new speech-rhythm prosody to *build up* large organic structures.

I had an apt on Nob Hill, got high on Peyote, & saw an image of the robot skullface of Moloch in the upper stories of a big hotel glaring into my window; got high weeks later again, the Visage was still there in red smokey downtown Metropolis, I wandered down Powell Street muttering, 'Moloch Moloch' all

night & wrote 'Howl' II nearly intact in cafeteria at foot of
Drake Hotel, deep in the hellish vale. Here the long line is used
as a stanza form broken within into exclamatory units punctuated by a base repetition, Moloch.

The rhythmic paradigm for Part III was conceived & half-
written same day as the beginning of 'Howl', I went back later &
filled it out. Part I, a lament for the Lamb in America with
instances of remarkable lamblike youths; Part II names the
monster of mental consciousness that preys on the Lamb; Part III
a litany of affirmation of the Lamb in its glory: 'O starry spang-
led shock of Mercy.' The structure of Part III, pyramidal, with a
graduated longer response to the fixed base. . . .

A lot of these forms developed out of an extreme rhapsodic
wail I once heard in a madhouse. Later I wondered if short quiet
lyrical poems could be written using the long line. 'Cottage in
Berkeley' & 'Supermarket in California' (written same day) fell in
place later that year. Not purposely, I simply followed my Angel
in the course of compositions.

What if I just simply wrote, in long units & broken short lines,
spontaneously noting prosaic realities mixed with emotional
upsurges, solitaries? *Transcription of Organ Music* (sensual
data), strange writing which passes from prose to poetry & back,
like the mind.

What about poem with rhythmic buildup power equal to
'Howl' without use of repeated base to sustain it? The 'Sunflower
Sutra' (composition time 20 minutes, me at desk scribbling,
Kerouac at cottage door waiting for me to finish so we could
go off somewhere party) did that, it surprised me, one long
Who . . .

Last, the Proem to 'Kaddish' (NY 1959 work)—finally, completely free composition, the long line breaking up within itself
into short staccato breath units—notations of one spontaneous
phrase after another linked within the line by dashes mostly: the
long line now perhaps a variable stanzaic unit, measuring
groups of related ideas, marking them—a method of notation.

Ending with a hymn in rhythm similar to the synagogue death lament. Passing into dactyllic? says Williams? Perhaps not: at least the ears hears itself in Promethian natural measure, not in mechanical count of accent. . . .

A word on Academies; poetry has been attacked by an ignorant & frightened bunch of bores who don't understand how it's made, & the trouble with these creeps is they wouldn't know Poetry if it came up and buggered them in broad daylight.

A word on the Politicians: my poetry is Angelical Ravings, & has nothing to do with dull materialistic vagaries about who should shoot who. The secrets of individual imagination—which are transconceptual & non-verbal—I mean unconditioned Spirit —are not for sale to this consciousness, are of no use to this world, except perhaps to make it shut its trap & listen to the music of the Spheres. Who denies the music of the spheres denies poetry, denies man, & spits on Blake, Shelley, Christ, & Buddha. Meanwhile have a ball. The universe is a new flower. America will be discovered. Who wants a war against roses will have it. Fate tells big lies, & the gay Creator dances on his own body in Eternity.

ROBERT GRAVES

From *The Poet and his Public**

Towards my poetry-reading public, however, I feel no such tenderness. By this I do not mean that I have stricter standards in
prose than in poetry. On the contrary, poems are infinitely more
difficult to write than prose, and my standards are correspond-
ingly higher. If I re-write a line of prose five times, I re-write a
line of verse fifteen times. The fact is that I could never say:
'Funds are low, I must write a dozen poems.' But I might well
say: 'Funds are low, it's time I wrote another novel.' Novels are
in the public domain, poems are not. I can make this last point
clear by talking about important letters. Most of the important
letters you write fall into two different categories. The first is the
business letter—'Sir: I beg to advise you in reply to your communication of the 5th ultimo . . .'—written with an eye on office
files. This sort of letter is in the public domain. But not the other
sort, the personal letter beginning: 'Darling Mavis, when we
kissed good-bye last night . . .' or: 'Dear Captain Dingbat, you
go to blazes!'—in each case written to convey a clear and passionate message, and without a thought for any libel suit, or
breach of promise action, in which it may one day be produced
as evidence against you. So with poems. We must distinguish
those written with a careful eye to the public files from those
written in private emotion. Of course, this comparison is not
quite exact. Though some poems (for example, most of Shakespeare's *Sonnets*) are in the love-letter category, and others (for
example, a couple of the same *Sonnets*) are in the 'You go to
blazes!' category; yet in most cases the poet seems to be talking
to himself, not either to his beloved or to his enemy.

---

* From *The Crowning Privilege* by Robert Graves.

Well, then, for whom does he write poems if not for a particular Mavis or Captain Dingbat? Don't think me fanciful when I say that he writes them for the Muse. 'The Muse' has become a popular joke. 'Ha, ha, my boy!' exclaims Dr Whackem, the schoolmaster, when he finds a rude rhyme chalked on the blackboard. 'So you have been *wooing the Muse*, have you? Take that, and that, and that!' But the Muse was once a powerful goddess. Poets worshipped her with as much awe as smiths felt for their god Vulcan; or soldiers for their god Mars. I grant that, by the time of Homer, the ancient cult of the Muse had been supplanted by the cult of the upstart Apollo, who claimed to be the god of poets. Nevertheless, both Homer's *Iliad* and Homer's *Odyssey* begin with a formal invocation to the Muse. When I say that a poet writes his poems for the Muse, I mean simply that he treats poetry with a single-minded devotion which may be called religious, and that he allows no other activity in which he takes part, whether concerned with his livelihood or with his social duties, to interfere with it. This has been my own rule since I was fourteen or fifteen, and has become second nature to me.

Poems should not be written, like novels, to entertain or instruct the public; or the less poems they. The pathology of poetic composition is no secret. A poet finds himsef caught in some baffling emotional problem, which is of such urgency that it sends him into a sort of trance. And in this trance his mind works, with astonishing boldness and precision, on several imaginative levels at once. The poem is either a practical answer to his problem, or else it is a clear statement of it; and a problem clearly stated is half-way to solution. Some poets are more plagued than others with emotional problems, and more conscientious in working out the poems which arise from them— that is to say more attentive in their service to the Muse.

Poems have been compared to pearls. Pearls are the natural reaction of the oyster to some irritating piece of grit which has worked its way in between its valves; the grit gets smoothed

over with layers of mother-of-pearl until it ceases to be a nuis-
ance to the oyster. Poems have also been compared to honey.
And the worker-bee is driven by some inner restlessness to
gather and store honey all summer long, until its wings are quite
worn out, from pure devotion to the queen. Both bee and oyster,
indeed, take so much trouble over their work that one finds the
geography books saying: 'The oysters of Tinnevelly yield the
most beautiful pearls on the Indian market', or: 'The bees of
Hymettus produce the sweetest honey in the world.' From this
it is only a step to the ridiculous assumption that the oyster is
mainly concerned in satisfying the Bombay pearl merchants'
love of beauty; and the bees in delighting gourmets at the
world's most expensive restaurants. The same assumption, almost equally ridiculous, is made about poets.

Though we know that Shakespeare circulated a few of his less
personal sonnets among his friends, he is unlikely to have had
any intention of publishing the remainder. It seems that a
bookseller-publisher, one Thorp, bought the manuscript from
the mysterious Mr W. H., to whom they were addressed, and
pirated the whole series. Nevertheless, a poem is seldom so personal that a small group of the poet's contemporaries cannot understand it; and if it has been written with the appropriate care
—by which I mean that the problem troubling him is stated as
truly and economically and detachedly as possible—they are
likely to admire the result. The poem might even supply the answer to a pressing problem of their own, because the poet is a
human being, and so are they. And since he works out his own
problems in the language which they happen to share, there is
a somewhat closer sympathy between his public and himself,
even though he does not write directly for it, than between the
oyster and the oyster's public, or the bee and the bee's public.

A poet's public consists of those who happen to be close
enough to him, in education and environment and imaginative
vision, to be able to catch both the overtones and the undertones
of his poetic statements. And unless he despises his fellow-men,

he will not deny them the pleasure of reading what he has written while inspired by the Muse, once it has served his purpose of self-information.

Young poets tend to be either ambitious, or anxious to keep up with fashion. Both these failings—failings only where poetry is concerned, because they are advantages in the business world and in most of the professions—encourage him to have designs on the public. The attempt to keep up with fashion will lead him to borrow the style of whatever poet is most highly approved at the time. . . . Now, I have known three generations of John Smiths. The type breeds true. John Smith ii and iii went to the same school, university and learned profession as John Smith i. Yet John Smith i wrote pseudo-Swinburne; John Smith ii wrote pseudo-Brooke; and John Smith iii is now writing pseudo-Eliot. But unless John Smith can write John Smith, however unfashionable the result, why does he bother to write at all? Surely one Swinburne, one Brooke, or one Eliot are enough in any age?

Ambition has even worse results. The young poet will try to be original; he will begin to experiment: a great mistake. It is true that if an unusually difficult problem forces a poet into a poetic trance, he may find himself not only making personal variations on accepted verse forms but perhaps (as Shakespeare and Hardy did) coining new words. Yet innovation in this sense is not experiment. Experimental research is all very well for a scientist. He carries out a series of routine experiments in the properties (say) of some obscure metallic compound, and publishes the results in a scientific journal. But poetry cannot be called a science; science works on a calm intellectual level, with proper safeguards against imaginative freedom.

And what is all this nonsense about poetry not paying? Why should it pay? Especially when it is experimental in the scientific sense? Poets today complain far too much about the economic situation, and even expect the State to support them. What social function have they? They are neither scientists, nor entertainers, nor philosophers, nor preachers. Are they then 'unac-

knowledged legislators' as Shelley suggested? But how can unacknowledged legislators be publicly supported by the legislature
itself? If a poet is obsessed by the Muse and privileged to satisfy
her demands when he records his obsessions in poetry, this in
itself should be sufficient reward. I doubt whether he should
even bargain with the public, like Wee MacGregor (wasn't it?)
with his school-friend: 'Gie me a bit of your apple, and I'll show
you my sair thumb!' It always surprises me to find that my
personal poems have a public at all; probably most of my readers buy them because of my novels—which I think is a very
poor reason.

So much for the poet in his unjustified search for a public.
Now about the public in its justified search for a poet. Public,
you sent me a one-man delegation the other day in the person of
a worthy, well-educated, intelligent, puzzled paterfamilias, who
happened to be closely connected with the publishing trade. This
is how he began: 'I must be getting old and stupid, Robert, but I
can't really follow more than an occasional line of this modern
poetry. I feel quite ashamed of myself in the presence of my boy
Michael and his friends.'

I asked him to explain. 'Well,' he said, 'when I was young and
keen on modern painting I had a fight with my father because he
couldn't appreciate Toulouse-Lautrec or the Douanier Rousseau. And now an important Toulouse-Lautrec fetches as much
as a Botticelli; and if you own a Douanier Rousseau, you have
to install a burglar alarm. . . . Michael and his friends take the
same line about Mr X and Mr Y; and so does everyone else at
Cambridge. Mr X's *Collected Poems* have recently sold ten
thousand copies, and Mr Y is regarded as the highest apple on
the tree. *All* the critics can't be wrong.'

'Why can't all the critics be wrong?' I asked. 'If you mean the
un-poets who set the Paris fashions. Who decides on this year's
skirt-length? Not the women themselves, but one or two clever
man-milliners in the Rue de la Paix. Similar man-milliners control the fashions in poetry. There will always be a skirt-length.

... And as William Blake said: 'In a Commercial Nation impostors are abroad in every profession.' How do you know that twenty years hence Messrs X and Y won't be as old-look as Humbert Wolfe and John Freeman, who were public idols twenty or thirty years ago?'

He said: 'Toulouse-Lautrec and Rousseau aren't old-look.'

I pacified him by agreeing that it would take a lot to kill either; or, for that matter, Botticelli. Then he asked the question that you are all itching to ask me: 'How can you tell good poetry from bad?'

I answered: 'How does one tell good fish from bad? Surely by the smell? Use your nose.'

He said: 'Yes, perhaps with practice one can tell the clumsy from the accomplished. But what about the real and the artificial?'

'Real fish will smell real, and artificial fish will have no smell at all.'

He thought this rather too slick an answer, so I explained: 'If you prefer the painting metaphor, very well. The test of a painting is not what it looks like in an exhibition frame on varnishing day; but whether it can hang on the wall of your dining-room a year or two after you bought it without going dead on you. The test of a poem is whether you can re-read it with excitement three years after the critics tell you it's a masterpiece. Well, the skirt-length of fashion has wandered up and down the leg from heel to knee since I first read my elder contemporaries Thomas Hardy and William Davies and Robert Frost; and my younger contemporaries Laura Riding, Norman Cameron, and James Reeves. They have all at times written below their best, and none of them are in fashion now, but their best does not go dead on the wall.'

To conclude. The only demands that a poet can make from his public are that they treat him with consideration, and expect nothing from him; and do not make a public figure of him—but rather, if they please, a secret friend. And may I take this opportunity for appealing to young poets: not to send me their poems for my opinion? If they are true poems, they will know this themselves and not need me to say so; and if they are not, why bother to send them?

From *Poetic Craft and Principle**

I find the standards of verse-craftsmanship offered by the *Oxford Book of English Verse* deplorably low, compared with those demanded from you undergraduates in, say, mathematics, physics, and biology. Real poems have a rhythmic pattern: the variation of emotional intensity from line to line, or stanza to stanza, can be drawn in the air with one's finger. The end usually provides the climax; though sometimes the climax comes earlier, and the end is what the Elizabethans called 'a dying fall'. Occasionally a calm level is sustained throughout, with only minor troughs and valleys. Donne was peculiar in often beginning with his climax, and letting the whole poem die away: like a Lenten sermon preached too long or on too stirring a text. Competent verse must also have a pattern of varying emphasis, skilfully maintained by the rhythmic control of words.

. . .

Poetry is the profession of private truth, supported by craftsmanship in the use of words; I prefer not to call it an art, because the art of Classical Verse from the time of Virgil onwards allied itself to the art of Rhetoric, which was a form of hypnotism designed to make a weak legal case seem strong, or a bad one good, or a trivial one important. From the first century B.C. onwards, the art of verse became the art of cozenage, not of truth.

. . .

Before closing, I must venture a view to which I do not ask you to subscribe, but which has forced itself on me more and more

---

* By Robert Graves.

strongly in the last few years. It is that both in England and the Commonwealth, and the United States, standards of verse-craftsmanship *seem* to have risen appreciably as the result of modern poems being included in school and college curricula. But is it not rather that far more attention is now paid to the standards of verse-craftmanship deduced by academic critics from certain fashionable modern poets? The rudiments of crafts-manship can be best learned, not by imitation but by personal experience in writing, after varied acquaintance with poems of different ages and styles; and by a gradual discovery of the need—which is my main insistence in these three lectures—to question every word and sound and implication in a poem either read or written.

Poetry is another matter altogether. The present trend in poli-tics, economics, and ethics seems wholly inimical to the appear-ance of new poets, or the honourable survival of those who may have already appeared; but this perhaps means that the occa-sional exception, the poet born with a light in his head, will be more surely tempered than before against departure from poetic principle; which is a simple, obstinate belief in miracle: an as-severation of personal independence against all collective codifi-cations of thought and behaviour.

. . .

An important rule of craftsmanship in English Verse is that a poet should never tell his readers how romantic, pathetic, awe-inspiring, tragic, mystic, or wondrous a scene has been. He must describe the details himself in such powerful but restrained lan-guage (nouns and verbs always outnumbering the adjectives), that it will be the reader who catches his breath, looks up from the page and says: 'How romantic, how pathetic, how awe-inspiring, how . . . !'

. . .

Throughout my lectures of the past four years I have dwelt on the difference between Muse Poetry and Apollonian poetry: a difference between the non-ecstatic and the ecstatic—*ecstasy* meaning in Greek a 'standing outside'. Outside what? I suppose outside the reality of our physical circumstances: so that any practical 'because' of a poem seems irrelevant to its nature.

In Muse poetry, the 'because' of a poem must be the poet's personal obsession with the Muse. Apollonian poetry is an arrangement of reasonable opinions in a memorizable verse form, with carefully chosen semi-archaic diction lending them authority: in fact, a form of rhetoric, which meets society's demand for the god of rational enlightenment rather than for the impractical Muse.

My views on the Muse Goddess are deduced from the multilingual corpus of love-poetry. I regard her as the primitive female who has separated herself from whatever laws have hitherto governed society, and whom man consistently fails to discipline. She is guardian of the love magic which all religious leaders, philosophers, and legalists in turn officiously attempt to define for her but which always eludes them. Only poets are convinced that a watchful trust in the undisciplined Muse Goddess will eventually teach them poetic wisdom and make them welcome to her secret paradise. Muse poetry is a distillation of love in its most unsocial, unphilosophical, unlegalistic, unliterary sense; written occasionally by those few women poets whom the Goddess possesses but, far more often, by men who have been granted access to her love-magic.

. . .

This is still with me, for I now realize that what overcame me that evening was a sudden awareness of the power of intuition, the supra-logic that cuts out all routine processes of thought and leaps straight from problem to answer. I did not in fact know everything, but became aware that in moments of real emergency the mind can weigh an infinite mass of imponderables and make immediate sense of them. This is how poems get written.

. . .

The qualities that make a poem durable are no mystery. If a

practising poet revises the canon of his poem every few years, passages of time will help him to recognize the derivative, the over-clever, the flawed, the repetitious, the didactic, the irrelevant. Durability implies that a poem was written for the right reasons, at the right time, and in the right state of mind. I mean that a poem had been forming unprompted in his imagination; that the time came when its nucleus suddenly appeared—the nucleus that predetermines the whole; and that he then fell into a trance that gave him full control of his faculties: that he did not view the poem as literature or as a saleable commodity, but as self-illumination. The poet alone knows how far any particular poem has obeyed these creative principles; indeed, the sole limitation he can put on the rejection of old work is the awareness that no perfect poem has ever been, or ever will be, written. To suppress his whole canon would mean inviting the old-clothes-men of literature to republish the bad along with the good, the durable with the impermanent, in ignorant selections of their own.

It is an act of social politeness to make one's will, because of the family's trouble in dealing with certain sentimental relics. It is equally polite for a poet to cut his canon down to a reasonable size. If all his predecessors had shown decent testamentary politeness, the required reading-list of the Oxford English School would be wholesomely curtailed. After all, what the student should know about is the poems themselves, not movements or fashions in style.

SEAMUS HEANEY

Feelings into Words*

I am uneasy about speaking under the general heading of 'innovation in contemporary literature'. Much as I would like to think of myself as breaking new ground, I find on looking at what I have done that it is mostly concerned with reclaiming old ground. My intention here is to retrace some of my paths into that ground, to investigate what William Wordsworth called 'the hiding places':

> the hiding places of my power
> Seem open; I approach, and then they close;
> I see glimpses now; when age comes on,
> May scarcely see at all, and I would give,
> While yet we may, as far as words can give,
> A substance and a life to what I feel:
> I would enshrine the spirit of the past
> For future restoration.

Implicit in those lines is a view of poetry which I think is also implicit in the few poems I have written that give me any right to be here addressing you: poetry as divination; poetry as revelation of the self to the self, as restoration of the culture to itself; poems as elements of continuity, with the aura and authenticity of archaeological finds, where the buried shard has an importance that is not obliterated by the buried city; poetry as a dig, a dig for finds that end up being plants.

'Digging' in fact, was the name of the first poem I wrote where I thought my feelings got into words, or, to put it more accu-

---

* A lecture delivered to The Royal Society of Literature, 17 October 1974.

rately, where I thought my *feel* had got into words. Its rhythms
and noises still please me, although there are a couple of lines
in it that have the theatricality of the gunslinger rather than
the self-absorption of the digger. I wrote it in the summer of
1964, almost two years after I had begun to dabble in verses,
and as Patrick Kavanagh said, a man dabbles in verses and
finds they are his life. This was the first place where I felt I
had done more than make an arrangement of words: I felt that
I had let down a shaft into real life. The facts and surfaces of
the thing were true, but more important, the excitement that
came from naming them gave me a kind of insouciance and a
kind of confidence. I didn't care who thought what about it:
somehow, it had surprised me by coming out with a stance and
an idea that I would stand over:

> The cold smell of potato mould, the squelch and slap
> Of soggy peat, the curt cuts of an edge
> Through living roots awaken in my head.
> But I've no spade to follow men like them.
>
> Between my finger and my thumb
> The squat pen rests.
> I'll dig with it.

As I say, I wrote it down ten years ago; yet perhaps I should
say that I dug it up, because I have come to realize that it was
laid down in me years before that even. The pen/spade analogy
was the simple heart of the matter, and *that* was simply a matter of almost proverbial common sense. People used to ask a
child on the road to and from school what class you were in
and how many slaps you'd got that day, and invariably they
ended up with an exhortation to keep studying because 'learning's easy carried' and 'the pen's lighter than the spade'. And
the poem does no more than allow that bud of wisdom to ex-
foliate, although the significant point in this context is that at

the time of writing I was not aware of the proverbial structure at the back of my mind. Nor was I aware that the poem was an enactment of yet another digging metaphor that came back to me years later. This was a rhyme that also had a currency on the road to school, though again we were not fully aware of what we were dealing with:

'Are your praties dry
And are they fit for digging?'
'Put in your spade and try,'
Says Dirty-Face McGuigan.

Well, digging there becomes a sexual metaphor, an emblem of initiation, like putting your hand into the bush or robbing the nest, one of the various natural analogies for uncovering and touching the hidden thing. I now believe that the 'Digging' poem had for me the force of an initiation: the confidence I mentioned arose from a sense that perhaps I could work this poetry thing, too, and having experienced the excitement and release of it once, I was doomed to look for it again and again.

I don't want to overload 'Digging' with too much significance. I know as well as you do that it is a big coarse-grained navvy of a poem, but it is interesting as an example—and not just as an example of what one reviewer called 'mud-caked fingers in Russell Square', for I don't think that the subject matter has any particular virtue in itself; it is interesting as an example of what we call 'finding a voice'.

Finding a voice means that you can get your own feeling into your own words and that your words have the feel of you about them; and I believe that it may not even be a metaphor, for a poetic voice is probably very intimately connected with the poet's natural voice, the voice that he hears as the ideal speaker of the lines he is making up. I would like to digress slightly in order to illustrate what I mean more fully.

In his novel *The First Circle*, Solzhenitsyn sets the action in a prison camp on the outskirts of Moscow where the inmates are all highly skilled technicians forced to labor at projects devised by Stalin. The most important of these is an attempt to invent a mechanism to bug a phone. But what is to be special about this particular bugging device is that it will not simply record the voice and the message, but that it will identify the essential sound patterns of the speaker's voice; it will discover, in the words of the narrative, 'what it is that makes every human voice unique' so that no matter how he disguises his accent or changes his language, the fundamental structure of his voice will be caught. The idea was that a voice is like a fingerprint, possessing a constant and unique signature that can, like a fingerprint, be recorded and employed for identification.

Now, one of the purposes of a literary education as I experienced it was to turn your ear into a poetic bugging device, so that a piece of verse denuded of name and date could be identified by its diction, tropes, and cadences. And this secret policing of English verse was also based on the idea of a style as a signature. But what I wish to suggest is that there is a connection between the core of a poet's speaking voice and the core of his poetic voice, between his original accent and his discovered style. I think that the discovery of a way of writing that is natural and adequate to your sensibility depends on the recovery of that essential quick which Solzhenitsyn's technicians were trying to pin down. This is the absolute register to which your proper music has to be tuned.

How, then, do you find it? In practice, you hear it coming from somebody else, you hear something in another writer's sounds that flows in through your ear and enters the echo chamber of your head and delights your whole nervous system in such a way that your reaction will be, 'Ah, I wish I had said that, in that particular way.' This other writer, in fact, has spoken something essential to you, something you recognize instinctively as a true sounding of aspects of yourself and your experience. And your first steps as a writer will be to imitate, consciously or unconsciously, those sounds that flowed in, that in-fluence.

.   .   .

I think technique is different from craft. Craft is what you can learn from other verse. Craft is the skill of making. It wins competitions in *The New Statesman*. It can be deployed without reference to the feelings or the self. It knows how to keep up a capable verbal athletic display; it can be content to be *vox et praeterea nihil*—all voice and nothing else, but not voice as in 'finding a voice'. Learning the craft is learning to turn the windlass at the well of poetry. Usually you begin by dropping the bucket halfway down the shaft and winding up a taking of air. You are miming the real thing until one day the chain draws unexpectedly tight, and you have dipped into waters that will continue to entice you back. You'll have broken the skin on the pool of yourself. Your praties will be 'fit for digging'.

At that point it becomes appropriate to speak of technique rather than craft. Technique, as I would define it, involves not only a poet's way with words, his management of meter, rhythm, and verbal texture; it involves also a definition of his stance toward life, a definition of his own reality. It involves the discovery of ways to go out of his normal cognitive bounds and raid the inarticulate: a dynamic alertness that mediates between the origins of feeling in memory and experience and the formal ploys that express these in a work of art. Technique entails the watermarking of your essential patterns of perception, voice, and thought into the touch and texture of your lines; it is that whole creative effort of the mind's and body's resources to bring the meaning of experience within the jurisdiction of form. Technique is what turns, in Yeats's phrase, 'the bundle of accident and incoherence that sits down to breakfast' into 'an idea, something intended, complete'.

It is indeed conceivable that a poet could have a real technique and a wobbly craft—I think this was true of Alun Lewis and Patrick Kavanagh—but more often it's a case of sure-enough craft and a failure of technique. And if I were asked for a figure who represents pure technique, I would say a water diviner. You can't learn the craft of dousing or divining—it's a gift for being in touch with what is there, hidden and real, a gift for mediating between the latent resource and the community that wants it current and released.

. . .

I suppose technique is what allows that first stirring of the mind round a word or an image or a memory to grow toward articulation, articulation not necessarily in terms of argument or explication but in terms of its own potential for harmonious self-reproduction. The seminal excitement has to be granted conditions in which, in Hopkins' words, it 'selves, goes itself . . . crying What I do is for me, for that I came.' Technique ensures that the first gleam attains its proper effulgence. And I don't just mean a felicity in the choice of words to flesh the theme— that is a problem also, but it is not so critical. A poem can survive stylistic blemishes, but it cannot survive a stillbirth. The crucial action is pre-verbal: to be able to allow the first alertness or come-hither, sensed in a blurred or incomplete way, to dilate and approach as a thought or a theme or a phrase. Frost put it this way: 'A poem begins as a lump in the throat, a homesickness, a lovesickness. It finds the thought and the thought finds the words.' As far as I'm concerned, technique is more vitally and sensitively connected with that first activity where the 'lump in throat' finds 'the thought' than with 'the thought' finding 'the words'. That first epiphany involves the divining, vatic, oracular function; the second, the making, crafting function. To say, as Auden did, that a poem is a 'verbal contraption' is to keep one or two tricks up your sleeve.

Traditionally, an oracle speaks in riddles, yielding its truths in

disguise, offering its insights cunningly. And in the practice of
poetry, there is a corresponding occasion of disguise, a protean,
chameleon moment when the lump in the throat takes protec-
tive coloring in the new element of thought. . . .
tive coloring in the new element of thought.

.   .   .

   In practice . . . you proceed by your own experience of what it
is to write what you consider a successful poem. You survive
in your own esteem not by the corroboration of theory but by
the trust in certain moments of satisfaction that you know intuitively are moments of extension. You are confirmed by the
visitation of the last poem and threatened by the elusiveness
of the next one, and the best moments are those when your
mind seems to implode and words and images rush of their own
accord into the vortex. Which happened to me once when the
line 'We have no prairies' drifted into my head at bedtime and
loosened a fall of images that constitute the poem 'Bogland',
the last one in *Door into the Dark*.
   I had been vaguely wishing to write a poem about bogland,
I had been vaguely wishing to write a poem about bogland,
chiefly because it is a landscape that has a strange assuaging
effect on me, one with associations reaching back into early
childhood. We used to hear about bog-butter, butter kept fresh
for a great number of years under the peat. Then when I was
at school the skeleton of an elk had been taken out of a bog
nearby, and a few of our neighbors had got their photographs
in the paper, peering out across its antlers. So I began to get an
idea of bog as the memory of the landscape, or as a landscape
that remembered everything that happened in and to it. In fact,
if you go round the National Museum in Dublin, you will realize that a great proportion of the most cherished material
heritage of Ireland was 'found in a bog'. Moreover, since memory was the faculty that supplied me with the first quickening
of my own poetry, I had a tentative unrealized need to make a
congruence between memory and bogland and, for the want of

a better word, our national consciousness. And it all released itself after 'We have no prairies . . .'—but we have bogs.

At that time I was teaching modern literature in Queen's University, Belfast, and had been reading about the frontier and the West as an important myth in the American consciousness, so I set up—or, rather, laid down—the bog as an answering Irish myth. I wrote it quickly the next morning, having slept on my excitement, and revised it on the hoof, from line to line, as it came.

.   .   .

Again, as in the case of 'Digging', the seminal impulse had been unconscious. I believe what generated the poem about memory was something lying beneath the very floor of memory, something I connected with the poem only months after it was written, which was a warning that older people would give us about going into the bog. They were afraid we might fall into the pools in the old workings, so they put it about (and we believed them) that *there was no bottom* in the bogholes. Little did they—or I—know that I would filch it for the last line of a book.

There was also in that book a poem called 'Requiem for the Croppies', which was written in 1966 when most poets in Ireland were straining to celebrate the anniversary of the 1916 Rising. Typically, I suppose I went farther back. Nineteen sixteen was the harvest of seeds sown in 1798, when revolutionary republican ideals and national feeling coalesced in the doctrines of Irish republicanism and in the rebellion of 1798 itself—unsuccessful and savagely put down. The poem was born of and ended with an image of resurrection based on the fact that some time after the rebels were buried in common graves, these graves began to sprout with young barley, growing up from barley corn the 'croppies' had carried in their pockets to eat while on the march. The oblique implication was that the seeds of violent resistance sowed in the Year of Liberty had flowered in what Yeats called 'the right rose tree' of 1916. I did not

realize at the time that the original heraldic murderous encounter between Protestant yeoman and Catholic rebel was to
be initiated again in the summer of 1969, in Belfast, two months
after the book was published.

From that moment, the problems of poetry moved from being
simply a matter of achieving the satisfactory verbal icon to
being a search for images and symbols adequate to our predica-
ment. I do not mean liberal lamentation that citizens should
feel compelled to murder one another or deploy their different
military arms over the matter of nomenclatures, such as British
or Irish. I do not mean public celebrations or execrations of resistance or atrocity—although there is nothing necessarily un-
poetic about such celebration, if one thinks of 'Easter 1916'. I
mean that I felt it imperative to discover a field of force in
which, without abandoning fidelity to the processes and experience of poetry as I have outlined them, it would be possible to
encompass the perspectives of a humane reason and, at the same
time, to grant the religious intensity of the violence its deplor-
able authenticity and complexity. And when I say religious, I am
not thinking simply of the sectarian division. To some extent the
enmity can be viewed as a struggle between the cults and devo-
tees of a god and a goddess. There is an indigenous territorial
numen, a tutelar of the whole island—call her Mother Ireland,
Kathleen Ni Houlihan, the poor old woman, the Shan Van
Vocht, whatever—and her sovereignty has been temporarily
usurped or infringed by a new male cult whose founding fathers were Cromwell, William of Orange, and Edward Carson,
and whose godhead is incarnate in a rex or caesar resident in a
palace in London. What we have is the tail end of a struggle in
a province between territorial piety and imperial power.

Now, I realize that this idiom is remote from the agnostic
world of economic interest whose iron hand operates in the velvet glove of 'talks between elected representatives', and remote
from the political maneuvers of power-sharing; but it is not
remote from the psychology of the Irishmen and Ulstermen who

do the killing, and not remote from the bankrupt psychology and mythologies implicit in the terms Irish Catholic and Ulster Protestant. The question, as ever, is 'How with this rage shall beauty hold a plea?' And my answer is, by offering 'befitting emblems of adversity'.

Some of those emblems I found in a book that was published here, appositely, the year the killing started, in 1969. And again appositely, it was entitled *The Bog People*. It was chiefly concerned with preserved bodies of men and women found in the bogs of Jutland, naked, strangled, or with their throats cut, disposed under the peat since early Iron Age times. The author, P. V. Glob, argues convincingly that a number of these, and, in particular, the Tollund Man, whose head is now preserved near Aarhus in the museum at Silkeborg, were ritual sacrifices to the Mother Goddess, the goddess of the ground who needed new bridegrooms each winter to bed with her in her sacred place, in the bog, to ensure the renewal and fertility of the territory in the spring. Taken in relation to the tradition of Irish political martyrdom for the cause whose icon is Kathleen Ni Houlihan, this is more than an archaic barbarous rite; it is an archetypal pattern. And the unforgettable photographs of these victims blended in my mind with photographs of atrocities, past and present, in the long rites of Irish political and religious struggles. When I wrote this poem, I had a completely new sensation: one of fear. It is a vow to go on pilgrimage, and I felt as it came to me—and again it came quickly—that unless I was deeply in earnest about what I was saying, I was simply invoking dangers for myself. It is called 'The Tollund Man'.

.   .   .

And just how persistent the barbaric attitudes are, not only in the slaughter but in the psyche, I discovered, again when the frisson of the poem itself had passed, and indeed after I had fulfilled the vow and gone to Jutland, 'the holy blisful martyr for to seeke'. I read the following in a chapter on 'The Religion of the Pagan Celts' by the Celtic scholar Anne Ross:

Moving from sanctuaries and shrines . . . we come now to consider the nature of the actual deities . . . But before going on to look at the nature of some of the individual deities and their cults, one can perhaps bridge the gap as it were by considering a symbol which, in its way, sums up the whole of Celtic pagan religion and is as representative of it as is, for example, the sign of the cross in Christian contexts. This is the symbol of the severed human head; in all its various modes of iconographic representation and verbal presentation, one may find the hard core of Celtic religion. It is indeed . . . a kind of shorthand symbol for the entire religious outlook of the pagan Celts.

My sense of occasion and almost awe as I vowed to go to pray to the Tollund Man and assist at his enshrined head had a longer ancestry than I had at the time realized.

I began by suggesting that my point of view involved poetry as divination, as a restoration of the culture to itself. In Ireland in this century it has involved for Yeats and many others an attempt to define and interpret the present by bringing it into significant relationship with the past, and I believe that effort in our present circumstances has to be urgently renewed. But here we stray from the realm of technique into the realm of tradition; to forge a poem is one thing, to forge the uncreated conscience of the race, as Stephen Dedalus put it, is quite another, and places daunting pressures and responsibilities on anyone who would risk the name of poet.   (1974)

TED HUGHES

On Poetry*

. . . In each poem, besides the principal subject—and in my
poems this is usually pretty easy to see, as, for instance, the
jaguar in the poem called 'The Jaguar'—there is what is not so
easy to talk about, even generally, but which is the living and
individual element in every poet's work. What I mean is the
way he brings to peace all the feelings and energies which, from
all over the body, heart, and brain, send up their champions
onto the battleground of that first subject. The way I do this, as
I believe, is by using something like the method of a musical
composer. I might say that I turn every combatant into a bit of
music, then resolve the whole uproar into as formal and balanced a figure of melody and rhythm as I can. When all the
words are hearing each other clearly, and every stress is feeling
every other stress, and all are contented—the poem is finished . . .

. . .

There is a great mass of English poetry in which the musical
element—the inner figure of stresses—is not so important as
other elements. To me—no matter what metaphysical persuasion or definable philosophy a poem may seem to subscribe to
—what is unique and precious in it is its heart, that inner figure
of stresses . . .   (1957)

---

* From Hughes' essays and interviews in Ekbert Faas's *Ted Hughes: The
Unaccommodated Universe* (1980).

The poet's only hope is to be infinitely sensitive to what his gift is, and this in itself seems to be another gift that few poets possess. According to this sensitivity, and to his faith in it, he will go on developing as a poet, as Yeats did, pursuing those adventures, mental, spiritual and physical, whatever they may be, that his gift wants, or he will lose its guidance, lose the feel of its touch in the workings of his mind, and soon be absorbed by the impersonal dead lumber of matters in which his gift has no interest, which is a form of suicide, metaphorical in the case of Wordsworth and Coleridge, actual in the case of Mayakovsky.

Many considerations assault his faith in the finality, wisdom and sufficiency of his gift. Its operation is not only shadowy and indefinable, it is intermittent, it has none of the obvious attachment to publicly exciting and seemingly important affairs that his other mental activities have and in which all his intelligent contemporaries have such confidence, and so it receives no immediate encouragement—or encouragement only of the most dubious kind, as a flagellant, questioning his illuminations, might be encouraged by a bunch of mad old women and some other half-dead gory flagellant; it visits him when he is only half suspecting it, and he is not sure it has visited him until some days or months afterwards and perhaps he never can be sure, being a sensible man aware of the examples of earlier poets and of the devils of self-delusion and of the delusions of whole generations. . . .   (1962)

. . . Technique is not a machine to do work, like a car engine that runs best of all with little or no load, but the act of work being done. So-called 'technique without substance' is our polite word for fakery, or the appearance of something happening that is not happening, and attracts our attention at all only because we will look for some minutes at absolutely anything that seems to say 'look at me', so humble and great is our hope.

•   •   •

In our time, the heroic struggle is not to become a hero but to remain a living creature simply. The Scientific Spirit has bitten so many of us in the nape, and pumped us full of its eggs, the ferocious virus of abstraction. We yield to the larvae, warmly numbed, and we all speak well of them and their parent. The Scientific Spirit, as we say, is hard-headed, it fears nothing, it faces the facts, and how it has improved our comforts! And yet what is this master of ours? The Scientific Spirit was born of the common hunt for the nourishing morsel, nursed by the benign search for objective truth, schooled in the pedagogic idolatry of the objective fact, graduated through old-maid specialised research, losing eyes, ears, smell, taste, touch, nerves and blood, adapting to the sensibility of electronic gadgets and the argument of numbers, to become a machine of senility, a pseudo-automaton in the House of the Mathematical Absolute. So it ousts humanity from man and he dedicates his life to the laws of the electron in vacuo, a literal self-sacrifice, and soon, by bigotry and the especially rabid evangelism of the inhuman, a literal world-sacrifice, as we all too truly now fear. Any artist who resists the suction into this galactic firestorm and holds to bodily wholeness and the condition of the creature, finds ranged against him the worldly powers of our age and everything that is not the suffering vitality of nature. The victims of radio-activity and of the death-camps, the corpse of a bird, an agony too private to name, become the only unequivocal portraits of life, of the Angel a hundred faces behind the human face. In this way, the particular misery and disaster of our time are, uniquely, the perfect conditions for the purest and most intense manifestation of the spirit, the Angel, the ghost of ashes, the survivor of the Creation. . . .   (1962)

Any form of violence—any form of vehement activity—invokes the bigger energy, the elemental power circuit of the Universe. Once the contact has been made—it becomes difficult to control.

Something from beyond ordinary human activity enters. When
the wise men know how to create rituals and dogma, the energy
can be contained. When the old rituals and dogma have lost
credit and disintegrated, and no new ones have been formed,
the energy cannot be contained, and so its effect is destructive—
and that is the position with us. And that is why force of any
kind frightens our rationalist, humanist style of outlook. In the
old world God and divine power were invoked at any cost—
life seemed worthless without them. In the present world we
dare not invoke them—we wouldn't know how to use them or
stop them destroying us. We have settled for the minimum practical energy and illumination—anything bigger introduces problems, the demons get hold of it. That is the psychological stu-
pidity, the ineptitude, of the rigidly rationalist outlook—it's a
form of hubris, and we're paying the traditional price. If you
refuse the energy, you are living a kind of death. If you accept
the energy, it destroys you. What is the alternative? To accept
the energy, and find methods of turning it to good, of keeping
it under control—rituals, the machinery of religion. The old
method is the only one.

. . .

Every writer if he develops at all develops either outwards into
society and history, using wider and more material of that sort,
or he develops inwards into imagination and beyond that into
spirit, using perhaps no more external material than before and
maybe even less, but deepening it and making it operate in the
many different inner dimensions until it opens up perhaps the
religious or holy basis of the whole thing. Or he can develop
both ways simultaneously. Developing inwardly, of course,
means organizing the inner world or at least searching out the
patterns there and that is a mythology. It may be an original
mythology. Or you may uncover the Cross—as Eliot did. The
ideal aspect of Yeats' development is that he managed to de-

velop his poetry both outwardly into history and the common imagery of everyday life at the same time as he developed it inwardly in a sort of close parallel . . . so that he could speak of both simultaneously. His mythology is history, pretty well, and his history is as he said 'the story of a soul'. . . .

You choose a subject because it serves, because you need it. We go on writing poems because one poem never gets the whole account right. There is always something missed. At the end of the ritual up comes a goblin. Anyway within a week the whole thing has changed, one needs a fresh bulletin. And works go dead, fishing has to be abandoned, the shoal has moved on. While we struggle with a fragmentary Orestes some complete Bacchae moves past too deep down to hear. We get news of it later . . . too late. In the end, one's poems are ragged dirty undated letters from remote battles and weddings and one thing and another.

. . .

The first idea of *Crow* was really an idea of a style. In folktales the prince going on the adventure comes to the stable full of beautiful horses and he needs a horse for the next stage and the king's daughter advises him to take none of the beautiful horses that he'll be offered but to choose the dirty, scabby little foal. You see, I throw out the eagles and choose the Crow. The idea was originally just to write his songs, the songs that a Crow would sing. In other words, songs with no music whatsoever, in a super-simple and a super-ugly language which would in a way shed everything except just what he wanted to say without any other consideration and that's the basis of the style of the whole thing. I get near it in a few poems. There I really begin to get what I was after. (1970)

. . . And my follow-up to 'View of a Pig' was 'Pike'. But that poem immediately became much more charged with particular memories and a specific obsession. And my sense of 'Hawk

Roosting' was that somehow or other it had picked up the proto-
type style behind 'View of a Pig' and 'Pike' without that over-
lay of a heavier, thicker, figurative language. Anyway, they
were written in that succession, so that I got to 'Hawk Roosting' through those other two poems. All three were written in
a mood of impatience, deliberately trying to destroy the ways
in which I had written before, trying to write in a way that
had nothing to do with the way in which I thought I ought to
be writing. But then, that too became deliberate and a dead end.

Almost all the poems in *Lupercal* were written as invocations
to writing. My main consciousness in those days was that it was
impossible to write. So these invocations were just attempts to
crack the apparent impossibility of producing anything. . . . it
culminated a deliberate effort to find a simple concrete language
with no words in it over which I didn't have complete owner-
ship: a limited language, but authentic to me. So in my ordinary
exercise of writing I felt that the *Lupercal* style simply excluded
too much of what I wanted to say. But the 'Hawk Roosting'
style offered infinite expansion and flexibility. It was just too
difficult a road, in my circumstances. It needed a state of concentration which I was evidently unable to sustain. So I preferred to look for a different way in. *Wodwo* was one way of
looking for the new ground with the old equipment. While
Crow was the discovery of a style as close and natural to me
as the *Lupercal* style, but then again I set off with an attempt
to simplify it . . . with idea of reintroducing, once I'd got control of it, all the perceptions and material I'd been able to use
in the *Lupercal* style. I never got that far.

. . .

I did that [*Oedipus*] in the middle of writing those Crow pieces.
And that turned out to be useful. Because it was a simple story,
so that at every moment the actual writing of it was under a

specific type and weight of feeling. It gave me a very sharp sense of how the language had to be hardened or deepened so it could take the weight of the feeling running in the story. After a first draft I realized that all the language I had used was too light. So there was another draft and then another one. And as I worked on it, it turned into a process of more and more simplifying, or in a way limiting the language. I ended up with something like three hundred words, the smallest vocabulary Gielgud had ever worked with. And that ran straight into *Crow*. However, it was a way of concentrating my actual writing rather than of bringing me to any language that was then useful in *Crow*. It simply concentrated me. That was probably its main use. It gave me a very clear job to work on continually, at top pressure. You knew when you had got it and when you hadn't and it was lots of hours you could put into it. And all that momentum and fitness I got from it, I could then use on those shorter sprints.

.   .   .

So it is not the story that I am interested in but the poems. In other words, the whole narrative is just a way of getting a big body of ideas and energy moving on a track. For when this energy connects with a possibility for a poem, there is a lot more material and pressure in it than you could ever get into a poem just written out of the air or out of a special occasion. Poems come to you much more naturally and accumulate more life when they are part of a connected flow of real narrative that you've got yourself involved in. . . .   (1977)

ROBERT LOWELL

From *An Interview*[*]

INTERVIEWER. But in *Lord Weary's Castle* there were poems moving toward a sort of narrative calm, almost a prose calm— 'Katherine's Dream', for example, or the two poems on texts by Edwards, or 'The Ghost'—and then, on the other hand, poems in which the form was insisted upon and maybe shown off, and where the things that were characteristic of your poetry at that time—the kind of enjambments, the rhyming, the metres, of course—seem willed and forced, so that you have a terrific log jam of stresses, meanings, strains.

LOWELL. I know one contrast I've felt, and it takes different forms at different times. The ideal modern form seems to be the novel and certain short stories. Maybe Tolstoy would be the perfect example—his work is imagistic, it deals with all experience, and there seems to be no conflict of the form and content. So one thing is to get into poetry that kind of human richness in rather simple descriptive language. Then there's another side of poetry: compression, something highly rhythmical and perhaps wrenched into a small space. I've always been fascinated by both these things. But getting it all on one page in a few stanzas, getting it all done in as little space as possible, revising and revising so that each word and rhythm though not perfect is pondered and wrestled with—you can't do that in prose very well, you'd never get your book written. 'Katherine's Dream' was a real dream. I found that I shaped it a bit, and cut it, and allegorized it, but still it was a dream someone had had. It was material that ordinarily, I think, would go into prose, yet it

---

[*] From *Writers at Work: The Paris Review Interviews*, Second Series, ed. by Malcolm Cowley. The interviewer is Frederick Seidel.

would have had to be much longer and part of something much longer.

INTERVIEWER. I think you can either look for forms, you can do specific reading for them, or the forms can be demanded by what you want to say. And when the material in poetry seems under almost unbearable pressure you wonder whether the form hasn't cookie-cut what the poet wanted to say. But you chose the couplet, didn't you, and some of your freest passages are in couplets.

LOWELL. The couplet I've used is very much like the couplet Browning uses in 'My Last Duchess', in *Sordello*, run-on with its rhymes buried. I've always, when I've used it, tried to give the impression that I had as much freedom in choosing the rhyme word as I had in any of the other words. Yet they were almost all true rhymes, and maybe half the time there'd be a pause after the rhyme. I wanted something as fluid as prose; you wouldn't notice the form, yet looking back you'd find that great obstacles had been climbed. And the couplet is pleasant in this way—once you've got your two lines to rhyme, then that's done and you can go on to the next. You're not stuck with the whole stanza to round out and build to a climax. A couplet can be a couplet or can be split and left as one line, or it can go on for a hundred lines; any sort of compression or expansion is possible. And that's not so in a stanza. I think a couplet's much less lyrical than a stanza, closer to prose. Yet it's an honest form, its difficulties are in the open. It really is pretty hard to rhyme each line with the one that follows it.

INTERVIEWER. Did the change of style in *Life Studies* have something to do with working away from that compression and pressure by way of, say, the kind of prose clarity of 'Katherine's Dream'?

LOWELL. Yes. By the time I came to *Life Studies* I'd been writing my autobiography and also writing poems that broke metre. I'd been doing a lot of reading aloud. I went on a trip to the West Coast and read at least once a day and sometimes twice for fourteen days, and more and more I found that I was simplifying my poems. If I had a Latin quotation I'd translate it into English. If adding a couple of syllables in a line made it clearer I'd add them, and I'd make little changes just impromptu as I read. That seemed to improve the reading.

INTERVIEWER. Can you think of a place where you added a syllable or two to an otherwise regular line?

LOWELL. It was usually articles and prepositions that I added, very slight little changes, and I didn't change the printed text. It was just done for the moment.

INTERVIEWER. Why did you do this? Just because you thought the most important thing was to get the poem over?

LOWELL. To get it over, yes. And I began to have a certain disrespect for the tight forms. If you could make it easier by adding syllables, why not? And then when I was writing *Life Studies*, a good number of the poems were started in very strict metre, and I found that, more than the rhymes, the regular beat was what I didn't want. I have a long poem in there about my father, called 'Commander Lowell', which actually is largely in couplets, but I originally wrote perfectly strict four-foot couplets. Well, with that form it's hard not to have echoes of Marvell. That regularity just seemed to ruin the honesty of senti-ment, and became rhetorical; it said, 'I'm a poem'—though it was a great help when I was revising having this original skele-ton. I could keep the couplets where I wanted them and drop them where I didn't; there'd be a form to come back to.

INTERVIEWER. Had you originally intended to handle all that material in prose?

LOWELL. Yes. I found it got awfully tedious working out transitions and putting in things that didn't seem very important but were necessary to the prose continuity. Also I found it hard to revise. Cutting it down into small bits, I could work on it much more carefully and make fast transitions. But there's an-other point about this mysterious business of prose and poetry, form and content, and the reasons for breaking forms. I don't think there's any very satisfactory answer. I seesaw back and forth between something highly metrical and something highly free; there isn't any one way to write. But it seems to me we've gotten in a sort of Alexandrian age. Poets of my generation and particularly younger ones have gotten terribly proficient at these forms. They write a very musical, difficult poem with tremendous skill, perhaps there's never been such skill. Yet the writings seem divorced from culture somehow. It's become too much something specialized that can't handle much experience. It's a craft, purely a craft, and there must be some breakthrough back into life. Prose is in many ways better off than poetry. It's quite hard to think of a young poet who has the vitality, say, of Salinger or Saul Bellow. Yet prose tends to be very diffuse. The novel is really a much more difficult form than it seems; few people have the wind to write anything that long. Even a short story demands almost poetic perfection. Yet on the whole prose is less cut off from life than poetry is. Now, some of this Alexandrian poetry is very brilliant, you would not have it changed at all. But I thought it was getting increasingly stifling. I couldn't get any experience into tight metrical forms.

INTERVIEWER. So you felt this about your own poetry, your own technique, not just about the general condition of poetry?

LOWELL. Yes. I felt that the metre plastered difficulties and mannerisms on what I was trying to say to such an extent that it terribly hampered me.

INTERVIEWER. This then explains, in part anyway, your admiration for Elizabeth Bishop's poetry. I know that you've said the qualities and the abundance of it's descriptive language reminded you of the Russian novel more than anything else.

LOWELL. Any number of people are guilty of writing a complicated poem that has a certain amount of symbolism in it and really difficult meaning, a wonderful poem to teach. Then you unwind it and you feel that the intelligence, the experience, whatever goes into it, is skin-deep. In Elizabeth Bishop's 'Man-Moth' a whole new world is gotten out and you don't know what will come after any one line. It's exploring. And it's as original as Kafka. She's gotten a world, not just a way of writing. She seldom writes a poem that doesn't have that exploratory quality; yet it's very firm, it's not like beat poetry, it's all controlled.

•   •   •

INTERVIEWER. Do you revise a very great deal?

LOWELL. Endlessly.

INTERVIEWER. You often use an idiom or a very common phrase either for the sake of irony or to bear more meaning than it's customarily asked to bear—do these come late in the game, do you have to look around for them?

LOWELL. They come later because they don't prove much in themselves, and they often replace something that's much more formal and worked-up. Some of my later poetry does have this quality that the earlier doesn't: several lines can be almost what you'd say in conversation. And maybe talking with a friend or with my wife I'd say, 'This doesn't sound quite right', and sort of reach in the air as I talked and change a few words. In that way the new style is easier to write; I sometimes fumble out a natural sequence of lines that will work. But a whole poem won't come that way; my seemingly relaxed poems are just about as hard as the very worked-up ones.

INTERVIEWER. That rightness and familiarity, though, is in 'Between the Porch and the Altar' in several passages which are in couplets.

LOWELL. When I am writing in metre I find the simple lines never come right away. Nothing does. I don't believe I've ever written a poem in metre where I've kept a single one of the original lines. Usually when I was writing my old poems I'd write them out in blank verse and then put in the rhymes. And of course I'd change the rhymes a lot. The most I could hope for at first was that the rhymed version wouldn't be much inferior to the blank verse. Then the real work would begin, to make it something much better than the original out of the difficulties of the metre.

INTERVIEWER. Have you ever gone as far as Yeats and written out a prose argument and then set down the rhymes?

LOWELL. With some of the later poems I've written out prose versions, then cut the prose down and abbreviated it. A rapidly written prose draft of the poem doesn't seem to do much good, too little pain has gone into it; but one really worked on is bound to have phrases that are invaluable. And it's a nice technical problem: how can you keep phrases and get them into metre?

. . .

INTERVIEWER. So you feel that the religion is the business of the poem that it's in and not at all the business of the Church or the religious person.

LOWELL. It shouldn't be. I mean, a religion ought to have objective validity. But by the time it gets into a poem it's so mixed up with technical and imaginative problems that the theologian, the priest, the serious religious person isn't of too much use. The poem is too strange for him to feel at home and make any suggestions.

INTERVIEWER. What does this make of the religious poem as a religious exercise?

LOWELL. Well, it at least makes this: that the poem tries to be a poem and not a piece of artless religious testimony. There is a drawback. It seems to me that with any poem, but maybe particularly a religious one where there are common interests, the opinion of intelligent people who are not poets ought to be useful. There's an independence to this not getting advice from religious people and outsiders, but also there's a narrowness. Then there is a question whether my poems are religious, or whether they just use religious imagery. I haven't really any idea. My last poems don't use religious imagery, they don't use symbolism. In many ways they seem to me more religious than the early ones, which are full of symbols and references to Christ and God. I'm sure the symbols and the Catholic framework didn't make the poems religious experiences. Yet I don't feel my experience changed very much. It seems to me it's clearer to me now than it was then, but it's very much the same sort of thing that went into the religious poems—the same sort of struggle, light and darkness, the flux of experience. The morality seems much the same. But the symbolism is gone; you couldn't possibly say what creed I believed in. I've wondered myself often. Yet what made the earlier poems valuable seems to be some recording of experience, and that seems to be what makes the later ones.

INTERVIEWER. So you end up saying that the poem does have some integrity and can have some beauty apart from the beliefs expressed in the poem.

LOWELL. I think it can only have integrity apart from the beliefs; that no political position, religious position, position of generosity, or what have you, can make a poem good. It's all to the good if a poem *can* use politics, or theology, or gardening, or anything that has its own validity aside from poetry. But these things will never *per se* make a poem.

INTERVIEWER. The difficult question is whether when the beliefs expressed in a poem are obnoxious the poem as a whole can be considered to be beautiful—the problem of the *Pisan Cantos*.

LOWELL. The *Pisan Cantos* are very uneven, aren't they? If you took what most people would agree are maybe the best hundred passages, would the beliefs in those passages be obnoxious? I think you'd get a very mixed answer. You could make quite a good case for Pound's good humour about his imprisonment, his absence of self-pity, his observant eye, his memories of literary friends, for all kinds of generous qualities and open qualities and lyrical qualities that anyone would think were good. And even when he does something like the death of Mussolini, in the passage that opens the *Pisan Cantos*, people debate about it. I've talked to Italians who were partisans, and who said that this is the only poem on Mussolini that's any

good. Pound's quite wily often: Mussolini hung up like an ox
—his brutal appearance. I don't know whether you could say
the beliefs there are wrong or not. And there are other poems
that come to mind: in Eliot, the Jew spelled with a small j in
'Gerontion', is that anti-Semitism or not? Eliot's not anti-Semitic
in any sense, but there's certainly a dislike of Jews in those early
poems. Does he gain in the fierceness of writing his Jew with a
small j? He says you write what you have to write and in criticism you can say what you think you should believe in. Very
ugly emotions perhaps make a poem.

INTERVIEWER. You were on the Bollingen Committee at the
time the award was made to Pound. What did you think of the
great ruckus?

LOWELL. I thought it was a very simple problem of voting for
the best book of the year; and it seemed to me Pound's was. I
thought the *Pisan Cantos* was the best writing Pound had ever
done, though it included some of his worst. It is a very mixed
book: that was the question. But the consequences of not giving
the best book of the year a prize for extraneous reasons, even
terrible ones in a sense—I think that's the death of art. Then
you have Pasternak suppressed and everything becomes stifling.
Particularly in a strong country like ours you've got to award
things objectively and not let the beliefs you'd like a man to
have govern your choice. It was very close after the war, and
anyone must feel that the poetry award was a trifling thing compared with the concentration camps. I actually think they were
very distant from Pound. He had no political effect whatsoever
and was quite eccentric and impractical. Pound's social credit,
his fascism, all these various things, were a tremendous gain to
him; he'd be a very Parnassan poet without them. Even if
they're bad beliefs—and some were bad, some weren't, and
some were just terrible, of course—they made him more human
and more to do with life, more to do with the times. They served
him. Taking what interested him in these things gave a kind of

realism and life to his poetry that it wouldn't have had otherwise.

•   •   •

INTERVIEWER. Have many of your poems been taken from real
people and real events?

LOWELL. I think, except when I've used myself or occasionally named actual people in poems, the characters are purely
imaginary. I've tried to buttress them by putting images I've
actually seen and in direct ways getting things I've actually experienced into the poem. If I'm writing about a Canadian nun the
poem may have a hundred little bits of things I've looked at, but
she's not remotely anyone I've ever known. And I don't believe
anybody would think my nun was quite a real person. She has a
heart and she's alive, I hope, and she has a lot of colour to her
and drama, and has some things that Frost's characters don't,
but she doesn't have their wonderful quality of life. His Witch of
Coös is absolutely there. I've gathered from talking to him that
most of the *North of Boston* poems came from actual people he
knew shuffled and put together. But then it's all-important that
Frost's plots are so extraordinary, so carefully worked out
though it almost seems that they're not there. Like some things in
Chekhov, the art is very well hidden.

INTERVIEWER. Don't you think a large part of it is getting the
right details, symbolic or not, around which to wind the poem
tight and tighter?

LOWELL. Some bit of scenery or something you've felt. Almost the whole problem of writing poetry is to bring it back to
what you really feel, and that takes an awful lot of manoeuvring.
You may feel the doorknob more strongly than some big personal event, and the doorknob will open into something that you
can use as your own. A lot of poetry seems to me very good in
the tradition but just doesn't move me very much because it
doesn't have personal vibrance to it. I probably exaggerate the
value of it, but it's precious to me. Some little image, some

detail you've noticed—you're writing about a little country shop, just describing it, and your poem ends up with an existentialist account of your experience. But it's the shop that started it off. You didn't know why it meant a lot to you. Often images and often the sense of the beginning and end of a poem are all you have—some journey to be gone through between those things; you know that, but you don't know the details. And that's marvelous; then you feel the poem will come out. It's a terrible struggle, because what you really feel hasn't got the form, it's not what you can put down in a poem. And the poem you're equipped to write concerns nothing that you care very much about or have much to say on. Then the great moment comes when there's enough resolution of your technical equipment, your way of constructing things, and what you can make a poem out of, to hit something you really want to say. You may not know you have it to say.

CHARLES OLSON

*Projective Verse**

* From *Selected Writings of Charles Olson*, ed. by Robert Creeley.

(projectile   (percussive   (prospective

vs.

The NON-Projective

(*or what a French critic calls 'closed' verse, that verse which print bred and which is pretty much what we have had, in English & American, and have still got, despite the work of Pound & Williams:*

it led Keats, already a hundred years ago, to see it (Words-worth's, Milton's) in the light of 'the Egotistical Sublime'; and it persists, at this latter day, as what you might call the private-soul-at-any-public-wall)

Verse now, 1950, if it is to go ahead, if it is to be of *essential* use, must, I take it, catch up and put into itself certain laws and possibilities of the breath, of the breathing of the man who writes as well as of his listenings. (The revolution of the ear, 1910, the trochee's heave, asks it of the younger poets.)

I want to do two things: first, try to show what projective or OPEN verse is, what it involves, in its act of composition, how, in distinction from the non-projective, it is accomplished; and II, suggest a few ideas about what stance toward reality brings such verse into being, what that stance does, both to the poet and to his reader. (The stance involves, for example, a change beyond, and larger than, the technical, and may, the way things look, lead to new poetics and to new concepts from which some sort of drama, say, or of epic, perhaps, may emerge.)

I

First, some simplicities that a man learns, if he works in OPEN, or what can also be called COMPOSITION BY FIELD, as opposed to inherited line, stanza, over-all form, what is the 'old' base of the non-projective.

(1) the *kinetics* of the thing. A poem is energy transferred from where the poet got it (he will have some several causations), by way of the poem itself to, all the way over to, the reader. Okay. Then the poem itself must, at all points, be a high energy-construct and, at all points, an energy-discharge. So: how is the poet to accomplish same energy, how is he, what is the process by which a poet gets in, at all points energy at least the equivalent of the energy which propelled him in the first place, yet an energy which is peculiar to verse alone and which will be, obviously, also different from the energy which the reader, because he is a third term, will take away?

This is the problem which any poet who departs from closed form is specially confronted by. And it involves a whole series of new recognitions. From the moment he ventures into FIELD COMPOSITION—puts himself in the open—he can go by no track other than the one the poem under hand declares, for itself. Thus he has to behave, and be, instant by instant, aware of some several forces just now beginning to be examined. (It is much more, for example, this push, than simply such a one as Pound put, so wisely, to get us started: 'the musical phrase', go by it, boys, rather than by, the metronome.)

(2) is the *principle*, the law which presides conspicuously over such composition, and, when obeyed, is the reason why a projective poem can come into being. It is this: FORM IS NEVER MORE THAN AN EXTENSION OF CONTENT. (Or so it got phrased by one, R. Creeley, and it makes absolute sense to me, with this possible corollary, that right form, in any

given poem, is the only and exclusively possible extension of content under hand.) There it is, brothers, sitting there, for USE.

Now (3) the *process* of the thing, how the principle can be made so to shape the energies that the form is accomplished. And I think it can be boiled down to one statement (first pounded into my head by Edward Dahlberg): ONE PERCEPTION MUST IMMEDIATELY AND DIRECTLY LEAD TO A FURTHER PERCEPTION. It means exactly what it says, is a matter of, at *all* points (even, I should say, of our management of daily reality as of the daily work) get on with it, keep moving, keep in, speed, the nerves, their speed, the perceptions, theirs, the acts, the split second acts, the whole business, keep it moving as fast as you can, citizen. And if you also set up as a poet, USE USE USE the process at all points, in any given poem always, always one perception must must must MOVE, INSTANTER, ON ANOTHER!

So there we are, fast, there's the dogma. And its excuse, its usableness, in practice. Which gets us, it ought to get us, inside the machinery, now, 1950, of how projective verse is made.

If I hammer, if I recall in, and keep calling in, the breath, the breathing as distinguished from the hearing, it is for cause, it is to insist upon a part that breath plays in verse which has not (due, I think, to the smothering of the power of the line by too set a concept of foot) has not been sufficiently observed or practised, but which has to be if verse is to advance to its proper force and place in the day, now, and ahead. I take it that PROJECTIVE VERSE teaches, is, this lesson, that that verse will only do in which a poet manages to register both the acquisitions of his ear *and* the pressures of his breath.

Let's start from the smallest particle of all, the syllable. It is the king and pin of versification, what rules and holds together the lines, the larger forms, of a poem. I would suggest that verse here and in England dropped this secret from the late Elizabethans to Ezra Pound, lost it, in the sweetness of metre and rime, in a honey-head. (The syllable is one way to distinguish the original success of blank verse, and its falling off, with Milton.)

It is by their syllables that words juxtapose in beauty, by these particles of sound as clearly as by the sense of the words which they compose. In any given instance, because there is a choice of words, the choice, if a man is in there, will be, spontaneously, the obedience of his ear to the syllables. The fineness, and the practice, lie here, at the minimum and source of speech.

> O western wynd, when wilt thou blow
> And the small rain down shall rain
> O Christ that my love were in my arms
> And I in my bed again

It would do no harm, as an act of correction to both prose and verse as now written, if both rime and metre, and, in the quantity words, both sense and sound, were less in the forefront of the mind than the syllable, if the syllable, that fine creature, were more allowed to lead the harmony on. With this warning, to those who would try: to step back here to this place of the elements and minims of language, is to engage speech where it is least careless—and least logical. Listening for the syllables must be so constant and so scrupulous, the exaction must be so complete, that the assurance of the ear is purchased at the highest—40 hours a day—price. For from the root out, from all over the place, the syllable comes, the figures of, the dance:

'Is' comes from the Aryan root, *as*, to breathe. The English 'not' equals the Sanskrit *na*, which may come from the root *na*, to be lost, to perish. 'Be' is from *bhu*, to grow.

I say the syllable, king, and that it is spontaneous, this way: the ear, the ear which has collected, which has listened, the ear, which is so close to the mind that it is the mind's, that it has the mind's speed . . .

it is close, another way: the mind is brother to this sister and

is, because it is so close, is the drying force, the incest, the sharp-
ener . . .

it is from the union of the mind and the ear that the syllable is
born.

But the syllable is only the first child of the incest of verse
(always, that Egyptian thing, it produces twins!). The other
child is the LINE. And together, these two, the syllable *and*
the line, they make a poem, they make that thing, the—what
shall we call it, the Boss of all, 'Single Intelligence'. And the
line comes (I swear it) from the breath, from the breathing of the
man who writes, at the moment that he writes, and thus is, it is
here that, the daily work, the WORK, gets in, for only he, the
man who writes, can declare, at every moment, the line its
metric and its ending—where its breathing, shall come to, termi-
nation.

The trouble with most work, to my taking, since the breaking
away from traditional lines and stanzas, and from such wholes
as, say, Chaucer's *Troilus* or S's *Lear*, is: contemporary workers
go lazy RIGHT HERE WHERE THE LINE IS BORN.

Let me put it baldly. The two halves are,
> the HEAD, by way of the EAR, to the SYLLABLE
> the HEART, by way of the BREATH, to the LINE

And the joker? that it is in the 1st half of the proposition that, in
composing, one lets-it-rip; and that it is in the 2nd half, surprise,
it is the LINE that's the baby that gets, as the poem is getting
made, the attention, the control, that it is right here, in the line,
that the shaping takes place, each moment of the going.

I am dogmatic, that the head shows in the syllable. The dance of
the intellect is there, among them, prose or verse. Consider the
best minds you know in this here business: where does the head
show, is it not, precise, here, in the swift currents of the syllable?
can't you tell a brain when you see what it does, just there? It is
true, what the master says he picked up from Confusion: all the

thots men are capable of can be entered on the back of a postage stamp. So, is it not the PLAY of a mind we are after, is not that that shows whether a mind is there at all?

And the threshing floor for the dance? Is it anything but the LINE? And when the line has, is, a deadness, is it not a heart which has gone lazy, is it not, suddenly, slow things, similes, say, adjectives, or such, that we are bored by?

For there is a whole flock of rhetorical devices which have now to be brought under a new bead, now that we sight with the line. Simile is only one bird who comes down, too easily. The descriptive functions generally have to be watched, every second, in projective verse, because of their easiness, and thus their drain on the energy which composition by field allows into a poem. *Any* slackness takes off attention, that crucial thing, from the job in hand, from the *push* of the line under hand at the moment, under the reader's eye, in his moment. Observation of any kind is, like argument in prose, properly previous to the act of contemporary to the acting-on-you of the poem? I would argue that here, too, the LAW OF THE LINE, which projective verse creates, must be hewn to, obeyed, and that the conventions which logic has forced on syntax must be broken open as quietly as must the too set feet of the old line. But an analysis of how far a new poet can stretch the very conventions on which communication by language rests, is too big for these notes, which are meant, I hope it is obvious, merely to get things started.

Let me just throw in this. It is my impression that *all* parts of speech suddenly, in composition by field, are fresh for both sound and percussive use, spring up like unknown, unnamed vegetables in the patch, when you work it, come spring. Now take Hart Crane. What strikes me in him is the singleness of the push to the nominative, his push along that one arc of freshness, the attempt to get back to word as handle. (If logos is word as thought, what is word as noun, as, pass me that, as Newman Shea used to ask, at the galley table, put a jib on the blood, will ya.) But there is a loss in Crane of what Fenollosa is so right about, in syntax, the sentence as first act of nature, as lightning, as passage of force from subject to object, quick, in this case, from Hart to me, in every case, from me to you, the VERB, between two nouns. Does not Hart miss the advantages, by such an isolated push, miss the point of the whole front of syllable, line, field, and what happened to all language, and to the poem, as a result?

I return you now to London, to beginnings, to the syllable, for the pleasures of it, to intermit:

> If music be the food of love, play on,
> give me excess of it, that, surfeiting,
> the appetite may sicken, and so die.
> That strain again. It had a dying fall,
> o, it came over my ear like the sweet sound
> that breathes upon a bank of violets,
> stealing and giving odour.

What we have suffered from, is manuscript, press, the removal of verse from its producer and its reproducer, the voice, a removal the poem, and, if allowed in, must be so juxtaposed, apposed, set in, that it does not, for an instant, sap the going energy of the content toward its form.

It comes to this, this whole aspect of the newer problems. (We now enter, actually, the large area of the whole poem, into the FIELD, if you like, where all the syllables and all the lines must be managed in their relations to each other.) It is a matter, finally, of OBJECTS, what they are, what they are inside a poem, how they got there, and, once there, how they are to be used. This is something I want to get to in another way in Part II, but, for the moment, let me indicate this, that every element in an open poem (the syllable, the line, as well as the image, the sound, the sense) must be taken up as participants in the kinetic of the poem just as solidly as we are accustomed to take what we call the objects of reality; and that these elements are to be seen as creating the tensions of a poem just as totally as do those other objects create what we know as the world.

The objects which occur at every given moment of composition (of recognition, we can call it) are, can be, must be treated exactly as they do occur therein and not by any ideas or preconceptions from outside the poem, must be handled as a series of objects in field in such a way that a series of tensions (which they also are) are made to *hold*, and to hold exactly inside the content and the context of the poem which has forced itself, through the poet and them, into being.

Because breath allows *all* the speech-force of language back in (speech is the 'solid' of verse, is the secret of a poem's energy), because, now, a poem has, by speech, solidity, everything in it can now be treated as solids, objects, things; and, though insisting upon the absolute difference of the reality of verse from that other dispersed and distributed thing, yet each of these elements of a poem can be allowed to have the play of their separate energies and can be allowed, once the poem is well composed, to keep, as those other objects do, their proper confusions.

Which brings us up, immediately, bang, against tenses, in fact against syntax, in fact against grammar generally, that is, as we have inherited it. Do not tenses, must they not also be kicked around anew, in order that time, that other governing absolute, may be kept, as must the space-tensions of a poem, immediate, by one, by two removes from its place of origin *and* its destination. For the breath has a double meaning which latin had not yet lost.

The irony is, from the machine has come one gain not yet sufficiently observed or used, but which leads directly on toward projective verse and its consequences. It is the advantage of the typewriter that, due to its rigidity and its space precisions, it can, for a poet, indicate exactly the breath, the pauses, the suspensions even of syllables, the juxtapositions even of parts of phrases, which he intends. For the first time the poet has the stave and the bar a musician has had. For the first time he can, without the convention of rime and metre, record the listening he has done to his own speech and by that one act indicate how he would want any reader, silently or otherwise, to voice his work.

It is time we picked the fruits of the experiments of Cummings, Pound, Williams, each of whom has, after his way, already used the machine as a scoring to his composing, as a script to its vocalization. It is now only a matter of the recognition of the conventions of composition by field for us to bring into being an open verse as formal as the closed, with all its traditional advantages.

If a contemporary poet leaves a space as long as the phrase before it, he means that space to be held, by the breath, an equal length of time. If he suspends a word or syllable at the end of a line (this was most Cummings's addition) he means that time to pass that it takes the eye—that hair of time suspended—to pick up the next line. If he wishes a pause so light it hardly separates the words, yet does not want a comma—which is an interruption of the meaning rather than the sounding of the line—follow him when he uses a symbol the typewriter has ready to hand:

> What does not change / is the will to change

Observe him, when he takes advantage of the machine's multiple margins, to juxtapose,

```
Sd he:
        to dream takes no effort
            to think is easy
                to act is more difficult
            but for a man to act after he has taken thought, this!
    is the most difficult thing of all
```

Each of these lines is a progressing of both the meaning and the breathing forward, and then a backing up, without a progress or any kind of movement outside the unit of time local to the idea.

There is more to be said in order that this convention be

recognized, especially in order that the revolution out of which it came may be so forwarded that work will get published to offset the reaction now afoot to return verse to inherited forms of cadence and rime. But what I want to emphasize here, by this emphasis on the typewriter as the personal and instantaneous recorder of the poet's work, is the already projective nature of verse as the sons of Pound and Williams are practising it. Already they are composing as though verse was to have the reading its writing involved, as though not the eye but the ear was to be its measurer, as though the intervals of its composition could be so carefully put down as to be precisely the intervals of its registration. For the ear, which once had the burden of memory to quicken it (rime & regular cadence were its aids and have merely lived on in print after the oral necessities were ended) can now again, that the poet has his means, be the threshold of projective verse.

II

Which gets us to what I promised, the degree to which the projective involves a stance toward reality outside a poem as well as a new stance towards the reality of a poem itself. It is a matter of content, the content of Homer or of Euripides or of Seami as distinct from that which I might call the more 'literary' masters. From the moment the projective purpose of the act of verse is recognized, the content does—it will—change. If the beginning and the end is breath, voice in its largest sense, then the material of verse shifts. It has to. It starts with the composer. The dimension of his line itself changes, not to speak of the change in his conceiving, of the matter he will turn to, of the scale in which he imagines that matter's use. I myself would pose the difference by a physical image. It is no accident that Pound and Williams both were involved variously in a movement which got called 'objectivism'. But that word was then used in some sort of a necessary quarrel, I take it, with 'subjectivism'. It is now too late to be bothered with the latter. It has excellently done itself to death, even though we are all caught in its dying. What seems to me a more valid formulation for present use is 'objectism', a word to be taken to stand for the kind of relation of man to experience which a poet might state as the necessity of a line or a work to be as wood is, to be as clean as wood is as it issues from the hand of nature, to be shaped as wood can be when a man has had his hand to it. Objectism is the getting rid of the lyrical interference of the individual as ego, of the 'subject' and his soul, that peculiar presumption by which western man has interposed himself between what he is as a creature of nature (with certain instructions to carry out) and those other creations of nature which we may, with no derogation, call objects. For a man is himself an object, whatever he may take to be his advantages, the more likely to recognize himself as such the greater his advantages, particularly at that moment that he achieves an humilitas sufficient to make him of use.

It comes to this: the use of a man, by himself and thus by others, lies in how he conceives his relation to nature, that force to which he owes his somewhat small existence. If he sprawl, he shall find little to sing but himself, and shall sing, nature has such paradoxical ways, by way of artificial forms outside himself. But if he stays inside himself, if he is contained within his nature as he is participant in the larger force, he will be able to listen, and his hearing through himself will give him secrets objects share. And by an inverse law his shapes will make their own way. It is in this sense that the projective act, which is the artist's act in the larger field of objects, leads to dimensions larger than the man. For a man's problem, the moment he takes speech up in all its fullness, is to give his work his seriousness, a seriousness sufficient to cause the thing he makes to try to take its place alongside the things of nature. This is not easy. Nature works from reverence, even in her destructions (species go down with a crash). But breath is man's special qualification as animal. Sound is a dimension he has extended. Language is one of his proudest acts. And when a poet rests in these as they are in himself (in his physiology, if you like, but the life in him, for all that) then he, if he chooses to speak from these roots, works in that area where nature has given him size, projective size.

It is projective size that the play, *The Trojan Women*, possesses, for it is able to stand, is it not, as its people do, beside the Aegean—and neither Andromache or the sea suffer diminution. In a less 'heroic' but equally 'natural' dimension Seami causes the Fisherman and the Angel to stand clear in *Hagoromo*. And Homer, who is such an unexamined cliché that I do not think I need to press home in what scale Nausicaa's girls wash their clothes.

Such works, I should argue—and I use them simply because their equivalents are yet to be done—could not issue from men who conceived verse without the full relevance of human voice, without reference to where lines come from, in the individual who writes. Nor do I think it accident that, at this end point of the argument, I should use, for examples, two dramatists and an epic poet. For I would hazard the guess that, if projective verse is practised long enough, is driven ahead hard enough along the course I think it dictates, verse again can carry much larger material than it has carried in our language since the Elizabethans. But it can't be jumped. We are only at its beginnings, and if I think that the *Cantos* make more 'dramatic' sense than do the plays of Mr Eliot, it is not because I think they have solved the problem but because the methodology of the verse in them points a way by which, one day, the problem of larger content and of larger forms may be solved. Eliot is, in fact, a proof of a present danger, of 'too easy' a going on the practice of verse as it has been, rather than as it must be, practised. There is no question, for example, that Eliot's line, from 'Prufrock' on down, has speech-force, is 'dramatic', is, in fact, one of the most notable lines since Dryden. I suppose it stemmed immediately to him from Browning, as did so many of Pound's early things. In any case Eliot's line has obvious relations backward to

the Elizabethans, especially to the soliloquy. Yet O. M. Eliot is
not projective. It could even be argued (and I say this carefully,
as I have said all things about the non-projective, having considered how each of us must save himself after his own fashion and
how much, for that matter, each of us owes to the non-
projective, and will continue to owe, as both go alongside each
other) but it could be argued that it is because Eliot has stayed
inside the non-projective that he fails as a dramatist—that his
root is the mind alone, and a scholastic mind at that (no high
intelletto despite his apparent clarities)—and that, in his listenings he has stayed there where the ear and the mind are, has
only gone from his fine ear outward rather than, as I say a
projective poet will, down through the workings of his own
throat to that place where breath comes from, where breath has
its beginnings, where drama has to come from, where, the coincidence is, all act springs.

Letter to Elaine Feinstein

DEAR E. B. FEINSTEIN

Your questions catch me athwart any new sense I might have of
a 'poetics'. The best previous throw I made on it was in *Poetry
NY* some years ago on Projective Open or Field verse versus
Closed, with much on the *line* and the *syllable*.

The basic idea anyway for me is that one, that form is never
any more than an extension of content—a non-literary sense,
certainly. I believe in Truth! (Wahrheit) My sense is that beauty
(Schönheit) better stay in the thingitself: das Ding—Ja!—
macht ring (the attack, I suppose, on the 'completed thought',
or, the Idea, yes? Thus the syntax question: what is the sentence?)

The only advantage of speech rhythms (to take your 2nd
question 1st) is illiteracy: the non-literary, exactly in Dante's
sense of the value of the vernacular over grammar—that speech

as a communicator is prior to the individual and is picked up as soon as and with ma's milk . . . he said nurse's tit. In other words, speech rhythm only as anyone of us has it, if we come on from the line of force as piped in as well as from piping we very much have done up to this moment—if we have, from, that 'common' not grammatical source. The 'source' question is damned interesting today—as Shelley saw, like Dante, that, if it comes in, that way, primary, from Ma there is then a double line of chromosomic giving (A) the inherent speech (thought, power) the 'species', that is; and (B) the etymological: this is where I find 'foreign' languages so wild, especially the Indo-European line with the advantage now that we have Hittite to back up to. I couldn't stress enough on this speech rhythm question the pay-off in *traction* that a non-literate, non-commercial and non-historical constant daily experience of tracking *any* word, practically, one finds oneself using, back along its line of force to Anglo-Saxon, Latin, Greek, and out to Sanskrit, or now, if someone wld do it, some 'dictionary' of roots which wld include Hittite at least.

I'll give in a minute the connection of this to form if capturable in the poem, that is, the usual 'poetics' biz, but excuse me if I hammer shortly the immense help archaeology, and some specific linguistic scholarship—actually, from my experience mainly of such completely different 'grammars' as North American Indians present, in the present syntax hangup: like Hopi. But also Trobriand space-Time premises. And a couple of North California tongues, like Yani. But it is the archaeology *behind* our own history proper, Hittite, for the above reason, but now that Canaanite is known (Ugaritic) and Sumerian, and the direct connection of the Celts to the Aryans and so to the Achaean-Trojan forbears which has *slowed* and opened the speech language thing as we got it, now, in our hands, to make it do more form than how form got set by Sappho & Homer, and hasn't changed much since.

I am talking from a new 'double axis': the replacement of the

Classical-representational by the *primitive-abstract* ((if this all sounds bloody German, excuse the weather, it's from the east today, and wet)). I mean of course not at all primitive in that stupid use of it as opposed to civilized. One means it now as 'primary', as how one finds anything, pick it up as one does new—fresh/first. Thus one is equal across history forward and back, and it's all levy, as present is, but sd that way, one states ... a different space-time. Content, in other words, is also shifted —at least from humanism, as we've had it since the Indo-Europeans got their fid in there (circum 1500 B.C.) ((Note: I'm for 'em on the muse level, and agin 'em on the content, or 'Psyche' side.

Which gets me to yr 1st question—'the use of the Image.' 'the Image' (wow, that you capitalize it makes *sense*: it is *all* we had (post-circum *The Two Noble Kinsmen*), as we had a sterile grammar (an unsufficient 'sentence') we had analogy only: images, no matter how learned or how simple: even Burns say, allowing etc and including Frost! Comparison. Thus representation was never off the dead-spot of description. Nothing was *happening* as of the poem itself—ding and zing or something. It was referential to reality. And that a p. poor crawling actuarial 'real'—good enough to keep banks and insurance companies, plus mediocre governments etc. But not Poetry's *Truth* like my friends from the American Underground cry and spit in the face of 'Time'.

The Image also has to be taken by a double: that is, if you bisect a parabola you get an enantiomorph (The Hopi say what goes on over there isn't happening here therefore it isn't the same: pure 'localism' of space-time, but such localism can now be called: what you find out for yrself (*'istorin*) keeps all accompanying circumstance.

The basic trio wld seem to be: topos/typos/tropos, 3 in 1. The 'blow' hits here, and me, 'bent' as born and of sd one's own decisions for better or worse (allowing clearly, by Jesus Christ, that you do love or go down)
if this sounds 'mystical' I plead so. Wahrheit, I find the contem-

porary substitution of society for the cosmos captive and deathly.

Image, therefore, is vector. It carries the trinity via the double to the single form which one makes oneself able, if so, to issue from the 'content' (multiplicity: originally, and repetitively, chaos—Tiamat: wot the Hindo-Europeans knocked out by giving the Old Man (Juice himself) all the lightning.

The Double, then, (the 'home'/heartland/of the post-Mesopotamians AND the post-Hindo Eees:

At the moment it comes out $\dfrac{\text{the Muse ('world'}}{\text{the Psyche (the 'life'}}$

You wld know already I'm buggy on say the Proper Noun, so much so I wld take it Pun is Rime, all from tope/type/trope, that built in is the connection, in each of us, to Cosmos, and if one taps, via psyche, plus a 'true' adherence of Muse, one does reveal 'Form'

in other words the 'right' (wahr-) proper noun, however apparently idiosyncratic, if 'tested' by one's own experience (out plus in) ought to yield along this phylo-line (as the speech thing, above) because—*decently* what one oneself can know, as well as what the word *means*—ontogenetic.

The other part is certainly 'landscape'—the other part of the double of Image to 'noun'. By Landscape I mean what 'narrative'; scene; event; climax; crisis; hero; development; posture; all that *meant*—all the substantive of what we call literary. To animate the scene today: wow: You say 'orientate me.' Yessir. Place it!

again

I drag it back: Place (topos, plus one's own bent plus what one *can* know, makes it possible to name.

O.K. I'm running out of appetite. Let this swirl—a bit like Crab Nebula—do for now. And please come back on me if you are interested. *Yrs.*

CHARLES OLSON

May 1959

SYLVIA PLATH

An Interview*

ORR. Sylvia, what started you writing poetry?

PLATH. I don't know what *started* me, I just wrote it from the time I was quite small. I guess I liked nursery rhymes and I guess I thought I could do the same thing. I wrote my first poem, my first published poem, when I was eight-and-a-half years old. It came out in *The Boston Traveller* and from then on, I suppose, I've been a bit of a professional.

ORR. What sort of thing did you write about when you began?

PLATH. Nature, I think: birds, bees, spring, fall, all those subjects which are absolute gifts to the person who doesn't have any interior experience to write about. I think the coming of spring, the stars overhead, the first snowfall and so on are gifts for a child, a young poet.

ORR. Now, jumping the years, can you say, are there any themes which particularly attract you as a poet, things that you feel you would like to write about?

PLATH. Perhaps this is an American thing: I've been very excited by what I feel is the new breakthrough that came with, say, Robert Lowell's *Life Studies*, this intense breakthrough into very serious, very personal, emotional experience which I feel has been partly taboo. Robert Lowell's poems about his experience in a mental hospital, for example, interested me very much. These peculiar, private, and taboo subjects, I feel, have been explored in recent American poetry. I think particularly the poetess Ann Sexton, who writes about her experiences as a mother, as a mother who has had a nervous breakdown, is an extremely emotional and feeling young woman and her poems are wonderfully

---

* From *The Poet Speaks*, ed. by Peter Orr.

craftsman-like poems and yet they have a kind of emotional and psychological depth which I think is something perhaps quite new, quite exciting.

ORR. Now you, as a poet, and as a person who straddles the Atlantic, if I can put it that way, being an American yourself. . .

PLATH. That's a rather awkward position, but I'll accept it!

ORR. . . . on which side does your weight fall, if I can pursue the metaphor?

PLATH. Well, I think that as far as language goes I'm an American, I'm afraid, my accent is American, my way of talk is an American way of talk, I'm an old-fashioned American. That's probably one of the reasons why I'm in England now and why I'll always stay in England. I'm about fifty years behind as far as my preferences go and I must say that the poets who excite me most are the Americans. There are very few contemporary English poets that I admire.

ORR. Does this mean that you think contemporary English poetry is behind the times compared with American?

PLATH. No, I think it is in a bit of a strait-jacket, if I may say so. There was an essay by Alvarez, the British critic: his arguments about the dangers of gentility in England are very pertinent, very true. I must say that I am not very genteel and I feel that gentility has a stranglehold: the neatness, the wonderful tidiness, which is so evident everywhere in England is perhaps more dangerous than it would appear on the surface.

ORR. But don't you think, too, that there is this business of English poets who are labouring under the whole weight of something which in block capitals is called 'English Literature'?

PLATH. Yes, I couldn't agree more. I know when I was at Cambridge this appeared to me. Young women would come up to me and say 'How do you dare to write, how do you dare to publish a poem, because of the criticism, the terrible criticism, that falls upon one if one does publish?' And the criticism is not of the poem *as poem*. I remember being appalled when someone criticized me for beginning just like John Donne, but not quite managing to finish like John Donne, and I first felt the full weight of English Literature on me at that point. I think the whole emphasis in England, in universities, on practical criticism (but not that so much as on historical criticism, knowing what period a line comes from) this is almost paralysing. In America, in university, we read—what?—T. S. Eliot, Dylan Thomas, Yeats, that is where we began. Shakespeare flaunted in the background. I'm not sure I agree with this, but I think that for the young poet, the writing poet, it is not quite so frightening to go to university in America as it is in England, for these reasons.

ORR. You say, Sylvia, that you consider yourself an American, but when we listen to a poem like 'Daddy', which talks about Dachau and Auschwitz and *Mein Kampf*, I have the impression that this is the sort of poem that a real American could not have written, because it doesn't mean so much, these names do not mean so much, on the other side of the Atlantic, do they?

PLATH. Well now, you are talking to me as a general American. In particular, my background is, may I say, German and Austrian. On one side I am a first generation American, on one side I'm second generation American, and so my concern with concentration camps and so on is uniquely intense. And then, again, I'm rather a political person as well, so I suppose that's what part of it comes from.

ORR. And as a poet, do you have a great and keen sense of the historic?

PLATH. I am not a historian, but I find myself being more and more fascinated by history and now I find myself reading more and more about history. I am very interested in Napoleon, at the present: I'm very interested in battles, in wars, in Gallipoli, the First World War and so on, and I think that as I age I am becoming more and more historical. I certainly wasn't at all in my early twenties.

ORR. Do your poems tend now to come out of books rather than out of your own life?

PLATH. No, no: I would not say that at all. I think my poems immediately come out of the sensuous and emotional experiences I have, but I must say I cannot sympathize with these cries from the heart that are informed by nothing except a needle or a knife, or whatever it is. I believe that one should be able to control and manipulate experiences, even the most terrifying, like madness, being tortured, this sort of experience, and one should be able to manipulate these experiences with an informed and an intelligent mind. I think that personal experience is very important, but certainly it shouldn't be a kind of shut-box and mirror-looking, narcissistic experience. I believe it should be *relevant*, and relevant to the larger things, the bigger things such as Hiroshima and Dachau and so on.

ORR. And so, behind the primitive, emotional reaction there must be an intellectual discipline.

PLATH. I feel that very strongly: having been an academic, having been tempted by the invitation to stay on to become a Ph.D., a professor, and all that, one side of me certainly does respect all disciplines, as long as they don't ossify.

ORR. What about writers who have influenced you, who have meant a lot to you?

PLATH. There were very few. I find it hard to trace them really. When I was at College I was stunned and astounded by the moderns, by Dylan Thomas, by Yeats, by Auden even: at one point I was absolutely wild for Auden and everything I wrote was desperately Audenesque. Now I again begin to go backwards, I begin to look to Blake, for example. And then, of course, it is presumptuous to say that one is influenced by someone like Shakespeare: one reads Shakespeare, and that is that.

ORR. Sylvia, one notices in reading your poems and listening to your poems that there are two qualities which emerge very quickly and clearly; one is their lucidity (and I think these two qualities have something to do one with the other), their lucidity and the impact they make on reading. Now, do you consciously design your poems to be both lucid and to be effective when they are read aloud?

PLATH. This is something I didn't do in my earlier poems. For example, my first book, *The Colossus*, I can't read any of the poems aloud now. I didn't write them to be read aloud. They, in fact, quite privately, bore me. These ones that I have just read, the ones that are very recent, I've got to say them, I speak them to myself, and I think that this in my own writing development is quite a new thing with me, and whatever lucidity they may have comes from the fact that I say them to myself, I say them aloud.

ORR. Do you think this is an essential ingredient of a good poem, that it should be able to be read aloud effectively?

PLATH. Well, I do feel that now and I feel that this development of recording poems, of speaking poems at readings, of having records of poets, I think this is a wonderful thing. I'm very excited by it. In a sense, there's a return, isn't there, to the old role of the poet, which was to speak to a group of people, to come across.

ORR. Or to sing to a group?

PLATH. To sing to a group of people, exactly.

ORR. Setting aside poetry for a moment, are there other things you would like to write, or that you have written?

PLATH. Well, I always was interested in prose. As a teenager, I published short stories. And I always wanted to write the long short story, I wanted to write a novel. Now that I have attained, shall I say, a respectable age, and have had experiences, I feel much more interested in prose, in the novel. I feel that in a novel, for example, you can get in toothbrushes and all the paraphernalia that one finds in daily life, and I find this more difficult in poetry. Poetry, I feel, is a tyrannical discipline, you've got to go so far, so fast, in such a small space that you've just got to turn away all the peripherals. And I miss them! I'm a woman, I like my little *Lares* and *Penates*, I like trivia, and I find that in a novel I can get more of life, perhaps not such intense life, but certainly more of life, and so I've become very interested in novel writing as a result.

ORR. This is almost a Dr Johnson sort of view, isn't it? What was it he said, 'There are some things that are fit for inclusion in poetry and others which are not'?

PLATH. Well, of course, as a poet I would say pouf! I would say everything should be able to come into a poem, but I *can't* put toothbrushes into a poem, I really can't!

ORR. Do you find yourself much in the company of other writers, of poets?

PLATH. I much prefer doctors, midwives, lawyers, anything but writers. I think writers and artists are the most narcissistic people. I mustn't say this, I like many of them, in fact a great many of my friends happen to be writers and artists. But I must say what I admire most is the person who masters an area of practical experience, and can teach me something. I mean, my local midwife has taught me how to keep bees. Well, she can't understand anything I write. And I find myself liking her, may I say, more than most poets. And among my friends I find people who know all about boats or know all about certain sports, or how to cut somebody open and remove an organ. I'm fascinated by this mastery of the practical. As a poet, one lives a bit on air. I always like someone who can teach me something practical.

ORR. Is there anything else you would rather have done than writing poetry? Because this is something, obviously, which takes up a great deal of one's private life, if one's going to succeed at it. Do you ever have any lingering regrets that you didn't do something else?

PLATH. I think if I had done anything else I would like to have been a doctor. This is the sort of polar opposition to being a writer, I suppose. My best friends when I was young were always doctors. I used to dress up in a white gauze helmet and go round and see babies born and cadavers cut open. This fascinated me, but I could never bring myself to disciplining myself to the point where I could learn all the details that one has to learn to be a good doctor. This is the sort of opposition: somebody who deals directly with human experiences, is able to cure, to mend, to help, this sort of thing. I suppose if I have any nostalgias it's this, but I console myself because I know so many doctors. And I may say, perhaps, I'm happier writing about doctors than I would have been being one.

ORR. But basically this thing, the writing of poetry, is something which has been a great satisfaction to you in your life, is it?

PLATH. Oh, satisfaction! I don't think I could live without it. It's like water or bread, or something absolutely essential to me. I find myself absolutely fulfilled when I have written a poem, when I'm writing one. Having written one, then you fall away very rapidly from having been a poet to becoming a sort of poet in rest, which isn't the same thing at all. But I think the actual experience of writing a poem is a magnificent one.

30 October 1962.

EZRA POUND

A Retrospect*

There has been so much scribbling about a new fashion in poetry, that I may perhaps be pardoned this brief recapitulation and retrospect.

In the spring or early summer of 1912, 'H. D.', Richard Aldington, and myself decided that we were agreed upon the three principles following:

(1) Direct treatment of the 'thing' whether subjective or objective.

(2) To use absolutely no word that does not contribute to the presentation.

(3) As regarding rhythm: to compose in the sequence of the musical phrase, not in sequence of a metronome.

Upon many points of taste and of predilection we differed, but agreeing upon these three positions we thought we had as much right to a group name, at least as much right, as a number of French 'schools' proclaimed by Mr Flint in the August number of Harold Monro's magazine for 1911.

This school has since been 'joined' or 'followed' by numerous people who, whatever their merits, do not show any signs of agreeing with the second specification. Indeed *vers libre* has become as prolix and as verbose as any of the flaccid varieties that preceded it. It has brought faults of its own. The actual language and phrasing is often as bad as that of our elders without even the excuse that the words are shovelled in to fill a metric pattern or to complete the noise of a rhyme-sound. Whether or no the phrases followed by the followers are musical

---

* A group of early essays and notes which appeared under this title in *Pavannes and Divisions* (1918). 'A Few Don'ts' was first printed in *Poetry*, I: 6 (March 1913). From *The Literary Essays of Ezra Pound*.

must be left to the reader's decision. At times I can find a marked metre in 'vers libres' as stale and hackneyed as any pseudo-Swinburnian, at times the writers seem to follow no musical structure whatever. But it is, on the whole, good that the field should be ploughed. Perhaps a few good poems have come from the new method, and if so it is justified.

Criticism is not a circumscription or a set of prohibitions. It provides fixed points of departure. It may startle a dull reader into alertness. That little of it which is good is mostly in stray phrases; or if it be an older artist helping a younger it is in great measure but rules of thumb, cautions gained by experience.

I set together a few phrases on practical working about the time the first remarks on imagisme were published. The first use of the word 'Imagiste' was in my note to T. E. Hulme's five poems, printed at the end of my *Ripostes* in the autumn of 1912. I reprint my cautions from *Poetry* for March 1913.

A FEW DON'TS

An 'Image' is that which presents an intellectual and emotional complex in an instant of time. I use the term 'complex' rather in the technical sense employed by the newer psychologists, such as Hart, though we might not agree absolutely in our application.

It is the presentation of such a 'complex' instantaneously which gives that sense of sudden liberation; that sense of freedom from time limits and space limits; that sense of sudden growth, which we experience in the presence of the greatest works of art.

It is better to present one Image in a lifetime than to produce voluminous works.

All this, however, some may consider open to debate. The immediate necessity is to tabulate A LIST OF DON'TS for those beginning to write verses. I can not put all of them into Mosaic negative.

To begin with, consider the three propositions (demanding

direct treatment, economy of words, and the sequence of the musical phrase), not as dogma—never consider anything as dogma—but as the result of long contemplation, which, even if it is someone else's contemplation, may be worth consideration.

Pay no attention to the criticism of men who have never themselves written a notable work. Consider the discrepancies between the actual writing of the Greek poets and dramatists, and the theories of the Graeco-Roman grammarians, concocted to explain their metres.

LANGUAGE

Use no superfluous word, no adjective which does not reveal something.

Don't use such an expression as 'dim lands *of peace*'. It dulls the image. It mixes an abstraction with the concrete. It comes from the writer's not realizing that the natural object is always the *adequate* symbol.

Go in fear of abstractions. Do not retell in mediocre verse what has already been done in good prose. Don't think any intelligent person is going to be deceived when you try to shirk all the difficulties of the unspeakably difficult art of good prose by chopping your composition into line lengths.

What the expert is tired of today the public will be tired of tomorrow.

Don't imagine that the art of poetry is any simpler than the art of music, or that you can please the expert before you have spent at least as much effort on the art of verse as the average piano teacher spends on the art of music.

Be influenced by as many great artists as you can, but have the decency either to acknowledge the debt outright, or to try to conceal it.

Don't allow 'influence' to mean merely that you mop up the particular decorative vocabulary of some one or two poets whom you happen to admire. A Turkish war correspondent was recently caught red-handed babbling in his dispatches of 'dove-grey' hills, or else it was 'pearl-pale', I can not remember.

Use either no ornament or good ornament.

RHYTHM AND RHYME

Let the candidate fill his mind with the finest cadences he can discover, preferably in a foreign language,[1] so that the meaning of the words may be less likely to divert his attention from the movement; e.g., Saxon charms, Hebridean Folk Songs, the verse of Dante, and the lyrics of Shakespeare—if he can dissociate the vocabulary from the cadence. Let him dissect the lyrics of Goethe coldly into their component sound values, syllables long and short, stressed and unstressed, into vowels and consonants.

It is not necessary that a poem should rely on its music, but if it does rely on its music that music must be such as will delight the expert.

Let the neophyte know assonance and alliteration, rhyme immediate and delayed, simple and polyphonic, as a musician would expect to know harmony and counterpoint and all the minutiae of his craft. No time is too great to give to these matters or to any one of them, even if the artist seldom have need of them.

Don't imagine that a thing will 'go' in verse just because it's too dull to go in prose.

Don't be 'viewy'—leave that to the writers of pretty little philosophic essays. Don't be descriptive; remember that the painter can describe a landscape much better than you can, and that he has to know a deal more about it.

When Shakespeare talks of the 'Dawn in russet mantle clad' he presents something which the painter does not present. There is in this line of his nothing that one can call description; he presents.

---

[1] This is for rhythm, his vocabulary must of course be found in his native tongue. (E.P.)

Consider the way of the scientists rather than the way of an advertising agent for a new soap.

The scientist does not expect to be acclaimed as a great scientist until he has *discovered* something. He begins by learning what has been discovered already. He goes from that point onward. He does not bank on being a charming fellow personally. He does not expect his friends to applaud the results of his freshman class work. Freshmen in poetry are unfortunately not confined to a definite and recognizable class room. They are 'all over the shop'. Is it any wonder 'the public is indifferent to poetry'?

Don't chop your stuff into separate *iambs*. Don't make each line stop dead at the end, and then begin every next line with a heave. Let the beginning of the next line catch the rise of the rhythm wave, unless you want a definite longish pause.

In short, behave as a musician, a good musician, when dealing with that phase of your art which has exact parallels in music. The same laws govern, and you are bound by no others.

Naturally, your rhythmic structure should not destroy the shape of your words, or their natural sound, or their meaning. It is improbable that, at the start, you will be able to get a rhythm-structure strong enough to affect them very much, though you may fall a victim to all sorts of false stopping due to line ends and cæsurae.

The Musician can rely on pitch and the volume of the orchestra. You can not. The term harmony is misapplied in poetry; it refers to simultaneous sounds of different pitch. There is, however, in the best verse a sort of residue of sound which remains in the ear of the hearer and acts more or less as an organ-base.

A rhyme must have in it some slight element of surprise if it is to give pleasure; it need not be bizarre or curious, but it must be well used if used at all.

Vide further Vildrac and Duhamel's notes on rhyme in *Technique Poétique*.

That part of your poetry which strikes upon the imaginative *eye* of the reader will lose nothing by translation into a foreign tongue; that which appeals to the ear can reach only those who take it in the original.

Consider the definiteness of Dante's presentation, as compared with Milton's rhetoric. Read as much of Wordsworth as does not seem too unutterably dull.[2]

If you want the gist of the matter go to Sappho, Catullus, Villon, Heine when he is in the vein, Gautier when he is not too frigid; or, if you have not the tongues, seek out the leisurely Chaucer. Good prose will do you no harm, and there is good discipline to be had by trying to write it.

Translation is likewise good training, if you find that your original matter 'wobbles' when you try to rewrite it. The meaning of the poem to be translated can not 'wobble'.

If you are using a symmetrical form, don't put in what you want to say and then fill up the remaining vacuums with slush.

Don't mess up the perception of one sense by trying to define it in terms of another. This is usually only the result of being too lazy to find the exact word. To this clause there are possibly exceptions.

The first three simple prescriptions will throw out nine-tenths of all the bad poetry now accepted as standard and classic; and will prevent you from many a crime of production.

'. . . *Mais d'abord il faut être un poète*', as MM. Duhamel and Vildrac have said at the end of their little book, *Notes sur la Technique Poétique.*

Since March 1913, Ford Madox Hueffer has pointed out that Wordsworth was so intent on the ordinary or plain word that he never thought of hunting for *le mot juste.*

John Butler Yeats has handled or man-handled Wordsworth and the Victorians, and his criticism, contained in letters to his son, is now printed and available.

---

[2] Vide infra. (E.P.)

I do not like writing *about* art, my first, at least I think it was my first essay on the subject, was a protest against it.

PROLEGOMENA[3]

Time was when the poet lay in a green field with his head against a tree and played his diversion on a ha'penny whistle, and Caesar's predecessors conquered the earth, and the predecessors of golden Crassus embezzled, and fashions had their say, and let him alone. And presumably he was fairly content in this circumstance, for I have small doubt that the occasional passerby, being attracted by curiosity to know why anyone should lie under a tree and blow diversion on a ha'penny whistle, came and conversed with him, and that among these passersby there was on occasion a person of charm or a young lady who had not read *Man and Superman*; and looking back upon this naive state of affairs we call it the age of gold.

Metastasio, and he should know if anyone, assures us that this age endures—even though the modern poet is expected to holloa his verses down a speaking tube to the editors of cheap magazines—S. S. McClure, or someone of that sort—even though hordes of authors meet in dreariness and drink healths to the 'Copyright Bill'; even though these things be, the age of gold pertains. Imperceivably, if you like, but pertains. You meet unkempt Amyclas in a Soho restaurant and chant together of dead and forgotten things—it is a manner of speech among poets to chant of dead, half-forgotten things, there seems no special harm in it; it has always been done—and it's rather better to be a clerk in the Post Office than to look after a lot of stinking, verminous sheep—and at another hour of the day one substitutes the drawing-room for the restaurant and tea is probably more palatable than mead and mare's milk, and little cakes than honey. And in this fashion one survives the resignation of Mr

---

[3] *Poetry and Drama* (then the *Poetry Review*, edited by Harold Monro), Feb. 1912. (E.P.)

Balfour, and the iniquities of the American customs-house, *e quel bufera infernal*, the periodical press. And then in the middle of it, there being apparently no other person at once capable and available one is stopped and asked to explain oneself.

I begin on the chord thus querulous, for I would much rather lie on what is left of Catullus's parlour floor and speculate the azure beneath it and the hills off to Salo and Riva with their forgotten gods moving unhindered amongst them, than discuss any processes and theories of art whatsover. I would rather play tennis. I shall not argue.

CREDO

Rhythm.—I believe in an 'absolute rhythm', a rhythm, that is, in poetry which corresponds exactly to the emotion or shade of emotion to be expressed. A man's rhythm must be interpretative, it will be, therefore, in the end, his own, uncounterfeiting, uncounterfeitable.

Symbols.—I believe that the proper and perfect symbol is the natural object, that if a man use 'symbols' he must so use them that their symbolic function does not obtrude; so that *a* sense, and the poetic quality of the passage, is not lost to those who do not understand the symbol as such, to whom, for instance, a hawk is a hawk.

Technique.—I believe in technique as the test of a man's sincerity; in law when it is ascertainable; in the trampling down of every convention that impedes or obscures the determination of the law, or the precise rendering of the impulse.

Form.—I think there is a 'fluid' as well as a 'solid' content, that some poems may have form as a tree has form, some as water poured into a vase. That most symmetrical forms have certain uses. That a vast number of subjects cannot be precisely, and therefore not properly rendered in symmetrical forms.

'Thinking that alone worthy wherein the whole art is employed'.[4] I think the artist should master all known forms and

---

[4] Dante, *De Volgari Eloquio*. (E.P.)

systems of metric, and I have with some persistence set about doing this, searching particularly into those periods wherein the systems came to birth or attained their maturity. It has been complained, with some justice, that I dump my note-books on the public. I think that only after a long struggle will poetry attain such a degree of development, or, if you will, modernity, that it will vitally concern people who are accustomed, in prose, to Henry James and Anatole France, in music to Debussy. I am constantly contending that it took two centuries of Provence and one of Tuscany to develop the media of Dante's masterwork, that it took the latinists of the Renaissance, and the Pleiade, and his own age of painted speech to prepare Shakespeare his tools. It is tremendously important that great poetry be written, it makes no jot of difference who writes it. The experimental demonstrations of one man may save the time of many—hence my furore over Arnaut Daniel—if a man's experiments try out one new rime, or dispense conclusively with one iota of currently accepted nonsense, he is merely playing fair with his colleagues when he chalks up his result.

No man ever writes very much poetry that 'matters'. In bulk, that is, no one produces much that is final, and when a man is not doing this highest thing, this saying the thing once for all and perfectly; when he is not matching Ποικιλόθρον', ἀθάνατ 'Αφρόδιτα,[5] or 'Hist—said Kate the Queen', he had much better be making the sorts of experiment which may be of use to him in his later work, or to his successors.

'The lyf so short, the craft so long to lerne.' It is a foolish thing for a man to begin his work on a too narrow foundation, it is a disgraceful thing for a man's work not to show steady growth and increasing fineness from first to last.

As for 'adaptations'; one finds that all the old masters of painting recommend to their pupils that they begin by copying masterwork, and proceed to their own composition.

---

[5] ['Splendid-throned, deathless Aphrodite': the opening line of Sappho's famous invocation.]

As for 'Every man his own poet', the more every man knows about poetry the better. I believe in every one writing poetry who wants to; most do. I believe in every man knowing enough of music to play 'God Bless Our Home' on the harmonium, but I do not believe in every man giving concerts and printing his sin.

The mastery of any art is the work of a lifetime. I should not discriminate between the 'amateur' and the 'professional'. Or rather I should discriminate quite often in favour of the amateur, but I should discriminate between the amateur and the expert. It is certain that the present chaos will endure until the Art of poetry has been preached down the amateur gullet, until there is such a general understanding of the fact that poetry is an art and not a pastime; such a knowledge of technique; of technique of surface and technique of content, that the amateurs will cease to try to drown out the masters.

If a certain thing was said once for all in Atlantis or Arcadia, in 450 Before Christ or in 1290 after, it is not for us moderns to go saying it over, or to go obscuring the memory of the dead by saying the same thing with less skill and less conviction.

My pawing over the ancients and semi-ancients has been one struggle to find out what has been done, once for all, better than it can ever be done again, and to find out what remains for us to do, and plenty does remain, for if we still feel the same emotions as those which launched the thousand ships, it is quite certain that we come on these feelings differently, through different nuances, by different intellectual gradations. Each age has its own abounding gifts yet only some ages transmute them into matter of duration. No good poetry is ever written in a manner twenty years old, for to write in such a manner shows conclusively that the writer thinks from books, convention, and cliché, and not from life, yet a man feeling the divorce of life and his art may naturally try to resurrect a forgotten mode if he finds in that mode some leaven, or if he think he sees in it some element lacking in contemporary art which might unite that art again to its sustenance, life.

In the art of Daniel and Cavalcanti, I have seen that precision which I miss in the Victorians, that explicit rendering, be it of external nature, or of emotion. Their testimony is of the eyewitness, their symptoms are first hand.

As for the nineteenth century, with all respect to its achievements, I think we shall look back upon it as a rather blurry, messy sort of a period, a rather sentimentalistic, mannerish sort of a period. I say this without any self-righteousness, with no self-satisfaction.

As for there being a 'movement' or my being of it, the conception of poetry as a 'pure art' in the sense in which I use the term, revived with Swinburne. From the puritanical revolt to Swinburne, poetry had been merely the vehicle—yes, definitely, Arthur Symon's scruples and feelings about the word not withholding—the ox-cart and post-chaise for transmitting thoughts poetic or otherwise. And perhaps the 'great Victorians', though it is doubtful, and assuredly the 'nineties' continued the development of the art, confining their improvements, however, chiefly to sound and to refinements of manner.

Mr Yeats has once and for all stripped English poetry of its perdamnable rhetoric. He has boiled away all that is not poetic —and a good deal that is. He has become a classic in his own lifetime and *nel mezzo del cammin*. He has made our poetic idiom a thing pliable, a speech without inversions.

Robert Bridges, Maurice Hewlett, and Frederic Manning are[6] in their different ways seriously concerned with overhauling the metric, in testing the language and its adaptability to certain modes. Ford Hueffer is making some sort of experiments in modernity. The Provost of Oriel continues his translation of the *Divina Commedia*.

As to Twentieth-century poetry, and the poetry which I expect to see written during the next decade or so, it will, I think, move against poppy-cock, it will be harder and saner, it will be what Mr Hewlett calls 'nearer the bone'. It will be as much like

---

[6] (Dec. 1911). (E.P.)

granite as it can be, its force will lie in its truth, its interpretative power (of course, poetic force does always rest there); I mean it will not try to seem forcible by rhetorical din, and luxurious riot. We will have fewer painted adjectives impeding the shock and stroke of it. At least for myself, I want it so, austere, direct, free from emotional slither.

What is there now, in 1917, to be added?

RE VERS LIBRE

I think the desire for vers libre is due to the sense of quantity reasserting itself after years of starvation. But I doubt if we can take over, for English, the rules of quantity laid down for Greek and Latin, mostly by Latin grammarians.

I think one should write vers libre only when one 'must', that is to say, only when the 'thing' builds up a rhythm more beautiful than that of set metres, or more real, more a part of the emotion of the 'thing', more germane, intimate, interpretative than the measure of regular accentual verse; a rhythm which discontents one with set iambic or set anapæstic.

Eliot has said the thing very well when he said, 'No *vers* is *libre* for the man who wants to do a good job.'

As a matter of detail, there is vers libre with accent heavily marked as a drum-beat (as par example my 'Dance Figure'), and on the other hand I think I have gone as far as can profitably be gone in the other direction (and perhaps too far). I mean I do not think one can use to any advantage rhythms much more tenuous and imperceptible than some I have used. I think progress lies rather in an attempt to approximate classical quantitative metres (NOT to copy them) than in a carelessness regarding such things.[7]

I agree with John Yeats on the relation of beauty to certitude. I prefer satire, which is due to emotion, to any sham of emotion.

---

[7] Let me date this statement 20 Aug. 1917. (E.P.)

I have had to write, or at least I have written a good deal about art, sculpture, painting, and poetry. I have seen what seemed to me the best of contemporary work reviled and obstructed. Can anyone write prose of permanent or durable interest when he is merely saying for one year what nearly every one will say at the end of three or four years? I have been battistrada for a sculptor, a painter, a novelist, several poets. I wrote also of certain French writers in *The New Age* in nineteen twelve or eleven.

I would much rather that people would look at Brzeska's sculpture and Lewis's drawings, and that they would read Joyce, Jules Romains, Eliot, than that they should read what I have said of these men, or that I should be asked to republish argumentative essays and reviews.

All that the critic can do for the reader or audience or spectator is to focus his gaze or audition. Rightly or wrongly I think my blasts and essays have done their work, and that more people are now likely to go to the sources than are likely to read this book.

Jammes's 'Existences' in *La Triomphe de la Vie* is available. So are his early poems. I think we need a convenient anthology rather than descriptive criticism. Carl Sandburg wrote me from Chicago, 'It's hell when poets can't afford to buy each other's books.' Half the people who care, only borrow. In America so few people know each other that the difficulty lies more than half in distribution. Perhaps one should make an anthology: Romains's 'Un Etre en Marche' and 'Prières', Vildrac's 'Visite'. Retrospectively the fine wrought work of Laforgue, the flashes of Rimbaud, the hard-bit lines of Tristan Corbière, Tailhade's sketches in 'Poèmes Aristophanesques', the 'Litanies' of De Gourmont.

It is difficult at all times to write of the fine arts, it is almost impossible unless one can accompany one's prose with many reproductions. Still I would seize this chance or any chance to reaffirm my belief in Wyndham Lewis's genius, both in his drawings and his writings. And I would name an out of the way prose book, the *Scenes and Portraits* of Frederic Manning, as well as James Joyce's short stories and novel, *Dubliners* and the now well-known *Portrait of the Artist*, as well as Lewis's *Tarr*, if, that is, I may treat my strange reader as if he were a new friend come into the room, intent on ransacking my bookshelf.

ONLY EMOTION ENDURES

'Only emotion endures.' Surely it is better for me to name over the few beautiful poems that still ring in my head than for me to search my flat for back numbers of periodicals and rearrange all that I have said about friendly and hostile writers.

The first twelve lines of Padraic Colum's 'Drover'; his 'O Woman shapely as a swan, on your account I shall not die'; Joyce's 'I hear an army'; the lines of Yeats that ring in my head and in the heads of all young men of my time who care for poetry: Braseal and the Fisherman, 'The fire that stirs about her, when she stirs'; the later lines of 'The Scholars', the faces of the Magi, William Carlos Williams's 'Postlude', Aldington's version of 'Atthis', and 'H. D.'s' waves like pine tops, and her verse in *Des Imagistes* the first anthology; Hueffer's 'How red your lips are' in his translation from Von der Vogelweide, his 'Three Ten', the general effect of his 'On Heaven'; his sense of the prose values or prose qualities in poetry; his ability to write poems that half-chant and are spoiled by a musician's additions; beyond these a poem by Alice Corbin, 'One City Only', and another ending 'But sliding water over a stone'. These things have worn smooth in my head and I am not through with them, nor with Aldington's 'In Via Sestina' nor his other poems in *Des Imagistes*, though people have told me their flaws. It may be that their content is too much embedded in me for me to look back at the words.

I am almost a different person when I come to take up the argument for Eliot's poems.

ALFRED PURDY

*An Interview**

INTERVIEWER. Somehow your poetry manages to be domestic and historical at the same time. Is this what critics mean by calling it epic?

PURDY. 'Rooms for rent in the outer planets.' Yes, but I don't think its epic. Epic sounds grandiose to me; and I don't think I'm grandiose. I certainly hope I'm not.

INTERVIEWER. In 'The Country North of Belleville' there is a sense of beauty and terror in the description. Do you find the Canadian landscape hostile?

PURDY. Landscapes hostile to man? I think man is hostile to himself. Landscapes, I think, are essentially neutral.

INTERVIEWER. But you travel a lot, as do many Canadian writers, and write about the places you visit. Is this because it is easier to control the elements of a newer, smaller area?

PURDY. Easier than Canada, you mean? No, it isn't that. I have the feeling that—before I worked at jobs and described the places where I was and the people that I met, etc.—that somehow or other one uses up one's past. It isn't that when one goes to another country one is consciously seeking for new poems, because it would get to sounding as goddam self-conscious as hell. For instance, if you go to Baffin Island to write poems (which I did, incidentally) . . . well, I don't like to look at it that way. I'm interested in going to Baffin Island because I'm interested in Baffin Island.

INTERVIEWER. And the poems just happen.

PURDY. I write poems like spiders spin webs, and perhaps for much the same reason: to support my existence. I talk, I eat, I

---

* This interview with Gary Geddes took place in the summer of 1968.

write poems, I make love—I do all these things self-consciously. The 'new area' bit . . . well, unless one is a stone one doesn't sit still. And perhaps new areas of landscape awake old areas of one's self. One has seen the familiar landscape (perhaps) so many times that one ceases to really see it. Maybe it's like the expatriate writers, Joyce and so on, who went to foreign countries in order to see their own.

INTERVIEWER. You have been called the great Canadian realist (to drag one from the bottom of the bag). Do you write any poems which *don't* have some base in actual experience?

PURDY. Aren't you talking about poets like Mallarmé? Very few poets do that. I've written poems about things, even doorknobs, but generally speaking it's out of my own life.

INTERVIEWER. Do you feel at ease to 'cook' your experiences for the sake of a poem?

PURDY. After you've lived your whole life writing poetry (and I started writing at thirteen), I think you've always got one ear cocked, listening to know if you're good enough to put it into a poem. Do you mean, to be wholly involved in the experience without seeing it as something else? No, I don't think so, if that's what you mean. I always know what I'm doing or feeling or seeing. I'm self-conscious about being self-conscious about being self-conscious.

INTERVIEWER. In your 'Lament for Robert Kennedy' there seems to be a qualitative difference between the first part of the poem, where you are dependent for the most part upon rhetoric and abstraction, and the second part, where the images and language become personal and concrete. Do you think that your poetry is strongest when it is attached to images from your own landscape?

PURDY. Yes, I think so. I was being pretty propagandist in the early part of that poem; but, also, when you say there's nothing concrete in it, how about the skidrow losers with the bottle of good booze in their hands like a lily? Yes, I generally stick to the concrete or get to it pretty quick. You can start from the concrete, but I don't think you can take off from no stance at all.

INTERVIEWER. I especially like your poem, 'Portrait', about Irving Layton. What did you mean in the last line?

PURDY. I don't remember the last line, frankly. What is it?

INTERVIEWER. 'And then again I'm a bit disappointed.'

PURDY. Well, I think the thought on my mind was that somebody had fixed themselves, pinned themselves down, taken a stance, identified themselves far too fully. I don't think . . . in my own case I like to think of a continual becoming and a changing and a moving. I feel that Irving takes such positive stances that I'm a little disappointed, because I think he could have done much better. For instance, now he's writing poems in *The Shattered Plinths* about various new events, about violence. Violence is a damned interesting subject, but not the way he's treated it somehow. Everything about Irving is positive; if you were to argue with him on any of these points, he'd defend them all vehemently. You wouldn't be able to win the argument, but he'd still be wrong.

INTERVIEWER. Is it a general characteristic of modern poets to *find* themselves too quickly? Creeley, for example, seems to have established a voice or a style which he exploits; one wonders whether the style reflects or *directs* the life-rhythms.

PURDY. I only know a bit about Creeley. I don't *like* his style very much; I don't like the deliberate ambiguities at the ends of his poems. But style is something that I was very hung up on a few years ago, when I kept noticing, or thought I did, that all the critics were insisting that you find your voice, that you find *a* consistency, and that you stick to it. Now this, of course, is what Creeley has done; and it's apparently something the critics still approve of. I disagree with it all along the line. I don't think that a man is consistent; he contradicts himself at every turn. Housman, for instance, takes a very dim view of life for the most part, is very depressing—but human life isn't like that *all* of the time. You wake up in the morning, the sun is shining and you feel good; this also is a time when Housman could have written a poem. I can't believe he never felt good once in his life. Anyway, I disagree with this consistency bit very strongly.

INTERVIEWER. Would you not say that the success of *The Cariboo Horses* has something to do with *your* having finally found some kind of voice or consistency?

PURDY. As far as I'm concerned, I found *a* voice (not necessarily a consistent one), but I thought that I was at my best beginning about 1961-2, when *Poems for All the Annettes* was first published; I was sure I had hit a vein in which I could say many more things. I'd been looking for ways and means of doing it; and finally, it got to the point that I didn't care what I said—I'd say anything—as long as it worked for me.

INTERVIEWER. How consciously are you concerned with technique? Do you share the recent technical interests of Williams and Olson, such as concern for the line, the syllable, the process of breathing?

PURDY. My technique, I suppose, takes a bit from Williams, a bit from Olson; for instance, I agree for the most part with using the contemporary, the modern, idiom. On the other hand, if I were writing a certain kind of poem I might avoid colloquialisms, idiosyncrasies, slang, and so on. It just depends; it all has to do with the poem. No, I pay no attention to the breathing bit; and I never compose on a typewriter, as Olson is supposed to do. Most of the time when I'm writing I don't think of how to write the thing at all, consciously; sometimes I do. When I wrote a poem about hockey players, I deliberately put in swift rhythms to simulate the players going down the ice. And there are times when I've mixed up rhythms deliberately. But other times, whatever rhythm you get in there seems accidental; though I don't suppose it is, because a poet writes a lot of poems. I'm concerned with techniques, yes, but I don't consciously spend so much time thinking of them as Williams and Olson do.

INTERVIEWER. What is it that makes a poem work?

PURDY. Technique? The language itself is part of that, also the various methods used to write a poem. But somehow saying that is not enough. There ought to be a quality in a good poet beyond any analysis, the part of his mind that leaps from one point to another, sideways, backwards, ass-over-the-electric-kettle. This quality is not logic, and the result may not be consistent with the rest of the poem when it happens, though it may be. I believe it is said by medicos that much of the human mind has no known function. Perhaps the leap sideways and backwards comes from there. At any rate, it seems to me the demands made on it cause the mind to stretch, to do more than it is capable of under ordinary and different circumstances. And when this happens, or when you think it does, that time is joyous, and you experience something beyond experience. Like discovering you can fly, or that relative truth may blossom into an absolute. And the absolute must be attacked again and again, until you find something that will stand up, may not be denied, which becomes a compass point by which to move somewhere else. I think that when you put such things into words they are liable to sound like pretentious jargon. Such things exist in your mind without conscious thought, perhaps in that unknown area. And sometimes—if you're lucky—a coloured fragment may slip through into the light when you're writing a poem.

INTERVIEWER. How do your poems generally take shape?

PURDY. Well, that's tough. I wrote the title poem of *The Cariboo Horses* in about twenty minutes, revised it a little, and that was about it; and I took about eight years to write another poem in the same book, which still isn't as good as it ought to be. In the hockey-player poem, I wanted a strong contrast between the metrics and prose; and I tried to make several passages about as prosy as possible in order to contrast with the swift metrical rhythms.

INTERVIEWER. Could you describe the evolution of a single poem?

PURDY. Well, there used to be an old grist mill in Ameliasburg village—four stories high with three-foot-thick walls of grey stone. In 1957-8 I explored that mill from top to bottom, trying to visualize the people who used to operate it. Marvelling at the 24-inch wide boards from nineteenth-century pine forests; peering curiously at wooden cogs and hand-carved gears, flour-sifting apparatus, bits of rotting silk-screens, and so on.

My interest in the mill grew to a strong curiosity about the people who built it—what were they like?—those old farmers, pioneers, dwellers in deep woods, men who worked from dawn to day's end, so tired the whole world wavered and reeled in their home-going vision. Most of the old ones were United Empire Loyalists, come here to the wilderness after the American Revolution because they had no other place to go. The man who built the village mill in 1842 was Owen Roblin. He lived to be ninety-seven, and lies buried in Ameliasburg graveyard near the black millpond, with wife and scattered brood of sons nearby.

I questioned the old people in the village about Owen Roblin. It seems . . . well, out of it all came my poem, 'Roblin's Mills'.

INTERVIEWER. More than thirty poems in *The Cariboo Horses* are open-ended, concluding with a dash or some other punctuation suggesting incompleteness. Is this simply a device?

PURDY. The open-endedness is both device and philosophy, but it doesn't bar formalism if I feel like it: i.e., I reject nothing. No form, that is, *if* I feel like it and the poem agrees. I was doing it a good deal at the time; maybe that owes something to Olson's 'in the field' bit—a line is as long as it's right for it to be. But I don't like periods very much; if I can work a lot using commas and semi-colons I will. It should just be taken as the reader takes it: I don't attach much more to it than just dispensing with punctuation. Its effect, of course, is different from punctuation, but I haven't gone into that. My own poems *without* this give me a peculiar feeling I can't explain.

INTERVIEWER. The experience that goes into a poem is changing even as the poem is written; in fact, the poem *changes* the experience.

PURDY. You mean *fixes* it.

INTERVIEWER. No, I mean that the open-endedness works against the final fixing of the experience.

PURDY. Well, yes, *you* said it. I have thought of that, but not in connection with these poems. One thinks of poems as little bits of life cut out, except that they are as one sees life with one's mind. You have the odd feeling that you can reach back and pick a poem that will take the place of that experience in the past. It does in one's life of course, but there are so many ifs and buts that when I say a thing I'm never sure if I'm right.

INTERVIEWER. Is poetry a way of exploring experience for you?

PURDY. Jesus Christ, that's an awful question! I've no idea. I like to write poetry; I get a kick out of writing poems. I suppose to a limited degree it does explore my own experience; but if anybody else was looking, they would deny that the poem described it, I expect, particularly my wife. I write poetry because I *like* to write poetry. It's much like getting drunk once in a while, especially if you write something you like. Exploring one's experience sounds like such a terrible way to describe a simple thing like writing a poem. Doesn't it though?

INTERVIEWER. As a descriptive poet, what is your response to external objects?

PURDY. In the first place, I don't consider myself any particular kind of poet. About objects in relation to myself, this is as subjective as hell. Any time any poet writes about an object, he's got to be subjective, no matter how objective he appears. I've sometimes thought that everybody sees the same colour differently. One isn't always able to express these differences in words, since words are so limited and have such large potential at the same time. No, I'm far more interested in objects in relation to something, in relation to people.

INTERVIEWER. You once asked Stephen Spender what he thought of Kenneth Patchen. Is Patchen a favourite? And which of your contemporaries do you admire?

PURDY. Did I ask that? That's a tough one, there are so very few. No, Patchen is not a favourite of mine. I like his 'Dirge'; that's about all I can think of. I like a lot of those poets who are producing in a consistent line, exactly as I said I would not like to do. Robert Bly has adopted a particular style and is writing pretty decent poems; but this style becomes very monotonous if he keeps it up—and he does keep it up. Charles Bukowski is writing in a style in which I also write; but that's just about his *only* style. I hope to get out of it once in a while.

There are so dammed few. I like some of James Dickey, for instance, quite a bit; but somehow or other, he lives at such intense white heat so much of the time that I don't believe he can possibly exist; he must burn up. He keeps being confounded, rivers keep boiling through his veins, he keeps becoming exalted all of the time.

In Canada? I like Newlove; I think he might have a chance to do something pretty good. Ian Young, George Jonas—maybe. Who else? They all seem to me—when they adopt some special way of writing, like bp Nichol and the concrete boys, or the *Tish* imitators of the Black Mountain—to be travelling down a dead end.

But in the world there are several, some living, some dead, that I like: I like Pierre Superveille very much and, of course, Pablo Neruda and Cesar Vallejo and one or two others. *Modern World Poetry*—in translation—is an awfully good book.

INTERVIEWER. What about earlier writers?

PURDY. I hope to find other poets to expend the same enthusiasms on as I did on Dylan Thomas and, to a certain extent, Robinson Jeffers; and also John Donne at one time. But enthusiasms pass. I was tremendously enthused over Layton about 1955; that enthusiasm has pretty well passed. I agree with my own line on Layton, that words no sooner said become clichés, though Layton is not all cliché. Somehow the immortal claptrap of poetry is a cliché,

INTERVIEWER. How much 'research' went into your poems in *North of Summer*?

PURDY. Actually, I didn't do a helluva lot of research. In fact, when I was up there I was reading E. M. Forster's *Passage to India* and about fifteen other pocket books, including that one I mentioned in 'When I Sat Down to Play the Piano', William Barrett's *Irrational Man*. The point at which books you read, or information from books you read, comes into your head is not when you are reading them, but sometime later. I always take off from any point or fact that seems relevant to the situation (in the North, say); I always take off on a personal expedition from there, though I may not know where I'm headed.

INTERVIEWER. I think of your 'In the Wilderness' as a Canadian 'Easter 1916'. Do other poems trigger you off to write?

PURDY. Yes, sometimes. Oddly enough, one poem called 'Dark Landscape', which will be in *Wild Grape Wine*, I twisted around to mean something other than what Vachel Lindsay means in 'Spring Comes on Forever'. That was almost a direct steal, except that I used it differently. Most of the time, when you read someone else's poem, it will give you your own thoughts on the same subject, which is much more valid, I think. This is why and how I wrote the bird poem in *North of Summer*. I think it was some Cuban poet that had written a poem about birds, so I started thinking about birds. And, incidentally, 'The Cariboo Horses' was written because I read in the Introduction to *New British Poetry* two quotes about horses by Ted Hughes and Philip Larkin and I thought they were terrible and .hat I could do better; so I started to write a poem. I think that if you write poems, your mind just knowingly or unknowingly casts around for subjects all of the time; I don't think a poet is ever not looking for subjects.

THEODORE ROETHKE

From *Some Remarks on Rhythm**

But what about the rhythm and the motion of the poem as a whole? Are there any ways of sustaining it, you may ask? We must keep in mind that rhythm is the entire movement, the flow, the recurrence of stress and unstress that is related to the rhythms of the blood, the rhythms of nature. It involves certainly stress, time, pitch, the texture of the words, the total meaning of the poem.

We've been told that a rhythm is invariably produced by playing against an established pattern. Blake does this admirably in 'A Poison Tree':

> I was angry with my friend,
> I told my wrath, my wrath did end.
> I was angry with my foe,
> I told it not, my wrath did grow.

The whole poem is a masterly example of variation in rhythm, of playing against metre. It's what Blake called 'the bounding line', the nervousness, the tension, the energy in the whole poem. And this is a clue to everything. Rhythm gives us the very psychic energy of the speaker, in one emotional situation at least.

. . .

Curiously, we find this primitiveness of the imagination cropping up in the most sophisticated poetry. If we concern ourselves with more primitive effects in poetry, we come inevitably to consideration, I think, of verse that is closer to prose. And here

* From *On the Poet and his Craft: Selected Prose of Theodore Roethke*, ed. by Ralph J. Mills Jr.

we jump rhythmically to a kind of opposite extreme. For many
strong stresses, or a playing against an iambic pattern to a loosening up, a longer, more irregular foot, I agree that free verse is
a denial in terms. There is, invariably, the ghost of some other
form, often blank verse, behind what is written, or the more
elaborate rise and fall of the rhythmical prose sentence. Let me
point up, to use Mr Warren's phrase, in a more specific way the
difference between the formal poem and the more proselike
piece. Mr Ransom has written his beautiful elegy, 'Bells for
John Whiteside's Daughter'; I'd like to read 'Elegy for Jane' on
the same theme, a poem, I'm proud to say, Mr Ransom first
printed.

I remember the neckcurls, limp and damp as tendrils;
And her quick look, a sidelong pickerel smile;
And how, once startled into talk, the light syllables leaped for her,
And she balanced in the delight of her thought,
A wren, happy, tail into the wind,
Her song trembling the twigs and small branches.
The shade sang with her;
The leaves, their whispers turned to kissing;
And the mold sang in the bleached valleys under the rose.

Oh, when she was sad, she cast herself down into such a pure depth,
Even a father could not find her:
Scraping her cheek against straw;
Stirring the clearest water.

My sparrow, you are not here,
Waiting like a fern, making a spiny shadow.
The sides of wet stones cannot console me,
Nor the moss, wound with the last light.

If only I could nudge you from this sleep,
My maimed darling, my skittery pigeon.
Over this damp grave I speak the words of my love:
I, with no rights in this matter,
Neither father nor lover.

But let me indicate one or two technical effects in my little piece.
For one thing, the enumeration, the favourite device of the more
irregular poem. We see it again and again in Whitman and Law-

rence. 'I remember', then the listing, the appositions, and the absolute construction. 'Her song trembling', etc. Then the last three lines in the stanza lengthen out:

> The shade sang with her;
> The leaves, their whispers turned to kissing;
> And the mold sang in the bleached valleys under the rose.

A kind of continuing triad. In the last two stanzas exactly the opposite occurs, the final lines being,

> Over this damp grave I speak the words of my love:
> I, with no rights in this matter,
> Neither father nor lover.

There is a successive shortening of the line length, an effect I have become inordinately fond of, I'm afraid. This little piece indicates in a way some of the strategies for the poet writing without the support of a formal pattern—he can vary his line length, modulate, he can stretch out the line, he can shorten. It was Lawrence, a master of this sort of poem (I think I quote him more or less exactly) who said, 'It all depends on the pause, the natural pause.' In other words, the breath unit, the language that is natural to the immediate thing, the particular emotion. Think of what we'd have missed in Lawrence, in Whitman, in Charlotte Mew, or, more lately, in Robert Lowell, if we denied this kind of poem. There are areas of experience in modern life that simply cannot be rendered by either the formal lyric or straight prose. We need the catalogue in our time. We need the eye close on the object, and the poem about the single incident —the animal, the child. We must permit poetry to extend consciousness as far, as deeply, as particularly as it can, to recapture, in Stanley Kunitz's phrase, what it has lost to some extent to prose. We must realize, I think, that the writer in freer forms must have an even greater fidelity to his subject matter than the poet who has the support of form. He must keep his eye on the object, and his rhythm must move as a mind moves, must be imaginatively right, or he is lost. Let me end with a simple and somewhat clumsy example of my own ['Big Wind'] in which we see a formal device giving energy to the piece, that device being, simply, participial or verbal forms that keep the action going.

From *Open Letter**

Rhythmically, it's the spring and rush of the child I'm after—and Gammer Gurton's concision: *mütterkin's* wisdom. Most of the time the material seems to demand a varied short line. I believe that, in this kind of poem, the poet, in order to be true to what is most universal in himself, should not rely on allusion; should not comment or employ many judgement words; should not meditate (or maunder). He must scorn being 'mysterious' or loosely oracular, but be willing to face up to genuine mystery. His language must be compelling and immediate: he must create an actuality. He must be able to telescope image and symbol, if necessary, without relying on the obvious connectives: to speak in a kind of psychic shorthand when his protagonist is under great stress. He must be able to shift his rhythms rapidly, the 'tension'. He works intuitively, and the final form of his poem must be imaginatively right. If intensity has compressed the language so it seems, on early reading, obscure, this obscurity should break open suddenly for the serious reader who can hear the language: the 'meaning' itself should come as a dramatic revelation, an excitement. The clues will be scattered richly—as life scatters them; the symbols will mean what they usually mean—and sometimes something more.

---

* From *On the Poet and his Craft: Selected Prose of Theodore Roethke*, ed. by Ralph J. Mills Jr.

GARY SNYDER

Poetry and the Primitive* NOTES ON POETRY AS AN

ECOLOGICAL SURVIVAL TECHNIQUE

BILATERAL SYMMETRY

'Poetry' as the skilled and inspired use of the voice and language to embody rare and powerful states of mind that are in immediate origin personal to the singer, but at deep levels common to all who listen. 'Primitive' as those societies which have remained non-literate and non-political while necessarily exploring and developing in directions that civilized societies have tended to ignore. Having fewer tools, no concern with history, a living oral tradition rather than an accumulated library, no overriding social goals, and considerable freedom of sexual and inner life, such people live vastly in the present. Their daily reality is a fabric of friends and family, the field of feeling and energy that one's own body is, the earth they stand on and the wind that wraps around it; and various areas of consciousness.

At this point some might be tempted to say that the primitive's real life is no different from anybody else's. I think this is not so. To live in the 'mythological present' in close relation to nature and in basic but disciplined body/mind states suggests a wider-ranging imagination and a closer subjective knowledge of one's own physical properties than is usually available to men living (as they themselves describe it) impotently and inadequately in 'history'—their mind-content programmed, and their caressing of nature complicated by the extensions and abstractions which elaborate tools are. A hand pushing a button may wield great power, but that hand will never learn what a hand can do. Unused capacities go sour.

---

*From *Earth House Hold* by Gary Snyder.

Poetry must sing or speak from authentic experience. Of all the streams of civilized tradition with roots in the paleolithic, poetry is one of the few that can realistically claim an unchanged function and a relevance which will outlast most of the activities that surround us today. Poets, as few others, must live close to the world that primitive men are in: the world, in its nakedness, which is fundamental for all of us—birth, love, death; the sheer fact of being alive.

Music, dance, religion, and philosophy of course have archaic roots—a shared origin with poetry. Religion has tended to become the social justifier, a lackey to power, instead of the vehicle of hair-raising liberating and healing realizations. Dance has mostly lost its connection with ritual drama, the miming of animals, or tracing the maze of the spiritual journey. Most music takes too many tools. The poet can make it on his own voice and mother tongue, while steering a course between crystal clouds of utterly incommunicable non-verbal states—and the gleaming daggers and glittering nets of language.

In one school of Mahayana Buddhism, they talk about the 'Three Mysteries'. These are Body, Voice, and Mind. The things that are what living *is* for us, in life. Poetry is the vehicle of the mystery of voice. The universe, as they sometimes say, is a vast breathing body.

With artists, certain kinds of scientists, yogins, and poets, a kind of mind-sense is not only surviving but modestly flourishing in the twentieth century. Claude Lévi-Strauss (*The Savage Mind*) sees no problem in the continuity: '. . . it is neither the mind of savages nor that of primitive or archaic humanity, but rather mind in its untamed state as distinct from mind cultivated or domesticated for yielding a return . . . We are better able to understand today that it is possible for the two to coexist and interpenetrate in the same way that (in theory at least) it is possible for natural species, of which some are in their savage state and others transfomed by agriculture and domestication, to coexist and cross . . . whether one deplores or rejoices in the fact, there are still zones in which savage thought, like savage species, is relatively protected. This is the case of art, to which our civilization accords the status of a national park.'

. . .

We all know what primitive cultures don't have. What they *do* have is this knowledge of connection and responsibility which amounts to a spiritual ascesis for the whole community. Monks of Christianity or Buddhism, 'leaving the world' (which means the games of society) are trying, in a decadent way, to achieve what whole primitive communities—men, women, and children —live by daily; and with more wholeness. The Shaman-poet is simply the man whose mind reaches easily out into all manners of shapes and other lives, and gives song to dreams. Poets have carried this function forward all through civilized times: poets don't sing about society, they sing about nature—even if the closest they ever get to nature is their lady's queynt. Class-structured civilized society is a kind of mass ego. To transcend the ego is to go beyond society as well. 'Beyond' there lies, inwardly, the unconscious. Outwardly, the equivalent of the unconscious is the wilderness: both of these terms meet, one step even farther on, as *one*.

. . .

Poetry, it should not have to be said, is not writing or books. Non-literate cultures with their traditional training methods of hearing and reciting, carry thousands of poems—death, war, love, dream, work, and spirit-power songs—through time. The voice of inspiration as an 'other' has long been known in the West as The Muse. Widely speaking, the muse is anything other that touches you and moves you. Be it a mountain range, a band of people, the morning star, or a diesel generator. Breaks through the ego-barrier. But this touching-deep is as a mirror, and man in his sexual nature has found the clearest mirror to be his human lover. As the West moved into increasing complexities and hierarchies with civilization, Woman as nature, beauty, and The Other came to be an all-dominating symbol; secretly striving through the last three millennia with the Jehovah or Imperator God-figure, a projection of the gathered power of anti-nature social forces. Thus in the Western tradition the Muse and Romantic Love became part of the same energy, and woman as nature the field for experiencing the universe as sacramental. The lovers' bed was the sole place to enact the dances and ritual dramas that link primitive people to their geology and the Milky Way. The contemporary decline of the cult of romantic is linked to the rise of the sense of the primitive, and the knowledge of the variety of spiritual practices and paths to beauty that cultural anthropology has brought us. We begin to move away now, in this interesting historical spiral, from monogamy and monotheism.

Some Yips & Barks in the Dark*

A NOTABLE UTTERANCE

The linguist Bloomfield once defined literature as 'notable utterances'. A poem is usually distinguished from other sorts of utterances by some characteristic arrangement of syllabic stress, pitch, vowel length, rhyming words, internal tone patterns, syllable count, initial or final consonants and so forth. In some cases there is a peculiar vocabulary the poem is couched in. All this is what critics call form. Another distinction is made on the basis of the nature of the message. Perhaps something other than 'words' is being communicated. Straight from the deep mind of the maker to the deep mind of the hearer. This is what poets call the Poem.

THE GRAIN OF THINGS

For me every poem is unique. One can understand and appreciate the conditions which produce formal poetry as part of man's experiment with civilization. The game of inventing an abstract structure and then finding things in experience which can be forced into it. A kind of intensity can indeed be produced this way—but it is the intensity of straining and sweating against self-imposed bonds. Better the perfect, easy discipline of the swallow's dip and swoop, 'without east or west'.

---

*From *Naked Poetry* edited by Stephen Berg and Robert Mezey.

Each poem grows from an energy-mind-field-dance, and has its own inner grain. To let it grow, to let it speak for itself, is a large part of the work of the poet. A scary chaos fills the heart as 'spir'itual breath— in'spir'ation; and is breathed out into the thing-world as a poem. From there it must jump to the hearer's under'stand'ing. The wider the gap the more difficult; and the greater the delight when it crosses. If the poem becomes too elliptical it ceases to be a poem in any usual sense. Then it may be a mantra, a koan, or a dharani. To be used as part of a larger walking, singing, dancing, or meditating practice.

THE POET

The poet must have total sensitivity to the inner potentials of his own language—pulse, breath, glottals nasals & dentals. An ear, an eye and a belly.

He must know his own unconscious, and the proper ways to meet with the beings who live there. As Confucius said, he should know the names of trees, birds, and flowers. From this knowledge and practice of 'body, speech, and mind' the poem takes form, freely.

It is a mistake that we are searching, now, for 'new forms'. What is needed is a totally new approach to the very idea of form. Why should this be? The future can't be seen on the basis of the present; and I believe mankind is headed someplace else.

Gary Snyder
Kyoto 22. VIII. 1966

WALLACE STEVENS

Selections from *Adagia**

Progress in any aspect is a movement through changes of terminology.

•

To give a sense of the freshness or vividness of life is a valid purpose for poetry. A didactic purpose justifies itself in the mind of the teacher; a philosophical purpose justifies itself in the mind of the philosopher. It is not that one purpose is as justifiable as another but that some purposes are pure, others impure. Seek those purposes that are purely the purposes of the pure poet.

The poet makes silk dresses out of worms.

•

Authors are actors, books are theatres.

•

Literature is the better part of life. To this it seems inevitably necessary to add, provided life is the better part of literature.

•

After one has abandoned a belief in God, poetry is that essence which takes its place as life's redemption.

•

Accuracy of observation is the equivalent of accuracy of thinking.

•

The relation of art to life is of the first importance especially in a skeptical age since, in the absence of a belief in God, the mind turns to its own creations and examines them, not alone from

---

* From *Opus Posthumous* by Wallace Stevens.

the aesthetic point of view, but for what they reveal, for what they validate and invalidate, for the support that they give.

Life is the reflection of literature.

As life grows more terrible, its literature grows more terrible.

Poetry and materia poetica are interchangeable terms.
•
The real is only the base. But it is the base.
•
The poem reveals itself only to the ignorant man.

The relation between the poetry of experience and the poetry of rhetoric is not the same thing as the relation between the poetry of reality and that of the imagination. Experience, at least in the case of a poet of any scope, is much broader than reality.
•
Not all objects are equal. The vice of imagism was that it did not recognize this.
•
All poetry is experimental poetry.

The bare image and the image as a symbol are the contrast: the image without meaning and the image as meaning. When the image is used to suggest something else, it is secondary. Poetry as an imaginative thing consists of more than lies on the surface.
•
It is the belief and not the god that counts.

What we see in the mind is as real to us as what we see by the eye.
•
There is nothing in life except what one thinks of it.

There is nothing beautiful in life except life.

There is no wing like meaning.

Consider: I. That the whole world is material for poetry; II. That there is not a specifically poetic material.

One reads poetry with one's nerves.

The poet is the intermediary between people and the world in which they live and also, between people as between themselves; but not between people and some other world.

Sentimentality is a failure of feeling.
•
The final belief is to believe in a fiction, which you know to be a fiction, there being nothing else. The exquisite truth is to know that it is a fiction and that you believe in it willing.

All of our ideas come from the natural world: trees = umbrellas.
•
Ethics are no more a part of poetry than they are of painting.

As the reason destroys, the poet must create.

The exquisite environment of fact. The final poem will be the poem of fact in the language of fact. But it will be the poem of fact not realized before.
•
To live in the world but outside of existing conceptions of it.
•
Poetry has to be something more than a conception of the mind. It has to be a revelation of nature. Conceptions are artificial. Perceptions are essential.
•

Money is a kind of poetry.

Poetry is an effort of a dissatisfied man to find satisfaction through words, occasionally of the dissatisfied thinker to find satisfaction through his emotions.

•

The poem is a nature created by the poet.

The aesthetic order includes all other orders but is not limited to them.

Religion is dependent on faith. But æsthetics is independent of faith. The relative positions of the two might be reversed. It is possible to establish æsthetics in the individual mind as immeasurably a greater thing than religion. Its present state is the result of the difficulty of establishing it except in the individual mind.

The ultimate value is reality.

Realism is a corruption of reality.

•

The world is the only thing fit to think about.

•

Poetry is a purging of the world's poverty and change and evil and death. It is a present perfecting, a satisfaction in the irremediable poverty of life.

•

The time will come when poems like Paradise will seem like very *triste* contraptions.

•

All men are murderers.

•

There must be something of the peasant in every poet.

•

Metaphor creates a new reality from which the original appears
to be unreal.

•

Description is an element, like air or water.

•

Poets acquire humanity.

Thought tends to collect in pools.

Life is not people and scene but thought and feeling.

•

God is a postulate of the ego.

•

Poetry must resist the intelligence almost successfully.

•

Literature is based not on life but on propositions about life, of
which this is one.

Life is a composite of the propositions about it.

A change of style is a change of subject.

•

Poetry is a pheasant disappearing in the brush.

We never arrive intellectually. But emotionally we arrive constantly (as in poetry, happiness, high mountains, vistas).

•

The poet represents the mind in the act of defending us against
itself.

•

Every poem is a poem within a poem: the poem of the idea
within the poem of the words.

•

Poetry is the gaiety (joy) of language.

To be at the end of fact is not to be at the beginning of imagination but it is to be at the end of both.

•

There is a nature that absorbs the mixedness of metaphors.

•

Imagination applied to the whole world is vapid in comparison to imagination applied to a detail.

•

Poetry is a response to the daily necessity of getting the world right.

•

The essential fault of surrealism is that it invents without discovering. To make a clam play an accordion is to invent not to discover. The observation of the unconscious, so far as it can be observed, should reveal things of which we have previously been unconscious, not the familiar things of which we have been conscious plus imagination.

•

French and English constitute a single language.

•

Reality is a cliché from which we escape by metaphor. It is only *au pays de la métaphore qu'on est poète.*

The degrees of metaphor. The absolute object slightly turned is a metaphor of the object.

Some objects are less susceptible to metaphor than others. The whole world is less susceptible to metaphor than a tea-cup is.

There is no such thing as a metaphor of a metaphor. One does not progress through metaphors. Thus reality is the indispensable element of each metaphor. When I say that man is a god it is very easy to see that if I also say that a god is something else, god has become reality.

In the long run the truth does not matter.

•

Poetry creates a fictitious existence on an exquisite plane. This definition must vary as the plane varies, an exquisite plane being merely illustrative.

DYLAN THOMAS

*Notes on the Art of Poetry**

You want to know why and how I just began to write poetry, and which poets or kinds of poetry I was first moved and influenced by.

To answer the first part of this question, I should say I wanted to write poetry in the beginning because I had fallen in love with words. The first poems I knew were nursery rhymes, and before I could read them for myself I had come to love just the words of them, the words alone. What the words stood for, symbolized, or meant, was of very secondary importance. What mattered was the *sound* of them as I heard them for the first time on the lips of the remote and incomprehensible grown-ups who seemed, for some reason, to be living in my world. And these words were, to me, as the notes of bells, the sounds of musical instruments, the noises of wind, sea, and rain, the rattle of milkcarts, the clopping of hooves on cobbles, the fingering of branches on a window pane, might be to someone, deaf from birth, who has miraculously found his hearing. I did not care what the words said, overmuch, nor what happened to Jack and Jill and the Mother Goose rest of them; I cared for the shapes of sound that their names, and the words describing their actions, made in my ears; I cared for the colours the words cast on my eyes. I realize that I may be, as I think back all that way, romanticizing my reactions to the simple and beautiful words of those pure poems; but that is all I can honestly remember, however much time might have falsified my memory. I fell in love— that is the only expression I can think of—at once, and am still

* Written in the summer of 1951, at Laugharne, in reply to questions posed by a student. From *Texas Quarterly* (winter 1961).

at the mercy of words, though sometimes now, knowing a little of their behaviour very well, I think I can influence them slightly and have even learned to beat them now and then, which they appear to enjoy. I tumbled for words at once. And, when I began to read the nursery rhymes for myself, and, later, to read other verses and ballads, I knew that I had discovered the most important things, to me, that could be ever. There they were, seemingly lifeless, made only of black and white, but out of them, out of their own being, came love and terror and pity and pain and wonder and all the other vague abstractions that make our ephemeral lives dangerous, great, and bearable. Out of them came the gusts and grunts and hiccups and heehaws of the common fun of the earth; and though what the words meant was, in its own way, often deliciously funny enough, so much funnier seemed to me, at that almost forgotten time, the shape and shade and size and noise of the words as they hummed, strummed, jugged, and galloped along. That was the time of innocence; words burst upon me, unencumbered by trivial or portentous association; words were their spring-like selves, fresh with Eden's dew, as they flew out of the air. They made their own original associations as they sprang and shone. The words, 'Ride a cock-horse to Banbury Cross', were as haunting to me, who did not know then what a cock-horse was nor cared a damn where Banbury Cross might be, as, much later, were such lines as John Donne's, 'Go and catch a falling star,/Get with child a mandrake root', which also I could not understand when I first read them. And as I read more and more, and it was not all verse, by any means, my love for the real life of words increased until I knew that I must live *with* them and *in* them always. I knew, in fact, that I must be a writer of words, and nothing else. The first thing was to feel and know their sound and substance; what I was going to do with those words, what use I was going to make of them, what I was going to *say* through them, would come later. I knew I had to know them most intimately in all their forms and moods, their ups and downs, their chops and changes, their needs and demands. (Here, I am afraid, I am beginning to talk too vaguely. I do not like writing *about* words, because then I often use bad and wrong and stale and woolly words. What I like to do is to treat words as a craftsman does his wood or stone or what-have-you, to hew, carve, mould, coil, polish, and plane them into patterns, sequences, sculptures, fugues of sound expressing some lyrical impulse, some spiritual doubt or conviction, some dimly-realized truth I must try to reach and realize). It was when I was very young, and just at school, that, in my father's study, before homework that was never done, I began to know one kind of writing from another, one kind of goodness, one kind of badness. My first, and greatest, liberty was that of being able to read everything and anything I cared to. I read indiscriminately, and with my eyes hanging out. I could never have dreamt that there were such goings-on in the world between the covers of books, such sand-storms and ice-blasts of words, such slashing of humbug, and humbug too, such staggering peace, such enormous laughter, such and so many blinding bright lights breaking across the just-awaking wits and splashing all over the pages in a million bits and pieces all of which were words, words, words, and each of which was alive forever in its own delight and glory and oddity and light (I must try not to make these supposedly helpful notes as confusing as my poems themselves). I wrote endless imitations, though I never thought them to be imitations but, rather, wonderfully original things, like eggs laid by tigers. They were imitations of anything I happened to be reading at the time: Sir Thomas Browne, de Quincey, Henry Newbolt, the Ballads, Blake, Baroness Orczy, Marlowe, Chums, the Imagists, the Bible, Poe, Keats, Lawrence, Anon., and Shakespeare. A mixed lot, as you see, and randomly remembered. I tried my callow hand at almost every poetical form. How could I learn the tricks of a trade unless I tried to do them myself? I learned that the bad tricks come easily; and the good ones, which help you to say what you think you wish to say in the most meaningful, moving way, I am still learning. (But in earnest company you must call these tricks by other names, such as technical devices, prosodic experiments, etc.)

The writers, then, who influenced my earliest poems and stories were, quite simply and truthfully, all the writers I was reading at the time, and, as you see from a specimen list higher up the page they ranged from writers of schoolboy adventure yarns to incomparable and inimitable masters like Blake. That is, when I began, bad writing had as much influence on my stuff as good. The bad influences I tried to remove and renounce bit by bit, shadow by shadow, echo by echo, through trial and error, through delight and disgust and misgiving, as I came to love words more and to hate the heavy hands that knocked them about, the thick tongues that [had] no feel for their multitudinous tastes, the dull and botching hacks who flattened them out into a colourless and insipid paste, the pedants who made them moribund and pompous as themselves. Let me say that the things that first made me love language and want to work *in* it and *for* it were nursery rhymes and folk tales, the Scottish Ballads, a few lines of hymns, the most famous Bible stories and the rhythms of the Bible, Blake's *Songs of Innocence,* and the quite incomprehensible magical majesty and nonsense of Shakespeare heard, read, and near-murdered in the first forms of my school.

You ask me, next, if it is true that three of the dominant influences on my published prose and poetry are Joyce, the Bible, and Freud. (I purposely say my 'published' prose and poetry, as in the preceding pages I have been talking about the primary influences upon my very first and forever unpublishable juvenilia.) I cannot say that I have been 'influenced' by Joyce, whom I enormously admire and whose *Ulysses,* and earlier stories I have read a great deal. I think this Joyce question arose because somebody once, in print, remarked on the closeness of the title of my book of short stories, *Portrait of the Artist as a Young Dog* to Joyce's title, *Portrait of the Artist as a Young*

Man. As you know, the name given to innumerable portrait paintings by their artists is, 'Portrait of the Artist as a Young Man'—a perfectly straightforward title. Joyce used the painting-title for the first time as the title of a literary work. I myself made a bit of doggish fun of the *painting*-title and, of course, intended no possible reference to Joyce. I do not think that Joyce has had any hand at all in my writing; certainly, his *Ulysses* has not. On the other hand, I cannot deny that the shaping of some of my *Portrait* stories might owe something to Joyce's stories in the volume *Dubliners*. But then, *Dubliners* was a pioneering work in the world of the short story, and no good story-writer since can have failed, in some way, however little, to have benefited by it.

The Bible, I have referred to in attempting to answer your first question. Its great stories, of Noah, Jonah, Lot, Moses, Jacob, David, Solomon, and a thousand more, I had, of course, known from very early youth; the great rhythms had rolled over me from the Welsh pulpits; and I read, for myself, from Job and Ecclesiastes; and the story of the New Testament is part of my life. But I have never sat down and studied the Bible, never consciously echoed its language, and am, in reality, as ignorant of it as most brought-up Christians. All of the Bible that I use in my work is remembered from childhood, and is the common property of all who were brought up in English-speaking communities. Nowhere, indeed, in all my writing, do I use any knowledge which is not commonplace to any literate person. I *have* used a few difficult words in early poems, but they are easily looked-up and were, in any case, thrown into the poems in a kind of adolescent showing-off which I hope I have now discarded.

And that leads me to the third 'dominant influence': Sigmund Freud. My only acquaintance with the theories and discoveries of Dr Freud has been through the work of novelists who have been excited by his case-book histories, of popular newspaper scientific-potboilers who have, I imagine, vulgarized his work beyond recognition, and of a few modern poets, including Auden, who have attempted to use psychoanalytical phraseology and theory in some of their poems. I have read only one book of Freud's, *The Interpretation of Dreams*, and do not recall having been influenced by it in any way. Again, no honest writer today can possibly avoid being influenced by Freud through his pioneering work into the Unconscious and by the influence of those discoveries on the scientific, philosophic, and artistic work of his contemporaries: but not, by any means, necessarily through Freud's own writing.

To your third question—Do I deliberately utilize devices of rhyme, rhythm, and word-formation in my writing—I must, of course, answer with an immediate, Yes. I am a painstaking, conscientious, involved, and devious craftsman in words, however unsuccessful the result so often appears, and to whatever wrong uses I may apply my technical paraphernalia. I use everything and anything to make my poems work and move in the direction I want them to: old tricks, new tricks, puns, portmanteau-words, paradox, allusion, paronomasia, paragram, catachresis, slang, assonantal rhymes, vowel rhymes, sprung rhythm. Every device there is in language is there to be used if you will. Poets have got to enjoy themselves sometimes, and the twisting and convolutions of words, the inventions and contrivances, are all part of the joy that is part of the painful, voluntary work.

Your next question asks whether my use of combinations of words to create something new, 'in the Surrealist way', is according to a set formula or is spontaneous.

There is a confusion here, for the Surrealists' set formula *was* to juxtapose the unpremeditated.

Let me make it clearer if I can. The Surrealists—(that is, super-realists, or those who work *above* realism)—were a coterie of painters and writers in Paris, in the nineteen twenties, who did not believe in the conscious selection of images. To put it in another way: they were artists who were dissatisfied with both the realists—(roughly speaking, those who tried to put down in paint and words an actual representation of what they imagined to be the real world in which they lived)—and the impressionists who, roughly speaking again, were those who tried to give an impression of what they imagined to be the real world. The Surrealists wanted to dive into the subconscious mind, the mind below the conscious surface, and dig up their images from there without the aid of logic of reason, and put them down, illogically and unreasonably, in paint and words. The Surrealists affirmed that, as three quarters of the mind was submerged, it was the function of the artist to gather his material from the greatest, submerged mass of the mind rather than from that quarter of the mind which, like the tip of an iceberg, protruded from the subconscious sea. One method the Surrealists used in their poetry was to juxtapose words and images that had no rational relationship; and out of this they hoped to achieve a kind of subconscious, or dream, poetry that would be truer to the real, imaginative world of the mind, mostly submerged, than is the poetry of the conscious mind that relies upon the rational and logical relationship of ideas, objects, and images.

This is, very crudely, the credo of the Surrealists, and one with which I profoundly disagree. I do not mind from where the images of a poem are dragged up; drag them up, if you like, from the nethermost sea of the hidden self; but, before they reach paper, they must go through all the rational processes of the intellect. The Surrealists, on the other hand, put their words down together on paper exactly as they emerge from chaos; they do not shape these words or put them in order; to them, chaos *is* the shape and order. This seems to me to be exceedingly presumptuous; the Surrealists imagine that whatever they dredge from their subconscious selves and put down in paint or in words must, essentially, be of some interest or value. I deny this. One of the arts of the poet is to make comprehensible and articulate what might emerge from subconscious sources; one of the great main uses of the intellect is to *select*, from the amorphous mass of subconscious images, those that will best further his imaginative purpose, which is to write the best poem he can.

And Question five is, God help us, what is my definition of Poetry?

I myself, do not read poetry for anything but pleasure. I read only the poems I like. This means, of course, that I have to read a lot of poems I don't like before I find the ones I do, but, when I *do* find the ones I do, then all I can say is 'Here they are', and read them to myself for pleasure.

Read the poems you like reading. Don't bother whether they're important, or if they'll live. What does it matter what poetry *is*, after all? If you want a definition of poetry, say: 'Poetry is what makes me laugh or cry or yawn, what makes my toenails twinkle, what makes me want to do this or that or nothing', and let it go at that. All that matters about poetry is the enjoyment of it, however tragic it may be. All that matters is the eternal movement behind it, the vast undercurrent of human grief, folly, pretension, exaltation, or ignorance, however unlofty the intention of the poem.

You can tear a poem apart to see what makes it technically tick, and say to yourself, when the works are laid out before you, the vowels, the consonants, the rhymes and rhythms. 'Yes, this is *it*. This is why the poem moves me so. It is because of the craftsmanship'. But you're back again where you began. You're back with the mystery of having been moved by words. The best craftsmanship always leaves holes and gaps in the works of the poem so that something that is *not* in the poem can creep, crawl, flash, or thunder in.

The joy and function of poetry is, and was, the celebration of man, which is also the celebration of God.

PHYLLIS WEBB

On The Line*

To whom am I talking? The awkward sound of that 'to whom'. Am I talking? No. My mouth is shut. Gary's letter arrives; I feel oppressed. It's Gary who wants the answers, though I put him up to it. Why did I start this dialogue which I now rebel against? On the poetic line. Let me discover the reasons for that as I try to find out to whom I am talking.

Last night, feeling uneasy, I turned again to Adrienne Rich, rereading her essays, 'The Tensions of Anne Bradstreet' and 'When We Dead Awaken: Writing as Re-vision'. I think I am trying to re-vision the approach to the line and all such matters. Gary, in Montreal, during that discussion we didn't tape, gave me the lead, talking about shorelines, tidelines. And Doug Barbour before that with his title *Shore Lines*. Sure lines.

I look again at the yellow dying tulip on the table. It is stretched out on an almost true horizontal. The flower has sliced itself exactly in half. I sympathize. The half tulip, halved tulip, hangs exposed. I was not there to hear the petals fall. They form a curve of yellow on the glass tabletop; they dropped to form a new line, a waxy curvature, unique to the forces that befell them. *Curvature.*

That is what I am coming to, the physics of the poem. Energy/Mass. Waxy splendour, the massive quiet of the fallen tulip petals. So much depends upon: the wit of the syntax, the rhythm and the speed of the fall, the drop, the assumption of a specific light, curved.

---

* From *Talking* by Phyllis Webb. Gary Geddes's letter, referred to in line 2 above, begins on page 672.

The oppression lifts as I draw the line on the page, like this

A hair-line, a hair's breadth. The wind in the willow. Hair's breath. Talking to myself on an April afternoon, my birth-day. The opening of that crack, of Duncan's field ('a wild field,' he says, 'I'm sort of interested in wild feelings, wild thoughts— and I don't mean like whoopee—but like wild life.') Or 'a series of fields folded.' Today, the fifty-fourth, the flowers arrive: roses, daisies, carnations, tulips (red), grape hyacinth, dead daffodils. Are falling into line, each one its own line, of its own accord, curved. Is that what we seek in sky, in field, in poem— *curvature?*

*   *   *   *   *   *

Enjambment: As bad as 'to whom'. Ugly, stupid, door-jamb. For closing. Foreclosing. Squashed.

*   *   *   *   *   *

The short line is 'for candor', says Duncan. Or terror, say I. Notes Toward a Poetics of Terror. Pull down thy vanity. The tulip is moving horizontally towards the light (tropos), cells burning brightly, dying out. Snuff out the poem. Stuff it. ('For flowers are peculiarly the poetry of Christ'—Christopher Smart.)

*   *   *   *   *   *

Syntactivity. Under the electron microscope. Oh look and see. Against this, an image pushes through of splicing tape. Janet in the listening room late at night at cBc. Listening room. The poem as listening room. Cut 20 seconds. Hear how they sound! Glossy plastic ribbon on the cutting room floor. Curling.

Ribbon at the end of the race. Break it. Ribbon at ceremonial opening of the bridge. Cut it with big authorial scissors. Champagne all around.

I am out of it. Cut. Splice. Play it again. To whom am I talking? Seriously. A fine line.

'The line has shattered,' Olson gasped in that interview I did with him in '63.

The water is boiling. Kenneth Koch's poem, 'The Boiling Water'. The seriousness of the boiling point for the water. For the tea, for me. The syntactivity (Geddes). So Gary forces me to this ebullience. The dance of the intellect in the syllables, for Olson. Knuckles of the articulate hand.

*   *   *   *   *   *

Certainties: that the long line (in English) is aggressive, with much 'voice'. Assertive, at least. It comes from assurance (or hysteria), high tide, full moon, open mouth, big-mouthed Whitman, yawp, yawp, and Ginsberg—howling. Male.

*   *   *   *   *   *

Modulations. Now take Kit Smart in *Jubilate Agno.* Yes, sure of himself, madly hurting. Sore lines. 'Silly Fellow, Silly Fellow.' Blessed. Based on Hebraic long-line psalmistry. (The short line, *au contraire,* private palmistry, heart line, cut to the quick). Gary, forget the commas, line breaks, caesura (plucked from the womb, untimely), the modes of measuring (though you are right about Levertov's ½ comma as frivolous), and look again at that idea: Behold, I am here. Even as the leaves of grass. Sexton *imitates* Smart (Behold, I am *almost* here). She was not

able to walk that line alone. Few women are, but they are learning. Anne, you took Christopher right into the poem for company.

In 'For Fyodor', the beetle is aggressive, enraged, monologu-
ing dramatically along the extended line. Poor Fyodor, foaming
at the mouth, harangued by this Trickster (yells and chuckles):
'You are mine, Dostoevsky.' Big-mouthed, proletarian, revolting
beetle. The balance of power unbalanced. (See also Wayman's
industrial poems.) Notes from the Insect Underground. Spider
Webb.

* * * * * *

Notes. The musical phrase, go with it, sd. Pound. Another
big mouth, or was it really a big ear, delicate as seashell or
tulipcup? He changed our borders, changed the shape of the
poem, its energy potential, for the 'data grid'? (Ed Sanders)
And presented us with the freedom we now mediate. Who are
'we'? To whom, etc.? Emily?

* * * * * *

—Emily—those gasps, those inarticulate dashes—those in-
citements—hiding what unspeakable—foul breath? But not revolting; *subversive.* Female. Hiding yourself—Emily—no, com-
pressing yourself, even singing yourself—tinily—with compact-
ed passion—a violent storm—

* * * * * *

Compare:

    Now you are sitting doubled up in pain.
    What's that for?

Doubled up I feel
small like these poems
the area of attack
is diminished.

I did not count the syllables or the ways. A hare's breath.

*   *   *   *   *   *

Sidelines. I play by ear. And the eye. The yellow tulip stretched on its stem, petals falling, a new moon, a phase.

I drink the tea. The seriousness of the moving line, for me. Detritus, the phenomenal world in Kenneth Koch. He cannot pull the wool over his eyes. Giving up on the weights and measures of the fine line to *hear* the water boiling, to overhear himself. Am I talking? Almost, to K.K. He lays himself bare in anxiety. Kroetsch sees anxiety as central to the short-lined *Naked Poems*—and the post-modern long poem generally. But the long-lined unyawping K.K. (unaggressive, relatively, unhysterical, relatively) fields his anxiety as you sprawl on your carpet, Kenneth, sprawl on the page, talking to me!

Comedian that he is, he throws away his lines. Hooray.

Hook, line and sinker.

*   *   *   *   *   *

Sound poetry. 'Open wide,' says doctor as he/she depresses your tongue to look down the little red lane.

From whence comes the dragon! Or the Four Horsemen. Whee. Whoa. Woe. Stop. Or that horse-thief Rothenberg. Technicians of the Sacred on the firing line.

But *no lines now*. Notes only. Notation. 'A new alphabet gasps for air'

Actually, an old alphabet

Shamanic

The Gutenberg Galaxy self-destructing under my hand and—

the mystical numbers come through the mail from Gwendolyn MacEwen, April 7, 1981:

1 - The Bond
3 - Divine Interception
5 - Impending Doom
7 - Weakness

'To control reality' when she was a child. Holding the line. The oppression of all that for the wild child.

Verse as numbers. Mystical systems. Music of the spheres. Curvature. Curlicue. Of the tulip of

Heraclitean fire.

'I am learning to be / a poet, caught in the / Divine Storm.' (Bowering, 'The Breath, Release'.)

*   *   *   *   *   *

Poundsound. Prosody: The articulation of the total sound of the poem. Or of the tulip, the yellow tulip, P.K.'s 'squeaky' flower.

*   *   *   *   *   *

And ultimately meaning, as you say, Gary, the movement of the meaning, the syntactivity, radioactivity, power.

When we dead arise.

I once complained about Adrienne Rich's line breaks, but when I read *The Dream of a Common Language*, I felt shame,

shame, ashamed, that I had ever been so petty, knowing that, like Marie Curie, your wounds, Adrienne, and your power come from the same source.

*   *   *   *   *   *

I talk like this only to myself with my mouth shut. Laying it on the line.

Edmonton.
April 8/9, 1981

Letter From Gary Geddes to Phyllis Webb

Dear Phyllis:

I'm looking forward to doing the interview with you, by mail *and* in person hopefully. It will help me formulate my own ideas too on the subject of the line. I think Levertov is right about the importance of the line, but less reliable on the ab-solute weight in terms of timing that it has. I'd say the weight of an end-line is very relative, depending almost entirely on context, the degree of syntactical activity (syntactivity?) and the momentum of sound and idea to hit the bearing-point of each line. Does a comma plus an end-line therefore equal 1½ commas? If so, what is the real duration of the comma—it all depends on the kind of noise, the buzz, each poem makes.

And the stanza. Lord, how to prescribe for its usage. Does the stanza have to be self-contained, with a closure either given by way of a full-stop or implied by spacing? Obviously not. Good poems break that convention often. And a comma hang-ing at the end of a stanza, what does that do, beyond keeping those words from sliding into the abyss that follows?

I wish Levertov would tell us more clearly how the line can be best used and then show how that method has been/must be broken to avoid tedium or predictability. I, for example, often separate the noun and adjective, precisely in order to *avoid* the sense of closure, of finality, or predictability that one associates with the phrasally determined line. The pause in many cases, then, is mainly eliminated or only hinted at. The advantage lies, I believe, in a subtle increase in energy *and* meaning that comes from making the noun and its qualifier appear separated in space but linked in time, thus giving a three-way focus on two words.

So I doubt if Levertov's theory of the line is any more reliable than Olson's breath-unit theory. We need, perhaps, to come at it via Olson, since one man's 4/4 time is another's 2/2 time, and then try to show how the material, the subject itself, calls up a certain momentum, as a lover does to one's pulse and breathing habits; this is where the question of tradition begins to get interesting, because one can see certain poets gaining strength by working against the iambic pentametre line with syllabics or some other mode of measuring.

Your own poem 'Poetics Against the Angel of Death' moves out onto the wide prairie in the last line, as a spacial pun and a manifesto, and in so doing it sits in the tradition of the free 20th and the more ordered 18th centuries. Pope could make the line crawl or leap or dance by virtue of his clever use of punctuation and syntax, so that the end of the line was less important than the main portion. Is that too Aristotelian—happiness of the line is more important—no, the means towards the end of the line is more important than the end itself? I want you 'to put yourself on the line' and say *what a line can't do without,* i.e., something for the ear, eye or mind, preferably all three.

That's all for now. Please drop me a *line* as you feel, the urge. . . .

WILLIAM CARLOS WILLIAMS

A New Measure*

I have never been one to write by rule, even by my own rules. Let's begin with the rule of counted syllables, in which all poems have been written hitherto. That has become tiresome to my ear.

Finally, the stated syllables, as in the best of present-day free verse, have become entirely divorced from the beat, that is the measure. The musical pace proceeds without them.

Therefore the measure, that is to say, the count, having got rid of the words, which held it down, is returned to the *music*.

The words, having been freed, have been allowed to run all over the map, 'free', as we have mistakenly thought. This has amounted to no more (in Whitman and others) than no discipline at all.

But if we keep in mind the *tune* which the lines (not necessarily the words) make in our ears, we are ready to proceed.

By measure I mean musical pace. Now, with music in our ears the words need only be taught to keep as distinguished an order, as chosen a character, as regular, according to the music, as in the best of prose.

By its *music* shall the best of modern verse be known and the *resources* of the music. The refinement of the poem, its subtlety, is not to be known by the elevation of the words but—the words don't so much matter—by the resources of the *music*.

To give you an example from my own work—not that I know anything about what I have myself written:

(count):—not that I ever count when writing but, at best, the
        lines must be capable of being counted, that is to

---

* From a letter written to Richard Eberhart, 23 May 1954. From *Selected Letters of William Carlos Williams*, ed. by John C. Thirlwall.

say, *measured*—(believe it or not).—At that I may, half consciously, even count the measure under my breath as I write.—

(approximate example)

    (1) The smell of the heat is boxwood
        (2) when rousing us
            (3) a movement of the air
    (4) stirs our thoughts
        (5) that had no life in them
            (6) to a life, a life in which

(or)

    (1) Mother of God! Our Lady!
        (2) the heart
            (3) is an unruly master:
    (4) Forgive us our sins
        (5) as we
            (6) forgive
    (7) those who have sinned against

Count a single beat to each numeral. You may not agree with my ear, but that is the way I count the line. Over the whole poem it gives a pattern to the metre that can be felt as a new measure. It gives resources to the ear which result in a language which we hear spoken about us every day.

On Measure — Statement for Cid Corman*

Verse—we'd better not speak of poetry lest we become confused —verse has always been associated in men's minds with 'measure', i.e., with mathematics. In scanning any piece of verse, you 'count' the syllables. Let's not speak either of rhythm, an aimless

---

* From *Selected Essays of William Carlos Williams.*

sort of thing without precise meaning of any sort. But measure implies something that can be measured. Today verse has lost all measure.

Our lives also have lost all that in the past we had to measure them by, except outmoded standards that are meaningless to us. In the same way our verses, of which our poems are made, are left without any metrical construction of which you can speak, any recognizable, any new measure by which they can be pulled together. We get sonnets, etc., but no one alive today, or half alive, seems to see anything incongruous in that. They cannot see that poems cannot any longer be made following a Euclidian measure, 'beautiful' as this may make them. The very grounds for our beliefs have altered. We do not live that way any more; nothing in our lives, at bottom, is ordered according to that measure; our social concepts, our schools, our very religious ideas, certainly our understanding of mathematics are greatly altered. Were we called upon to go back to what we believed in the past we should be lost. Only the construction of our poems —and at best the construction of a poem must engage the tips of our intellectual awareness—is left shamefully to the past.

A relative order is operative elsewhere in our lives. Even the divorce laws recognize that. Are we so stupid that we can't see that the same things apply to the construction of modern verse, to an art which hopes to engage the attention of a modern world? If men do not find in the verse they are called on to read a construction that interests them or that they believe in, they will not read your verses and I, for one, do not blame them. What will they find out there that is worth bothering about? So, I understand, the young men of my generation are going back to Pope. Let them. They want to be read at least with some understanding of what they are saying and Pope is at least understandable; a good master. They have been besides scared by all the wild experimentation that preceded them so that now they want to play it safe and to conform.

They have valid reasons for what they are doing—of course

not all of them are doing it, but the English, with a man such as Christopher Fry prominent among the.., lead the pack. Dylan Thomas is thrashing around somewhere in the wings but he is Welsh and acknowledges no rule—he cannot be of much help to us. Return as they may to the classics for their models it will not solve anything for them. They will still, later, have to tackle the fundamental problems which concern verse of a new construction to conform with our age. Their brothers in the chemical laboratory, from among whom their most acute readers will come if they know what is good for them, must be met on a footing that will not be retrograde but equal to their own. Though they may recognize this theoretically there is no one who dares overstep the conventional mark.

It's not only a question of daring, no one has instructed them differently. Most poems I see today are concerned with what they are *saying*, how profound they have been given to be. So true is this that those who write them have forgotten to make poems at all of them. Thank God we're not musicians, with our lack of structural invention we'd be ashamed to look ourselves in the face otherwise. There is nothing interesting in the construction of our poems, nothing that can jog the ear out of its boredom. I for one can't read them. There is nothing in their metrical construction to attract me, so I fall back on e. e. cummings and the disguised conventions that he presents which are at least amusing—as amusing as 'Doctor Foster went to Gloucester, in a shower of rain.' Ogden Nash is also amusing, but not amusing enough.

The thing is that 'free verse' since Whitman's time has led us astray. He was taken up, as were the leaders of the French Revolution before him with the abstract idea of freedom. It slopped over into all their thinking. But it was an idea lethal to all order, particularly to that order which has to do with the poem. Whitman was right in breaking our bounds but, having no valid restraints to hold him, went wild. He didn't know any better. At the last he resorted to a loose sort of language with no discipline about it of any sort and we have copied its worst feature, just that.

The corrective to that is forgetting Whitman, for instinctively he was on the right track, to find a new discipline. Invention is the mother of art. We must invent new modes to take the place of those which are worn out. For want of this we have gone back to worn-out modes with our tongues hanging out and our mouths drooling after 'beauty' which is not even in the same category under which we are seeking it. Whitman, great as he was in his instinctive drive, was also the cause of our going astray. I among the rest have much to answer for. No verse can be free, it must be governed by some measure, but not by the old measure. There Whitman was right but there, at the same time, his leadership failed him. The time was not ready for it. We have to return to some measure but a measure consonant with our time and not a mode so rotten that it stinks.

We have no measure by which to guide ourselves except a purely intuitive one which we feel but do not name. I am not speaking of verse which has long since been frozen into a rigid mould signifying its death, but of verse which shows that it has been touched with some dissatisfaction with its present state. It is all over the page at the mere whim of the man who has composed it. This will not do. Certainly an art which implies a discipline as the poem does, a rule, a measure, will not tolerate it. There is no measure to guide us, no recognizable measure.

Relativity gives us the cue. So, again, mathematics comes to the rescue of the arts. Measure, an ancient word in poetry, something we have almost forgotten in its literal significance as something measured, becomes related again with the poetic. We have today to do with the poetic, as always, but a *relatively* stable foot, not a rigid one. That is all the difference. It is that which must become the object of our search. Only by coming to that realization shall we escape the power of these magnificent verses of the past which we have always marveled over and still be able to enjoy them. We live in a new world, pregnant with tremendous possibility for enlightenment but sometimes, being old, I despair of it. For the poem which has always led the way to the other arts as to life, being explicit, the only art which is explicit, has lately been left to fall into decay.

Without measure we are lost. But we have lost even the ability to count. Actually we are not as bad as that. Instinctively we have continued to count as always but it has become not a conscious process and being unconscious has descended to a low level of the invention. There are a few exceptions but there is no one among us who is consciously aware of what he is doing. I have accordingly made a few experiments which will appear in a new book shortly. What I want to emphasize is that I do not consider anything I have put down there as final. There will be other experiments but all will be directed toward the discovery of a new measure, I repeat, a new measure by which may be ordered our poems as well as our lives.

1953

WILLIAM BUTLER YEATS

From *Magic**

I cannot now think symbols less than the greatest of all powers whether they are used consciously by the masters of magic, or half unconsciously by their successors, the poet, the musician, and the artist. At first I tried to distinguish between symbols and symbols, between what I called inherent symbols and arbitrary symbols, but the distinction has come to mean little or nothing. Whether their power has arisen out of themselves, or whether it has an arbitrary origin, matters little, for they act, as I believe, because the Great Memory associates them with certain events and moods and persons. Whatever the passions of man have gathered about, becomes a symbol in the Great Memory, and in the hands of him who has the secret it is a worker of wonders, a caller-up of angels or of devils. The symbols are of all kinds, for everything in heaven or earth has its association, momentous or trivial, in the Great Memory, and one never knows what forgotten events may have plunged it, like the toadstool and the ragweed, into the great passions. Knowledgeable men and women in Ireland sometimes distinguish between the simples that work cures by some medical property in the herb, and those that do their work by magic. Such magical simples as the husk of the flax, water out of the fork of an elm-tree, do their work, as I think, by awaking in the depths of the mind where it mingles with the Great Mind, and is enlarged by the Great Memory, some curative energy, some hypnotic command. They are not what we call faith cures, for they have been much used and successfully, the traditions of all lands affirm, over children and over animals, and to me they seem the only medicine that could

---

* From *Ideas of Good and Evil* by William Butler Yeats.

have been committed safely to ancient hands. To pluck the wrong leaf would have been to go uncured, but, if one had eaten it, one might have been poisoned.

. . .

And surely, at whatever risk, we must cry out that imagination is always seeking to remake the world according to the impulses and the patterns in that Great Mind, and that Great Memory? Can there be anything so important as to cry out that what we call romance, poetry, intellectual beauty, is the only signal that the supreme Enchanter, or some one in His councils, is speaking of what has been, and shall be again, in the consummation of time?

1901

From *The Symbolism of Poetry**

All sounds, all colours, all forms, either because of their preordained energies or because of long association, evoke indefinable and yet precise emotions, or, as I prefer to think, call down among us certain disembodied powers, whose footsteps over our hearts we call emotions; and when sound, and colour, and form are in a musical relation, a beautiful relation to one another, they become, as it were, one sound, one colour, one form, and evoke an emotion that is made out of their distinct evocations and yet is one emotion. The same relation exists between all portions of every work of art, whether it be an epic or a song, and the more perfect it is, and the more various and numerous the elements that have flowed into its perfection, the more powerful will be the emotion, the power, the god it calls among us.

---

* From *Ideas of Good and Evil* by William Butler Yeats.

Because an emotion does not exist, or does not become percep-
tible and active among us, till it has found its expression, in
colour or in sound or in form, or in all of these, and because no
two modulations or arrangements of these evoke the same emotion, poets and painters and musicians, and in a less degree
because their effects are momentary, day and night and cloud
and shadow, are continually making and unmaking mankind. It
is indeed only those things which seem useless or very feeble
that have any power, and all those things that seem useful or
strong, armies, moving wheels, modes of architecture, modes of
government, speculations of the reason, would have been a little
different if some mind long ago had not given itself to some
emotion, as a woman gives herself to her lover, and shaped
sounds or colours or forms, or all of these, into a musical relation, that their emotion might live in other minds. A little lyric
evokes an emotion, and this emotion gathers others about it and
melts into their being in the making of some great epic; and at
last, needing an always less delicate body, or symbol, as it grows
more powerful, it flows out, with all it has gathered, among the
blind instincts of daily life, where it moves a power within powers, as one sees ring within ring in the stem of an old tree. This
is maybe what Arthur O'Shaughnessy meant when he made his
poets say they had built Nineveh with their sighing; and I am
certainly never sure, when I hear of some war, or of some
religious excitement, or of some new manufacture, or of anything else that fills the ear of the world, that it has not all
happened because of something that a boy piped in Thessaly. I
remember once telling a seeress to ask one among the gods who,
as she believed, were standing about her in their symbolic
bodies, what would come of a charming but seeming trivial
labour of a friend, and the form answering, 'the devastation of
peoples and the overwhelming of cities'. I doubt indeed if the
crude circumstance of the world, which seems to create all our
emotions, does more than reflect, as in multiplying mirrors, the
emotions that have come to solitary men in moments of poetical

contemplation; or that love itself would be more than an animal hunger but for the poet and his shadow the priest, for unless we believe that outer things are the reality, we must believe that the gross is the shadow of the subtle, that things are wise before they become foolish, and secret before they cry out in the market-place. Solitary men in moments of contemplation receive, as I think, the creative impulse from the lowest of the Nine Hierarchies, and so make and unmake mankind, and even the world itself, for does not 'the eye altering alter all'?

> Our towns are copied fragments from our breast;
> And all man's Babylons strive but to impart
> The grandeurs of his Babylonian heart.

The purpose of rhythm, it has always seemed to me, is to prolong the moment of contemplation, the moment when we are both asleep and awake, which is the one moment of creation, by hushing us with an alluring monotony, while it holds us waking by variety, to keep us in that state of perhaps real trance, in which the mind liberated from the pressure of the will is unfolded in symbols. If certain sensitive persons listen persistently to the ticking of a watch, or gaze persistently on the monotonous flashing of a light, they fall into the hypnotic trance; and rhythm is but the ticking of a watch made softer, that one must needs listen, and various, that one may not be swept beyond memory or grow weary of listening; while the patterns of the artist are but the monotonous flash woven to take the eyes in a subtler enchantment. I have heard in meditation voices that were forgotten the moment they had spoken; and I have been swept, when in more profound meditation, beyond all memory but of those things that came from beyond the threshold of waking life. I was writing once at a very symbolical and abstract poem, when my pen fell on the ground; and as I stooped to pick it up, I remembered some fantastic adventure that yet did not seem fantastic, and then another like adventure, and when I asked myself when these things had happened, I found that I was remembering my dreams for many nights. I tried to remember what I had done the day before, and then what I had done that morning; but all my waking life had perished from me, and it was only after a struggle that I came to remember it again, and as I did so that more powerful and startling life perished in its turn. Had my pen not fallen on the ground and so made me turn from the images that I was weaving into verse, I would never have known that meditation had become trance, for I would have been like one who does not know that he is passing through a wood because his eyes are on the pathway. So I think that in the making and in the understanding of a work of art, and the more easily if it is full of patterns and symbols and music, we are lured to the threshold of sleep, and it may be far beyond it, without knowing that we have ever set our feet upon the steps of horn or of ivory.

Besides emotional symbols, symbols that evoke emotions alone, —and in this sense all alluring or hateful things are symbols, although their relations with one another are too subtle to delight us fully, away from rhythm and pattern,—there are intellectual symbols, symbols that evoke ideas alone, or ideas mingled with emotions; and outside the very definite traditions of mysticism and the less definite criticism of certain modern poets, these alone are called symbols. Most things belong to one or another kind, according to the way we speak of them and the companions we give them, for symbols, associated with ideas that are more than fragments of the shadows thrown upon the intellect by the emotions they evoke, are the playthings of the allegorist or the pedant, and soon pass away. If I say 'white' or 'purple' in an ordinary line of poetry, they evoke emotions so exclusively that I cannot say why they move me; but if I bring them into the same sentence with such obvious intellectual symbols as a cross or a crown of thorns, I think of purity and sovereignty. Furthermore, innumerable meanings, which are held to 'white' or to 'purple' by bonds of subtle suggestion, and

alike in the emotions and in the intellect, move visibly through
my mind, and move invisibly beyond the threshold of sleep,
casting lights and shadows of an indefinable wisdom on what
had seemed before, it may be, but sterility and noisy violence. It
is the intellect that decides where the reader shall ponder over
the procession of the symbols, and if the symbols are merely
emotional, he gazes from amid the accidents and destinies of the
world; but if the symbols are intellectual too, he becomes himself a part of pure intellect, and he is himself mingled with the
procession. If I watch a rushy pool in the moonlight, my emotion at its beauty is mixed with memories of the man that I have
seen ploughing by its margin, or of the lovers I saw there a night
ago; but if I look at the moon herself and remember any of her
ancient names and meanings, I move among divine people, and
things that have shaken off our mortality, the tower of ivory, the
queen of waters, the shining stag among enchanted woods, the
white hare sitting upon the hilltop, the fool of Faery with his
shining cup full of dreams, and it may be 'make a friend of one
of these images of wonder', and 'meet the Lord in the air'. So,
too, if one is moved by Shakespeare, who is content with emotional symbols that he may come the nearer to our sympathy,
one is mixed with the whole spectacle of the world; while if one
is moved by Dante, or by the myth of Demeter, one is mixed
into the shadow of God or of a goddess. So, too, one is furthest
from symbols when one is busy doing this or that, but the soul
moves among symbols and unfolds in symbols when trance, or
madness, or deep meditation has withdrawn it from every impulse but its own. 'I then saw,' wrote Gérard de Nerval of his
madness, 'vaguely drifting into form, plastic images of antiquity,
which outlined themselves, became definite, and seemed to represent symbols of which I only seized the idea with difficulty.' In
an earlier time he would have been of that multitude whose
souls austerity withdrew, even more perfectly than madness
could withdraw his soul, from hope and memory, from desire
and regret, that they might reveal those processions of symbols

that men bow to before altars, and woo with incense and offer-
ings. But being of our time, he has been like Maeterlinck, like
Villiers de l'Isle-Adam in *Axël*, like all who are preoccupied
with intellectual symbols in our time, a foreshadower of the new
sacred book, of which all the arts, as somebody has said, are
beginning to dream. How can the arts overcome the slow dying
of men's hearts that we call the progress of the world, and lay
their hands upon men's heartstrings again, without becoming the
garment of religion as in old times?

If people were to accept the theory that poetry moves us because
of its symbolism, what change should one look for in the manner
of our poetry? A return to the way of our fathers, a casting out
of descriptions of nature for the sake of nature, of the moral law
for the sake of the moral law, a casting out of all anecdotes and
of that brooding over scientific opinion that so often extinguished the central flame in Tennyson, and of that vehemence
that would make us do or not do certain things; or, in other
words, we should come to understand that the beryl stone was
enchanted by our fathers that it might unfold the pictures in its
heart, and not to mirror our own excited faces, or the boughs
waving outside the window. With this change of substance, this
return to imagination, this understanding that the laws of art,
which are the hidden laws of the world, can alone bind the
imagination, would come a change of style, and we would cast
out of serious poetry those energetic rhythms, as of a man running, which are the invention of the will with its eyes always on
something to be done or undone; and we would seek out those
wavering, meditative, organic rhythms, which are the embodi-
ment of the imagination, that neither desires nor hates, because
it has done with time, and only wishes to gaze upon some reality, some beauty; nor would it be any longer possible for anybody to deny the importance of form, in all its kinds, for although you can expound an opinion, or describe a thing, when
your words are not quite well chosen, you cannot give a body to

something that moves beyond the senses, unless your words are as subtle, as complex, as full of mysterious life, as the body of a flower or of a woman. The form of sincere poetry, unlike the form of the 'popular poetry', may indeed be sometimes obscure, or ungrammatical as in some of the best of the *Songs of Innocence and Experience*, but it must have the perfections that escape analysis, the subtleties that have a new meaning every day, and it must have all this whether it be but a little song made out of a moment of dreamy indolence, or some great epic made out of the dreams of one poet and of a hundred generations whose hands were never weary of the sword.

1900

From *A General Introduction to my Work**

STYLE AND ATTITUDE

Style is almost unconscious. I know what I have tried to do, little what I have done. Contemporary lyric poems, even those that moved me—'The Stream's Secret', 'Dolores'—seemed too long, but an Irish preference for a swift current might be mere indolence, yet Burns may have felt the same when he read Thomson and Cowper. The English mind is meditative, rich, deliberate; it may remember the Thames valley. I planned to write short lyrics or poetic drama where every speech would be short and concentrated, knit by dramatic tension, and I did so with more confidence because young English poets were at that time writing out of emotion at the moment of crisis, though their old slow-moving meditation returned almost at once. Then, and in this English poetry has followed my lead, I tried to make the

---

* From *Essays and Introductions* by William Butler Yeats.

language of poetry coincide with that of passionate, normal speech. I wanted to write in whatever language comes most naturally when we soliloquize, as I do all day long, upon the events of our own lives or of any life where we can see ourselves for the moment. I sometimes compare myself with the mad old slum women I hear denouncing and remembering; 'How dare you,' I heard one say of some imaginary suitor, 'and you without health or a home!' If I spoke my thoughts aloud they might be as angry and as wild. It was a long time before I had made a language to my liking; I began to make it when I discovered some twenty years ago that I must seek, not as Wordsworth thought, words in common use, but a powerful and passionate syntax, and a complete coincidence between period and stanza. Because I need a passionate syntax for passionate subject-matter I compel myself to accept those traditional metres that have developed with the language. Ezra Pound, Turner, Lawrence wrote admirable free verse, I could not. I would lose myself, become joyless like those mad old woman. The translators of the Bible, Sir Thomas Browne, certain translators from the Greek when translators still bothered about rhythm, created a form midway between prose and verse that seems natural to impersonal meditation; but all that is personal soon rots; it must be packed in ice or salt. Once when I was in delirium from pneumonia I dictated a letter to George Moore telling him to eat salt because it was a symbol of eternity; the delirium passed, I had no memory of that letter, but I must have meant what I now mean. If I wrote of personal love or sorrow in free verse, or in any rhythm that left it unchanged, amid all its accidence, I would be full of self-contempt because of my egotism and indiscretion, and foresee the boredom of my reader. I must choose a traditional stanza, even what I alter must seem traditional. I commit my emotion to shepherds, herdsmen, camel-drivers, learned men, Milton's or Shelley's Platonist, that tower Palmer drew. Talk to me of originality and I will turn on you with rage. I am a crowd, I am a lonely man, I am nothing. Ancient salt is best packing. The heroes of Shakespeare convey to us through their looks, or through the metaphorical patterns of their speech, the sudden enlargement of their vision, their ecstasy at the approach of death: 'She should have died hereafter', 'Of many thousand kisses, the poor last', 'Absent thee from felicity awhile'. They have become God or Mother Goddess, the pelican, 'My baby at my breast', but all must be cold; no actress has ever sobbed when she played Cleopatra, even the shallow brain of a producer has never thought of such a thing. The supernatural is present, cold winds blow across our hands, upon our faces, the thermometer falls, and because of that cold we are hated by journalists and groundlings. There may be in this or that detail painful tragedy, but in the whole work none. I have heard Lady Gregory say, rejecting some play in the modern manner sent to the Abbey Theatre, 'Tragedy must be a joy to the man who dies.' Nor is it any different with lyrics, songs, narrative poems; neither scholars nor the populace have sung or read anything generation after generation because of its pain. The maid of honour whose tragedy they sing must be lifted out of history with timeless pattern, she is one of the four Maries, the rhythm is old and familiar, imagination must dance, must be carried beyond feeling into the aboriginal ice. Is ice the correct word? I once boasted, copying the phrase from a letter of my father's, that I would write a poem 'cold and passionate as the dawn'.

When I wrote in blank verse I was dissatisfied; my vaguely medieval *Countess Cathleen* fitted the measure, but our Heroic Age went better, or so I fancied, in the ballad metre of *The Green Helmet*. There was something in what I felt about Deirdre, about Cuchulain, that rejected the Renaissance and its characteristic metres, and this was a principal reason why I created in dance plays the form that varies blank verse with lyric metres. When I speak blank verse and analyse my feelings, I stand at a moment of history when instinct, its traditional songs and dances, its general agreement, is of the past. I have been cast up out of the whale's belly though I still remember the

sound and sway that came from beyond its ribs, and, like the
Queen in Paul Fort's ballad, I smell of the fish of the sea. The
contrapuntal structure of the verse, to employ a term adopted by
Robert Bridges, combines the past and present. If I repeat the
first line of *Paradise Lost* so as to emphasize its five feet I am
among the folk singers—'Of mán's first dísobédience ánd the
frúit', but speak it as I should cross it with another emphasis,
that of passionate prose—'Of mán's fírst disobédience and the
frúit', or 'Of mán's fírst dísobedience and the frúit'; the folk
song is still there, but a ghostly voice, an unvariable possibility,
an unconscious norm. What moves me and my hearer is a vivid
speech that has no laws except that it must not exorcise the
ghostly voice. I am awake and asleep, at my moment of revelation, self-possessed in self-surrender; there is no rhyme, no echo
of the beaten drum, the dancing foot, that would overset my
balance. When I was a boy I wrote a poem upon dancing that
had one good line: 'They snatch with their hands at the sleep of
the skies'. If I sat down and thought for a year I would discover
that but for certain syllabic limitations, a rejection or acceptance
of certain elisions, I must wake or sleep.

The Countess Cathleen could speak a blank verse which I had
loosened, almost put out of joint, for her need, because I
thought of her as medieval and thereby connected her with the
general European movement. For Deirdre and Cuchulain and all
the other figures of Irish legend are still in the whale's belly.

Notes

MARGARET ATWOOD (b. 1939)

'We must resist. We must refuse to disappear', Margaret Atwood writes
in 'Roominghouse, Winter': 'In exile / survival / is the first necessity.'
Atwood is profoundly aware of the elements in modern life that conspire
to engulf us, to make us disappear both psychically and physically. She
has a keen sense of the isolation, or alienation, at the centre of experience:
the anguish of thinking man, who is separated by his rationality from the
objects (things, events or people) he perceives in the world external to his
ego; the feeling of permanent rootlessness or exile that, as Camus argues
so eloquently in *The Myth of Sisyphus*, constitutes the meaning of the
Absurd; the basic aggressiveness, the struggle for power or dominance,
that permeates all levels of human activity from the sexual to the political.

Atwood is interested primarily in poetry that is *affective*, like Brecht's
poetry and plays—that stimulates a response in the reader. Brecht spoke
of a smoking-man's theatre, where members of the audience would stay
behind to thrash out the issues being dramatized; in his ideal theatre art
would have a revolutionary influence, be a call to arms rather than a
cathartic. Atwood's aims are not dissimilar, as she suggests in an interview
with Chris Levenson in *Manna*: 'I would say that I don't think what poetry
does is express emotion. What poetry does is to evoke emotion from the
reader, and that is a very different thing. As someone once said, if you
want to express emotion, scream. If you want to evoke emotion it's more
complicated.'

Like Brecht, Atwood uses various distancing, or alienating, techniques to
stimulate the interest of the reader, to keep his full attention; she is an
illusionist who employs perceptual tricks, such as interjecting non-sequiturs
or off-hand comments that distract the reader from the apparent content
of the poem or suddenly shifting the point of view in the middle of a
poem. Atwood eschews traditional romantic stances and vocabulary except
for purposes of parody; instead of lyrical outbursts, displays of auditory
and emotional excess, and the use of familiar names or characterization,
she depends upon understatement, the creation of a voice that is wry and
prosaic, the shock-value of disarming or surreal images. As she explains
in *Manna*: 'There are always concealed magical forms in poetry. By
"magic" I mean a verbal attempt to accomplish something desirable. You
can take every poem and trace it back to a source in either prayer, curse,
charm or incantation—an attempt to make something happen. Do you
know anything about autistic children? One of the symptoms of that is
they mistake the word for the thing. If they see the word "clock" on the
paper they pick it up to see if it ticks. If you write "door" they try to
open it. That sort of thing is inherent in language in some funny way
and poetry is connected with that at some level.'

Atwood was born in Ottawa. A good part of her childhood was spent
with her parents in the wilds of Northern Quebec. She studied at the
University of Toronto and Harvard, travelled widely, and alternated between writing and teaching at various institutions in Canada. She lives in

Toronto. Atwood has written several novels, including *The Edible Woman* (1969), *Surfacing* (1972), *Life Before Man* (1979), and *Bodily Harm* (1981); numerous books of poetry, including *The Circle Game* (1966, Governor General's Award), *The Animals in That Country* (1968), *The Journals of Susanna Moodie* (1970), *Power Politics* (1973), *Two-Headed Poems* (1978), *True Stories* (1981), and *Interlunar* (1984); three books of short stories: *Dancing Girls* (1977), *Murder in the Dark* (1983), and *Bluebeard's Egg* (1984); and two books of criticism: *Survival: A Thematic Guide to Canadian Literature* (1972) and *Second Words: Selected Critical Prose* (1982). She is also editor of *The New Oxford Book of Canadian Verse in English* (1982).

W. H. AUDEN (1907-73)

Auden led an extremely restless and productive life. He was born in York, England, and educated at Oxford. He married Erika Mann (daughter of Thoman Mann) in 1936, participated in the Spanish Civil War as an ambulance driver for the Loyalists in 1937, and travelled to China with Christopher Isherwood in 1938. He took up residence in the United States, becoming a citizen in 1946, and divided his time between New York and Austria. He was professor of poetry at Oxford in 1955.

Auden's intellectual restlessness took him from Marxism, Freudian psychoanalysis, and Existentialism to Anglo-Catholicism. Poetically he experimented with Anglo-Saxon verse forms, ballad rhythms, epigram, and blues. Auden was associated with the Oxford poets C. Day Lewis, Stephen Spender, and Louis MacNeice, who turned to communism in the thirties in reaction to the economic depression and the rise of fascism. The pressures of economic and political commitment dominated Auden's early poetry, giving it a public rather than a private character. In the poems of this period Auden is primarily a topical poet who, like Dryden, is most at ease with a 'subject' upon which he can turn his unfailing eye for significant detail and his wonderful control of language. 'Musée des Beaux Arts', for example, is a masterpiece of understatement in which, through the ironic tension between stark images and a painfully matter-of-fact tone, Auden captures the tragic sense of indifference to human suffering and aspiration that informs Breughel's 'The Fall of Icarus'.

Like the confessional poetry of Robert Lowell, Auden's more recent verse is personal and relaxed; it is refreshingly meditative and conversational. Ultimately Auden's analysis of the human condition is seldom deep, but his evocation of the surfaces and moods of the political and intellectual life of his times is unquestionably brilliant.

Auden is the author of several volumes of poetry, including *Poems* (1930), *The Double Man* (1941), *For the Time Being, a Christmas Oratorio* (1945), *The Age of Anxiety: A Baroque Eclogue* (1948, Pulitzer Prize), *Nones* (1951), *The Shield of Achilles* (1955), *Homage to Clio* (1960). His collections include *Collected Shorter Poems* (1967), *Collected Longer Poems* (1969), *Collected Poems* (1976), as well as *The English Auden* (1977), which also includes several of his plays. Important collections of his critical work are *The Enchaféd Flood: The Romantic Iconography of the Sea* (1950), three critical essays on the romantic spirit, and *The Dyer's Hand*, a volume of essays that appeared in 1962.

MARGARET AVISON (b. 1918)

Margaret Avison makes one think of Isaac Babel's image of the poet as a meditative figure with 'spectacles on his nose and autumn in his heart'. Born in Galt, Ontario, and educated at the University of Toronto, she has been a secretary, a librarian, a research assistant, a lecturer in English, and a worker in a relief mission. She has gone about her work as a poet with a quiet intensity, avoiding the facile and the sensational. She is neither prolific nor wide-ranging in subject matter. Her interest, as she explains in 'Voluptuaries and Others', is in depth, in 'that other kind of lighting up/which shows the terrain comprehended'.

There is in Avison's poetry an intellectual probing that is characteristic of the metaphysical poets of the seventeenth century. In *Winter Sun* (1960, Governor General's Award), for example, she explores the landscape of the mind, charting with considerable detail the withdrawal of a delicate sensibility from the external world:

> But as the weeks pass I become accustomed
> To failing more and more
> In credence of reality as others
> Must know it, in a context, with a coming
> And going marshalled among porticos,
> And peacock-parks for hours of morning leisure.

In the halting prose rhythms and photographic images that she owes to Eliot, one senses Avison's concern to describe not only the 'truth' of experience, but also the *process* of arriving at that truth.

The winter terrain of Avison's first book gives way to warmer climates in *The Dumbfounding* (1966), marking a deepening of religious experience and a reconciliation to the physical world. Consequently the book is more concrete and humble in its explorations and pronouncements. Avison's consciousness of the nature and dynamics of perception is here turned to good advantage: her capacity for rapid shifts of perspective within a single poem is replaced by careful observation of minutiae, such as the faces of loiterers and the industry of insects; her sensitivity to the subtleties of language and to the fine distinctions of logic now encompasses the sound of raindrops, 'letting the ear experience this/discrete, delicate clicking.' Whether it marks the passage from despair to belief or, on a technical level, from Eliot to William Carlos Williams, her poetry has undergone a remarkable transformation.

Avison's more recent collections are *Sunblue* (1978) and *Winter Sun/The Dumbfounding: Poems 1940-1966* (1982). Her translated poems from the Hungarian appear in *The Plough and the Pen: Writings from Hungary 1930-1956* (1963) edited by Ilona Duczynska and Karl Polanyi.

JOHN BERRYMAN (1914-72)

In 1954 Geoffrey Moore wrote in *The Penguin Book of Modern American Verse* that Berryman's work had been described by critics as cerebral: 'This is true,' he said, 'and there is also a kind of compressed intellectual savagery. There is a grim vividness . . . in these poems; a damned soul might have written them.' The voice of prophecy: in 1972 Berryman leapt from a bridge to his death, thus ending the long, agonized struggle that was his life. He was born John Allyn Smith in McAlester, Oklahoma, the son of a banker and schoolteacher. When he was ten his family moved to Tampa, Florida, where, two years later, the father shot himself to death outside his son's window. His mother settled in New York and married a Wall Street banker named Berryman, who adopted the boy. His mother and stepfather were divorced after ten years. Berryman himself was married three times. He studied at Columbia and Cambridge, gained recognition as a writer and critic and editor of *Partisan Review*, and taught at Harvard, Wayne State, Princeton, and the University of Minnesota. His poetry won various awards, including the Pulitzer Prize (1965), the Bollingen Prize (1968), and the National Book Award (1969).

Berryman paid heavily for his success. As he once said in connection with his poem 'The Dispossessed': 'I wanted something that would be both very neat, contained, and at the same time thoroughly mysterious. . . . Particularly because I used the poem as title-piece for a book, I have been sensitive (as indeed I was long before) to the word "dispossessed": and there can be no harm in saying here that I have come on it not dozens but hundreds of times used in the specially emphatic and central way I tried myself to achieve. The concept reaches deep into the modern agony.' *Deep into the modern agony*—that is where Berryman's poems, like those of Roethke and Plath, may be said to begin, and end.

Berryman's short poems are of uneven quality; they have a certain stiffness and self-consciousness, as if the poet were uneasy with his medium. He seems, in fact, always to have been working towards the larger canvasses of *Homage to Mistress Bradstreet* and *77 Dream Songs*; it is only in these later works that he comes near achieving a verse that is 'neat', 'contained', and 'mysterious'. Berryman's poetry has been called confessional because it explores such psychic states as neurosis and schizophrenia and because it is sprinkled liberally with very personal references and biographical details. The triumph of *Mistress Bradstreet* and the *Dream Songs*, however, lies in another direction—in Berryman's discovery of a comfortable mask or persona. In *Mistress Bradstreet* he identifies himself with seventeenth-century poet Anne Bradstreet, with her physical and psychic travail and her contradictory yearnings for chaos and form. At times his own voice merges with hers in lines that have a choric intensity; at times the voices are separate and doomed. *77 Dream Songs* follows naturally from *Mistress Bradstreet:* Berryman replaces the 8-line stanza with three 6-line stanzas to create a kind of modern sonnet sequence; he maintains the tortured, distorted syntax that seems so suitable for rendering states of mental disturbance; and he creates a kind of unholy or infernal trinity—Henry, Mr. Bones, and I—a composite persona that embraces the tragic, the comic, and the sentimental. Here is a marriage of Faust, Prufrock, and Joe Christmas—damned figures, like those in Beckett, wandering through the rubble of our century, through Hiroshima, into whom Berryman pours his own despair and the despair of his age. If this poetry is confessional, it is a confession for all mankind.

Berryman's books of poetry include *The Dispossessed* (1948), *Homage to Mistress Bradstreet* (1956; rev. 1968), *77 Dream Songs* (1964), *Short Poems* (1967), *His Toy, His Dream, His Rest* (1968), and *Delusions, Etc.* (1972). He also wrote considerable prose, including a critical biography, *Stephen Crane* (1950), and a novel, *Recovery* (1973).

EARLE BIRNEY (b. 1904)

Born in Calgary, Birney spent most of his youth in Banff and in Creston, British Columbia. He graduated from the University of British Columbia in 1926. His graduate studies in California were interrupted by difficulties, mostly financial, which took him to Utah to teach, and to New York to work for the Trotskyites. With a grant from the Royal Society he completed his doctoral studies in London and at the University of Toronto, where he lectured for several years. He was literary editor of the *Canadian Forum* until 1940, when he went overseas as a Personnel Selection Officer. For a short time he was Supervisor of Foreign Language Broadcasts to Europe for the CBC, after which he became a Professor of English at U.B.C. There he established and headed the department of creative writing. Recently Birney has been poet-in-residence at universities in Canada and the United States.

Since his early radical days, Birney has exhibited a wide range and depth of social criticism in his poetry. He has constantly exposed instances of exploitation, such as the rape of the B.C. forests by industry, the suppression of minorities, or the mass murder of innocents in time of war. For a time Birney's primary response was that of moral outrage, seen, for example, in his mock-heroic satire on bigotry and smallmindedness in 'Anglo-Saxon Street'. Recently he has found newer and subtler ways of expressing his contempt for injustice and his concern for brotherhood. He has created the persona of a sensitive tourist, a kind of twentieth-century Gulliver, whose curiosity and wry sense of self make him an ideal commentator on the human condition. In 'A Walk in Kyoto' and 'Cartagena de Indias' the poet explores his own reactions to unfamiliar environments and, through self-analysis and careful attention to nuance and detail, discovers something fundamental about his relation to these people and places.

'Living art', Birney explains in *The Creative Writer* (1966), 'like anything else, stays alive only by changing.' He has mastered such traditional forms as the narrative, the meditative lyric, verse satire, the descriptive nature poem, and has experimented with Anglo-Saxon verse rhythms. But he has also been interested in experiments with typography and orthography and in the theories and practice of the Black Mountain and concrete poets. Birney constantly reworks his poems; in his *Selected Poems* he has revised extensively and removed most of the traditional punctuation.

Birney's reputation as a poet was established with *David and Other Poems* (1942) and *Now Is Time* (1945), both of which won Governor General's Awards. Further poetry books include *The Strait of Anian* (1948), *Trial of a City and Other Verse* (1952; the narrative poem of the title eventually reprinted as *The Damnation of Vancouver*), *Near False Creek Mouth* (1964), *Collected Poems* (1975), *The Ghost in the Wheels: Selected Poems* (1977), and *Fall by Fury* (1978). He has also published two novels, *Turvey* (1949) and *Down the Long Table* (1955), and three books about his life and art: *The Creative Writer* (1966), *The Cow Jumped Over the Moon* (1972), and *Spreading Time: Book I, 1940-1949* (1980).

ELIZABETH BISHOP (1911-79)

Elizabeth Bishop was born in Worcester, Massachusetts, to parents of Canadian origin and spent a number of impressionable years as a child living with her grandparents in Great Sands, Nova Scotia. Her father's early death, her mother's mental breakdown, and the unstable conditions of life with a series of relatives, led her to describe herself as a 'country mouse' and to see her childhood as a series of 'tiny tragedies and grotesque grieves'; not surprisingly, she took refuge in the imaginative worlds of fantasy and books. She attended Vassar College, travelled to Paris, and lived for nine years in Key West, Florida; but, despite friendships with Marianne Moore, Randall Jarrell, and Robert Lowell, she never established permanent roots in the U.S. and eventually settled in Brazil, where she lived until her death. Her published works include *North & South* (1946), *A Cold Spring* (1955), *Questions of Travel* (1965), *Geography III* (1977), *The Complete Poems, 1927-1979* (1980), and *The Collected Prose* (1984). She co-edited an anthology of Brazilian poetry translated into English and has written (with the editors of *Life*) a book about Brazil.

The search for home, 'wherever that may be', led Bishop to examine in great detail not only the bleak, almost elemental landscapes of her childhood and the exotic surfaces of the Brazil of her maturity, but also to question the function of travel and the nature of reality itself, where the world of the senses cannot always be trusted and where 'there are too many waterfalls'. Her poems have a highly charged quality that reminds one of the effect of the camera slowly panning objects in a gothic film, or of the unsettling and unnerving lighting and sense of stasis or suspended animation experienced in the paintings of magic realists such as Andrew Wyeth. Bishop had no program to follow. She was not a nature poet, though few poets have given so impressive an account of the colours and textures of human and physical nature; neither was she a symbolist, though her best lyrics rise to a symbolic level. She preferred 'glimpses of the always-more-successful surrealism of everyday life'. Though she often begins with the particulars of the natural world, she will occasionally reverse her process, as in '12 O'Clock News', where she makes the flotsam of her writing desk an everywhere—a complex moral and political landscape mined with meaning and significance.

Bishop was an exacting poet. In her memoir of Marianne Moore she claims that Moore's concern for felicity of sound and exactness of expression 'made me realize more than I ever had the rarity of true originality and also the sort of alienation it might involve.' She came to believe that poetry must be 'effortlessly rhetorical' and that there is 'no detail too small' for the serious poet. In other words she found her home at last in art, in language itself, the medium that possesses a more 'watery, dazzling rhetoric' than an Amazon village, that 'resolves and dissolves' the contradictions and contrarieties of ordinary life.

LEONARD COHEN (b. 1934)

Leonard Cohen was born in Montreal and educated at McGill University, where he published his first volume of poetry, *Let Us Compare Mythologies* (1956), in the McGill Poetry Series. He dropped out of graduate studies at Columbia to write and perform, in Montreal nightclubs and for the CBC, the poems and songs collected in *The Spice-Box of Earth* (1961). While living abroad, mostly in Greece, Cohen produced two novels, *The Favourite Game* (1963) and *Beautiful Losers* (1966), and two books of poetry: *Flowers for Hitler* (1964) and *Parasites of Heaven* (1966). His career as a folk-singer led to several albums, including *Songs of Leonard Cohen* (1968), *Songs from a Room* (1969), and *The Best of Leonard Cohen* (1975). *Selected Poems* appeared in 1968, followed by *The Energy of Slaves* (1972), *Death of a Lady's Man* (1978), and *Small Expectations* (1984).

Cohen inherited the mantle of the Beat poets, including their spiritual questing, anti-establishment sentiments, and attraction to the subject of decadence, to which he added his own fascination with power and violence. This combination gave him great popularity in the mid-sixties among audiences who were struggling to define their values and discover new strategies for living. 'We are on the threshold of a great religious age,' he said, 'an age of discipleship. All our spiritual vocabulary has been discredited.' Cohen played secular priest to the individualism of that generation; however, a more committed, politically aware age emerged from the racial protests and political activism of the late sixties, for which Cohen's decadent and disengaged verses seemed to have little relevance. As a result, his popularity declined radically.

Now it is possible to look at Cohen's work apart from the fashions of the mid-sixties and to see the link between the religious quest underlying the poetry and the poetics that inform it. The struggle for a pure heart goes hand in hand with the search for a simple, unadorned style; and the sense of underlying mystery implies a view of art as a means of conjuring, as ritual or magic that will change lives:

> I think that a decent man who has discovered valuable secrets is under some obligation to share them. But I think that the technique of sharing them is a great study. . . .
>
> Now, you can reveal secrets in many ways. One way is to say this is the secret I have discovered. I think that this way is often less successful because when that certain kind of conscious creative mind brings itself to bear on this information, it distorts it, it makes it very inaccessible. Sometimes it's just in the voice, sometimes just in the style, in the length of the paragraph; it's in the tone, rather than in the message.

Following his own artistic advice Cohen has sought a style, or styles, that would best reveal his secrets, moving from traditional lyricism to surrealism to the self-reflexive and anti-poetic strategies of postmodernism. Beneath all of his experiments lie the basic religious forms of address that a man makes to his God: prayer praise, confession, and incantation.

ROBERT CREELEY (b. 1926)

Creeley's belief that ' "Peace comes of communication" ' grows out of a wish to discover the essential rhythms of the self, the poet's own *life*-tone, and to transmit these rhythms to the printed page. This discovery cannot be made by imitating the language patterns and poetic forms of other poets, but must come from close attention to the pressures of one's own breathing and the rhythms of one's own speech. 'Speech,' he insists, 'is an assertion of one man, by one man, "Therefore each speech having its own character, the poetry it engenders will be peculiar to that speech also in its own intrinsic form." '

Creeley is an imagist of the emotions; he turns his acute attention not upon objects in the external world but upon the fine discriminations of the heart and mind. The rhythms of his life, which find their way into poems, are often delicate and lyrical; many of the poems are punctuated in a manner that directly reflects the quiet, almost halting deliberation of the man. His poetry, which is restrained and unpretentious, is accessible to most readers. His sharply etched, compressed lyrics seem perfectly suited to his desire to avoid 'any *descriptive* act . . . which leaves the attention outside the poem.'

Creeley was born in Arlington, Massachusetts. He left Harvard to join the American Field Service in India and Burma, returned briefly to the United States, was married, and departed for France and Majorca, where he started the Divers Press. Creeley completed his degree and taught from 1954-6 at the short-lived Black Mountain College in North Carolina, where he edited the *Black Mountain Review*. He has taught on a coffee *finca* in Guatemala, at the State University of New York at Buffalo, and at the University of New Mexico, where he completed his M.A. Since *Le Fou* (1952), Creeley has published extensively. His books of poetry include *For Love* (1962), *Words* (1967), *Charm: Early and Uncollected Poems* (1968), *St. Martin's* (1971), *Presences* (1976), *Selected Poems* (1976), and *The Collected Poems of Robert Creeley* (1983). In addition to publishing a novel, *The Island* (1963), and a volume of short stories, *The Gold Diggers* (1954; repr. 1965), he has edited the *Selected Writings of Charles Olson*. His non-fiction writings and interviews are available in *A Quick Graph* (1970), *The Collected Prose of Robert Creeley* (1984) and *Contexts of Poetry* (1973).

E. E. CUMMINGS (1894-1962)

cummings wrote many kinds of poetry: the delicate, almost sentimental lyricism in 'somewhere i have never travelled gladly beyond'; the engaging puns and humour in 'may i feel'; and the savage criticism of cant and hypocrisy in 'i sing of Olaf'. His poetic experiments—dispensing with punctuation, distorting typography, using lower-case type, ignoring the rules of grammar and syntax—are an important aspect of his fight against established ideas and systems that threaten the spontaneity and joy cummings valued most in his life. His painter's preoccupation with the visual dimensions of poetry and his curiosity about the letter and syllable as units of meaning look forward to the work of the concrete poets and have been a liberating force in modern poetry. His humour and his unabashed celebration of the simple pleasures of the body and emotions of the heart are an antidote to the cynicism and despair so evident in the work of his contemporaries.

cummings was born in Cambridge, Massachusetts. He was educated at Harvard before joining the Norton Harjes Ambulance Corps in France during the First World War. His imprisonment in a detention camp for three months, due to the error of a military censor, is recorded in his novel, *The Enormous Room* (1922). After studying art in Paris, cummings lived with his wife, the photographer and fashion model Marion Morehouse, in Greenwich Village and at Silver Lake, New Hampshire, where he wrote poetry and painted. He delivered the Eliot Norton Lectures at Harvard in 1952-3 and received the Bollingen Prize for Poetry in 1957.

cummings has written a play, *him* (1927), and a book about his travels in Russia, *Eimi* (1933). His poetry is available in *Poems, 1923-1954* (1954), *95 Poems* (1958), *100 Selected Poems* (1959), and *Complete Poems* (1972).

T. S. ELIOT (1888-1965)

Eliot was born in St. Louis, Missouri. After completing his M.A. at Harvard, he studied philosophy, Sanskrit, and Pali at the Sorbonne, Harvard, and Merton College, Oxford. In London, Eliot taught at Highgate School, worked in Lloyd's Bank, published his first volume of poetry, *Prufrock and Other Observations* (1917), and edited *Criterion*, a quarterly review. Eliot became a British subject in 1927. He distinguished himself as a poet, dramatist, and critic, became director of Faber and Faber, and won the Nobel Prize for Literature in 1948.

Yeats once said of Eliot: 'He wrings the past dry and pours the juice down the throats of those who are either too busy, or too creative, to read as much as he does. I believe that in time he will be regarded as an interesting symptom of a sick and melancholy age.' Although Yeats's statement is limited in the extreme, it anticipates the reaction against Eliot's poetry, which has begun to be felt in critical circles. We now feel less obliged, for example, to understand *all* of Eliot's French sources and esoteric references. In fact many readers have come to regard *The Waste Land* (1922) less as a sacred text and more as an interesting literary collage. It remains true, however, that there are many levels on which Eliot's poetry may be appreciated. For the literati, there is Eliot's relation to tradition, his insistence that the poet exist not only in the present but also in 'the present moment of the past'. From this stems his deliberate quotation from, and allusion to, great literature and events of the past, his ironic juxtaposition of past and present—of Prufrock and John the Baptist, or Hamlet. For the less sophisticated, there is the interest and challenge of Eliot's image-puzzles. In this respect it is perhaps useful to see him as a Tennyson strained through the filter of imagism: that is, he is essentially a narrative poet, but one who has (for reasons of economy and suggestiveness) removed most of the logical connectives from his narrative, leaving only the 'distillation' of his original conception. Keeping this in mind, the reader who immerses himself in the highly charged imagery of 'The Love Song of J. Alfred Prufrock' cannot fail to perceive the emotional state that is being dramatized.

Eliot's verse has its own peculiar music—nursery rhymes, jazz rhythms, dissonance, prose rhythms. Most striking is the sense of the *speaking* voice that characterizes such poems as 'Journey of the Magi' and the cycle that comprises *Four Quartets*. The strength of this speaking voice comes, in part, from Eliot's intellectual confidence, but also from his assured use of the persona and his sense of the dramatic play of feelings and ideas.

Eliot's vision and language have become part of the consciousness of this age. He has made a spiritual pilgrimage from alienation and solitude in *The Waste Land* and 'The Hollow Men' to liberation and community in *Ash Wednesday* (1930) and finally to the vision of God through self-knowledge in *Four Quartets* (1943). But the Eliot of 'Prufrock', who has measured out his life with coffee spoons, still speaks to us most convincingly.

Eliot's poetry is available in *Complete Poems and Plays* (1969). Of his plays, the most famous are *Murder in the Cathedral* (1935), *The Family Reunion* (1939), and *The Cocktail Party* (1950). His literary criticism includes *Selected Essays* (1932, 1951), *The Use of Poetry and the Use of Criticism* (1933), and *On Poetry and Poets* (1957).

LAWRENCE FERLINGHETTI (b. 1919)

Ferlinghetti was born in New York. During the Second World War he was connected with the Free French and Norwegian Underground. He received his B.A. from the University of North Carolina, his M.A. from Columbia, and his doctorate from the Sorbonne, where he studied fine art. In 1951 he moved to San Francisco, where he started City Lights Bookstore, the first all paper-bound bookstore in the U.S. City Lights began to publish in 1955, and brought out Ginsberg's *Howl* in its Pocket Poets Series.

Ferlinghetti rejects common assumptions concerning the detachment of the beats; he believes that the poet must be *engagé*. His love affair with America has been turbulent: he has been both an articulator of its dreams and a severe critic, publicly denouncing the Eisenhower administration and satirizing, in his poetry, almost every cliché of American life. As a publisher he has tried to promote a hearing for modern poetry; as a poet he has been instrumental in returning poetry from the academies to the marketplace. To accomplish this he has stressed heavily the auditory dimension of poetry and has composed poems (the 'oral messages' in *A Coney Island of the Mind*) for jazz accompaniment. Although he is not an academic poet, Ferlinghetti is the most self-consciously eclectic of the beats; to read his poetry is to rediscover Keats, Yeats, Eliot, and Thomas in excitingly unusual contexts and juxtapositions.

In addition to *Pictures of a Gone World* (1955), *A Coney Island of the Mind* (1958), *Secret Meaning of Things* (1969), *Love Is No Stone on the Moon* (1972), *Who Are We Now?* (1976), *Landscapes of Living & Dying* (1979), and *Endless Life: The Selected Poems* (1981), Ferlinghetti has written a novel, *Her* (1960), and several travel journals.

ROBERT FROST (1874-1963)

Robert Lee Frost was born in San Francisco to a Scottish mother and an outspoken father who championed the South and States' Rights. This combination may explain the mixture of rebelliousness and restraint that were to characterize Frost's life and art. After his father's death, Frost and his mother moved to Lawrence, Massachusetts. Before marrying his childhood sweetheart, Elinor White, Frost worked as a bobbin boy and reporter in Lawrence. After two years at Harvard, Frost tried farming, which he hated, and teaching, for which he was temperamentally unsuited. In 1912 he went to England with his wife and four children, where he moved in literary circles and where his poetry first found recognition. With the success of *A Boy's Will* (1913) and *North of Boston* (1914), he returned to America, where he was poet-in-residence at Amherst College from 1916 to 1938. Frost spent his last years in New England, widely known and honoured as a poet and lecturer.

In 'The Figure a Poem Makes' Frost declares that a poem 'begins in delight and ends in wisdom'. Initially, few readers progressed in their appreciation beyond the deceptively simple surfaces of Frost's poems. But Frost writes symbolic poetry; to arrive at certain basic truths about life, he explores feelings and thoughts *obliquely* through the use of simple bucolic incidents. Poems as immediately accessible as 'Stopping by Woods', 'Mending Wall', and 'Birches' possess levels of meaning that are dark and profound—like subtle literary parables.

Although few of his early readers ever went beyond the delight to the wisdom of Frost's poetry, the notion of him as merely the singer of a benevolent nature is no longer acceptable. He was a passionate and troubled man, who sought in his poems 'a momentary stay against confusion'; and his skilfully constructed poems testify to his mastery over that confusion.

Most of Frost's poetry is available in *Collected Poems of Robert Frost* (1930, Pulitzer Prize; new edition, 1939) and *Complete Poems of Robert Frost* (1949). In addition there is a useful collection, *Collected Poems of Robert Frost* (1983).

704

ALLEN GINSBERG (b. 1926)

Ginsberg was born in Paterson, New Jersey, to Naomi Ginsberg, a Russian immigrant, and Louis Ginsberg, a lyric poet and schoolteacher. His life from age seventeen until the publication of *Howl and Other Poems* in 1956 included Columbia, the merchant service, dishwashing, market research, book reviewing, drugs, travel to Texas, Denver, Mexico City, and Yucatán. Between *Howl* and *Kaddish and Other Poems* (1961), Ginsberg travelled to the Arctic by sea, to Venice, Tangiers, Amsterdam, Paris and London, and read poems at Oxford, Columbia, and Chicago. After 'Kaddish', a long poem written about the death of his mother, he recorded his poems in San Francisco and departed for the Orient.

Ginsberg's friend, John Clellon Holmes, describes the problem at the core of the beat philosophy in this way: 'Beyond all laws, it is our stunted consciousness that imprisons us, and we suffer from a consequent hunger of the spirit for which all our perversions and our politics are only a kind of ugly stomach cramp. How are we to break out of the prison? How do we let the spirit prosper so that the blistered desert we are making of the world can flower again?' For Ginsberg, of course, the answer is to widen the area of consciousness, which involves a conscientious rejection of all copied forms and responses, of all values and institutions that are not oriented towards psychic liberation.

Starting from William Carlos Williams' idea of the new American measure and reaching back to Whitman, Ginsberg arrived at what he calls his 'romantic inspiration—Hebraic-Melvillian bardic breath'. What this means in terms of *Howl* and *Kaddish* is the freedom to be exuberant and incantatory, to catalogue at will, and to employ free association of ideas in the context of a sweeping, religious utterance. Ultimately, Ginsberg is the natural heir to Whitman—in his further exploration of Whitman's long line ('Howl'), and in terms of his preoccupation with transcending the ego by *containing*, or partaking of, all experience, a kind of osmosis of the imagination.

Ginsberg's *Collected Poems 1947-1980* appeared in 1984. He has also published a steady stream of books and pamphlets, including *Reality Sandwiches* (1963), *Indian Journals* (1970), *Mind Breaths: Poems 1972-1977* (1978), *Plutonian Ode: Poems 1977-1980* (1982), and *Many Loves & Other Poems* (1983). *The Yage Letters*, his correspondence with William Burroughs, was published in 1963.

ROBERT GRAVES (b. 1895)

Robert Graves was born in Wimbledon, England, to Alfred Percival Graves, the Irish writer, and Amalia von Ranke. From school he went directly into the First World War, where he became a captain in the Royal

Welsh Fusiliers. Apart from spending a year as a professor of English at Cairo University in 1926 and succeeding W. H. Auden as professor of poetry at Oxford in 1961, Graves has earned his living by writing. In his prolific lifetime, he has published an autobiography, *Good-bye to All That* (1929; rev. 1957), many historical novels, including *I, Claudius* and *Wife to Mr Milton*, translations, critical essays, *The White Goddess* (studies in mythology that present a new view of the poetic impulse), and *The Greek Myths* (the first modern dictionary of Greek mythology). His permanent home is on Majorca, Spain.

Graves's highly organic poetry may well seem out of place, if not anachronistic, in the age of permanent literary revolution that Kathleen Raine describes in *Defending Ancient Springs:* 'It might seem that revolution for its own sake, transformation as such, an instantaneous gesture which expresses finally nothing but its own instantaneity, process as such, has become the be-all and end-all of art; process so accelerated that all images have dissolved into the flux of continuous transformation, so much so that form, in such art, can no longer be said to exist.' Although he defends the poet's right to use whatever means he requires to make good poems, Graves depends upon traditional metres and forms rather than on the verbal and typographical gymnastics of the moderns. But he uses tradition gracefully and unobtrusively. Graves's poetry does have a formal beauty that is rare in this age; and yet he is careful to insist that 'Method in poetry is not something that can be discussed in terms of purely physical form.' He prefers to emphasize other qualities in his verse, especially its originality of thought and image. In his poems the images have not been 'dissolved into the flux'; they are highly charged and have an unusual psychological impact on the reader. In 'The Cool Web' and 'Warning to Children', for example, Graves taps some secret spring of human passion and knowledge; he seems to draw on the vast reservoir of images that Jung calls the 'collective unconscious'.

With his devotion to the craft and his painstakingly honed poems, Graves is a poet's poet. He regularly revises, reprinting in successive versions of his *Collected Poems*—which first appeared in 1938 and last appeared in 1977—only his newest revisions of his own favourites. His individual volumes include *More Poems 1961* (1961), *New Poems* (1962), *Man Does Woman Is* (1964), *Love Respelt* (1965), *My Head, My Head* (1974), and *Watch the North Wind Rise* (1982). His lectures as professor of poetry at Oxford are collected in *Poetic Craft and Principle* (1967); and a number of his critical essays appear in *The Crowning Privilege* (1955).

THOM GUNN (b. 1929)

Thom Gunn was born in Gravesend, England. He attended school in Hampstead before taking his degree at Trinity College, Cambridge. Gunn served in the British army from 1948 to 1950 and lived in Paris and Rome for several years before going to the United States on a Fulbright scholarship. He studied and later taught at Stanford before joining the English department at the University of California in 1958.

Gunn's reputation rests in part on non-literary factors: his attraction to violence and his participation in the world of motorcycles and black jackets. 'I think the whole question of energy and violence isn't particularly modern,' he says. 'I think we live in an extremely unviolent world, really. I know this is not the *cliché*, but if you compare somebody's day in London or in San Francisco now with what it would have been a hundred years ago, let alone two hundred years ago, it's extremely mild and pacific. You don't see any fights around you, or anything. I think our particular generation is obsessed with the idea of violence—maybe it misses it; it has a kind of nostalgia for violence. I think it's terribly unhealthy, actually, like most nostalgias.' Asked to explain his interest in violence, Gunn says: 'I think we start with a kind of life energy, and this is obviously in an elementary sense good, since this is the whole of life. At the same time, this energy, in so far as it expresses us, is often going to infringe on other people's energy, and so it becomes negative; it becomes destructive. And I think the kind of thing I am searching for is a way of defining a type of energy that *doesn't* infringe on other people's energy —that possibly may even help other people. This is asking rather a lot.'

As if to control his highly charged subject matter, Gunn has developed a remarkable facility with traditional metrics and syllabics. As he explains in the same BBC interview: 'I would like to be able to write free verse, but I can't write free verse that is any good. So I find that writing syllabics (which I didn't invent, by any means) enables me to preserve some kind of discipline that apparently I need in the writing of a poem; and at the same time I am able to get certain free-verse effects—a kind of free-verse tone which is often more relaxed and casual than the kind which I have when I am writing metrical verse. This enables me to take up different kinds of subjects, rather smaller subjects, often; or to take up the small, noticed, rather casual detail.'

In addition to his *Selected Poems* (1962) with Ted Hughes, Gunn has published *Fighting Terms* (1954; rev. 1962), *The Sense of Movement* (1957), *My Sad Captains and Other Poems* (1967), *Poems 1950-1966* (1971), *Selected Poems* (1979), and *The Passages of Joy* (1982). His nonfiction writings are available in *The Occasions of Poetry: Essays in Criticism and Autobiography* (1982).

SEAMUS HEANEY (b. 1939)

Raised on a farm in County Derry, Northern Ireland, Heaney received his B.A. from Queen's University, Belfast, in 1961. He taught in schools and colleges for several years and has been a guest lecturer at Berkeley and Harvard. Since 1972 he has lived principally in the Republic of Ireland. His publications include *Death of a Naturalist* (1966), *Door into the Dark* (1969), *Wintering Out* (1972), *North* (1975), *Field Work* (1979), *Selected Poems 1965-1975* (1980), *Station Island* (1984), *Preoccupations: Selected Prose 1968-1978* (1980). He has also written a short critical work, *The Fire i' the Flint: Reflections on the Poetry of Gerard Manley Hopkins* (1975).

Heaney speaks of poetry 'as a point of entry into the buried life of the feelings or as a point of exit from it.' Much of his work as a poet has been to dig up material from his personal and collective past; this has taken him from grainy close-ups of farm life, as he experienced and remembered it, to symbolic narratives and meditations on the moral and cultural significance of archeological discoveries in the bogs of Ireland and Northern Europe. He believes in 'poetry as divination; poetry as revelation of the self to the self, as restoration of the culture to itself; poems as elements of continuity, with the aura and authenticity of archeological finds, where the buried shard has an importance that is not obliterated by the buried city; poetry as a dig, a dig for finds that end up being plants.'

Much of the power of Heaney's work resides in its sound, in the grunt of his diction and the torque of his syntax. He writes a richly textured verse with great density of sound, which owes as much to the examples of Hopkins, Dylan Thomas, and Ted Hughes as to the Irish contribution to the English language. Not surprisingly, Heaney accepts Rimbaud's notion 'of vowels as colours and poetry as an alchemy of sounds.' The range of his sound is narrower and less multi-coloured than that of Yeats or Hopkins; but it is not without power. In fact, the deliberately blunt rhythms and gutteral sounds seem particularly suited to Heaney's view of the poetic process and to the rural and subterranean nature of his materials.

TED HUGHES (b. 1930)

Born in Mytholmroyd, Yorkshire, Ted Hughes was a ground wireless mechanic in the Royal Air Force before studying at Cambridge, where he met and married the American poet Sylvia Plath. Hughes first attracted attention during his stay in America when his *Hawk in the Rain* won the first publication award for the Poetry Centre of the New York City YM-YWHA in 1957. This volume was followed by *Lupercal* (1960), *Selected Poems* (1962) with Thom Gunn, *Wodwo* (1967), and a steady flow of new work, including *Crow: From the Life and Songs of the Crow* (1970; rev. 1972), *Selected Poems: 1957-1967* (1974), *Gaudette* (1977), *Moortown* (1980), *Under the North Sea* (1981), *New Selected Poems* (1982), and *River* (1984). His poetics and non-fiction writings appear in *Poetry in the Making: An Anthology of Poems and Programmes from Listening and Writing* (1969) and interviews in *Ted Hughes: The Unaccommodated Universe* (1980) by Ekbert Faas. Hughes received first place in the Guinness Poetry Awards (1958), a Guggenheim fellowship (1959-60), and the Hawthornden Prize (1961). Hughes' latest achievement is his appointment as Poet Laureate.

Hughes is one of the most original and powerful English poets in the second half of this century. He has a special talent for dramatizing the dynamics of man's encounters with the animal world; he captures (in thrush, otter, and pike) both the indefinable threat and the mixture of attraction and repulsion that one associates with D. H. Lawrence's animals. Hughes' success in rendering this tension results from a remarkable imaginative sympathy—his ability to take part in the existence of things outside the self. The early poems are heavily textured in terms of image and sound, giving the reader a deeply sensuous involvement in the poem's form and content. In the *Crow* poems Hughes denudes his language for a verse that is stark and elemental, in keeping with the symbolic nature of the creation parable. However, even in *Crow*, with its comic-opera aspect, he manages to sustain a high degree of versatility, a ritual intensity, and a shamanistic sense of mystery and play.

Hughes speaks of the making of a poem in terms of musical composition: 'I might say that I turn every combatant into a bit of music, then resolve the whole uproar into as formal and balanced a figure of melody and rhythm as I can. When all the words are hearing each other clearly, and every stress is feeling every other stress, and all are contented— the poem is finished.' Although he is a very conscious craftsman, Hughes values vision and truth more than craft, and admits that 'in the end, one's poems are ragged dirty undated letters from remote battles and weddings and one thing and another.'

A. M. KLEIN (1909-72)

Abraham Moses Klein was born in Montreal to immigrant parents who were orthodox Jews. He graduated from McGill University in 1929 and studied law at the University of Montreal. From 1933 Klein practised law in Montreal, edited the *Canadian Zionist*, taught English literature part time, worked on a still-unfinished study of James Joyce (to be found in unfinished form in *Accent*, x, 3, 1950 and *New Directions 13*), and ran unsuccessfully as a CCF candidate for federal parliament.

Klein's poetic heritage is extremely rich. He draws from his knowledge of the French, English, and Hebrew languages and their respective cultures. He is as familiar with the writings of T. S. Eliot and James Joyce and the literature of the English Renaissance as he is with Jewish history and religious teachings. In the best of Klein's poetry these diverse elements are fused by a penetrating social consciousness, which is compounded of great rage and compassion. In 'In re Solomon Warshawer', for example, the Jew who declaims against the 'unfuturity' of the S.S. men is, in fact, addressing himself to all such emanations of evil in the history of mankind:

> O I have known them all,
> The dwarf dictators, the diminutive dukes,
> The heads of straw, the hearts of gall,
> Th' imperial plumes of eagles covering rooks!

The brilliance of this poem lies not only in its exploration of 'the heart's depths, how it may sink/Down to the deep and ink of genesis', but also in the incredible range of reference that the poet exhibits.

Klein's poetic stance is not merely declamatory; he is capable of lyricism, religious rhapsody, reminiscence, and confession, as well as varying degrees of humour and satire. His aim as a poet, as stated in 'Portrait of the Poet as Landscape', is 'to say the word that will become sixth sense', 'to bring/new form to life'.

Klein's volumes of poetry include *Hath Not a Jew* (1940), *The Hitleriad* (1944), *Poems* (1944), and *The Rocking Chair and Other Poems* (1948), for which he received a Governor General's Award, and *The Collected Poems of A. M. Klein* (1974) edited by Miriam Waddington. His novel, *The Second Scroll*, was published in 1951. *Beyond Sambation: Selected Essays and Editorials 1928-1955*, edited by M. W. Steinberg and Usher Caplan, appeared in 1982, and *A. M. Klein: Short Stories*, edited by M. W. Steinberg, in 1983.

PHILIP LARKIN (b. 1922)

Philip Larkin was born in Coventry, Warwickshire, and educated at King Henry VIII School and St John's College, Oxford. He makes his living as librarian in the University of Hull. In addition to *The North Ship* (1945), Larkin has published *The Less Deceived* (1955); *The Whitsun Weddings* (1964); *High Windows* (1974); two novels, *Jill* (1946) and *A Girl in Winter* (1947); and a book of critical and biographical writings, *Required Reading: Miscellaneous Pieces, 1955-1982* (1984).

Larkin is the poet of the emotionally underprivileged, of the vast majority of mankind for whom life is a progressive disillusionment. His poetic personae are invariably unimposing figures: a solitary man, with bicycle clips on his trousers, ruminating in an empty church, an outsider looking in on the merrymaking of others, and an unfortunate who has literally and figuratively missed the boat. If Larkin's lot is the short end of the stick, one can only say that he has a firm grasp on it. He is not a shallow cynic but, like Thomas Hardy (one of his early influences), an intelligent skeptic.

Larkin's distaste for the spectacular extends also to the *manner* of his poetry, which is traditional rather than experimental. His small output reflects his concern for careful observation, and for clarity and precision of statement—something learned from the poetry of Yeats. Larkin's is a grey world, but it is a compellingly frank and honest one, to be understood, as the title of his second volume suggests, only by the less deceived.

IRVING LAYTON (b. 1912)

Layton was born in Rumania but has spent most of his life since early childhood in Montreal. He studied agriculture at Macdonald College and economics and political science at McGill University. Layton has taught in Montreal secondary schools and at Sir George Williams University and has travelled extensively in Europe. Perhaps the most prolific poet in Canada, his numerous readings and his outspoken opinions on current affairs have made him a well-known, though little understood, public figure.

To many readers Layton is a paradox. His poetry is violent and aggressive, shocking 'delicate' sensibilities with its bombast, satire, and blatantly self-conscious erotica (which is basically asexual), and espousing what Layton considers dark truths about mankind. This is the Layton of 'Misunderstanding' and 'Whom I Write For', the poet who (intending no irony) dedicates a volume of poetry to Lyndon Johnson. The other side of Layton's poetry is sentimental and reflective, as in the warmly elegaic 'Cain' and 'The Bull Calf' or the naturalistic 'The Cold Green Element' and 'A Tall Man Executes a Jig'.

Layton's poetry has suffered from his inability to reconcile two opposing conceptions of the poet's function: the public spokesman who storms up and down the market-place, like Christ and the prophets, railing at vice and folly; and the clear-thinking analyst and articulator of the human condition. In a number of superb poems, such as 'Sacrament by Water', 'Berry Picking', and 'Keine Lazarovitch', Layton does manage to direct his aggressions and sentiments towards poetic excellence. The superiority of these poems indicates that Layton can write with both passion and restraint, that by finding the 'right' subject the contradictions of his nature can be resolved.

Since the publication of his first two volumes of poetry, *Here and Now* (1945) and *Now Is the Place* (1948), Layton has produced a steady stream of books, including *The Long Pea-Shooter* (1954) and *The Cold Green Element* (1955). In addition to two volumes of selected poems, *The Im-*

proved Binoculars (1956) and *A Red Carpet for the Sun* (1959), for which
he received the Governor General's Award, Layton has published *Balls for
a One-Armed Juggler* (1963), *The Laughing Rooster* (1964), *Collected
Poems* (1965), *Periods of the Moon* (1967), *The Shattered Plinths* (1968),
The Collected Poems of Irving Layton (1971), *The Pole-Vaulter* (1974),
For My Brother Jesus (1976), *The Covenant* (1977), *Droppings from
Heaven* (1979), *A Wild Peculiar Joy* (1982), and *The Gucci Bag* (1983).

ROBERT LOWELL (1917-77)

Born in Boston into one of the famous families of New England, Robert
Lowell received his formal education at Harvard, at Kenyon College where
he studied classics and worked with writer John Crowe Ransom, and at
Louisiana State University. During the Second World War Lowell was
drafted, after trying twice unsuccessfully to enlist in 1943, but refused to
serve on the grounds that the allied bombing of enemy civilians was unjustified and that America was out of danger. His imprisonment is recorded in some of his later poems ('Given a year,/I walked on the roof
of West Street Jail . . .'). Early in his poetic career Lowell became a
Catholic, adding to the burden and complications of a New England Puritan conscience. He was married twice, to Jean Stafford (1940) and Elizabeth Hardwick (1948), and was an occasional teacher.

Lowell's early poetry is mannered and formal, employing rhyme and
metrics, and is steeped in the lore and landscape of New England. In this
environment, Lowell finds abundant correlatives for the turmoil of his
young manhood: in 'The Quaker Graveyard in Nantucket' the tortuous
moral terrain of New England is brilliantly realized; and in 'Mr Edwards
and the Spider' the Puritan obsession with sin and damnation is rendered
in the form of a dramatic monologue by the famous preacher, Jonathan
Edwards. In the later *Life Studies* (1959), however, Lowell's poems are
confessional and conversational, without the apparent formality and objectivity of *Lord Weary's Castle* (1946). Instead of rhyme and metrics, one
finds in 'For the Union Dead', for example, continuously shifting speech
rhythms in conjunction with strikingly appropriate images:

> Their monument sticks like a fishbone
> in the city's throat.
> Its Colonel is as lean
> as a compass-needle.

These poems are neither casual nor relaxed; Lowell's early restraint is still
there, but it is apparent in a new spareness, a strength and clarity of outline, that is the legacy of the imagists.

Lowell has published *Land of Unlikeness* (1944), *Lord Weary's Castle*
(1946, Pulitzer Prize), *Poems, 1938-49* (1950), *The Mills of the Kavanaughs*
(1951), *Life Studies* (1959), *Imitations* (1961), *For the Union Dead* (1964),

Near the Ocean (1967), *The Dolphin* (1973), *History* (1973), *Selected Poems* (1976; rev. 1977), and *Day By Day* (1977).

CHARLES OLSON (1910-1970)

Born in Worcester, Massachusetts, Olson claims to have been 'uneducated' at Wesleyan, Yale, and Harvard, where he completed a PH.D. in American Studies. He taught at Clarke and Harvard Universities (1936-9) and at Black Mountain College in North Carolina (1951-6), where he was instructor and rector. With the assistance of a Guggenheim fellowship, Olson completed his unique critical study of Melville, *Call Me Ishmael* (1947). In 1952 another grant took him to Yucatán to study Mayan hieroglyphics. His influence on the North American literary scene, including his intervention on behalf of Ezra Pound, his contact with young poets, his teaching, and his well-known poetic manifestos, has been immense.

In a note to *Human Universe and Other Essays* (1965), Olson writes:

It's as though you were hearing this for the first time—who knows what a poem ought to sound like? until it's thar? And how do you get it thar except as you do—*you*, and nobody else (who's
a poet
  What's
a poem?
  It ain't dreamt until it walks   It talks   It spreads its green barrazza
  Listen closely, folks, this poem comes to you by benefit of its own Irish green bazoo. You take it, from here.

This note explains somewhat whimsically what Olson believes seriously to be the nature of poetic composition. He rejects formal order as such, especially the tight imagistic modes and cross-fertilization of metaphor favoured by New Criticism. Instead he insists that a poem is a *thing*, a unit of energy passed from writer to reader, and that it has its own laws, the most important being that form and content must be realized simultaneously. This, in the hands of an inexperienced writer, results only in formlessness; but not for the poet with a fine ear to discriminate among possible syllables as particles of sound and sense and a fine eye to determine the placing of these syllables.

Olson's rejection of the closed form for what he calls composition by field reflects his conception of poetry as an act of being. The poet must dispense with all intellectual trappings, all systems of thought (including abstractions such as space and time) that interfere with his experience of himself and other *objects* in his world. The result of this denuding process, which Olson describes as 'objectism', is that the individual is faced with the bare fact of his existence as an object in the physical world: 'It

is his own physiology he is forced to arrive at.' In his poetry Olson begins with the literal fact of being. Thus his unusual awareness, in the act
of creation, of the discriminations of his senses and the pressure of his
breathing. To ignore this awareness, Olson would say, is to ignore what
is most fundamental, most personal, in the creative process.

Following *Call Me Ishmael* (1947), Olson's publications include *Y & X*
(1948), *Letter for Melville* (1951), *In Cold Hell, in Thicket* (1953), *Maximus
Poems / 1-10* (1953), *Maximus Poems / 11-22* (1956), *O'Ryan* (1958), *The
Distances* (1960), *The Maximus Poems* (1983). A fine selection of his best
poetry and prose, including his important essay 'Projective Verse' (1959),
is available in *Selected Writings of Charles Olson* (1967), edited with an
introduction and bibliography by Robert Creeley.

MICHAEL ONDAATJE (b. 1943)

Michael Ondaatje was born and spent his first eleven years in Sri Lanka
(Ceylon). He was educated in Dulwich, England, before coming in 1963
to Canada, where he studied at Bishop's University, the University of
Toronto, and Queen's. His collections of poetry include *The Dainty
Monsters* (1967); *The Man with Seven Toes* (1969); *The Collected Works
of Billy the Kid* (1970), which won a Governor General's award; *Rat
Jelly* (1973); *There's A Trick With A Knife I'm Learning To Do* (1979),
which won a second Governor General's award; and *Secular Love* (1984).
He has also made films, written scripts, published a book of criticism of
Leonard Cohen's work, and composed two long prose works: *Coming
Through Slaughter* (1976), a novel about the madness and death of jazz
musician Buddy Bolden, and *Running in the Family* (1983), a fictionalized
biography of his family in Sri Lanka.

Ondaatje's poetry ranges from tender poems of friendship and domes-
ticity to explosive portrayals of violence and psychic upheaval. Thus
duality is present also in terms of form, in writing that ranges from
conventional lyrics and short narratives rooted in the traditions of formal
elegance to aggressive and unstable pieces that push against the limits
of established form, threatening to turn into anti-art. In such poetry
Ondaatje expresses the two impulses Roland Barthes identifies in *The
Pleasure of the Text* as being at war in contemporary art: a safe, imitative edge, which treads ground that is familiar, and a subversive edge
that is violent, unpredictable, and always moving towards that frontier
where 'the death of language is glimpsed'.

In longer poems, such as *The Collected Works of Billy the Kid*, Ondaatje
explores and explodes popular myths, ransacks contemporary culture for
documents, tales, interviews, jokes, gossip, and ads, and carries on a
running battle with the accepted sense of what is 'poetic'. Just as he is
drawn to the outlandish, the surreal, and the chaotic as a safeguard

against worn-out forms, so too does he cultivate a music and diction that are slightly off-beat and out-of-kilter. Aspects of the new grammar he seeks may be found in avant-garde cinema, which is fragmentary and discontinuous, or in music, particularly jazz, which is improvisational, pushing the familiar in unexpected directions.

WILFRED OWEN (1893-1918)

Owen was born in Shropshire and educated at Birkenhead and the University of London. From 1913 to 1915 he was tutor to a French family near Bordeaux. After two years in the British army during the First World War, he was killed at the Sambre Canal just seven days before Armistice. His *Collected Poems* were edited in 1920 with an introduction by Siegfried Sassoon. A new edition, edited by Edmund Blunden, including a number of previously unpublished pieces and notices of his life and work, was published in 1931. A third edition, published in 1963, was edited by C. Day Lewis.

Owen's poetry encompasses one of the fundamental issues of twentieth-century life: war. His descriptions of the mutilation of body and mind are shocking and immediate, even in an age accustomed to a steady diet of violence and obsessed with the atrocities of war. That he should have experienced war from the trenches rather than the administrative offices makes all the more remarkable the fact that he responded with such profound pity and restraining irony. His verse first came to the attention of the young poets with Blunden's edition in 1931, and its impact may be felt in the war poems of Spencer, Auden, Jarrell, and many others.

Owen's verse has a rugged beauty. The naturalness of his idiom and his substitution of assonance for rhyme are the work of an original and skilful technician. Beyond this, his poetry, because it is a prologue to death, is unavoidably passionate.

P. K. PAGE (b. 1916)

P. K. Page was born in England but raised in Calgary and Winnipeg. She lived briefly in the Maritimes before moving to Montreal, where she worked at the National Film Board and in 1942 became associated with Patrick Anderson and F. R. Scott on the board of the 'little magazine' *Preview*. She married Arthur Irwin and, as the wife of the Canadian ambassador, lived from 1953 to 1964 in Mexico, Brazil, and Australia. Her poetry collections are *As Ten as Twenty* (1946), *The Metal and the Flower* (1954, Governor General's Award), *Cry Arrarat!* (1967), *Poems New and Selected* (1974), *Leviathan in a Pool* (1974), and *Evening Dance of the Grey Flies* (1981). A novel, first published in 1944, was reissued in *The Sun and the Moon and Other Fictions* (1973).

Page is a fascinating example of the poet as psychic traveller for whom poetry and painting are two possible vehicles. She began her work under the influence of Eliot, Auden, and the neo-Metaphysical poets for whom the poem was largely a closed form, a performance. In this realm she produced a number of brilliant lyrics. Then, under the influence of travel, new languages, painting, age, and a reading of the mystics, she came to see poetry as a form of exploration and conjuring. Her sojourn in Brazil, according to an interview in *The Canadian Forum*, strengthened her belief that 'certain proportions, the right proportions, can actually alter human perception'. To this end she endeavoured, in her poems and drawings, to discover the magical combinations and forms that would open perceptual doors.

Not surprisingly her poems, early and late, contain many explicit references to the kinds, tricks, and limits of human perception. Even her account of the poetic process makes use of the optical illusion of a vanishing point: 'The idea diminishes to a dimensionless point in my absolute centre. If I can hold it steady long enough, the feeling which is associated with that point grows and fills a larger area as perfume permeates a room. It is from here that I write—held within that luminous circle, that locus which is at the same time a focusing glass, the surface of a drum' (*Canadian Literature* 46, Autumn 1970).

SYLVIA PLATH (1932-63)

Sylvia Plath was born in Boston of Austrian and German parentage. After graduating from Smith College in 1955, she studied at Cambridge on a Fulbright fellowship in 1957, where she met and married Ted Hughes. She had two children and taught briefly at Smith before her death by suicide in London. Her first collection of poems, *The Colossus* (1960), attracted considerable critical attention; it was followed by a novel, *The Bell Jar* (1963), and the posthumous collections *Ariel* (1965), *Crossing the Water* (1972), and *Winter Trees* (1972).

Sylvia Plath expressed excitement at what she called Robert Lowell's 'intense breakthrough into very serious, very personal, emotional experience which I feel has been partly taboo.' Her own poetry explores an intense inner world. One aspect of this world is a morbid fascination with death and the grotesque:

> The eye of the blind pianist
>
> At my table on the ship.
> He felt for his food.
> His fingers had the noses of weasels.
> I couldn't stop looking.

The strength of such poems lies precisely in the poet's inability to 'stop looking'. In 'Lady Lazarus', Plath dramatizes a bitterness and self-contempt that border on masochism; but in 'Tulips' she conveys a painful reaching out for life and sanity.

These poems are as carefully crafted and as finely chiselled as they are bizarre. Both her diaries and the comments of Ted Hughes indicate that the apparently confessional aspect of her poetry was considerably less important to her than the most detailed formal considerations.

EZRA POUND (1885-1972)

Pound was born in Hailey, Idaho, 'in a half savage country, out of date', to use his own words. He attended the University of Pennsylvania and Hamilton College, taking his M.A. in romance languages. Pound was too much of a bohemian for the Indiana authorities and was asked to resign his teaching post, after which he left for Europe on a cattle ship. He married Dorothy Shakespear in 1914. During his stay in England, Pound edited with Richard Aldington the first imagist anthology and was active in literary circles. He went to Paris and then to Rapallo, Italy, where he worked on the *Cantos* and tried to advance the reputations of several artists, including James Joyce. In 1945 Pound was imprisoned in Rome by American troops for his support of the fascists; then he was removed to the United States to be tried for treason. He was declared insane and committed instead of being tried (an experience that is described in *The Pisan Cantos* and in William Carlos Williams's *Autobiography*). In 1948 Pound was awarded the Bollingen Prize for Poetry, a much-disputed and long-overdue recognition of his genius and contribution to literature. Following his release from hospital in 1958, Pound returned to Italy, where he remained in relative seclusion.

As a poet, Pound is often accused of being both 'archaic' and self-consciously 'modern'. He has been a constant innovator, not only in inventing new forms but also in reviving old forms and in introducing into English elements from the poetry of other languages. Paradoxically, when Pound's poetry is most 'archaic' it is most modern in its psychology; for he seems to achieve in his historical subjects a freedom and objectivity that are denied to him in the pressing matters of his own age. Pound brought about a revolution in poetic attitudes and practice. He anticipated the objectivism of Williams, the rhythmical preoccupations of Olson and Creeley, and the technical experiment that characterizes poetry in this century. His own verse is lyrical, crudely didactic, satirical, esoteric, rambling, witty, colloquial, ranging in form from the epic to the epigram, in manner from the autobiographical to the classically objective. With the imagists he sought for concentration and clarity of expression, to reduce poetry to its essentials. His poetry bears the mark of his early interest in the Chinese ideogram, which he describes as 'a vivid shorthand picture of the operations of nature'. On the other hand, his poetry can also be vast and sprawling, as in the *Cantos*, a profoundly moving and amusing case history of our civilization.

Pound believed 'in technique as the test of a man's sincerity'; but he also insisted that in art 'only emotion endures'. His own poetry, if one travels from the epigrams to the translations to the *Cantos*, reveals at every turn both his technical virtuosity and his emotional intensity.

Since *A Lume Spento* (1908), Pound's publications include *Personae* and *Exultations* in 1909, *Canzoni* (1911), *Ripostes* (1912), *Lustra* (1916), *Hugh Selwyn Mauberley* (1920), *Homage to Sextus Propertius* (1934), and a series of drafts of the *Cantos* dating from 1925. Useful collections of Pound's poems are *Selected Poems* (1928, up to and including *Mauberley*), *Personae: Collected Shorter Poems* (1971), *The Cantos of Ezra Pound* (1970), and *Collected Early Poems* (1976). Also available are *Letters of Ezra Pound, 1907-41* (1950) and *The Literary Essays of Ezra Pound* (1954). *The Translations of Ezra Pound* was published in 1954.

ALFRED PURDY (b. 1918)

Purdy is a maverick. Born in Wooler, Ontario, he left Albert College at the age of sixteen to take up the life of a transient worker, apple-picking and riding the rods to western Canada. He enlisted in the RCAF in January 1940, but his independence of mind resulted in his being 'busted' from the rank of sergeant while in British Columbia. After the war, Purdy started a taxi business (which folded), bootlegged, and worked in a steel factory. From 1949 to 1955 he lived in Vancouver with his wife, working in a mattress factory and making himself unpopular by trying to organize a union. After selling his first play to the CBC in 1955, Purdy moved to Montreal and then to Roblin Lake at Ameliasburg, where he has lived for the last few years. He has travelled to the Cariboo, the Arctic, and Greece with the aid of writing fellowships.

Purdy's first book of poetry appeared in 1944 and his second in 1955. With the publication of *Poems for All the Annettes* (1962) and *The Cariboo Horses*, (1965, Governor General's Award) Purdy's reputation was established. In these volumes he revealed a rich sense of humour and a delightful capacity for self-mockery. In *North of Summer* (1967), and *Wild Grape Wine* (1968), however, the engaging, boisterous Purdy gives way to the more restrained descriptive and meditative poet. His earlier poetry owes something to North American poets, such as Creeley, Layton, and Ferlinghetti, but his recent influences are European and academic. The best of Purdy's recent poems, such as 'Lament for the Dorsets' and 'The Runners', are historical meditations, delicate renderings of vanishing moments from the past. Like Philip Larkin, he has an unusual sensitivity to change, a time-consciousness; his imagination is attuned to the subtle ironies and nuances produced by juxtaposing past and present.

Since the mid-sixties Purdy has published numerous books of poetry, including *Wild Grape Wine* (1968), *Love in a Burning Building* (1970), *Selected Poems* (1972), *Sex & Death* (1973), *Sundance At Dusk* (1976), *The Poems of Al Purdy* (1976), *Being Alive* (1978), and *Piling Blood* (1984). He also edited the anthologies *Fifteen Winds* (1969), *Storm Warning I* (1972), and *Storm Warning II* (1976).

ADRIENNE RICH (b. 1916)

Adrienne Rich was born in Baltimore, attended Radcliffe College, Harvard University, and has spent most of her adult life in Cambridge, Massachusetts, and New York. She has won many awards for her poetry collections, which include: *A Change of World* (1951), *The Diamond Cutters* (1952), *Snapshots of a Daughter-in-Law* (1963), *Necessities of Life* (1966), *Leaflets* (1969), *The Will to Change* (1971), *Diving into the Wreck* (1973, National Book Award, which she rejected personally but accepted on behalf of all women), *Poems Selected and New* (1975), *The Dream of a Common Language* (1978), *A Wild Patience Has Taken Me This Far* (1981), and *The Fact of a Doorframe: Poems Collected and New, 1950-1984* (1984).

Adrienne Rich's early poetry resonates with an intense consciousness of the weight of history and the relentless passage of time. The poems abound in images of change, loss, and extinction: from ice ages and mammoths to the decay of the flesh and human relationships, where every day is the 'end of an era'. In the midst of this life sentence, this imprisonment in endless change, where the past is irretrievable and 'the present breaks our hearts', poetry provides a solace, an anchor, an 'unsought amnesty'. The repressed anger of her early work gives way to a more positive, politically engaged, and at times even joyous confrontation with time and its allies. Proving Tillie Olson's view that 'Every woman who writes is a survivor', Rich has been in the vanguard of feminist activities for almost two decades, addressing issues of education, sexual orientation, and women's rights. A moving record of her prose writings on these subjects is to be found in *On Lies, Secrets and Silence* (1979).

Rich has rejected, for the most part, the rhetoric and literary trappings of the poetic tradition in favour of a 'common language', which will bring her struggles home to the hearts of ordinary readers. In this respect she distinguishes herself from writers such as Sylvia Plath and Diane Wakoski, who, she says, demonstrate 'a subjective, personal rage never before seen in women's poetry. If it is unnerving, it is also cathartic, the blowtorch of language cleansing the rust and ticky tacky and veneer from an entire consciousness.' Instead, she identifies with the means by which Robin Morgan makes her anger serve artistic purposes: 'In Morgan's *Monsters* this same force is politicized, shared with other women, offered to them as a sounding board, a voice at the end of some hotline.

Morgan writes not simply out of her own intention to survive, but out of a vision of the survival and transformation of all women.'

The sexual and political transformations in Rich's life find parallels in her search not only for an adequate language, but also for a degree of formal flexibility and openness. 'I would think that a really good poem opens up a possibility for other poems, rather than being the end of a succession of things,' she says. 'Instead of wrapping something up it explodes the possibilities.'

THEODORE ROETHKE (1908-63)

Roethke's odyssey in search of the self involved many emotional and financial hardships, many painful self-revelations. As a sensitive but unfortunately vulnerable and insecure man, he suffered considerable frustration as a result of his loneliness and his initial lack of recognition as a poet. 'I learn by going where I have to go', he admits in 'The Waking'. Roethke's poetry traces with frankness and honesty this long journey towards self-knowledge and fulfilment, recording sensations of childhood, mental breakdown, bereavement, and, finally, love. To use his own words, it is the poetry of a man 'naked to the bone'.

Roethke was born in Saginaw, Michigan. He grew up around the greenhouses and sanctuary started by his grandfather, who had been Bismark's head forester in Prussia. From these impressionable years and, perhaps, in reaction to his own troubled life, he found power and order in the world of growing things, which he felt and loved deeply. His profound reverence for life is reflected not only in his delightfully fresh and immediate nature poems, but also in poems about friends, students, and shared experiences. Before embarking on a life of teaching and writing, Roethke attended Harvard. He taught at Lafayette, Pennyslvania State, Bennington, and the University of Washington, where he received the honorary title of poet-in-residence in 1962. His awards include a Pulitzer Prize, a Ford Foundation grant, the Bollingen Prize, two National Book Awards, and a Fulbright lectureship in Italy.

In his poetry, Roethke reveals an affection (unusual in the mid twentieth century) for formal rhythm and rhyme. He considered free verse a 'denial in terms' and was continuously searching for new rhythms and forms of expression. As he said concerning a poem by Blake, 'Rhythm gives us the very psychic energy of the speaker, in one emotional situation at least.' Undoubtedly the vitality of his poetry in comparison with much of the verse now printed in literary magazines stems from his search for appropriate rhythms. Roethke's technical excellence and his depth of emotion are evident in 'Big Wind', an extended metaphor of great lyrical intensity and beauty, and 'I Knew a Woman', a love poem that is a masterpiece of wit and feeling. Each is a rhythmical *tour de force*.

Roethke has published numerous volumes of poetry, including *Open House* (1941), *The Lost Son* (1948), *Praise to the End!* (1951), *The Waking: Poems, 1933-1953* (1953, Pulitzer Prize), *Words for the Wind* (1958, Bollingen Prize), *I am! Says the Lamb* (1961), and *The Far Field* (1964). Available now are *The Collected Poems of Theodore Roethke* (1966), *On the Poet and His Craft: Selected Prose of Theodore Roethke* (1965), and *Selected Letters of Theodore Roethke* (1968).

GARY SNYDER (b. 1930)

Born in San Francisco, Synder was raised on a farm north of Seattle. He studied mythology at Reed College, linguistics at Indiana University, and moved from bumming, logging, and forestry to Chinese studies at Berkeley. From there Snyder went to Japan and to the Mediterranean on a tanker and then studied Buddhism in a Zen monastery in Kyoto. He is one of an increasing number of poets who are turning to studies of social and cultural anthropology. At one level this appears to be a contemporary version of the attraction of the Romantic poet to the gothic, to the seemingly simpler and more vital life of medieval times; at another level, however, this attraction to the primitive way may be seen as the beginnings of some sort of psychic revolution in the West.

Snyder is a peculiar mixture of priest and lumberjack. He believes in the value of physical labour, in contact with animals and the land; yet he urges his readers in the direction of a *back country* that exists beyond and through a simple physical return to the land. In its aims and styles his poetry reflects this strange mixture. Some of the books have a controlled mythic structure, while others have the flavour of a diary or Whole Earth Catalogue, with poems that serve as maps, recipes, or tips on survival in the wilderness. Snyder views poetry as an ecological survival technique, which explains his legendary status in the American subculture. He is less interested in the *contrived* poem than in poetry that is like 'the clear spring—it reflects all things and feeds all things but is itself transparent'. His early poems are extremely transparent, seemingly naïve and artless renderings of observation and event that have none of the sense of self and pride of craft that such experiential verse often engenders. 'Riprap', Snyder explains, 'is really a class of poems I wrote under the influence of the geology of the Sierra Nevada and the daily trail-crew work of picking up and placing granite stones in tight cobble patterns on hard slab. "What are you doing?" I asked old Roy Marchbanks.—"Riprapping," he said. His selection of natural rocks was perfect—the result looked like dressed stone fitting to hair-edge cracks. Walking, climbing, placing with the hands. I tried writing poems of tough, simple, short words, with the complexity far beneath the surface texture. In part the line was influenced by the five-and seven-character line Chinese poems I'd been reading, which work like sharp blows on the mind.'

It is difficult to convey a sense of Snyder's range and complexity in a short space; some of his most ambitious and extended work, such as *Myths & Texts*, consists of poem-sequences that must be read as a whole. These, and the recent poems, are more clearly symbolic; they are rooted in actual experience, but extend beyond their frames. In *Manzanita* Snyder begins to draw the lines from which his revolutionary work will be done; and the poems are exciting for their commitment and sensuality, as much as for their concreteness and economy. Poetry, Snyder says, is to '*give access* to persons—cutting away the fear and reserve and cramping of social life' and proclaiming joyfully 'this is what I have seen'. Snyder rejects the Romantic conception of the poet: 'In the new way of things the community is essential to the creative act; solitary poet figure and "name" author will become less and less relevant. Hence I prefer to be with my friends—which is the creative context'.

Snyder lives with his family and friends in the Sierra Nevadas. His books include *Riprap* (1958); *Myths & Texts* (1960); *Six Sections from Mountains and Rivers Without End* (1961); *A Range of Poems* (1966), his collected poems; *The Back Country* (1967); *Regarding Wave* (1967); *Manzanita* (1972), *Turtle Island* (1974), *Myths and Texts* (1978), *Passage Through India* (1983), and *Axe Handles* (1983). Because many of Snyder's poems have appeared as chapbooks and in small editions, it is difficult to provide an accurate chronology of his work. His poetry ought to be read in conjunction with his remarkable essays on culture, religion, ecology, and literature in *Earth House Hold: Technical Notes & Queries to Fellow Dharma Revolutionaries* (1957) and *The Real Work: Interviews and Talks* (1980).

WALLACE STEVENS (1879-1955)

Stevens was born in Reading, Pennsylvania. Educated at Harvard and the New York Law School, he was admitted to the Bar in 1904. After practising in New York City, he joined the legal department of the Hartford Accident and Indemnity Company in 1916 and became vice-president in 1934. In the years between the publication of his first volume, *Harmonium* (1923, reissued 1931), and his death in 1955, he published *Ideas of Order* (1935), *Owl's Clover* (1936), *The Man With the Blue Guitar* (1937)), *Parts of a World* (1942), *Notes Toward a Supreme Fiction* (1942), *Esthétique du Mal* (1944), *Transport to Summer* (1947), and *The Auroras of Autumn* (1950). His *Selected Poems* first appeared in England in 1953. Two further publications are *Collected Poems* (1954) and his prose work, *The Necessary Angel: Essays on Reality and the Imagination* (1951). *Opus Posthumous*, a collection of plays, essays, some poems, and epigrams, was published in 1957.

Stevens was a philosophical poet. His poems are primarily analytical rather than descriptive, pressing towards discovery, towards a more profound apprehension of reality. As he explains in 'A Collect of Philosophy': 'Theoretically, the poetry of thought should be the supreme poetry. . . . A poem in which the poet has chosen for his subject a philosophic theme should result in the poem of poems. That the wing of poetry should also be the rushing wing of meaning seems to be an extreme aesthetic good; and so in time and perhaps, in other politics, it may come to be.' Stevens shares with Coleridge a conviction that imagination is the 'sum of all our faculties' and an interest in defining that particular intersection of imagination and reality that is the poetic process. His poems have their base in reality, the familiar world of feelings and objects and events, but they move towards the unreal, the unfamiliar: 'one may find intimations of immortality in an object on the mantlepiece; and these intimations are as real in the mind in which they occur as the mantlepiece itself.' He writes, as he explains, about 'a particular of life thought of for so long that one's thoughts have become an inseparable part of it or a particular of life so intensely felt that the feeling has entered into it.'

Ultimately it is not the naturalistic subject-matter in Stevens' poems that interests the reader, but the sensibility that perceives and defines it. Stevens writes with wit and elegance. In his meditative poems there are depth and insight that one associates with a 'study' by the Dutch Masters, a profundity that comes of great concentration and compassion. 'One of the consequences of the ordination of style', he wrote, 'is not to limit it, but to enlarge it, not to impoverish it, but to enrich and liberate it.' Considering the beauty and control of such poems as 'Sunday Morning' and 'The Idea of Order at Key West', it is difficult not to agree with Stevens that, if liberty is attainable in life and art, it is most likely to be achieved through the pursuit of order, or the 'idea of order'.

DYLAN THOMAS (1914-53)

Dylan Thomas was born in Swansea, Wales. After attending Swansea Grammar School he set out for London, where he worked as a reporter and broadcaster, wrote radio and movie scripts, and published his first volume of verse, *18 Poems* (1934). Thomas's unique combination of charisma, eloquence, and incorrigibility made him a sensational success on the reading and lecture circuit in America. But he could never entirely reconcile his needs as a creative artist with the destructive forces in his personality; and, consequently, he was exploited by people who had no interest in his art and was reduced to a state of constant financial and social turmoil. He died in New York on his third reading tour.

Thomas reserved his weaknesses and buffoonery for life; in his poetry he was a conscientious craftsman. He had an unparalleled ear for language and believed that poetry must be read aloud: 'a poem on a page is only half a poem.' The magic of his words has caused the less astute critics to accuse Thomas of being 'all sound and no sense'; and it has moved many of his most enthusiastic admirers to consider his poems somehow *above* analysis. Each of Thomas's poems is carefully wrought, a 'formally watertight compartment of words', controlled by either a narrative or an associative logic. Thomas's metaphors are the most startling thing about his poetry. He has the kind of wit that Samuel Johnson ascribed to the 'metaphysical' poets of the seventeenth century, *discordia concors:* the ability to combine dissimilar images or to discover the resemblances in things apparently different. While the metaphysical poets preferred the extended metaphor (i.e., comparing two lovers to the fixed arms of a compass), Thomas's great strength lies in the *compressed* metaphor: 'green age', 'the weather of the heart', 'windy boy', 'holy streams', 'fields of praise', 'lamb white days', 'fire green as grass'.

The best poems of Thomas's first six volumes of poetry may be found in his *Collected Poems 1934-52* (1952). In addition to his play, *Under Milk Wood* (1954), Thomas wrote a number of prose works, including *Portrait of the Artist as a Young Dog* (1940), *Quite Early One Morning* (1954), and *Adventures in the Skin Trade* (1955).

PHYLLIS WEBB (b. 1927)

Born in Victoria, B.C., Phyllis Webb graduated in English and Philosophy from the University of British Columbia in 1949. She ran as a CCF candidate in provincial elections before moving to Montreal, where she was associated with F. R. Scott, Louis Dudek, Irving Layton, and Miriam Waddington. Webb's publications include *Even Your Right Eye* (1956), which contains poems written while travelling and living in England and Ireland; *The Sea is Also a Garden* (1962); *Naked Poems* (1965); *Selected Poems 1954-1965* (1971); *Wilson's Bowl* (1980); *Sunday Water: Thirteen Anti Ghazals* (1982); *The Vision Tree: Selected Poems* (1982), winner of a Governor General's Award; and *Water and Light: Ghazals and Anti Ghazals* (1984). Webb's work with CBC radio as reviewer, broadcaster, and executive director of the program 'Ideas', is recorded in *Talking* (1982), which also contains essays on the poetic process. She now lives on Saltspring Island, B.C.

Though Webb's voice is passionate and witty, she brings to her work a rigorous, questioning intellect. In fact questioning is central to her writing, not only in essays and poems about curiosity, interrogation, and torture, as well as in her long involvement with Amnesty International, but also in her view of the poem as a vehicle of analysis and discovery. Her poetry is often concerned with philosophical issues, fine discriminations of conscience, and the nature of art itself.

Obviously the idea of a poet as inquisitor implies great attention to means, to the techniques of persuasion. Webb is meticulous in matters of technique, struggling with the patterning of sound, the intricacies of diction and line-length, and what she calls 'the intuitive sense of form'. 'When I speak of long lines and short lines,' she writes in an essay called 'Polishing Up the View', 'I am not merely thinking of the effect of the line on the page, of its typographical effect—in fact, that is probably secondary. I am thinking of the phrasing, of the measure of the breath, of what is natural to the phrase. . . .' The absolute precision one observes in a poem such as 'Poetics Against the Angel of Death' is reflected over and over again in her painstaking analysis of the creative process in the essays in *Talking*. Webb's technical preoccupations, along with her general disinterest in narrative and parochial subjects, have cost her a certain popular attention; but they have made her a great favourite among poets.

RICHARD WILBUR (b. 1921)

Wilbur was born in New York City. He graduated from Amherst in 1942 and, after military service, did postgraduate studies at Harvard. Wilbur has taugnt at Harvard and Wellesley College and is now professor of English at Wesleyan University. He is married and has four children. Wilbur has received two Guggenheim awards, the Prix de Rome, the Pulitzer Prize for poetry, and has made an extended trip to Russia as a representative of the U.S. State Department.

Wilbur shares with the early Robert Lowell and contemporary English poets, such as Thom Gunn and Ted Hughes, a willingness to explore and extend the usefulness of traditional poetic forms. His poetic grammar and syntax are often Miltonic and his habit of mind resembles that of the metaphysical poets. He employs the decasyllabic line with iambics but nevertheless achieves a conversational ease that is remarkable. Wilbur's poetry ranges from the beautifully lyrical to the heavily rhetorical and ironic. He uses traditional forms with the grace and control that one associates with the poetry of Robert Graves. Whether he is celebrating the richness and beauty of life or contemplating the process of disillusionment and decay, Wilbur's observations are acute, often penetrating, the product of an informed and exploring intelligence.

In addition to editing *A Bestiary*, translating Molière's *Le Misanthrope* (1955) and *Tartuffe* (1963), and collaborating with Lillian Hellman on *Candide* (a comic opera based on Voltaire's work), he has published *The Beautiful Changes* (1947), *Ceremony and Other Poems* (1950), *Things of This World* (1956), and *Advice to a Prophet* (1960), most of which are collected in *The Poems of Richard Wilbur* (1963). His recent titles include *Walking to Sleep: New Poems & Translations* (1970), *Digging For China* (1970), *Opposites: Poems & Drawings* (1973), *Responses: Prose Pieces, 1948-1976* (1976), and *The Mind-Reader* (1977).

WILLIAM CARLOS WILLIAMS (1883-1963)

Williams was born in Rutherford, New Jersey, to an English father and a Puerto Rican mother of French and Basque parentage. He was educated in New York, Paris, the University of Pennsylvania (where he met Ezra Pound in 1906), and Leipzig, where he did postgraduate work in pediatrics. Married, with two sons, Williams practised medicine in Rutherford until a few years before his death. From the publication of *Poems* (1909), he went on to become one of the most prolific and influential American poets.

Williams was nurtured in the same soil of revolutionary romanticism as Whitman and cummings. He began by rejecting the expatriate life and the preoccupation with tradition that characterized Pound and Eliot. In reaction to what he described as 'the order that cuts off the crab's feelers to make it fit into the box', Williams immersed himself in the American scene, in search of a distinctly American idiom and measure. In *Paterson*, an epic poem to be placed alongside *The Waste Land* and Hart Crane's *The Bridge*, he worked out his linguistic and stylistic theories and attempted the 'rediscovery of a primary impetus, the elemental principle of all art, in the local conditions'.

There can be little doubt about the extent to which Williams's ideas— his assertion of the importance of feeling and physical environment as shaping factors in a poet's work, and his rejection of poetic formalism— have influenced the directions of modern poetry. One has only to look at the work of Olson and Creeley and the poets of the Black Mountain group. But Williams's early concern to be anti-poetic shows an underlying preoccupation with form, a preoccupation that was to characterize his later work. He soon tired of the free verse and so-called objectivity of imagism, developing instead the 'variable foot', to be used in creating what he referred to as *versos sueltos* or loose verses. 'The key to modern poetry is measure,' he finally admitted, 'which must reflect the flux of modern life. You should find a variable measure for the fixed measure; for man and the poet must keep pace with this world.' Williams's own triadic stanza and measured line enabled him during the last ten years of his life to produce some of his finest poems, those in *Pictures from Breughel*.

After *Poems* (1909), Williams's chief poetical works are *Collected Earlier Poems* (1951), *Collected Later Poems* (1950), *Journey to Love* (1955), *Paterson* (1946-58), and *Pictures from Breughel and Other Poems* (1962, Pulitzer Prize). His prose includes *In the American Grain* (1925), *Autobiography* (1951), *Make Light of It: Collected Stories* (1950), *Selected Essays* (1954), and *Yes, Mrs Williams* (1959). Also available is *The Selected Letters of William Carlos Williams* (1957).

WILLIAM BUTLER YEATS (1865-1939)

Yeats was born at Sandymount, near Dublin. He was educated in London
and Dublin, spending his summers at his parents' birthplace in Sligo.
After the publication of his first book, *Mosada: A Poem* (1886), Yeats
lived for a time in London, where he founded the Rhymers' Club and
associated with various writers, including William Morris, Oscar Wilde,
and Arthur Symons (who introduced him to the writing of Mallarmé and
the French Symbolists). In 1902 he helped found the Irish National Theatre
Society, out of which the Abbey Theatre grew. He was greatly interested
in the myths and legends of Ireland and became the leading figure of the
Irish renaissance, which revived the ancient lore and traditions of Ireland
in works of literature. Yeats's role in the Irish rebellions was largely insignificant; he was more of a cultural than a political force, although
later, as a senator, he promoted Ireland's liberal copyright laws. Yeats received the Nobel Prize for Literature in December 1923.

Perhaps the most subtle and provocative tribute to Yeats's genius is
W. H. Auden's elegy, 'In Memory of W. B. Yeats'. Auden describes the
day of Yeats's death as 'a dark cold day', a day on which 'the dogs of
Europe bark' and human pity has given way to hatred and intellectual dis-
honesty. To many Europeans the death of Yeats must have seemed symbolic of the death of all that is best in civilization. Yeats had looked
clearly at the myths of 'science' and 'progress', which we have created to
justify the dehumanization of our fellow man, and the myth of 'self determination', by which we justify exploitation and mass-murder. Years before the Second World War, he had warned that 'Things fall apart; the
centre cannot hold/Mere anarchy is loosed upon the world'. Above all,
Yeats had integrity—as a man and as an artist. He continually demon-
strated the critical intelligence and natural skepticism without which freedom is impossible.

Although Yeats admitted that his poetry 'all comes from rage or lust',
he directed his rage towards truths *outside* the self: 'all that is personal
soon rots; it must be packed in ice or salt.' Yeats believed that in order
to escape the limitations of purely subjective statement the poet must
write out of his 'antithetical self', that he must explore the tension that
exists between opposing ideas. Much of the success of 'The Second Coming' stems from the superb coincidence of simple diction, passionate syntax, and contending opposites (Christ and anti-Christ, order and anarchy,
etc.). In order to achieve an indirect mode of expression, Yeats experimented with the mask, or persona, and employed the techniques of the
Symbolists. Another of his methods is that of literary and historical allusion, as in 'Leda and the Swan', where contemporary history is illuminated through reference to events in classical mythology.

Yeats had no use for sloppiness of sentiment and expression. He was
an untiring craftsman, a self-critic who respected his own observations

and emotions enough to give them artistic shape. He revised all that he wrote, took great care in the placing of his poems in collections, and strove constantly for simplicity. 'I tried to make the language of poetry coincide with that of passionate, normal speech,' he wrote. 'Because I need a passionate syntax for passionate subject-matter I compel myself to accept those traditional metres that have developed with the language.' Most poets aim for diction and rhythms reflecting ordinary speech, but few can claim to have achieved in their verse the unusual degree of intensity that Yeats's poems support.

Yeats's poems are available in *The Poems of W. B. Yeats* (1983), ed. Richard J. Finneran, and in the variorum edition of P. Allt and R. K. Alspach (1957); his plays in *The Collected Plays of William Butler Yeats* (1952); and much of his important prose in *A Vision* (rev. 1937), *Autobiography* (1938), *Letters* (1954), ed. by Allan Wade, and *Essays and Introductions* (1961).

INDEX